RESHAPING THE EQUITY MARKETS

A Guide for the 1990s

Robert A. Schwartz

With the assistance of Laura M. Cohen

BUSINESS ONE IRWIN
Homewood, Illinois 60430

For Emily

Sponsoring editor: Ralph Rieves
Production manager: Dennis Mendenhall
Designer: Tim Kaage
Printer: Malloy Lithographing

Library of Congress Cataloging-in-Publication Data

Schwartz, Robert A. (Robert Alan), date
    Reshaping the equity markets: a guide for the 1990s / Robert A. Schwartz; with the assistance of Laura M. Cohen.
      p.   cm.
    Includes index.
    ISBN 1-55623-682-4
    1. Securities.   2. Stock-exchange.
   HG4521.S357835   1993
   332.63'2 — dc20   93–18582

Printed in the United States of America
1 2 3 4 5 6 7 8 9 0 ML 0 9 8 7 6 5 4 3

Contents

Preface

This book is about current and impending developments in the equity markets. It analyzes the systems, procedures, and protocols that define a market's architecture and determine how orders are handled and translated into trades. Two themes in particular are emphasized: (1) accurate price discovery is an important function of a marketplace, and (2) the liquidity of a market can be enhanced—and the costs of trading reduced—by the way a market is structured.

Market professionals and investors are affected by three attributes of securities: risk, return, and liquidity. Commonly, only risk and return are assessed in a systematic fashion, and liquidity is almost entirely ignored in the literature on investment analysis and portfolio theory. A major reason for this neglect is that the concept is neither subject to precise definition nor readily quantified. Consequently, we have only an intuitive understanding of the term, of the effect of illiquidity on share prices, and of the trade-offs that exist among the risk, return, and liquidity characteristics of different assets.

Liquidity and accurate price determination are of paramount importance for market participants individually and for the economy as a whole. Illiquidity reduces the frequency of trading; imposes costs that lower portfolio performance; and distorts asset prices, thereby sending erroneous signals to the broad market. Illiquidity also depresses share prices, reducing the financial wealth of the economy and increasing the cost of capital for issuing firms. The higher cost of raising capital in turn leads to a lower investment in real assets (plant, equipment, human capital, and so on) and thus to a smaller aggregate output of goods and services.

The market crash on 19 October 1987 brought widespread attention to problems attributable to illiquidity and underscored the fact that markets cannot provide unlimited liquidity to investors and traders. On Black Monday large positions could not be sold without causing prices to tumble further; desired hedges could not be instantly put on or unwound so as to control risk; and share valuations fluctuated widely. The events of October 19 and 20 evidenced that specialists and other market maker firms cannot or will not supply enough capital to the market to keep price movements orderly under conditions of severe stress. Two years later the mini-crash on

13 October, 1989 again highlighted the existence of serious structural defects in the market's architecture that reduce liquidity and cause excessive price volatility.

The 1987 and 1989 crashes are extreme examples of what can happen. Equally important, the impact of illiquidity on trading decisions, transaction costs, and asset prices is felt every trading second of every trading day. However, the illiquidity of a market can be controlled by the design of the trading system. Recent experience has made it clear that an efficient system enhances liquidity and an inefficient system impairs liquidity.

Part I of this book contains descriptive material on various market centers and trading systems. Issues concerning market design, new trading systems, and innovative procedures are discussed in Part II. Models of share valuation, trading, and price determination, and an assessment of market and informational efficiency, are presented in Part III.

Acknowledgments

Parts of this book contain material from its predecessor, *Equity Markets: Structure, Trading, and Performance* (Harper & Row, 1988). I again thank those whose comments improved that earlier work, and my coauthors with whom I have pursued much of my research for many years. In particular, I thank Corinne Bronfman and Randolph Mann for the assistance they have given me with the current manuscript; their efforts on my behalf are deeply appreciated. A number of people from various market centers have been most helpful to me. I especially thank James Cochrane, Gene Finn, Helen Hogarth, James Shapiro, and Deborah Sosebee. Anthony Neuberger's participation in the London study is also gratefully acknowledged.

PART I

The Equity Markets Today

1

Securities Markets Under Stress

October 1987

For the nation, 1987 marked the fifth year of economic expansion. Inflation was low, and stock market indexes had risen to record levels. The Dow reached its peak of 2,722.42 on August 25 of that year. In the fall of 1987, expectations of quarterly earnings reports were bullish.

But along with the optimism were major economic uncertainties. Of particular concern was the federal budget deficit that, although at the time somewhat lower, had reached $22 billion in 1986 and a trade deficit that stood at $169.7 billion in 1986. Interest rates had risen substantially throughout most of 1987, and there was a threat of renewed inflation. Foreign buying at the U.S. Treasury auctions had helped to finance the federal budget deficit, and large sums of foreign capital had been invested in U.S. equities during the market's rise; these funds could be withdrawn rapidly if U.S. interest rates or the U.S. dollar fell.

On October 6 the Dow dropped a record 91.55 points to 2,548.63 because of mounting fears of higher interest rates and a wave of computerized sell programs. On October 14 a trade deficit of $15.68 billion was announced for the month of August. Although lower than the previous month's figure of $16.47 billion, the deficit was larger than expected, and the news rattled an increasingly nervous investment community. The dollar declined in foreign exchange markets, interest rates surged, and the Dow responded with another record point drop of 95.46.

Table 1.1 shows the Dow Jones Industrial Average (DJIA) of 30 industrial stocks, close-to-close changes in the index, percentage changes in the index, and trading volume for the four-week period from Monday, October 12, through Friday, November 6. Table 1.2 shows how the index changed over hourly intervals during the four most turbulent days of the period, October 16 and October 19–21. As shown in Table 1.1, the market experienced

---

This chapter draws on material from Schreiber and Schwartz (1986) and Schwartz (1990) and (1991), used with permission.

TABLE 1.1   *Dow Jones Industrial Average and NYSE Trading Volume, 12 October 1987 to 6 November 1987*

Day	Dow Jones Industrial Index	Point Change from Previous Close	Percentage Change from Previous Close	Number of Shares Traded (Millions)
Mon. Oct.12	2471.44	−10.77	−0.43	141.9
Tues. Oct.13	2508.16	+36.72	+1.49	172.9
Wed. Oct.14	2412.70	−95.46	−3.81	207.4
Thur. Oct.15	2355.09	−57.61	−2.39	263.2
Fri. Oct.16	2246.74	−108.35	−4.60	338.5
Mon. Oct.19	1738.74	−508.00	−22.61	604.3
Tues. Oct.20	1841.01	+102.27	+5.88	608.1
Wed. Oct.21	2027.85	+186.84	+10.15	449.4
Thur. Oct.22	1950.43	−77.42	−3.82	392.2
Fri. Oct.23	1950.76	+.33	+0.02	245.6
Mon. Oct.26	1793.93	−156.83	−8.04	308.8
Tues. Oct.27	1846.49	+52.56	+2.93	260.2
Wed. Oct.28	1846.82	+0.33	+0.02	279.4
Thur. Oct.29	1938.33	+91.51	+4.96	258.1
Fri. Oct.30	1993.53	+55.20	+2.85	303.4
Mon. Nov. 2	2014.09	+20.56	+1.03	176.0
Tues. Nov. 3	1963.53	−50.56	−2.51	227.8
Wed. Nov. 4	1945.29	−18.24	−0.93	202.5
Thur. Nov. 5	1985.41	+40.12	+2.06	226.0
Fri. Nov. 6	1959.05	−26.36	−1.33	228.3
Change from Oct. 12 close		−512.39	−20.73	

its first substantial drop on October 14, yet another substantial decrease on October 15, and then a sharp decline on Friday, October 16. The decline on the sixteenth, as shown in Table 1.2, occurred mainly between 1:00 P.M. and 2:00 P.M. and in the last hour of trading before the weekend. The Dow lost 235 points for the week and closed 476 points below its August peak. Pressures that would push the market far lower were building.

Three other developments jolted the market at this time. First, a tax bill under consideration by Congress contained provisions that could have seriously hindered corporate takeover activity, particularly the leveraged takeovers. Second, comments over the weekend from Washington suggesting that the United States would let the dollar fall if West Germany did not reverse a recent rise in interest rates reinforced concern that *anticipation* of

TABLE 1.2 *Dow Jones Industrial Index at Hourly Intervals, October 16 and October 19–21*

		Dow Jones Industrial Index	Point Change from Previous Value	Percentage Change from Previous Value
Fri., October 16	open	2363.90	+8.81	+0.37
	10 A.M.	2355.09	−8.81	−0.37
	11 A.M.	2347.91	−7.18	−0.30
	12 noon	2340.40	−7.51	−0.32
	1 P.M.	2323.11	−17.29	−0.74
	2 P.M.	2268.44	−54.67	−2.35
	3 P.M.	2297.00	+28.56	+1.26
	close	2246.74	−50.26	−2.19
Mon., October 19	open	2046.67	−200.07	−8.90
	10 A.M.	2178.69	+132.02	+6.45
	11 A.M.	2040.63	−138.06	−6.34
	12 noon	2103.79	+63.16	+3.10
	1 P.M.	2061.85	−41.94	−1.99
	2 P.M.	1974.54	−87.31	−4.23
	3 P.M.	1958.88	−15.66	−0.79
	close	1738.74	−220.14	−11.24
Tues., October 20	open	1949.77	+211.03	+12.14
	10 A.M.	1863.06	−86.71	−4.45
	11 A.M.	1858.75	−4.31	−0.23
	12 noon	1726.46	−132.29	−7.12
	1 P.M.	1825.27	+98.81	+5.72
	2 P.M.	1760.28	−64.99	−3.56
	3 P.M.	1878.98	+118.70	+6.74
	close	1841.01	−37.97	−2.02
Wed., October 21	open	2016.08	+175.07	+9.51
	10 A.M.	1947.28	−68.80	−3.41
	11 A.M.	2036.14	+88.86	+4.56
	12 noon	2003.15	−32.99	−1.62
	1 P.M.	2008.12	+4.97	+0.25
	2 P.M.	2028.35	+20.23	+1.01
	3 P.M.	1992.21	−36.14	−1.78
	close	2027.85	+35.64	+1.79

a declining dollar would drive foreign money from U.S. markets. Third, at 8:33 A.M., on Monday, October 19, before the NYSE opened, news was reported that warships thought to be American had bombed an Iranian oil platform in the Persian Gulf. For the markets, the tinder was dry and the match had been lit.

On Monday in Tokyo, prices fell from the opening bell. Then the London market opened sharply down. In New York a barrage of sell orders rocked the NYSE even before opening trades were made on the Big Board. For instance, the indicated opening price for IBM was $125, compared to a Friday close of $134.50; the indicated opening price for Merck was $170, compared to a Friday close of $184. As shown in Table 1.2, the New York market opened on October 19 at 2,046.67, down 200.07 points, or 8.90%. Takeover stocks plummeted. Portfolio insurance sell programs triggered in Chicago put enormous pressure on index futures. The price of the futures fell below the price of shares on the NYSE, and arbitrage programs were activated that drove the New York prices lower. Volume exploded; traders began losing track of what was happening. As prices spiraled downward, new rounds of portfolio insurance programs were activated in Chicago. In response, selling pressure was intensified in New York by traders anticipating that more arbitrage programs would be run. The market was in full flight.

A trader described the scene as follows:

> Half of the Dow stocks couldn't open for trading this morning. They didn't open for an hour or more. We were frozen in front of our screens. There were just no bids. I.B.M., General Electric, Merck—some of the biggest blue-chip stocks in the Dow—and we couldn't open them! I did some trades on Merck today. You know what a downtick is? When a stock goes down an eighth of a point, a quarter of a point? I was watching Merck on my screen, and it started trading on downticks four points at a time. Then it downticked eight points.[1]

The following passage from *The New York Times* quotes Donald Stone, specialist and senior partner of Lasker, Stone, and Stern, a leading NYSE specialty firm:

> I was in combat during World War II and the feeling you had in your stomach was the same as when you were under fire, except here you didn't risk your life—just all your assets.[2]

The *Times* further reported that Stone traded over a million shares of Johnson & Johnson on Monday and another 1.2 million on Tuesday, in the process "committing some $75 million in just that one stock."

In one 15-minute period on the nineteenth, the Dow dropped 50 points. In a 45-minute period it fell 100 points. From 10 A.M. to 11 A.M. it fell 138 points. Between 3 P.M. and the market's close the Dow plunged 220 points. Laszlo Birinyi, Jr., then chief equity strategist at Salomon Brothers, was quoted by *Newsweek* as saying, "What does the market know that we don't?" *Newsweek* added, "He got no answers. Just blank stares and shrugs."[3]

Only once before had the market experienced an equivalent fall—in October 1929. But the 1987 drop was faster. The Dow had declined 23% in a two-day period in 1929, October 28 and 29. In October 1987, the Dow lost 22.6% of its value in a single day. And the fall was worldwide.

In London the Financial Times average of 30 stocks fell 10%. In Tokyo the Nikkei 225-share index was down 7.3%. The market index dropped 7.1% in Frankfurt, 11.3% in Zurich, 4.6% in Paris, 7.8% in Amsterdam, 10.5% in Brussels, 12.2% in Singapore, and 11.1% in Toronto. In Hong Kong, the market fell 11.1% on October 19, at which point the exchange was closed. When it reopened on October 26, Hong Kong's Hang Seng index lost one-third of its value in one of the most severe session-to-session declines in stock market history.

Trading on the U.S. markets remained extremely heavy, and enormous price fluctuations continued for the next several days. On October 20, after several wild swings (see Table 1.2), the Dow closed up 102.27 points. On October 21, the market opened up 175.07 points and held on to close with a 186.84-point gain for the day. Thus, in two days the Dow had recouped almost 300 points of the 508-point loss. On Friday the market closed up 0.33 points; traders were exhausted; the Exchange was closed at 2:00 P.M. to ease back office operations; and the session was quiet by then-current standards—only 245.6 million shares were traded.

The price swings remained large through the last week of October and then dampened somewhat during the first week in November. On Friday, November 6, the market closed at 1,959.05, about where it had been on Friday, October 23, at the end of the most tumultuous week in the Exchange's history.

October 1989

The markets experienced dramatic price fluctuations once again in October 1989. More than in 1987, not just the sizes of the jumps were of concern, but so too was the fact that many were followed by reversals.

On Friday, October 13, the Dow declined 190 points in the closing hour of trading. The plunge was triggered by an announcement that debt financing had been denied for the buyout of United Air Lines (UAL). News concerning one company presumably cannot, by itself, explain a 190-point move unless it was the catalyst that caused a broad spectrum of investors to question whether the level the market had reached was sustainable.

Then, despite all the publicity, discussion, and analysis over the weekend, nobody knew on Monday the sixteenth, the next trading day, if the NYSE market would open up or down, or by how much, until the opening bell rang at 9:30 A.M. and trading began. On that day the market fell an additional 63.9 points in the first 41 minutes of trading, but bounced back 152 points to close up 88.1.

Another large swing occurred on October 24, a day the DJIA lost only 3.1 points from open to close. By 10:30 A.M., the market was down 84.3. Once again, bad news concerning UAL was the cause: the company had issued a statement after the preceding day's close that its board wanted to maintain the firm's independence.

UAL had closed on October 23 at 178. Before trading on the twenty-fourth, the UAL specialist on the NYSE gave an opening indication of between $135 and $155. The stock finally opened at $150 at 10:08 A.M. According to *The Wall Street Journal* of October 25, takeover speculators immediately started selling other stocks and S&P futures; then program traders were selling stocks in the Major Market Index and S&P 500 index.

Some large brokerage firms suddenly entered the S&P futures pit in Chicago as buyers. A turnabout occurred and was transmitted back to New York; in five minutes the Dow rose almost 30 points. Later in the afternoon, some hundred-thousand-share buy orders came in for UAL and, as the stock climbed back to 170 (down only 8⅜ for the day), the Dow actually crept into the black before closing down a mere 3.1 points for the day.

What did the traders think of the 81-point swing? According to *The Wall Street Journal* of October 25,

> Some institutional traders loved the wild ride. "This is fun," asserted Susan Del Signore, head equity trader at Travelers Investment Management Co. She said she used the market's wild swings to buy shares cheaply on the sell-off. On the comeback, Ms. Del Signore unloaded shares she has been aiming to get rid of.

> But traders who risk money handling big blocks of stock were shaken. "This market is eating away my youth," said Chung Lew, head equity trader at Kleinwort Benson North America Inc. . . . "I think we are losing credibility because when the market does this, it doesn't present itself as a rational investment."

The crash of 1987 and extreme turbulence in October 1989 showed participants that the equity markets can, under stressful conditions, get out of control. Unfortunately, this realization can turn into a self-fulfilling prophesy. *The Wall Street Journal* article of October 25 quoted Jack Solomon, technical analyst for Bear Stearns:

> October 13th left us with a cut and exposed nerve. . . . People are fearful and sensitive. Everybody's finger is one inch closer to the button. I have never had as many calls as I had this morning. Volatility is here to stay. (p. C1)

Intraday Price Movements

NYSE S&P 500 Issues

Even under relatively normal conditions, short-run price changes are appreciable. Table 1.3 shows how individual NYSE-listed S&P 500 issues are distributed according to the range over which their prices varied on three selected trading days: 19 January, 26 January, and 7 February 1990. Range is measured both by the absolute value of the difference between a stock's

TABLE 1.3 *NYSE Listed S&P 500 Firms' Distribution by Price Range, Expressed in Dollars for a $50 Stock[a]*

| | High to Low Range | | | | | | | | | | Cumulative |
Open to Close Range	0.00 to 0.25	0.26 to 0.50	0.51 to 0.75	0.76 to 1.00	1.01 to 1.50	1.51 to 2.00	2.01 to 3.00	Over 3.00	Total	%	%
					19 January 1990 — A Flat Day						
0.00 to 0.25	4	36	51	25	15	0	2	2	135	29.7	100.0
0.26 to 0.50		22	38	34	9	1	1	1	106	23.3	70.3
0.51 to 0.75			19	23	30	4	0	0	76	16.7	47.0
0.76 to 1.00				26	21	6	2	0	55	12.1	30.3
1.01 to 1.50					32	13	2	1	48	10.5	18.2
1.51 to 2.00						14	4	1	19	4.2	7.7
2.01 to 3.00							5	3	8	1.7	3.5
Over 3.00								8	8	1.7	1.7
Total	4	58	108	108	107	38	16	16	455	100.0	
%	0.9	12.7	23.7	23.7	23.5	8.4	3.5	3.5	100.0		
Cumulative %	100.0	99.1	86.4	62.6	38.9	15.4	7.0	3.5			

(continued)

9

TABLE 1.3 (Continued)

Open to Close Range	High to Low Range								Total	%	Cumulative %
	0.00 to 0.25	0.26 to 0.50	0.51 to 0.75	0.76 to 1.00	1.01 to 1.50	1.51 to 2.00	2.01 to 3.00	Over 3.00			
				26 January 1990 — A Reversal Day							
0.00 to 0.25	2	6	22	27	48	23	12	3	143	31.9	100.0
0.26 to 0.50		4	19	21	37	17	7	1	106	23.7	68.1
0.51 to 0.75			9	10	29	11	13	1	73	16.3	44.3
0.76 to 1.00				5	18	13	6	2	44	9.8	28.0
1.01 to 1.50					14	15	13	5	47	10.5	18.2
1.51 to 2.00						6	9	7	22	4.9	7.7
2.01 to 3.00							3	9	12	2.6	2.8
Over 3.00								1	1	0.2	0.2
Total	2	10	50	63	146	85	63	29	448	100.0	
%	0.4	2.2	11.2	14.1	32.6	19.0	14.1	6.5	100.0		
Cumulative %	100.0	99.7	97.5	86.3	72.2	39.6	20.6	6.5			

High to Low Range

Open to Close Range	0.00 to 0.25	0.26 to 0.50	0.51 to 0.75	0.76 to 1.00	1.01 to 1.50	1.51 to 2.00	2.01 to 3.00	Over 3.00	Total	%	Cumulative %
					7 February 1990 — A Trending Day						
0.00 to 0.25	1	16	18	10	14	3	0	2	64	14.1	100.0
0.26 to 0.50		6	20	20	23	5	0	0	74	16.3	85.9
0.51 to 0.75			9	14	36	10	0	0	69	15.2	69.5
0.76 to 1.00				11	41	16	1	0	69	15.2	54.3
1.01 to 1.50					38	42	14	3	97	21.3	39.1
1.51 to 2.00						17	28	2	47	10.3	17.8
2.01 to 3.00							12	9	21	4.6	7.5
Over 3.00								13	13	2.9	2.9
Total	1	22	47	55	152	93	55	29	454	100.0	
%	0.2	4.8	10.4	12.1	33.4	20.5	12.1	6.4	100.0		
Cumulative %	100.0	99.8	94.9	84.5	72.4	39.0	18.5	6.4			

a Issues that went ex-dividend on one of the dates or which no trade was recorded by 10:00 A.M. are excluded from the table.

opening and closing price (in rows) and by the stock's high-low spread for the day (in columns). Adjustments are made for differences in the price level for different securities by measuring the ranges in percentage terms and then computing the comparable dollar amounts for a $50 stock.

The aggregate market was flat on January 19; the DJIA closed 2.35 points below its opening value of 2,680.25 and had a high-low spread for the day of 18.1 points. Even on that flat day, the prices of many individual issues moved considerably: 15% of the companies had a high-low range of $1.50 or more, and for 7% the range was $2.00 or more.

January 26 was a reversal day; the DJIA closed 2.48 points below its opening value of 2,561.71 and had a high-low spread of 59.5 points. On that reversal day, 40% of the companies had a high-low range of $1.50 or more, and for 21% the range was $2.00 or more.

February 7 was a trending day; the DJIA closed 47.07 points above its opening value of 2,561.04 and had a high-low spread of 55.2 points. On that day, 39% of the companies had a high-low range of $1.50 or more, and for 18% the range was $2.00 or more.

The matrix format used to present the distributions suggests that, as one would expect, the size of the high-low range is positively related to the absolute size of the open-to-close price change, particularly on the trending day (many of the observations lie close to or on the diagonal). For the flat day and the reversal day, however, a substantial proportion of the observations are distributed away from the diagonal. On the reversal day 38 securities had a high-low range of $1.50 or more, but closed within $0.25 of their opening price.

CBS Common

The magnitude of price volatility under normal conditions can also be seen with reference to a specific transaction record. Table 1.4 presents a transaction record for CBS stock for the first half hour of trading on 11 January 1988. No press release or unusual news event concerning the company occurred around this period. Table 1.4 shows the bid and ask quotations; the bid-ask spread; the price of each transaction for the period; an indication of whether each transaction was at the bid (B), the ask (A), or within the spread (M); the size of each transaction (volume); and the time of each transaction.

The market opened for CBS at 9:33:59 at a price of 159.25. The opening trade comprised all crossing orders from (a) the limit order book, (b) the trading crowd on the floor, and (c) orders delivered to the specialist's post by the Exchange's Opening Automated Report System (OARS). (The NYSE's opening procedure is discussed in Chapter 2.) The opening price reflected these orders and the specialist's assessment of the market at the time. After the opening trade, the quotes were established at 159.75 ask, 159.00 bid.

TABLE 1.4 *Transaction Record for CBS First Half Hour of Trading, 11 January 1988*

Bid	Ask	Spread	Price	Transaction Location[a]	Transaction Volume	Time
			159.25	M	5400	9:33:59
159.00	159.75	0.75				9:34:55
			159.75	A	900	9:35:25
159.25	160.00	0.75				9:35:26
			160.00	A	100	9:36:21
159.50	160.50	1.00				9:36:24
			160.00	M	100	9:36:45
			160.00	M	500	9:36:52
			160.50	A	800	9:37:09
160.00	161.00	1.00				9:37:13
160.00	160.50	0.50				9:37:56
			160.50	A	100	9:38:57
			160.50	A	400	9:39:00
160.00	160.75	0.75				9:39:01
			160.75	A	500	9:39:11
			160.75	A	600	9:39:25
160.25	161.25	1.00				9:39:28
160.25	161.00	0.75				9:40:01
			161.00	A	500	9:40:34
160.50	161.50	1.00				9:40:35
			160.50	B	500	9:41:05
160.00	161.00	1.00				9:41:08
			161.00	A	500	9:41:36
160.50	161.00	0.50				9:41:39
160.50	161.00					9:41:59
			160.50	B	100	9:42:07
160.00	161.00	1.00				9:42:09
			160.00	B	100	9:44:13
159.50	161.00	1.50				9:44:15
159.50	160.00	0.50				9:44:57
			160.00	A	1500	9:45:10
159.50	160.00	0.50				9:45:11
			160.00	A	400	9:45:29
159.50	160.50	1.00				9:45:30
			159.50	B	400	9:48:57
159.00	160.00	1.00				9:48:58
159.00	159.625	0.625				9:49:16
			159.00	B	300	9:50:21
158.50	159.50	1.00				9:50:24

(continued)

TABLE 1.4   (*Continued*)

Bid	Ask	Spread	Price	Transaction Location[a]	Transaction Volume	Time
			158.75	M	400	9:50:32
158.25	159.25	1.00				9:50:35
			158.875	M	1000	9:51:01
158.375	159.375	1.00				9:51:04
			158.875	M	200	9:51:11
158.50	159.375	0.875				9:52:28
			158.875	M	600	9:52:38
			158.875	M	100	9:52:51
			159.25	M	500	9:53:28
158.75	159.75	1.00				9:53:29
159.00	159.75	0.75				9:54:06
			159.25	M	1000	9:54:47
			159.125	M	1300	9:57:03
159.00	159.50	0.50				9:57:22
			159.00	B	600	9:57:31
159.00	159.50	0.50				9:58:11
			159.25	M	300	9:59:45

[a] B = bid; A = ask; M = within the spread.

CBS's price changed appreciably as trading progressed for the next half hour. By 9:40 the stock was trading up 1.75 points (1.1%) to 161.00; by 9:50 it had fallen back 2.25 points (1.4%) to 158.75; and by the end of the period it had returned to its opening value of 159.25. Thus, for the 26-minute period, the open-to-close range was zero and the high-low was 2.25.[4]

Short-Run Price Changes Matter

Portfolio managers presumably do not alter their expectations of future share values with every price variation on the market, and consequently price movements of the magnitude shown in Tables 1.3 and 1.4 can have a substantial impact on longer-run returns. Thus short-run price movements must be taken into account to achieve long-run objectives. As an example, consider the hypothetical ABC fund.

ABC has a portfolio valued at $1 billion that includes XYZ common. XYZ common pays no dividend, has a forecasted end-of-year price of $58.00, and is currently trading at $51.25. The expected return of 13.17% [($58.00 ÷ $51.25) − 1] is enough for the fund to hold 300,000 shares, an investment that would be 1.54% of ABC's portfolio ($15,375,000).

TABLE 1.5 *The ABC Fund's Alternative Investment Decisions for XYZ Common* Future expectation of share @ $58 constant

Current price	$51.25	$51.00	$50.00
Expected return	13.17%	13.72%	16.00%
Desired share holdings	300,000	400,000	800,000
Value of share holdings (000)	$15,375	$20,400	$40,000
Percentage of the total portfolio	1.54%	2.04%	4.00%

ABC, recognizing that prices are volatile over brief periods, also assesses its desired holdings at $51.00 and $50.00. Table 1.5 contains the relevant information. We assume that, in the absence of new information, the fund's forecast of the end-of-year price remains fixed at $58.00 a share even when the current price of shares changes; that is, there is no price signaling. A 2.44% price reduction (from $51.25 to $50.00) increases the expected return on the investment by 21.49% (from 13.17% to 16.00%) and, consequently, the fund would invest more in the company at the lower price (4.00% of its

TABLE 1.6 *The ABC Fund's Trading Alternatives*

	Action	Reason
1.	**Market Order Strategy:** Buy 200,000 shares at market ($51.25)	Unwilling to risk missing an execution relatively more stable mkt.
2A.	**Scaled Limit Order Strategy:** Wait, hoping to buy 300,000 shares at $51 and 400,000 shares at $50	Transaction price is sufficiently variable
2B.	**Limit Order Strategy:** Wait, hoping to buy 700,000 shares at $50	Transaction price is *very* variable volatile mkt.
3.	**Do Nothing**	Transaction costs too high

Note: Because of the size of its desired purchase, the ABC fund would also be concerned about market impact. Reduction of this execution cost might require negotiating in the upstairs market, giving a floor trader a not held (NH) order, giving the specialist a percentage order, etc. We ignore these possibilities and the market impact problem to emphasize the underlying relationship between individual trading decisions and price discovery.

portfolio instead of 1.54%). That an annual return can be increased by more than 21% by reducing the purchase price from $51.25 to $50.00 is simple arithmetic. The striking fact is that a portfolio manager may indeed realize this profit enhancement by properly handling his or her orders in a volatile market.

Intraday price volatility gives an asset manager trading alternatives. Table 1.6 highlights three of these alternatives: (1) trade immediately at market to ensure receiving an execution, (2) place a limit order in the hope of executing at a better price, or (3) do not attempt to trade at all if transaction costs are too high. (These decisions are considered in greater detail in Chapter 14.) A market can be stabilized or destabilized, depending on the alternatives asset managers select.

Causes of Short-Run Price Volatility

Extensive attention was given to the turbulent markets of October 1987 and October 1989 in the financial press, and a number of government and industry reports have been issued. One of the most influential and widely cited is *The Report of the Presidential Task Force on Market Mechanisms*, commonly known as the "Brady Report."[5] The reports have recognized that volatility has been excessive and that the structure of the market is flawed, but the causes have not been well understood.

Informational Change

The major cause of stock price changes should ideally be news concerning the fundamental determinants of share value. Let us consider the October 1987 crash in this light. Information concerning the earnings power of individual companies was relatively constant during the period, and, as noted, expectations for fourth quarter financial reports were generally bullish through the first two weeks of the month. According to a report in *Newsweek*,[6] "Few of the nation's thousands of financial gurus had called the crash correctly; by one count, a mere five newsletters came anywhere close."

But prospects for higher interest rates and renewed inflation were strengthening, uncertainty in the financial markets had increased, and the market had responded. Future earnings were discounted at a higher rate, and share prices were adjusted down. By Friday, November 6, the market closed at 1,959.05, some 512 points and 21% below the value it had closed at on Monday, October 12. If the Dow on October 12 and on November 6 reflected reasonable assessments of the market at these times, the 512-point decrease was a reasonable assessment of the informational change that had occurred over the four-week period.

How accurately did the specific path that prices followed reflect the pattern of informational change? The wild swings experienced, particularly during the week of October 19, suggest that investor expectations were changing, not only because of new information concerning the basic determinants of ※ share value, but also in reaction to the order flow itself and in response to the market's dynamics.

Electronic Technology

During the wildest moments on 19 October 1987 the pace at which market events occurred had so accelerated that traders could not remain sufficiently informed about market conditions. Nor could they adequately digest the import of the events that were taking place so rapidly. Electronic technology had increased the speed with which sell decisions were made, the speed with which the orders were transmitted to the market, and the speed with which the resulting trades were reported. In this context, the widespread use of electronic technology could have contributed to the instability of the market.

But it is easy to point an accusing finger at a new and highly sophisticated technology. The computer has changed broker/dealer operations dramatically and affected the economic fortunes of many market professionals. Perhaps by speeding up the pace at which events can occur, it has put new stress on the market. Nevertheless, the clock cannot be turned back on technology. In a global environment any attempt by a market center to do so would only cause orders to flow across borders to other markets.

The continuous market was unnecessarily destabilized by traders overresponding to the stressful conditions.[7] Because of this, the Brady Commission proposed that circuit breakers be instituted to halt trading in destabilized conditions. A reasonable procedure to do so might have helped in October 1987 if one had already been in place. But to have suddenly closed the NYSE during the crisis could have created panic. John Phelan, Jr., the Exchange's chairman and CEO at the time, showed courage by keeping the market open.

Derivative Products

In recent years, sharp price changes and reversals have been associated with the program trading of institutional investors and large brokerage houses. When the sell programs are activated, share prices can be beaten down across the board, regardless of fundamental information concerning the individual stocks included in the baskets. During the October 1987 crash, arbitrage programs interacting with portfolio insurance programs transmitted massive selling pressure from the Chicago futures market back to the New York cash market, and prices that kept falling were fed into electronic systems that in turn kept spitting out additional sell orders.

The destabilizing interaction between portfolio insurance and index arbitrage programs will probably not be a recurring phenomenon. Portfolio insurance did not work at the time, and the cost to those firms that relied on it was high. The strategy is not widely used today.

The futures markets have traditionally played an important price discovery function for commodities, and they should for equities as well. A futures contract for a stock index enables the aggregate market to be traded as a single product, rather than issue by issue. This provides an alternative approach to evaluating the market and is a useful pricing guide for individual shares. If futures trading has in fact destabilized the cash market, the problem must lie with the specific system being used, not with the existence of the market per se.

Institutional Investors

The marketplace today is dominated by institutional investors. The investment managers can alter their decisions and submit orders with electronic speed. Programs are now being run that bring basket orders directly to the exchange floor, where they can execute with considerable market impact (although block trades for individual issues continue to be negotiated in the upstairs market). And, while they may not state it in these terms, portfolio managers act *as if* they think markets can make mistakes and then suddenly correct themselves.

These managers are assessed according to their trades, and their portfolios are scrutinized. They strive to avoid buying at or near the high for the day (or selling at or near the low). Moreover, the fund managers are reluctant to maintain large positions in securities that have suddenly dropped in value even if, in their opinion, long-run prospects remain bright. This puts additional pressure on the asset managers to make decisions in anticipation of how the market will behave in the very short term.

Errors in Price Discovery

Intraday price changes are not due to news only. They are also attributable to market impact effects and to errors in price discovery. Little attention has been paid to price discovery, even in relation to such turbulent events as the market crash in October 1987 and the mini-crash in October 1989.

Price discovery is not a simple matter of inaccurate quotes attracting orders that restore desired values. Rather, investors place their orders with regard to their eagerness to trade and expectations of what transaction prices will be in the short run. This strategic action can cause inflated or depressed prices to persist for some time. But if the level a market has reached starts to look questionable, sell orders triggered by expectations that prices will suddenly fall can cause prices to drop precipitously. Similarly, buy orders triggered by expectations that prices will suddenly rise can cause sharp price increases.

Market Structure

Excessive price volatility in brief time intervals cannot be adequately understood by focusing myopically on program trading, on the new and highly sophisticated technology that is required for its implementation, or on financial futures that enable the aggregate market to be traded quickly as a single product. The underlying problem is that shareholders do not seek to trade unless they are sufficiently dissatisfied with their portfolio holdings to incur the costs of transacting, and consequently the markets are relatively thin on any given day. There simply are not many orders on the trading floor or on the specialists' limit order books, and small transaction volume (vis-à-vis the number of shares outstanding) can have a sizable impact on a security's price. This was demonstrated dramatically on 19 October 1987: according to the Brady Report, "Only 3 percent of the total shares of publicly traded stock in the U.S. changed hands during this period, but it resulted in the loss in stock value of $1 trillion."

Another factor contributing to volatility is that price discovery is more difficult in today's market, which is increasingly dominated by institutional investors. The existence of large traders is not the cause, however, and accessibility of the market to them should not be restricted. Instead, the trading system must be altered in some very fundamental ways to bring needed liquidity to the market and to handle the institutional order flow properly.

Issues concerning the restructuring of the market are central to this book. Our recommendations are set forth in Part II. In brief, we suggest that consolidating orders in an electronic call market, where all crossing orders execute at a single price in a multilateral trade, will provide an environment where price discovery is facilitated, transactions costs are reduced, and short-run price movements are stabilized. Further, we suggest that listed corporations participate in the electronic calls to ensure that the secondary markets for their issues are sufficiently liquid and adequately stabilized.

Suggested Reading

Blume, M., Mackinlay, C., and Terker, B. "Order Imbalances and Stock Price Movements on October 19 and 20, 1987." *Journal of Finance,* September 1989.
Edwards, F. "The Crash: A Report of the Reports." In *The Challenge of Information Technology for the Securities Markets,* H. Lucas and R. Schwartz, eds. Homewood, IL: Dow Jones-Irwin, 1989.

"Final Report on Stock Index Futures and Cash Market Activity During October 1987." Commodity Futures Trading Commission, Division of Economic Analysis and Division of Trading and Markets, Washington, DC: GPO, January 1988.

General Accounting Office. *Financial Markets: Preliminary Observations on the October 1987 Crash.* Washington, DC: GPO, January 1988.

Harris, L. "The October 1987 S&P 500 Stock-Futures Basis." *Journal of Finance,* March 1989.

Leland, H., and Rubenstein, M. "Comments on the Market Crash: Six Months After." *Journal of Economic Perspectives,* Summer 1988.

Mendelson, M., Peake, J., and Williams, R. "Black Monday: Market Structure and Market-Making." In *The Challenge of Information Technology for the Securities Markets,* H. Lucas and R. Schwartz, eds., Homewood, IL: Dow Jones-Irwin, 1989.

Miller, M., Hawke, Jr., J., Malkiel, B., and Scholes, M. "Preliminary Report of the Committee of Inquiry Appointed by the Chicago Mercantile Exchange To Examine the Events Surrounding October 19, 1987." Chicago Mercantile Exchange, December 1987.

The Presidential Task Force on Market Mechanisms. *Report of the Presidential Task Force on Market Mechanisms.* Washington, DC: GPO, January 1988.

Roll, R. "The International Crash of October 1987." *Financial Analysts Journal,* September 1988.

Schreiber, P., and Schwartz, R. "Price Discovery in Securities Markets." *Journal of Portfolio Management,* Spring 1988.

Schwartz, R. "Price Discovery, Instability, and Market Structure." In Appendix G of report of the New York Stock Exchange's *Panel on Market Volatility and Investor Confidence.* New York: New York Stock Exchange, Inc., 1990.

Schwartz, R. "Institutionalization of the Equity Markets." *The Journal of Portfolio Management,* Winter 1991.

U.S. Congress, Office of Technology Assessment, *Electronic Bulls & Bears: U.S. Securities Markets & Information Technology,* OTA-CIT-469, Washington, DC: GPO, September 1990.

U.S. Securities and Exchange Commission, Division of Market Regulation. *The October 1987 Market Break,* Washington, DC: GPO, February 1988.

Notes

1. "Talk of the Town—Notes and Comments," *The New Yorker,* November 2, 1987, pp. 33, 34.
2. Robert J. Cole, *"Specialists Man the Ramparts,"* *The New York Times,* October 22, 1987, p. D14.
3. *Newsweek,* November 2, 1987, p. 24.
4. Data for CBS for the first half hour of trading on 1 March 1985 are given in R. Schwartz, *Equity Markets: Structure, Trading and Performance*, New York: Harper and Row, 1988. The pattern described is remarkably similar to that shown in Table 1.4. In the earlier period the stock opened at 86.00, rose to 87.125 after 14 minutes of trading, and then dropped back to 86.625 after 30 minutes.

5. Other reports include those of the Commodity Futures Trading Commission, the Securities and Exchange Commission, the General Accounting Office, the Office of Technology Assessment, the New York Stock Exchange, and the Chicago Mercantile Exchange. For further discussion, see Franklin Edwards, "The Crash: A Report on the Reports," in H. Lucas and R. Schwartz, eds., *The Challenge of Information Technology for the Securities Markets: Liquidity, Volatility & Global Trading,* Homewood, IL: Dow Jones-Irwin, 1989.
6. *Newsweek,* November 2, 1987, p. 16.
7. Some observers believe that some of the recent price movements may be attributable to price manipulation. Certain brokerage houses and institutional investors are indeed large enough to impact the aggregate market. But clear evidence of this has not been presented in the various crash reports, and we do not consider the possibility further.

2

The New York Stock Exchange

The NYSE is an agency market in which orders for the purchase and sale of listed securities are consolidated on a trading floor where they interact in an auction environment. Orders are routed to the exchange specialist who acts both as a dealer and as a broker's broker, matches orders received with other public orders or professional trader's orders, and controls the execution of orders held by floor traders. The floor traders compete with the specialist and the limit order book in the purchase and sale of shares.

Intermarket Competition

NYSE-listed securities are also traded on other U.S. exchanges, in the over-the-counter market, directly between investors, and overseas. Comprehensively, the U.S. secondary markets are classified as follows:

- The First Market refers to trades in exchange-listed issues that are made on the floor of an exchange.
- The Second Market refers to trades in non-exchange-listed securities that are made over-the-counter (OTC).
- The Third Market refers to trades in exchange-listed issues that take place off the exchange floor with the aid of brokers.
- The Fourth Market refers to trades in exchange-listed issues that are made by buyers and sellers, off the exchange floor, without the aid of brokers. (This does not refer to the "upstairs market," the network of trading desks that negotiates block transactions; these trades are generally taken to a market center to be executed.)

There are two national stock exchanges:

- The New York Stock Exchange (NYSE)
- The American Stock Exchange (Amex)

and five regional exchanges:

- Boston Stock Exchange (B)
- Cincinnati Stock Exchange (C)
- Midwest Stock Exchange (M)
- Pacific Stock Exchange (P)
- Philadelphia Stock Exchange (X)

Price discovery generally occurs at the NYSE, and many traders prefer to have their orders routed to the Big Board. On the other hand, commission charges may be lower in other markets and, in some cases, the execution of a block trade may be easier. Consequently, of all trades in NYSE-listed issues that were reported on the Consolidated Tape in 1989, only 84.1% of share volume took place on the NYSE (compared with 87.8% of total share volume in 1980). In 1989, only 69.2% of the trades took place on the NYSE (compared with 85.4% in 1980).[1] The NYSE's market share of all trades is less, however, when fourth market and overseas (primarily London) transactions that are not reported on the consolidated tape are also taken into account. According to a *Business Week* article,[2] the NYSE's share of the market is currently less than 60%.

This trend, if it continues, could have serious consequences for the Exchange's survival. Implications for trading costs and the quality of price discovery depend on the characteristics of the alternative market center (or centers) that could then become dominant. It would, however, be desirable for the NYSE, through change and innovation, to remain a premier marketplace for its securities.

Organizational Structure of the NYSE

NYSE Board

The NYSE is a not-for-profit corporation governed by a 27-person Board of Directors that both sets NYSE policy and supervises its operations. The Board is comprised of 12 industry directors (NYSE members) and 12 public directors (nonmembers) who are elected by the members of the NYSE. The exchange's Chairman, two Executive Vice Chairmen, and President also serve on the Board.

NYSE Members

Members of the NYSE are either individuals who own or lease a membership (called a "seat") or nominees (partners or employees) of member firms that own seats. The number of seats has been fixed at 1,366 since 1953. Seats can be bought, sold, or leased, and their price, as set by buyers and sellers, reflects the demand to hold a seat.[3] In addition to the regular NYSE members, 60 individuals have obtained either physical or electronic access to the trading floor by paying an annual membership fee. Unlike regular members, electronic or physical access members have no rights to the distributive assets of the NYSE. Because NYSE member firms are also members of the National Association of Security Dealers (NASD, the self-regulatory organization of broker/dealers that regulates the OTC market), many broker/dealer firms are simultaneously members of the NYSE, customers of the NYSE, and competitors of the NYSE.

NYSE members who operate on the trading floor include the following:

- *Specialists:* Specialists supply immediacy to the market by providing two-way quotes in the absence of other trading interest. As dealers, specialists post quotes on the market and buy for and sell from their inventory. As agents (broker's brokers), specialists handle limit orders for the stocks assigned to their trading posts. As of 31 December 1989, there were 438 individual specialists on the NYSE representing 49 *specialist units*. Specialist units have traditionally been private corporations or partnerships; however, several are subsidiaries of publicly held corporations or brokerage houses.

- *Commission-House Brokers:* Employed by the brokerage houses, commission-house or floor brokers link the brokerage houses with the specialist posts. The commission-house brokers operate from booths along the outside walls of the trading floor where they receive orders from their firms' clients and either execute them with the specialist, with each other or cross the trades. A cross trade occurs when the broker has both a buy and a sell order of the same size and completes the trade. All floor trades must be reported to and approved by the specialist.

- *Two-Dollar Brokers:* These brokers perform the same functions as the commission-house brokers but are not employed by a brokerage house. Rather, for a commission (that at one time was two dollars per order), they execute orders for commission-house brokers who are not able to handle all of the orders that have been transmitted to their firms. Two-dollar brokers may also be used by firms to disguise their interest in buying or selling a particular stock.

- *Competitive Traders:* These traders deal for their own accounts. They may also be two-dollar brokers or even specialists, but they may not act as both principal and agent for the same stock on the same day. Competitive traders operate on the trading floor to give the market greater depth through larger order flow. Their trading activities are constrained by various stabilization tests. These traders are typically given advantages in the form of lower trading costs and preferred access to some floor information.

- *Registered Competitive Market-Makers (RCMMs):* Like competitive traders, RCMMs may deal for their own accounts, and they cannot act as both principal and agent for the same stock on the same day. As a nonspecialist floor member, an RCMM can be called upon by a floor official to aid a specialist firm by adding liquidity to the market at times of particular stress.

The Listed Companies

As of June 1990, there were 1,721 listed companies, 87 of which were foreign. To be listed, a company must satisfy minimum standards of quality and size, must be willing to release adequate information about its operations, and must attract sufficient public interest. The following minimum requirements are imposed by the NYSE for domestic corporations (alternative standards are applied to foreign corporations):

- 1.1 million publicly held shares with public market value of at least $18 million. (Public market value does not include shares held by individuals within the organization.)
- Net tangible assets of $18 million. (This requirement may be relaxed at the discretion of the NYSE. In practice, more importance is placed on the market value criteria.)
- $2.5 million in earnings before federal income tax for the latest fiscal year and $2 million in earnings before federal income tax for each of the two preceding years, or an aggregate for the last three fiscal years of $6.5 million and a minimum in the most recent fiscal year of $4.5 million.
- 2,000 or more round lot shareholders (holding 100 or more shares each) or 2,200 total stockholders together with average monthly trading volume for the most recent six months of 100,000 shares.

Stock Allocation. Interested specialist firms apply for the allocation of newly listed securities. The Stock Allocation Committee allocates the securities to a specialist unit that then becomes responsible for making a market in that stock. The committee's allocation procedure takes into account the specialist firm's prior performance record, the firm's score on the Specialist Performance Evaluation Questionnaires (SPEQ), which is filled out quarterly by floor brokers, and the characteristics (such as industry type) of the issues currently assigned to the specialist firm. Requests made by the newly listed companies are also considered by the allocation committee.

Delisting. Delisting of a stock is possible, but occurs very infrequently and only with difficulty as long as a stock continues to satisfy the listing criteria. The NYSE will grant a delisting request if the following conditions are all met:

- At least two-thirds of the holders of outstanding shares vote in favor of delisting.
- No more than 10% of the shareholders object.
- Delisting is approved by a majority of the company's board of directors.

Revenues.   A large portion of the NYSE's revenues are generated by fees paid by the listed companies and from trading fees paid by members or member firms. Total revenues in 1989 were $349 million, made up of the following:

Listing Fees	$107,431,000
Trading Fees	80,449,000
Market Data Fees	54,777,000
Regulatory Fees	39,031,000
Facility and Equipment Fees	37,420,000
Membership Fees	8,007,000
Investment and Other Income	22,156,000

After expenses of $339 million, the NYSE had income before taxes of $10 million in 1989.

Trading Arenas

The NYSE comprises three major trading arenas:

1. *Main Trading Floor:* The largest, most important trading arena on the NYSE is the main trading floor, where stocks, warrants, options, and American Depository Receipts (ADRs) are traded.[4] The trading floor is divided into four separate rooms: the Main Room, the Garage, the Blue Room, and the Expanded Blue Room. Each stock is traded at a specific specialist's location around one of seventeen trading posts. Trading takes place from 9:30 A.M. to 4:00 P.M.

2. *Fixed Income Trading Floor:* The NYSE has over 2,900 listed bonds, including corporate and government issues. However, the major market for corporate and government bonds is Over-the-Counter. Approximately 85% of all NYSE bond trading is done through the *Automated Bond System (ABS),* a computerized system that provides current quotations and trade information and gives electronic executions for NYSE listed bonds. In addition to ABS, the NYSE has cabinet trading for

infrequently traded bonds and crowd trading for a few actively traded issues.

3. *New York Futures Exchange (NYFE):* NYFE, the seventh largest futures exchange in the U.S. and the most recent of the NYSE's operations, commenced operations in August 1980. On NYFE, contracts are exchanged in pit trading, a form of crowd trading in which traders stand in a tiered semicircle and call out buy and sell orders to each other in order to transact bilaterally. This type of trading can be sustained in NYFE due to the heavy volume of trading in the index options. The contracts traded are futures on the NYSE Composite Index, options on the NYSE Composite Index futures,[5] CRB Index futures and options on the futures,[6] and U.S. Treasury Bond futures. The most popular equity index future contract, the S&P 500 futures contract, which proxies 500 NYSE, Amex, and OTC stocks, is traded at the Chicago Mercantile Exchange.

Trading hours for NYFE are 9:30 A.M. to 4:15 P.M. for stock index futures and options on the futures; 9:30 A.M. to 3:30 P.M. for CRB Index futures and options on the futures; and 8:20 A.M. to 4:15 P.M. for U.S. Treasury Bond futures.

The Specialists

In a system that, except for the Toronto Stock Exchange, is unique to the U.S. exchanges, trading is structured around the specialist, a market professional who functions as both a principal (dealer) and an agent (broker's broker). As the key market makers in the NYSE, specialists handle most of the order flow for the stocks assigned to them.

Specialist Responsibilities and Restrictions

With regard to a listed corporation, the specialist is bound by certain responsibilities and restrictions:

- the specialist must make at least one annual contact with an official of the corporation.
- neither the specialist nor anyone associated with the specialist (for example, a partner or clerk) may participate in a proxy contest or in a contest for a change of management of the corporation.
- a specialist may not be an officer or a director of the corporation.
- the specialist may not accept orders directly from officers, directors, principal stockholders of the corporation or from the corporation itself.

With regard to his or her own trades as a dealer, the specialist:

- cannot buy for his or her own account while holding unexecuted market orders to buy, and cannot sell for his or her own account while holding unexecuted market orders to sell, and must always give priority to equally priced limit orders.
- cannot by his or her own buying or selling activate a customer's stop order on the book.
- may not charge a brokerage commission and be a dealer in the same trade.
- with the permission of a floor official, a specialist can trade with an order he or she is holding on the order book.
- may not solicit orders in stock in which he or she specializes.
- may not accept orders from an institution or deal directly with an institutional investor.
- is restricted in his or her freedom to buy shares at a price higher than the last transaction price (on an "up-tick") or to sell shares at a price lower than the last transaction price (on a "down-tick"). This "tick-test rule" prevents the specialist from accentuating a market imbalance.

The Specialist as Auctioneer

As discussed, all orders for a stock that are sent to the NYSE converge at the specialist post to which that stock is assigned. When trading is heavy, floor traders pack in about the post and the specialist conducts an auction. As auctioneer, the specialist is responsible for ensuring that orders are handled in conformity with acceptable auction practice and for determining who gets a trade. In this regard, the market maker is responsible for enforcing trading priority rules by determining the orders that have priority, parity or precedence (refer to the section, "Order Execution," later in this chapter). Any member may call upon a floor official to make a ruling in the event of a dispute.

As auctioneer, the specialist may "stop a stock," but only when the market spread is greater than the minimum tick size of one-eighth. When the specialist *stops a stock* he or she has guaranteed execution at the *stop price*. The request to stop a stock may be initiated at a floor broker's request for a public trader. Once it is granted, the specialist is obliged to honor the request. If the specialist succeeds in finding a better price, the stop is off. Once an order is executed in the crowd at the guaranteed price, the specialist must execute the stopped order and inform the floor broker that the stop has been "elected."

The Specialist's Affirmative Obligation

Specialists have an affirmative obligation to make "a fair and orderly market" for the stocks assigned to them. "Fair and orderly" is viewed as the absence of excessively large and erratic price changes relative to the number of shares traded. This means that the specialist must intervene in trading to keep price changes *acceptably* small by buying and selling from his or her own account against a prevailing market trend. What is acceptable has been defined by the NYSE with reference to the price level at which the stock is trading, the stock's trading activity, and so forth. Thus, specialists dampen the short-run volatility of prices, but they do not peg prices. If the underlying pressure exists for a price to increase or decrease to a new level, the price does change to the new level. The specialist simply makes the transition more orderly. Specialist intervention, either to make stabilizing trades or to halt trading, mutes swings that occur either as a result of thinness on one side of the market or because the market has overreacted to news. This is of value to market-order traders because it gives them greater assurance that prices will not jump away from them while their orders are being transmitted to the specialist posts.

At times the specialist is not expected to keep price changes within usual limits. When sizable price movements occur because of major stock-specific informational change, the market may not efficiently be able to find a new price and handle trades at the same time. Under this condition, the specialist may, with the permission of a floor official, *halt trading*. During a trading halt, the specialist has time to assess market conditions and traders have time to digest news and to revise their orders.

At times of marketwide price changes, specialists may be unable to keep price changes for their issues within normal limits. The extreme market volatility in October 1987 and the precipitous decline on October 19th, showed that the liquidity specialists can provide to a market under stress is limited, and that trading halts for specific issues may not arrest a broad decline.

During the crash of 1987, specialist capital proved inadequate relative to the liquidity demands of institutional traders. Furthermore, the NYSE's criteria for a fair and orderly market was unsupportable when the market dropped over 500 points in a single day.

Following the crash, the NYSE took some steps to improve specialists' ability and incentive to cope with volatile conditions. Eleven stocks were reallocated because of inadequate specialist performance. The NYSE also increased minimum capital requirements per assigned specialist unit to the greater of $1 million or 25% of position requirements of 450 round lots in each stock in which the specialist is registered to make a market (from the greater of $100,000 or 25% of position requirements of 150 round lots). These steps are insufficient to deal with the broader systemic problems.

Price Discovery During Market Opening/Reopening Procedures

Specialist operations are particularly critical at the start of the trading day. The NYSE opening bell rings at 9:30 A.M.; the market for a stock opens when the specialist finds a price that balances the buy and sell orders for the issue. The specialist does this by matching market orders that come in through OARS (see the next section), public limit orders and non-OARS-eligible market orders that come into the electronic display book or printers, and orders from the trading crowd. This special opening procedure of the NYSE resembles call market trading; call market trading is the batching of orders for execution only at specific predetermined times instead of continuously. The specialist establishes a price that best balances the accumulated buy and sell pressures and reflects the market's aggregate desire to hold shares of the stock. In setting a price, the specialist usually must commit his or her own capital by buying or selling from his or her own account to balance the orders.

When an opening price is not determined within fifteen minutes due to major informational change, opening is *delayed* and the specialist sends out price indications. When an acceptable price is found, the market for the stock is opened and trading begins. As trading proceeds during the trading day, the specialist continues to assess market conditions in order to establish prices that best balance buy and sell pressures in the market.

Specialists' Profits

Specialists derive their profits from negotiated commission revenue and from trading gains. Commissions, a relatively riskless source of income, are earned when the specialist assumes the role of broker and handles public orders. With the advent of SuperDOT and negotiated commissions, commission income is of dwindling importance; except for short sales, market orders and limit orders that execute within two minutes through SuperDOT are ineligible for commission billing by the specialists. Trading gains, a much riskier source of income, are realized because, as a dealer, the specialist buys for and sells from his or her own account. Specialists' up-to-the-second knowledge of the limit order book and location on the exchange floor gives them a good vantage point from which to trade. But, in certain respects they are at a disadvantage: a public order at a price must be executed before a specialist's order, and the affirmative obligation to make a fair and orderly market forces specialists to trade under conditions they would not otherwise accept.

Specialist profits are not derived from a monopoly power over the order flow because the specialist does not have a monopoly position. As discussed, anyone is free to submit a limit order and thereby establish a quote at which anyone else may trade. Furthermore, investors may negotiate their orders with each other, in the upstairs market, or via commission house-brokers on the trading floor, thereby by-passing the specialist. In addition, public limit orders are exposed directly to other traders, and all orders are exposed to the crowd of floor traders. In 1989, specialists participated as either buyers or sellers in transactions that involved only 19% of total transaction volume on the NYSE.

Order-Routing and Information Systems

SuperDOT

In 1976, the NYSE developed the Designated Order Turnaround (DOT) system to route orders directly to specialists' posts on the trading floor. DOT has been upgraded significantly since its introduction, and the improved electronic order-routing system is known as SuperDOT. SuperDOT accepts market orders of up to 30,099 shares and limit orders of up to 99,999 shares. SuperDOT is widely used to handle program trades. In 1989, SuperDOT processed an average of 149,000 orders per day; this is estimated to be between 75% and 85% of all NYSE orders.

The NYSE experienced dramatic growth during the 1980s; average daily volume increased from 32 million shares in 1979 to more than 165 million shares in 1989. Entering the fourth quarter of 1987, the NYSE's maximum capacity was estimated to be about 425 million shares, yet on both 19 and 20 October 1987, more than 600 million shares changed hands. In fact, between Friday, October 16 and Friday, October 23 of that year, more than 2.6 billion shares were traded. Following this period of extreme volume, the NYSE escalated its capacity-building efforts, setting a goal of being able to handle peak daily volume of one billion shares in the early 1990s. The NYSE opened the Expanded Blue Room in January 1988, thereby enlarging its trading floor by 23%. Various system upgrades have helped speed order flow through the NYSE's SuperDOT System.

OARS. A feature of SuperDOT, the Opening Automated Report Service (OARS), accepts preopening market orders. OARS facilitates orderly openings by helping specialists determine an opening price for a stock that best balances supply and demand. At the opening, OARS automatically pairs buy and sell orders and presents the imbalance to the specialist.

IIEDS. Addressing the concern that small investors might be unable to gain fair access to the market during periods of heavy activity, the NYSE introduced the Individual Investor Express Delivery Service (IIEDS) in

October 1988. IIEDS gives priority to individual investor orders of up to 2,099 shares that are submitted through SuperDOT, thereby accelerating their routing through the system. The system was initially activated only on days when the Dow Jones Industrial Average (DJIA, a weighted index comprised of 30 industrial stocks) moved 25 points from its previous close; following the extreme volatility in October 1989, IIEDS was made available to individual investors whenever the market is open. (On 16 October 1989, that year's most active day, 96,000 orders from individuals were executed via IIEDS.)

CMS.   The Common Message Switch is the electronic port of entry into SuperDOT. As part of the NYSE's capacity-building effects, the message-handling capacity of the NYSE's order-routing systems was upgraded to 210 messages per second in 1989. (CMS must be able to handle 240 messages per second to process a billion shares per day.)[7] More than 600 direct lines connect approximately 190 member firms to the NYSE trading floor via SuperDOT. Orders are sorted by type and transmitted to the floor. A *Floor Switch* enables member firms to route orders directly to the appropriate specialist's post or to the firm's broker booth location on the trading floor for manual execution by floor brokers.

For member firms, a primary advantage of using SuperDOT is that specialists cannot charge a commission for pre–opening market orders of up to 30,099 shares or for post–opening market orders of up to 2,099 shares. (Market orders for short sales are not commission free.) Limit orders of up to 2,099 shares that are executed within two minutes are also exempted from commissions, as are all limit orders where the specialist is on the contra side of a trade.

Another advantage of SuperDOT is the automatic transmission of a transaction report (upon execution) to the member firm that submitted the order. Over 98% of all market orders handled by SuperDOT in 1989 were executed and reported back to the originating member firm within two minutes.[8]

The Consolidated Tape

The Consolidated Tape displays current transaction prices and volume. It consists of two networks:

Network A provides transaction data for NYSE-listed issues executed either on the NYSE, regional exchanges or over-the-counter. (Transactions made in the third market must be reported to the Consolidated Tape within 90 seconds of the trade.)

Network B provides transaction data for American Stock Exchange (Amex) transactions on Amex, regional exchanges, and over-the-counter.

Transactions in regional issues not listed on Amex are also reported on this network.

A sequence of entries on the Consolidated Tape may appear as follows:

CBS	T	ITT	GM
197⅞	5s43	11.000s56	40.4s40⅛

The transactions occurred from left to right and the tape advances from the right to the left. The issue's trading symbol is at the top of the tape and transaction data are at the bottom and to the right of the symbol. The sequence of trades shown above are interpreted as follows:

- The first entry shows that 100 shares of CBS traded at 197⅞. Only the transaction price is shown if the transaction is for 100 shares (one round lot).

- The second entry shows that 500 shares of AT&T (ticker symbol T) traded at 43. For transactions of two or more round lots (but less than 100 round lots), the number of round lots is followed by an *s* preceding the price.

- The third entry shows that 11,000 shares (110 round lots) of ITT traded at 56. For transactions of 100 roundlots or more, the entire volume is displayed.

- The last entry shows that 100 shares of General Motors traded at 40, and then 400 shares traded at 40⅛. Information for back-to-back trades in the same stock is given after the symbol with a decimal point separating the trades.

Errors on the Consolidated Tape are corrected in the following types of entries:

NO.T	WAS
5s43	5s44

This indicates that a previous trade in AT&T was at 44, not 43.

CANCEL LAST GM
40⅛

This indicates that the most recently reported trade in GM was canceled.

LUV.SLD

17 ¼

This indicates that the reported trade in SouthWest Airlines is being reported out of order.

UAL.OPD

99 ½

This indicates a delayed opening and an indicated opening price for United Airlines stock.

TOY   S

35 ⅛

T

This indicates that the specialist "stopped the stock" of Toys R Us to guarantee a price. The tape also contains special entries for information on inactive stocks, trading halts, stock splits, and block transactions.

The Consolidated Tape can print at speeds of up to 900 characters per minute depending on the trading activity on the NYSE. In addition, several delete modes can be activated when heavy trading volume necessitates. For example, volume data and the whole number portion of the stock price (the handle) other than the last digit, may be deleted, except on opening prices and for trades at integer multiples of 10. For example, if the sequence of trades for GM is 400 at 39 ⅞ then 100 at 39 ¾; 200 at 39 ⅞; 100 at 40 ⅛; 300 at 40 ¼, the tape entries would be the following:

GM	GM	GM	GM	GM
4s39 ⅞	9 ¾	9 ⅞	40 ⅛	40 ¼

If trading for all issues is halted on the floor of the NYSE due to weather (for example, a snowstorm) or for governmental reasons (for example, due to the assassination of a President) or as a result of a power failure, and so forth, other market centers may not close. If this occurs, trade reports for other market places are not shown on the Consolidated Tape as they occur, but are displayed after the NYSE close.

The Intermarket Trading System

The Intermarket Trading System (ITS) is an electronic network that links the NYSE, the American Stock Exchange (Amex), the National Association of Securities Dealers Automatic Quotation System (NASDAQ) and the five regional exchanges. ITS started as a pilot program between the New York and Philadelphia stock exchanges on 17 April 1978. Gradually, other exchanges and more issues have been added to the system. The number of shares executed through ITS increased from 209.4 million in 1979, its first complete year of operation, to 2.3 billion in 1989. As of 31 December 1989, 2,082 issues were eligible for trading through ITS.[9]

Orders routed by ITS are commitments to trade a given number of shares at a stated price. The commitments have an expiration time of one to two minutes. A broker on the floor of any of the seven U.S. stock exchanges can observe the quotes for an ITS stock on a CRT at the specialist's post. After obtaining the specialist's quotes, if the broker chooses the ITS, a commitment is sent to the specialist at the exchange where the best ITS quote has been posted. This commitment is either accepted or rejected (if it has been filled or withdrawn).[10]

The NYSE (or regional) specialist has an opportunity to match the best quote shown in the ITS and thus to capture the order because no secondary (time) priority trading rule is enforced in the system. Therefore, an order initially submitted to one exchange is likely to be executed on that exchange.

Order Handling and Execution

A varied set of orders and order qualifications can be written on the NYSE, and the rules of order execution are relatively complex. This is largely because of the fiduciary responsibilities inherent in an agency/auction environment. In practice, most orders are written as either *market orders* or *limit orders*.

NYSE Order Types

Market Orders. A *market order* is an order to buy or to sell that is executed at the current market price, namely at the best price currently established on the market. For a market order *seller,* the best price is often the highest bid posted by a buyer. For a market order *buyer,* the best price is often the lowest ask posted by a seller. Market orders are commonly executed within the quotes, however, when the spread is greater than $\frac{1}{8}$ of a point. Market order traders usually face some uncertainty concerning the exact price at which they will transact, but unlike limit order traders, they are under normal conditions assured of transacting.

Limit Orders.   A *limit order* sets a limit on the price at which the order can be executed. A *limit buy order* states the maximum price at which the trader will buy. A *limit sell order* states the minimum price at which the trader will sell. Price limits for buy orders are usually set at or below current market prices, and price limits for sell orders are usually set at or above current market prices.

Limit orders that do not execute upon arrival are put in a *limit-order book,* a file of orders sequenced by price and time of arrival. These orders are kept on an electronic display book rather than on paper. These "books" are in theory closed to all but the specialists, specialists clerks, and, if necessary, floor officials. As a practical matter, the CRTs are located on the specialists' posts and can be seen by others on the trading floor.

Day Orders are automatically cancelled if not executed or withdrawn by the end of the day on which they are submitted. *Good 'Til Canceled (GTC)* orders remain on the book until executed or canceled.

Not Held Orders.   A *not held order* (marked NH) indicates that the broker is not held responsible if the order is not executed while the broker attempts to obtain a better price. A *not held limit order* and *not held market order* give the commission broker the freedom to "work" the order on the floor. A not held limit order also instructs the broker not to go beyond the limit price. Orders may not be given to the specialist on a not held basis; a broker holding an NH order may, on his or her own judgment, give all or part of it to the specialist, but only on a "held" basis.

Percentage Orders.   A *percentage order* states how much of an order will be activated based upon trading volume in the issue. A percentage order allows the public trader to have an order "worked" without requiring that a floor trader stand continuously by the specialist's post. In essence, it enables a specialist to fulfill the role of a floor trader without exercising his or her own discretion (as noted, specialists are not allowed to handle customer orders on a not held basis).

A percentage order must be "elected" (turned into a limit order) before it can be executed. It is elected when another transaction occurs for the same issue and on the same exchange to which the order has been submitted. The stated percentage establishes the amount of the order that is elected relative to trading volume for the issue on the exchange.

For example, if a 50% order for 8,000 shares is specified, 100 shares of the order become a limit order with each 100 shares that transact on the exchange. This guarantees that the trader who placed the percentage order will participate in no more than 50% of the trades in the stock. If the ask quotation on the market decreases below the limit price of a buy percentage order, or if the bid quotation rises above the limit price of a sell percentage order, the elected portion of the percentage order in effect becomes a market order and executes immediately to the extent possible.

A percentage order may, if a public trader so instructs, be converted into a limit order without an electing trade. For example, an investor may submit a percentage order to buy 8,000 shares of an issue at $40, with instructions that the order be converted, in whole or in part, into a limit order at that price if any order to sell 10,000 or more shares comes on the market. This conversion arrangement allows the trader who submits the order to participate in a block transaction. A percentage order may also give the specialist permission to be on parity with the order (that is, to buy or to sell stock along with the elected portion of the percentage order). In this case the percentage order is known as a "CAP" (convert and parity) order.

Percentage orders are commonly used by institutional traders to minimize price impact and to ensure that the average prices of their executions are in reasonable conformity with the average prices of all trades in an issue for a trading session.

Stop Orders. A *stop order* is usually transmitted to the specialist and entered on the limit-order book. Stop orders to buy at market are written at prices above the current quotes, and stop orders to sell at market are written at prices below the current quotes. The prices at which the orders are written are *stop prices*. A stop order is activated when the price on the market reaches the stop price. Assume, for example, that the market ask quote for XYZ stock is 50, and that a stop order to buy 100 shares has been entered at 55 (the order would be written "Buy 100 XYZ stop 55"). If the market price rises to 55, the stop order is activated by being converted into a market order and then executed against the best available ask on the market.

Stop orders can also be written as *stop limit orders*. When a stop limit order is activated, it is converted into a limit rather than a market order. A stop limit order to buy 100 shares of XYZ stock might read, "buy 100 XYZ at 55 stop, limit 55." Assume XYZ is currently trading at 50. The order would be activated if the price of XYZ were to rise to 55. It would then become an order to buy 100 shares at a maximum (limit) price of 55.

The term "stop order" reflects the defensive use to which these orders are commonly put: to stop the loss that can occur in the advent of an adverse price movement. For instance, assume an investor has sold a stock short. If the price of the stock were to go down, the investor would buy it back cheaply, repay his or her debt, and enjoy a profit. The risk the investor runs is that the stock might go up in price. The investor can obtain some protection against this risk by placing a stop order to buy at a higher price. Then, if the price of the stock starts to rise, the order is automatically activated and the investor's loss is limited.

The stop order can also be used to protect a gain. Assume an investor has already made paper profits on a short position and, for some reason, expects the price of a stock to go down in the short run and then later to rise. Thus, while the investor is holding out for a better price, the gains from the short sale can be protected by placing a stop order to buy. Similarly, an investor who has made paper profits on a long position can achieve some protection against an unexpected downturn by placing a stop order to sell at a stop price below the current market price.

Order Qualifications and Instructions

The following qualifications and instructions are used for orders submitted to the exchanges: (Other qualifications may also be specified regarding the terms of settlement.)

- *Fill or Kill (FOK)* The order to buy (sell) at a particular price must either be entirely filled immediately, or entirely cancelled.

- *Immediate or Cancel (IOC)* IOC orders are similar to FOK orders, except that partial execution is acceptable, and only the unexecuted portion of the order is cancelled.

- *All or None (AON)* AON orders are similar to FOK orders in that they do not allow for partial execution; however, they are not cancelled if they do not execute immediately.

- *At the Opening* Orders placed "at the opening" are to be executed only at the opening; any unfilled portion of the order that remains after the opening is cancelled.

- *Market-on-Close* The order is to be executed as close to the market closing as possible.

- *Limit or Market-on-Close* The order is placed as a limit order, but if it does not execute during the trading day, it is to be executed as a market order as near to the close as possible.

- *Limit or Better* Assume the market bid for a stock is 40. A limit or better order to sell might be written at 39 OB. The customer expects to sell at 40, but is protected by the limit of 39; the "or better" identification is added so that the floor broker will not think the price was a mistake.

- *Do Not Reduce (DNR)* Ordinarily, the prices of limit buy orders and of stop orders to sell are automatically reduced for dividends on the ex-dividend date; the DNR instruction tells the specialist not to do this. The instruction applies only to the cash dividend adjustment, however;

the price of the order will still be reduced for other distributions (stock dividends or rights).

Trading Priority Rules

Price Priority Rule. With *price priority,* buyers posting higher bids have priority over buyers posting lower bids; sellers posting lower asks have priority over sellers posting higher asks. This assures that traders who are willing to pay the highest prices will be the first to receive shares, and that sellers willing to accept the lowest prices will be the first to sell shares.

Secondary Trading Priority Rules. A *secondary trading priority rule* specifies the sequence to be followed for orders that have been submitted at the same price. The secondary priority rule most commonly used is *time priority:* the first order placed is the first to execute. An alternative rule is *size priority* where the largest order is the first to execute.

Orders on the NYSE display book are handled according to time priority. To determine the sequence in which they are executed along with orders held by floor traders, the set of display book orders at each price is treated as one order that is executed along with orders in the crowd according to a mixture of time and size priorities that comprise the rules of priority, parity and precedence.

Strict time priority applies to the first order placed (this is the rule of priority); time priority continues to apply if the limit buy order that was placed next in the sequence is large enough to absorb the remainder of the sell order entirely. Size priority applies if the limit buy order that was placed next in the sequence cannot absorb the remainder of the sell order entirely. By combining size and time priorities, the NYSE minimizes the number of separate transactions that a large order can generate, while still adhering to time priority as closely as possible. The procedure also facilitates the execution of block transactions that have been negotiated in the upstairs market.

To see how the rules of priority, parity, and precedence work, assume that five limit buy orders for XYZ stock have been placed at 42, and that they have been entered in the following sequence:

Time	Buy Order	Size of Buy Order
11:05	A	1,000 shares
11:30	B	1,000 shares
11:32	C	3,000 shares
12:00	D	3,000 shares
12:15	E	5,000 shares

Assume a trade at 12:20 eliminates a limit buy order at 42 ⅛, and that the market bid becomes 42. Now let a market order to sell 4,000 shares arrive at 12:30.

Priority. Priority is given to the first limit order placed at a price. The first counterpart order that triggers a trade at the price must be executed against the limit order that has priority. In the above example, order A has priority, and 1,000 shares of the 4,000-share market sell order will be executed against order A.

Parity. The rule of parity applies to all orders, at a price, that are large enough to satisfy the remaining part of a market order. In the above example, orders C, D, and E have parity. The orders that have parity are executed according to the time sequence in which they were placed; therefore, order C (which was placed before orders D and E) will be executed against the remaining 3,000 shares of the market sell order.

Precedence. If the market order to sell had been for 7,000 shares, order A would still have priority and so would be executed first. But no other order would be large enough to satisfy the remainder, and consequently none would have parity. In this case the rule of precedence would apply. By the rule of precedence, the sequence is determined by order size. In the above example, order E (for 5,000 shares) is the largest, and it will be executed after order A according to the rule of precedence. Following the execution of order E, 1,000 shares of the market sell order still remain. Orders B, C, and D are each large enough to satisfy the remainder, and thus the rule of parity once again applies; order B, having been placed first, will absorb the remainder of the market sell order.

If a public limit order is not executed at a price at which trades have been made, the specialist reports either *stock ahead* (that is, other orders were executed first on the basis of priority, parity, or precedence), *matched and lost* (if two orders arrive at the same time, their time sequence is assigned by random selection), or in the case of a short sale, that a tick-test rule has prevented the execution.

Special Rules of Order Execution

The Priority of Public Orders. The specialist or any floor trader who handles customer orders as agent and who also trades from his or her own account as principal must give way to public orders at a price. This rule is applied before the rules of priority, parity, and precedence.

Tick-Test Rule. The tick-test rule is applied to tick-sensitive orders such as orders marked "buy minus" or "sell plus" and short sales. A sell order is marked "short" if the seller does not own the shares (that is, has a long position) he or she is selling and therefore must deliver borrowed shares.

A short sale can be executed only on a plus tick or a zero plus tick. (Orders marked "short exempt" are exempt from the short sales rules.) The tick-test rule is applied to short sales to prevent public traders from destabilizing the market by selling into a falling market.

Buy-minus and sell-plus designations are commonly used for index arbitrage trades to protect against market impact effects in the cash market. If the market moves up or down by 50 points or more in any one day, the NYSE itself requires that the buy-minus or sell-plus tick test rule is imposed for all index arbitrage trades.

Partial Execution. The rules of priority, parity, and precedence determine the limit orders that will execute against a counterpart order, regardless of whether or not the limit orders execute totally (unless the limit order is FOK or AON). For example, if a limit order is for 4,000 shares, a market order for 1,000 shares can execute against it, reducing its size to 3,000 shares. The remaining portion of the limit order does not lose its place on the book.

Handling Block Trades

Any transaction of 10,000 shares or more is considered a block trade. Block transactions accounted for 51.1% of NYSE share volume in 1989, but only 2% of the trades.[11] In 1989, 872,811 blocks were executed on the NYSE (representing 21.3 billion shares) for an average of 3,464 blocks per day. On an average day in 1989, in total, 165,470 trades were made on the NYSE. The 10 largest block trades that year each exceeded 5 million shares. Because large orders are destabilizing if presented to the market in the same way that smaller orders are presented, block orders are handled differently. Whether an order will be handled as a block depends upon the size of the trade in relation to the normal trading volume for the stock and the broker's opinion of the market's ability to absorb the trade.

Assume that an institutional investor wants to sell 600,000 shares of XYZ stock at a minimum price of 35. There are basically six ways the large block may be sold:

1. Sell the shares at the market. Some large buy orders may be behind the quotes on the NYSE limit order book and some orders may be worked on the NYSE floor. But if the daily trading volume of XYZ is only 700,000 shares, the market for XYZ would not be sufficiently liquid to absorb the sell order without a substantial price decrease.

2. Place a huge limit order on the book (perhaps at 35 ⅜). The sell order would be highly visible and, correctly or erroneously, would be

interpreted as a signal of informational change. Buyers would respond to the signal by lowering their bids. Compounding the problem, the seller's limit order would extend to all other traders a **free** option to call the stock at the limit price. This would prevent an increase in the stock's price as buyers would likely lower their bids and gamble that selling pressure will decrease the price of the stock.

3. Convey the order to a broker on the NYSE floor. Medium size orders are worked on the exchange to avoid the price impact of a market order or the price impact attributable to the option value of a revealed limit order. This approach is not viable, however, for a 600,000 share order because the contra orders on the floor (other traders or the limit order book) simply would not be large enough to provide the liquidity required.

4. Convey the order to the fourth market (for example, Instinet). The buyer and a seller can meet electronically, obtain privacy on the screen, and submit tentative bids and offers to each other in an electronic negotiation. When agreement is reached, the trade is revealed to other subscribers in the fourth market.

5. Break the order into smaller pieces to be sold over a period of a day or more. This approach can be very time consuming.

6. Negotiate the order in the *upstairs market*. Refer to section *Block Trading* in Chapter 6, "Behind the Scenes," for further discussion of this procedure.

Handling Odd Lots

An odd lot is an order to trade less than one round lot of 100 shares. For example, an order to buy 50 shares of LMC is an odd lot. A partial round lot is a round lot with an odd lot portion, for example, if the order is for 150 shares of LMC.

Odd lot orders are handled in an electronic system that executes the orders against the specialist's account. The specialist does not see them or even become informed about them as they occur. The specialist is only informed of his or her cumulative odd lot transactions whenever net purchases or sales hits a quantity trigger that the specialist sets.

Odd lot market orders are priced at the quoted bid or ask. Because they are system executed, they are never stopped and are never executed within the spread.

An odd lot limit order is executed at its limit price when that price has been penetrated by one-eighth of a point. For example, a limit order to buy 50 shares of TOY at 25 requires a trade of 24 7/8 to be executed at 25.

The odd lot part of a partial round lot order is priced and executed with the round lot portion regardless of the counterparty to the trade. The specialist, however, is always the counterparty to the odd lot portion. For example, a market order to buy 2,008 shares of LUV may be matched within the quotes with a 2,000-share sell order held by a floor broker. The specialist will sell the odd lot portion of eight shares, but not be informed until the trigger has been reached.

Regulation

Congress established of the Securities and Exchange Commission (SEC) in 1934 to oversee and regulate the issuance and trading of securities in the United States. The SEC in turn delegated certain regulatory responsibility to the market centers themselves (the Stock Exchanges and the National Association of Securities Dealers). In this capacity, the market centers are known as "self-regulatory organizations" (SROs).

Self-Regulatory Organization

The NYSE has primary responsibility for the day-to-day surveillance of trading activity. In its SRO capacity, the NYSE also imposes, monitors, and enforces a variety of regulatory rules, requirements and controls on its member firms. The Exchange further requires that information be provided by the issuers of listed securities and can discipline its members for breaches of conduct. With regard to its various constituencies the following conditions hold:

1. Specialists are monitored to ensure adequate compliance with their affirmative obligation to make a fair and orderly market.
2. All trading is monitored to guard against unfair practices such as price manipulation and exploitation of information that has not been made public.
3. Broker/dealer firms are monitored with regard to minimum net capital requirements, various standards and licensing requirements, and training and disciplinary procedures.
4. Various listing and disclosure requirements are enforced on the listed companies, as discussed above.

Market Surveillance

Several automated facilities support market surveillance at the Exchange:

StockWatch. StockWatch is an automated surveillance system that monitors every NYSE trade and alerts analysts when certain price and/or volume parameters are violated. If a legitimate reason for any unusual activity is not apparent (a news release, for example), an investigation is initiated.

Intermarket Surveillance Information System (ISIS).   ISIS is a collection of electronic databases of trading and audit trail information. ISIS files contain transactions data from the members of the Intermarket Surveillance Group, which was set up in 1981 by the major U.S. securities markets to facilitate the monitoring of trading activity across markets. During an investigation, ISIS enables analysts to reconstruct a transaction and helps to identify the member firms involved in a suspicious activity.

Automated Search and Match (ASAM).   This system automatically matches trade data submissions against the ASAM investigative tree, enabling NYSE to determine quickly if suspected insider traders are officers or directors of the same company, members of the same clubs, or residents of the same area. The ASAM data base contains the names of approximately 500,000 business executives, and has been expanded to include names of lawyers, accountants, and investment bankers.

Intermarket Coordination

Following the October 1987 market crash, the NYSE has undertaken a series of initiatives to dampen "excess" volatility and to improve the performance of the market during periods of extreme stress. Improvements have been concentrated in the areas of trading capacity and NYSE specialist performance requirements (discussed above), program trading reforms (discussed in Chapter 6), and intermarket cooperation.

To coordinate more effectively the equity and derivative markets, the NYSE and the Chicago Mercantile Exchange (CME) agreed in July 1988 on a series of joint initiatives. Most notably, a set of coordinated "circuit breakers" have been adopted. When the S&P 500 future contract traded on the CME falls 12 points (approximately 96 DJIA points), the price of the future is not permitted to fall further for 30 minutes. During this time, market orders for program trades of the S&P 500 stocks are collected in a blind file. After five minutes, buy and sell orders are paired off and only the matched orders are eligible for execution. If orderly trading cannot be resumed, trading is halted, and the imbalance is publicly announced.

In its June 1990 report, the New York Stock Exchange's Panel on Market Volatility and Investor Confidence proposed a coordinated set of circuit breakers for the cash, futures, and options markets. Triggers for the New York Stock Exchange were set at 100, 200, 300, and 400 DJIA points (up or down). Triggers for the Chicago Mercantile Exchange were set at 12, 24, 36, and 48 S&P points (up or down). If the first Dow trigger is hit, trading would be halted for 60 minutes in both the New York and Chicago markets.

If the successive triggers are hit, trading would be halted for 90 minutes, then for 120 minutes, and then for another 120 minutes. If an S&P trigger is hit before a Dow trigger, trading is not halted, but a price limit is set in the Chicago market. After any halt, trading is resumed using the NYSE's and CME's usual opening procedures. However, at least 50% of the stocks (weighted by market capitalization) must reopen in the cash market for the index futures market to reopen.

The NYSE, NYFE, and the CME have also developed a common policy to prevent frontrunning and manipulative self-frontrunning between the cash market and the market for equity index futures and options on index futures. Trading in front of the customer has traditionally been prohibited. In the 1980's the definitions of frontrunning and manipulative self-frontrunning were expanded to prohibit trading in equity derivative products with prior knowledge of an upcoming trade in the underlying cash market. To implement this policy of prevention, futures and equities exchanges have agreed to share audit trail and surveillance information.

On the other hand, the NYSE has instituted NYSE Rule 80A that stipulates that, whenever the Dow Jones Industrial Average falls more than 50 points in a trading session, index arbitrage sell programs can be executed only on a plus or zero-plus tick, and when the Dow rises by more than 50 points, index arbitrage buy programs can be executed only on a minus or zero-minus tick. This constraint effectively prevents index arbitrage when the Dow moves by more than 50 points, but is not an explicit circuit breaker and is not coordinated with the futures markets. Consequently, the two markets are separated rather than coordinated.[12]

If properly constructed, circuit breakers can help to dampen price swings. Nevertheless, considerably more fundamental changes in market structure need be made to deal appropriately with an order flow that is dominated by institutional investors and to ensure the provision of adequate liquidity and stability under stressful conditions.

Suggested Reading

Amihud, Y., Ho, T., and Schwartz, R., eds. *Market Making and the Changing Structure of the Securities Industry.* Lexington, MA: Lexington Books, 1985.

Cohen, K., Maier, S., Schwartz, R., and Whitcomb, D. *The Microstructure of Securities Markets.* Englewood Cliffs, NJ: Prentice Hall, 1986.

Miller, M. "Volatility, Episodic Volatility and Coordinated Circuit-Breakers." In Pacific-Basin *Capital Market Research,* volume 2, S. G. Rhee and R. Chang, eds. New York: North Holland, March 1991.

New York Stock Exchange, Inc. "The Rule 80A Index Arbitrage Tick Test: Interim Report to the U.S. Securities and Exchange Commission," January 1991.

Schwert, G. W., Stock Exchange Seats as Capital Assets. *Journal of Financial Economics,* January 1977.

Shapiro, J. The NYSE Market System Background and Issues, in *NYSE: 1989 and Beyond: An Overview of an Academic Seminar, May 5, 1989,* New York Stock Exchange, Inc., 1989.

Smidt, S. Trading Floor Practices on Futures and Securities Exchanges: Economics, Regulation and Policy Issues. In *Futures Markets: Regulatory Issues,* A. Peck, ed. Washington, DC: American Enterprise Institute, 1985.

Stoll, H. *The Stock Exchange Specialist System: An Economic Analysis.* Monograph Series in Finance and Economics, 1985-2, Salomon Brothers Center for the Study of Financial Institutions, New York University Graduate School of Business Administration, 1985.

Stone, D. "The View from the Trading Floor." In Amihud, Ho, and Schwartz (1985).

West, R., and Tinic, S. *The Economics of the Stock Market.* New York: Praeger, 1971.

Notes

1. The New York Stock Exchange *Fact Book 1990.*
2. "The Future of Wall Street," *Business Week,* 5 November 1990, pp. 118–131.
3. The highest price ever paid to own a seat on the NYSE was $1,150,000 on 21 September 1987, just prior to the October 1987 stock market crash. The price reached a five-year low of $250,000 in December 1990.
4. An ADR is a certificate, issued by a U.S. bank, that represents ownership of a foreign security in the bank's possession. ADRs facilitate trading in foreign stocks; they are registered in the name of the individual owner, pay dividends declared on the underlying stock, but do not convey voting rights to the holder.
5. The NYSE Composite Index is a capitalization weighted index that reflects the movement of all common stocks listed on the NYSE.
6. The CRB Index is based on the Commodity Research Bureau's Futures Price Index that is an unweighted geometric average of 21 nonfinancial commodity futures prices. Trading began on the CRB Index future 12 June 1986 and on the option on the future on 28 October 1988.
7. The 1989 NYSE Annual Report and "NYSE: 1989 and Beyond, An Overview of an Academic Seminar."
8. NYSE *Fact Book 1990,* p. 23.
9. NYSE *Fact Book 1990.*
10. ITS trades are typically executed in about 26 seconds. See D. Stone, "The View from the Trading Floor," in Amihud, Ho, and Schwartz (1985).
11. NYSE *Fact Book 1990,* p. 17.
12. See M. Miller, "Volatility, Episodic Volatility, and Coordinated Circuit-Breakers," in Pacific-Basin *Capital Market Research,* volume 2, S.G. Rhee and R. Chang, eds., New York: North Holland, 1991.

3

The Over-The-Counter Market

The OTC is a decentralized, electronically linked market that comprises thousands of geographically dispersed, competitive dealer and member firms that are linked together by telephones and computer screens. The term *over-the-counter* originated in an era when stocks were bought and sold in banks and the physical certificates were passed "over-the-counter." Although many OTC securities in today's sophisticated markets are traded in electronic screen-based systems equivalent to exchanges, the term has nevertheless remained to describe all trading other than the trading that takes place on an exchange.

Organizational Structure

The National Association of Securities Dealers (NASD) is the self-regulatory organization (SRO) for the OTC markets. The NASD owns and operates NASDAQ, its automated quotations system. The NASD also has surveillance and overview responsibilities for the OTC markets, OTC market makers, and member securities firms. The NASD's premiere market is NASDAQ/NMS (NMS stands for "National Market System"); other NASD markets are the regular NASDAQ market, the NASDAQ Bulletin Board for less active securities, the PORTAL private placement market, and the NASDAQ International Market operating in London.

The philosophy behind these NASDAQ markets is very different from the one that characterizes the New York Stock Exchange. Rules of order handling and trade execution are simplier. The NASD relies more on competitive forces and less on explicit regulation to promote liquid, fair, and orderly markets. The OTC and NYSE are similar in one respect, however. Both of these competing market centers are better suited to handling small orders than large orders. For both markets, large block trades are negotiated. In 1989, total block volume (transactions of 10,000 shares or more), accounted for 42.7% of total NASDAQ/NMS share volume, compared with 51.1% for the NYSE.[1]

The International Stock Exchange (ISE) in London also uses a competitive dealer system for equity trading. Prior to the Big Bang in October 1986, the ISE comprised a small number of competitive jobber firms that functioned as competing dealers. The ISE carefully considered the competing market-maker and specialist systems but patterned its new system after NASDAQ. Operationally, however, the London market is quite different—its order flow is dominated by institutional investors who expect and receive immediate liquidity from the British market makers, even for large block orders. This has forced change in London's competitive dealer market and has highlighted aspects of the system that are not so apparent in the U.S. environment (for further discussion, see Chapter 4, "London's International Stock Exchange").

To understand fully the operations of a NASDAQ market, one must appreciate the services provided by dealers, the costs the market makers incur, and the dynamic pricing and inventory policies they employ. These are discussed in Chapter 8, "The Role of Market Makers."

Intermarket Competition

A dealer market, by its very nature, is physically fragmented across the various competitive market maker firms. The benefit is that competition helps to keep bid-ask spreads tight. A disadvantage is that price discovery may not be as accurate. But any firm can make a market for any given issue with only minimal entry barriers, and the dealer market is indeed competitive.

As of 31 December 1989, 458 firms were making markets in OTC stocks. Typically between three and thirty dealers make a market in any one stock, with the more actively traded issues attracting a larger number of dealers. A minimum of two market makers is required for each stock. In 1989, the number of market makers per NASDAQ/NMS security averaged 11.5. The more market makers for an issue, the larger the amount of capital that can be committed to providing liquidity and, all else constant, the tighter the stock's bid-ask spread.

NASDAQ faces additional competition for order flow for its listed securities. Trades in NASDAQ issues can be made via Instinet, an electronic block trading and order-handling facility owned by Reuters. Like NASDAQ's SOES (small order execution system), SelectNet, and other competing systems, Instinet accepts limit orders for NASDAQ issues, which means that public orders can compete with the dealers' quotes. In addition, regional stock exchanges now have unlisted trading privileges (UTP) that allow them to make markets in NASDAQ issues.

TABLE 3.1 *Comparison of NYSE, Amex, and NASDAQ Equity Markets*

(a) 9-year comparison

Year	Number of companies			Share volume (000,000)		
	NYSE	Amex	NASDAQ	NYSE	Amex	NASDAQ
1981	1,565	867	3,353	11,854	1,343	7,823
1982	1,526	834	3,264	16,458	1,338	8,432
1983	1,550	822	3,901	21,590	2,081	15,909
1984	1,543	792	4,097	23,071	1,545	15,159
1985	1,540	783	4,136	27,511	2,101	20,699
1986	1,573	796	4,417	35,680	2,979	28,737
1987	1,647	869	4,706	47,801	3,506	37,890
1988	1,681	896	4,451	40,850	2,515	31,070
1989	1,719	859	4,293	41,699	3,125	33,530

(b) Comparison of the order flow for 1988 and 1989

Market Center	Share Volume (000,000)		Dollar Volume (000,000)	
	1988	1989	1988	1989
NYSE	40,850	41,699	$1,356,050	$1,542,800
NASDAQ	31,070	33,530	347,089	431,381
Amex	2,515	3,125	29,786	44,401
Regionals	5,808	6,733	172,325	216,773
NASDAQ/OTC	1,206	1,794	40,025	66,378
Totals	81,449	86,881	1,945,275	$2,301,733

The major source of competition for the NASDAQ market, however, is not competition for trade execution of its own securities, but competition for the listings. Table 3.1 contains data on the overall size of the NASDAQ, NYSE, and Amex (American Stock Exchange) markets. It shows the number of companies listed in each of the three market centers, along with share volume for the years 1981–1989. As shown in the table, the NASDAQ market has grown appreciably in the 1980s, in terms of both the number of companies and share volume. A growing number of companies that would meet the requirements for exchange listing have chosen to remain on the NASDAQ market. Share volume has also increased on the

NYSE and Amex, but the number of exchange-listed companies has remained relatively flat.

The Markets

The OTC equities market is divided into four segments: NASDAQ/NMS, regular NASDAQ, NASD Bulletin Board, and pink sheet securities (other inactive issues). NASDAQ and NASDAQ/NMS combined constitute the second largest stock market in the United States (exceeded only by the NYSE) and it is among the five largest in the world (exceeded also by the Tokyo Stock Exchange). It is the major market for stocks with regional appeal and for the stocks of newer firms that do not meet the listing requirements of the exchanges. In addition, these markets include several hundred major companies that qualify for exchange listing, but have elected to remain on NASDAQ. In 1983 over 600 companies whose shares traded OTC qualified for an NYSE listing. Competition between NASDAQ and the NYSE is attributable to the markedly improved quality of the OTC.[2]

Most corporate bonds, municipal bonds, government securities, mutual funds, bank stocks (except for large money center banks), insurance company stocks, and Real Estate Investment Trusts (REITs) also trade in the OTC. Some listed stocks, warrants, preferred stock, and ADRs as well trade OTC (along with being traded on the exchanges).

The NASDAQ/NMS Market

The OTC's premiere market is the National Association of Security Dealers Automated Quotation/National Market System (NASDAQ/NMS). The approximately 2,700 issues on this list are the largest and most actively traded of the OTC stocks. Along with the publication of bid and ask quotations, stocks traded in the NASDAQ/NMS are subject to last sale price and volume reporting: NASDAQ/NMS market makers must report transaction prices and size to the NASD within 90 seconds of a transaction's occurrence. Additionally, NASDAQ terminals provide high, low, last-sale, and cumulative volume figures for NASDAQ/NMS issues. This information is reported daily in newspapers across the country.

The listing requirements for NASDAQ/NMS stocks are shown in Table 3.2.

The NASDAQ Market

This segment of the OTC comprises approximately 2,300 smaller, less actively traded OTC stocks that do not meet the minimum standards of NMS

TABLE 3.2 NASDAQ/NMS Listing Requirements

Standard	Initial NASDAQ/NMS Inclusion		Continued NASDAQ/NMS Inclusion
	Alternative 1	Alternative 2	
Registration under Section 12(g) of the Securities Exchange Act of 1934 or equivalent	Yes	Yes	Yes
Net Tangible Assets[a]	$4 million	$12 million	$2 million or $4 million[b]
Net Income (in last fiscal year or two of last three fiscal years)	$400,000	—	—
Pretax Income (in last fiscal year or two of last three fiscal years)	$750,000	—	—
Public Float (Shares)[c]	500,000	1 million	200,000
Operating History	—	3 years	—
Market Value of Float	$3 million	$15 million	$1 million
Minimum Bid	$5	—	—
Shareholders	—	—	—
—if between 0.5 and 1 million shares publicly held	800	400	400[d]
—if more than 1 million shares publicly held	400	—	—
—if more than 0.5 million shares publicly held and average daily volume in excess of 2,000 shares	400	—	—
Number of Market Makers	2	2	2

[a] "Net tangible assets" means total assets (excluding goodwill) minus total liabilities.
[b] Continued NASDAQ/NMS inclusion requires net tangible assets of at least $2 million if the issuer has sustained losses from continuing operations and/or net losses in two of its three most recent fiscal years or $4 million if the issuer has sustained losses from the continuing operations and/or net losses in three of its four most recent fiscal years.
[c] Public float is defined as shares that are not "held directly or indirectly by any officer or director of the issuer and by any person who is the beneficial owner of more than 10% of the total shares outstanding..."
[d] Or 300 shareholders of round lots.

securities. To become a dealer on NASDAQ, an OTC market maker must satisfy the following requirements:

- Maintain capital of the lesser of $2,500 for each security in which it makes a market, or $100,000
- Report daily and monthly trading volume to the NASD

For an issue to be included in the NASDAQ system, the issuing company must comply with the disclosure requirements of Section 12(g) of the Securities and Exchange Act of 1934 and have the following characteristics:

- $2 million in total assets
- $1 million in capital and retained earnings
- 100,000 publicly held shares (with no minimum market value)
- 2 market makers for its shares
- 300 shareholders of record

The Pink Sheet Market

Bid and ask quotations for approximately 11,000 thinly traded stocks that do not qualify for a NASDAQ listing are reported in the "pink sheets." This publication is distributed daily to brokers by the National Quotation Bureau. Traders must telephone market makers to find the most favorable price for a "pinkie."

Recently, the NASD developed an electronic bulletin board for non-NASDAQ OTC (NNOTC) stocks that allows market makers to enter indications of interest electronically, and to post firm or subject quotes. The bulletin board currently lists almost 9,000 securities, and has the potential of accommodating up to 42,159 issues. This easily accessed on-line system with up-to-date pricing adds visibility and leads to greater liquidity. The bulletin board also permits better monitoring of the NNOTC stocks, thus allowing superior compliance and regulation.

Information Dissemination

The NASD's Automated Quotation System, NASDAQ, did not begin as an order execution system, but as a nationwide electronic system that displays the dealer's quotes for NASDAQ and NASDAQ/NMS issues on terminals in brokerage offices across the country. Prior to NASDAQ's introduction in 1971, the OTC market was linked by telephone lines among market-making and member firms. The real-time electronic NASDAQ system has had a tremendous impact on the efficiency of the market. It has integrated the dealer markets, causing spreads to tighten and improving the quality of price discovery and trade execution. NASDAQ has made the OTC competitive with the exchanges as an alternative market system.

OTC dealer firms at first feared the competition the system would introduce and were reluctant to display their quotes on the screen. However, to do business, a dealer firm must receive orders from brokers, and NASDAQ has enabled those firms that make the best markets to receive more of the order flow. A dealer firm can now successfully make a market in a stock it has not previously traded: simply by registering with the NASD a day in advance and then posting quotes on the NASDAQ screen, it can get order flow.

Today, NASDAQ quotes are available on over 200,000 terminals in brokerage offices and trading rooms worldwide. Compared to the pre-NASDAQ era, NASDAQ firms make markets in many more issues, and NASDAQ market makers include most large national firms. All told, NASDAQ has been of tremendous value to the OTC market.

There are three different NASDAQ levels of service:

- *Level 1 service* This service displays the inside quotes (the highest bid and the lowest ask); high, low, and last prices; and volumes for NASDAQ/NMS stocks. It does not reveal the origin of the quotes or trade reports. It is used primarily by account executives in branch offices and the public to follow the market and to ascertain the market before submitting orders to market makers.

- *Level 2 service* This service displays the current quotes and the names of the market makers who have entered the quotes. It is used primarily by market makers and trading desks, order entry brokers, and institutional investors that commonly deal on a net basis with market makers.

- *Level 3 service* This service is used by the market makers and order entry brokers; it displays the same information as the level 2 service and also allows the market makers to enter and to update their quotes in the system and order entry firms to enter orders for the various NASDAQ automated execution systems and the Limit Order File (LOF).

A *firm quote* is posted by a dealer who is willing to buy or to sell at least one round lot (equivalent to 1,000, 500, or 200 shares, depending on the stock's order size parameter for automatic execution in SOES) at the quote. All NASDAQ quotes are firm quotes. A dealer that does not honor a firm quote is said to have "backed away" and will be censured or fined by the NASD if discovered.

Order Handling and Execution

In the OTC, public investors generally trade with a dealer who serves as intermediary. Dealers are allowed to handle public limit orders, but they do not do so in the normal course of business. However, limit orders are permitted on stocks traded in the NASDAQ market and are accepted in SOES. Some brokerage firms (but not all) can also place stop orders for OTC securities. For the most part, however, only market orders have thus far been used in OTC trading.

OTC market makers do not have a franchise in the stocks they handle, as do NYSE specialists. Issues are not assigned to, but are selected by, the dealer firms. When a dealer firm is registered as a market maker for an issue, it must make a continuous two-sided market by continuously posting both bid and ask quotations for the issue. To be competitive, NASDAQ market makers must also execute at the market quotes when a market is temporarily affected by a buy/sell imbalance; otherwise they will lose client order flow. Unlike NYSE specialists, OTC dealers do not have a regulatory obligation to maintain a fair and orderly market. A dealer firm is also free to stop making a market for an issue, but if it does so, it is not allowed to resume market making in that issue for 20 business days, and it risks the loss of all its regular clients in the stock.

Order execution for NASDAQ and NASDAQ/NMS stocks is accomplished through the electronic systems described below, and via telephone. When a customer places an order with a broker for an OTC issue, it is routed, usually automatically, to the OTC trading department of the securities firm. If a brokerage firm does not have an OTC trading operation (many discount brokers, for example, do not have their own OTC trading desks), the broker routes his or her order flow to OTC member firms that do. Approximately 70% of NASDAQ orders are eligible for automatic execution through SOES. It can be assumed that at least these orders are executed automatically in one of several competing automated execution systems. For larger orders the trader uses a level 3 service to locate the lowest ask or the highest bid among the competing dealers. He or she then contacts the market maker advertising the best available price.

The NASDAQ system has been upgraded many times since its inception in 1971. It can now execute trades automatically and also handle limit orders.

Small Order Execution System (SOES)

Introduced in December 1984, SOES allows brokers to execute customers' small orders automatically at the best current quotes. SOES trades are automatically reported to the NASD and entered into the clearing cycle on a "locked-in" basis. The system reduces paperwork and eliminates the need to contact market makers by telephone. *non pinksheets*

Up to 1,000 share orders for NASDAQ/NMS issues, and up to 500 share orders for non-NMS issues, can be traded in SOES. If two or more market makers have entered quotes at the best price, orders are rotated among them. In 1989, 1.4% of NASDAQ/NMS volume and 9.4% of NASDAQ/NMS trades were executed through SOES; but because 70% of trades are "SOES eligible," it can be assumed that 60–70% are being executed automatically.

Any NASDAQ market maker in a NASDAQ/NMS security must be a SOES market maker for that security as well. In addition, SOES Order Entry Firms (NASD member firms that so register) can enter customer orders for execution against the SOES market makers.

Limit-Order Service.   Prior to the introduction of the limit order service in January 1989, OTC brokers could choose to accept or reject customer limit orders on an individual basis. The Limit-Order Service, an extension of SOES, allows both GTC (good till canceled) and day limit orders of 1,000 shares or less to be accepted, stored, and automatically executed when a market maker's quote reaches or exceeds a limit order price. As of 10 December 1990 an enhancement to the Limit-Order Service permits the direct matching of limit orders that are priced within the best dealer quotes on the market, if market makers elect not to participate within a specified period.

Advanced Computerized Execution System (ACES).   Introduced in January 1989, ACES is a dealer service that automates executions with broker-dealer customers, controls market makers' inventories, and maintains files of open limit orders (either day, good-till-canceled, or good-till-date orders). A limit order is automatically filled when an inside quote reaches the order's limit price. ACES allows order entry plans to be set up in advance that confirm and formalize arrangements between dealers and customers, and it allows NASD members to direct orders to market makers of their choice. The system gives locked-in trades that are sent to the clearing corporation for entry into the settlement cycle.

Automated Confirmation Transaction (ACT).   ACT was implemented in 1989 to allow self-clearing firms to compare their locked-in telephone trades within five minutes.

SelectNet.   Introduced in November 1990, SelectNet provides a fast, efficient, low-cost means of negotiating trades and executing orders. Both agency and principle orders can be entered in SelectNet. Members can preference their orders (that is, direct them to a specific market maker), send an unpreferenced order to all market makers in an issue, or preference an order and then broadcast any unfilled part of that order to all other market makers. Market makers can also use SelectNet to broadcast an order to all NASDAQ subscribers.

In addition to showing size and price, users can identify themselves if they so choose (market makers must disclose their identifies), specify that the order is good for up to 99 minutes or a day, and indicate whether the size or the price of an order is negotiable. Market makers may accept, counter, or decline SelectNet orders. If they counter an order, a negotiation is considered "in progress." Counters are exchanged until agreement is reached or the transaction is dropped. During a negotiation, all other possible counters are queued and then sent according to time priority to the order entry firm if the first negotiation is not successful.

SelectNet orders are shown on NASDAQ Workstation screens. Users can control the information they receive by placing specific securities in a "watch file." Market makers can register specific traders, and non–market makers can register to view the orders of specific market makers. Trades executed in SelectNet are processed through ACT.

Portal

In response to the passage of SEC Rule 144a in April 1990, the NASD developed PORTAL, an acronym for *Private Offerings, Resales and Trading Through Automated Linkages*. Rule 144a essentially creates a separate secondary market for private placements of both debt and equity. The 144a market, unencumbered by normal SEC registration requirements, should appeal primarily to foreign issuers. PORTAL is intended to increase the efficiency of the currently global, but fragmented, private placement market. Operating much like the NASDAQ system, it allows these institutions to advertise bid and ask quotations for listed private placement issues. Participation in PORTAL will be limited to qualified institutional investors (defined by the SEC as institutions with over $100 million in invested securities). Since its launching in the summer of 1990, major changes in the system that would make it more open have been under consideration.

Block Trading

Block trades (trades involving 10,000 shares or more) are generally negotiated in the *upstairs market* as they are for NYSE issues (refer to Chapter 6 for discussion).

Global Trading

The NASD is planning an international quotation system that will link London's International Stock Exchange (ISE) to the NASDAQ system and will include NYSE listings. The system will operate from 4:00 A.M. to 9:00 A.M. (Eastern Standard Time) for trading approximately 40 NYSE issues while the NYSE is closed, and will trade about 300 major OTC issues in London from 4:00 A.M. to 4:00 P.M. (EST) while the ISE is open. A debate concerning whether British or U.S. transaction reporting standards will be used is currently delaying the opening of this NASD facility.

Regulatory Organization

The 1938 Maloney Act Amendments to the Securities and Exchange Act of 1934 created the NASD as a self-regulatory organization (SRO). The NASD, headquartered in Washington, D.C., has primary responsibility for regulating brokers and dealers. In this capacity, it has imposed a uniform set of rules for its members.

Rules of Fair Practice

The NASD has established the *Rules of Fair Practice*. These apply to the financial integrity of member firms, sales practices (including a 5% markup policy, which prevents NASD members from profiting unreasonably at the expense of their customers),[3] market making, and underwriting activities.

Surveillance

The NASD's Market Surveillance Department (MSD) maintains surveillance of the OTC market. In 1990, the NASD introduced a new system for monitoring prices and volume, called StockWatch and Automated Tracking (SWAT). The SWAT system captures news items along with prices and volume, to determine if price quotations are reasonable in relationship to "legitimate market forces." In the event of unusual trading activity, the NASDAQ companies are required by MSD to disclose "news" upon request that they might not otherwise provide. Violation of this disclosure requirement may result in suspension or termination of listing privileges.

Quotes may be halted while the NASD seeks an explanation for unusual price or volume fluctuations. The MSD may also impose trading halts to permit the dissemination of material news to all market participants. Once the news is widely disseminated, trading resumes.

The NASD conducts field examinations of its member firms at least once a year. Infractions are brought to one of the 14 District Business Conduct Committees (DBCCs). A DBCC can censure, fine, suspend, or expel a broker/dealer firm from the NASD.

Contrast of the OTC and NYSE

The OTC and NYSE represent very different approaches to market making. The NASD points to the advantages of its competitive dealer system. The NYSE stresses its advantages as an agency/auction market and emphasizes the importance of its specialist system. Differences between the two markets are summarized in Table 3.3 and discussed in the following text.

TABLE 3.3 *OTC Market Versus NYSE*

	OTC Market	NYSE
Trade Initiation	Dealer market Quote driven Active interaction with the order flow	Agency/auction market Order driven Passive interaction with the order flow
Competition	Multiple dealers	Single dealer and public order flow
Flexibility	Freedom to select stocks Primary and Secondary market operations	Stocks are assigned Secondary market operations only
Information Flows	Deal directly with customers Close contact with firms Emphasis on quotation reporting	Consolidated order flow and floor information Emphasis on transaction price reporting
Price Discovery	No formal procedure Competitive firm quotations centrally displayed	Market opening procedure Consolidation of the order flow
Regulation	SRO for member firms Obligation to continuously quote firm two-sided market Rely on competition to limit abuses	SRO for member firms Affirmative obligation Specialist trading restrictions

Trade Initiation

The OTC market is quote driven, compared with the NYSE's order-driven, agency/auction market. The dealers are allowed to take the initiative in finding buyers and sellers, whereas NYSE specialists must assume a more passive position—they post their quotes and wait for other traders to respond.

Competition

The OTC is a dealer market. The dealers compete with each other, and have been reluctant to accept additional competition from the public order flow. The NASD depends on this interdealer competition to keep markets fair, orderly, and liquid. The NYSE, with just one market maker per issue (the specialist), depends on competition from public limit orders, floor traders, specialists on other exchanges linked by the Intermarket Trading System (ITS), and its own surveillance system to keep markets fair, orderly, and liquid.

Flexibility

OTC dealers are free to select the stocks they make markets in. They face no significant regulatory impediments to becoming, or ceasing to be, market makers for an issue. A specialist firm, on the other hand, must apply for the right to be the market maker for a newly listed issue. Once assigned by the Exchange's stock allocation committee, an issue is rarely given up by a specialist firm and is almost never taken away.

An OTC dealer firm is free to participate in the new issues market, although it must temporarily give up market making for an issue in the secondary market when it acts as underwriter for the same company in the primary market. NYSE specialists operate in the secondary market only.

OTC dealers' freedom to participate in the lucrative primary markets gives large brokerage houses that make OTC markets an incentive to provide liquidity that NYSE specialists do not have. This happens because brokerage houses that make better secondary markets are more likely to be favored by firms when they issue new securities in the primary markets.

Information Flows

Specialists are prohibited by NYSE Rule 113 from dealing with institutions. OTC dealers, on the other hand, can receive orders directly from customers, including institutional traders. This direct contact gives OTC dealers an informational advantage NYSE specialist do not enjoy. The orders are generally transmitted by telephone, which enables the dealer houses to sense the motive behind an order—namely, whether it is informationally motivated or instead is an "informationless" order (for example, if it is from an index fund).

Some OTC dealers maintain close contact with the firms whose securities they trade, and brokerage houses with OTC trading operations commonly act in an advisory capacity for these firms. NYSE specialist firms have no such relationship with their listed companies. The specialists, on the other hand, have an informational advantage that is not shared by the OTC dealers—they see a larger fraction of the order flow because the order flow is more consolidated in exchange trading.

An agency/auction market places much emphasis on transaction price reporting, while a competitive dealer market places more emphasis on quote reporting. This is clearly the case both for London's International Stock Exchange (see Chapter 4), and for the U.S. OTC, even though a transaction tape now exists in London and last sale reporting is required for NASDAQ/NMS trades.

The informational signal transmitted by a quote differs significantly from that transmitted by a transaction price. A quote reflects one market participant's willingness to trade, is firm only up to a given size, and may be improved on (in terms of price and/or quantity). Quotes also reflect trading strategy and "gaming" by market participants.

A transaction price is a price that has actually been accepted by both counterparties to a trade. A transaction price, however, relates to the past and does not necessarily reflect the price at which one can trade in the present (as does a bid or an ask quotation). Nevertheless, transaction prices may better reflect current market conditions, particularly in an agency/auction environment where quotes can be set by very different types of market participants (specialists, floor traders, and public limit order traders), and where transactions do occur frequently.

Price Discovery

The OTC does not have an explicit price discovery mechanism such as the call market opening procedure used by the NYSE. Furthermore, consolidation of the public order flow on the trading floor of the NYSE gives exchange specialists a more comprehensive knowledge of buy/sell propensities in the broader market for an issue.

OTC dealers sense the public's buy/sell propensities by posting quotes and observing the market's response. For instance, if a dealer opens a market with quotes that are unrealistically low, one might expect that public buy orders will trigger transactions at the ask, and that both the bid and the ask quotes will be raised until an equilibrium level is attained. However, public orders depend on the informational signal transmitted by the quotes, and quotes that are too high can, until they are adjusted, attract orders (both to buy and to sell) that execute at the relatively high price. Similarly, quotes that are too low can attract orders that execute at the relatively low price. This complicates the dealer's task of inferring equilibrium prices, just as it complicates the task of an NYSE specialist.[4]

Problems associated with accurate price discovery have not been adequately recognized. In the academic dealer literature, for instance, it is commonly assumed that a dealer knows an equilibrium price (see Chapter 8). Consequently, little attention has been given to the fact that fragmentation of the order flow across different dealer firms can obscure its informational content (for further discussion, see Chapter 9). For the most part, attention has been focused on tightening bid-ask spreads. Unfortunately, dealers may tend to set wider spreads when they are less certain about the equilibrium price level for an issue. Conversely, the specialist markets close down until a public order balance can be determined.

Regulation

Competing OTC dealers face fewer regulatory restrictions than NYSE specialists because the NASD relies more on the constraints of a competitive environment to discipline dealer firms. Furthermore, because specialist firms also execute public orders on an agency basis, they have a fiduciary responsibility to give executions that are consistent with exchange auction rules. Lastly, competing OTC dealers do not have the affirmative (although unquantifiable) obligations to maintain a fair and orderly market as do the exchange specialists. They do not have an exclusive franchise, and thus need not be subjected to continuity or stabilization tests. Consequently, the rules, regulations, and surveillance of specialist operations are of necessity more elaborate on the exchanges than in the OTC.

Nevertheless, OTC markets need to be, and are, regulated. Recent experiences with price volatility, particularly during the stressful days of October 1987 and October 1989, have underscored the inherent instability of the OTC as well as the exchange markets. Of particular importance, a dealer firm's freedom to withdraw from market making under stressful conditions must be constrained.

At the time of the 1987 crash, SOES was a completely automated execution system. Hence, NASDAQ market makers were not obligated to participate in SOES, and those market makers who were participating could withdraw for any reason, at any time. Between 16 and 21 October 1987, the average number of SOES market makers per security declined by 75%.[5] Of course, only about 1% of NASDAQ volume is executed through SOES. Overall market positions declined about 11%. More importantly, trading continued in all stocks at all times although many phone calls did not get through, unlike the specialist markets, where trading was halted in hundreds of stocks for lengthy periods. But at that time, a dealer firm could totally cease to make a market in a particular issue without a valid excuse and be prevented for only two days from resuming market making for the issue. A similar but more subtle problem concerning "fair weather market making" has also arisen in the London market (see Chapter 4).

The NASD has taken a number of initiatives in response to problems underscored by the 1987 crash. These include making participation in SOES mandatory for NASDAQ/NMS market makers, tightening the set of acceptable excuses for a dealer firm to withdraw from market making in a particular stock, and making a dealer firm that ceases to make a market without a valid excuse subject to a twenty-business-day, rather than the two-day, suspension.

The NASD also instituted a limit order facility, and a similar facility is being contemplated for the London equity market. This will help increase liquidity in the market and will provide investors in the OTC with an alternative way to write orders and have them handled by the system. With the introduction of the limit order facility, transaction price reporting, and enhanced surveillance of the dealers, the OTC is starting to resemble an exchange market in certain important respects. This may turn out to be very desirable. But OTC could go further; in principle, it could also incorporate a formal market opening procedure (such as an electronic call) into its competitive dealer system to enhance the accuracy of price discovery.

Demands made by the institutionalization of the order flow are increasingly being felt in major market centers around the world, and problems of price discovery are beginning to be appreciated. Whatever unexpected developments the future might bring, the relentless demand to reduce transaction costs, to supply adequate liquidity, to ensure reasonably accurate price discovery, and to be competitive in a global environment will generate continuous pressures to innovate. This will generate new regulatory demands for the NASD, as it already has for Britain's competitive dealer system. We turn to the issues involved in the next chapter.

Suggested Reading

Amihud, Y., Ho, T., and Schwartz, R., eds. *Market Making and the Changing Structure of the Securities Industry.* Lexington, MA: Lexington Books, 1985.

Bronfman, C., and Schwartz, R. Order Placement and Price Discovery in a Securities Market. Paper delivered at the meetings of the American Finance Association, Washington, DC, December 1990.

Sanger, G., and McConnell, J. "Stock Exchange Listings, Firm Value, and Security Market Efficiency: The Impact of NASDAQ." *Journal of Financial and Quantitative Analysis.* March 1986.

Wall, J. "The Competitive Environment of the Securities Market." In *Market Making and the Changing Structure of the Securities Industry.* Y. Amihud, T. Ho, and R. Schwartz, eds. Lexington, MA: Lexington Books, 1985.

Notes

1. NASDAQ *Fact Book, 1990*
2. J. Wall, "The Competitive Environment of the Securities Market," in Y. Amihud, T. Ho, and R. Schwartz, eds. *Market Making and the Changing Structure of the Securities Industry.* Lexington, MA: Lexington Books, 1985.
3. *A markup* is the percentage difference between a market maker's share purchase price and the higher price at which the shares are subsequently sold.
4. For further discussion see C. Bronfman, and R. Schwartz, *Order Placement and Price Discovery in a Securities Market.* Paper delivered at the meetings of the American Finance Association,Washington, DC, December 1990.
5. See SEC Report (1988, p. 9–14), Washington, DC: GPO.

4

London's International Stock Exchange

London's International Stock Exchange (ISE) is a competitive dealer market, similar in structure to the OTC's NASDAQ. Both are geographically dispersed markets where information is displayed on computer screens and trades are made predominantly by telephone. The ISE market differs from NASDAQ in certain key respects, however. Most importantly, ISE trading is dominated by institutional investors. Institutional orders for the largest, most liquid stocks (referred to as "alphas") are generally not negotiated in an upstairs market (as in the U.S.), but rather are brought to the market makers and filled immediately. Furthermore, unlike the more retail-oriented NASDAQ market, transactions are commonly made within the spread. This has a major effect on the operations of the competitive dealer market.

Prior to Big Bang, there were two principal types of exchange members — brokers and jobbers. Under the single capacity system, brokers acted as agents for clients and could not take principal positions, and jobbers took principal positions but were not permitted to deal with clients except through the brokers. Enormous change has characterized the London equity market since the advent of Big Bang in October 1986. The change spans technology (the rapid introduction of computer-based information systems), broker/dealer and jobber operations (the move from single to dual capacity), the competitive environment (the elimination of fixed commissions and opening of exchange membership to foreign firms), the regulatory environment (the establishment of the Securities and Investment Board, or SIB, London's equivalent to the SEC), and the enforcement of a more prescribed set of insider trading restrictions. These changes have transformed what had been a closed market into an open system, and have resulted in the trading

This chapter has been adapted from Neuberger, A. and Schwartz, R. "Current Developments in the London Equity market," *Finanzmarkt und Portfolio Management*, 1990, used with permission.

floor being replaced by the SEAQ screen. The open, competitive environment has also attracted massive capital to market making from the integrated financial firms. However, at the heart of today's market are the market makers, professionals not unlike the jobbers of old, but required to operate in a far more transparent way.

Market Design

Membership

There is no serious entry barrier to market making in London. The ISE is a competitive environment where any adequately capitalized firm that is prepared to abide by the rules may participate.

There is no obligation for investors to execute their securities business on the ISE or for securities dealers to join the Exchange. Because the ISE has no rule equivalent to NYSE Rule 390, members and non-members are free to deal directly with each other. Market makers also trade among themselves through an interdealer broker network (IDB). However, all trades in London in U.K. equities are reported to the ISE and are subject to its surveillance and reporting rules.

Market Makers

Market makers are required to post firm, two-way quotes for shares in the securities for which they are registered. The minimum firm quote size is 5,000 shares for alpha stocks and 1,000 shares for beta stocks (the second group of stocks in liquidity sequence). Minimum capital requirements must be satisfied and rules obeyed, but market makers are not obliged to smooth prices, to ensure an orderly market, or to maintain tight spreads. Failure to post quotes for an issue results in the loss of the market maker's registration in that stock, and a three-month reregistration delay. In return for making a market, the market making firms receive certain privileges, notably relief from stamp tax (a duty of 0.5% paid by buyers in a trade), facilitated stock borrowing for short sales, and access to the interdealer broker (IDB) system.

The number of market maker firms increased appreciably after Big Bang. Over 90% of the "alpha" stocks (the 100–150 most liquid, highly capitalized issues) have at least 10 registered market makers. Currently, 30 firms are registered as market makers. Many of these are part of well-capitalized financial institutions for whom market making in the U.K. fits into a wider strategic plan. Commissions and spreads have both been driven down by competition as large integrated financial firms have fought for position in the strategically important London market.

Broker/Dealers

Broker/dealers are free to act as principals or to cross customers' orders. Their only obligation is to ensure that customers do at least as well in agency trades as they would have if they had dealt with a market maker, or that they get a better execution in principal trades. This means trading at or within the *touch* (the spread) for agency trades and strictly within the touch for principal trades. Market makers are not informed of trades between broker/dealers and clients, but are lobbying for exposure to, and publication of, these trades.

The Order Flow

The ISE's order flow is characterized by large, infrequent trades, as a consequence of being dominated by institutional investors. Over 80% of customer turnover in U.K. equities are institutional trades over £100,000, 18% of which are over £1 million in value. Order flow is low, even in liquid stocks. In the 100 or so most liquid stocks, approximately 150 transactions occur per day, of which perhaps 10 to 15 are over £100,000 in value.

The institutions generally expect immediacy and tend to generate a "one-way" order flow. A "one-way" market occurs when public customers arrive sequentially on the same side of the market, either as buyers or sellers. One-way markets are thought to exist in London because of a "herd instinct" on the part of institutional clients who tend to respond in similar ways to the same research reports and economic conditions.

Stock Exchange Automatic Quotation System (SEAQ)

SEAQ is the ISE's computerized quote display system. Like NASDAQ, SEAQ is a billboard; market makers have to be contacted by telephone or, for small orders, via SEAQ's *Automatic Execution Facility (SAEF)* for a trade to be executed. The SEAQ screen displays each competing market maker's bid and ask quotes for an issue and the sizes for which the quotes are firm. The screen also shows cumulative volume and the size and price of the most recent transactions. The quotes of market makers offering the best bid and ask prices are highlighted by being listed on a prominent "yellow strip" on the SEAQ screen.

SEAQ is based on the principle that investors should be able to see the prices at which they can trade with individual market makers (the market should be transparent). The system allows each market maker to post only one set of quotes (a single bid and a single ask). Market makers must make firm two-way quotes for at least 5,000 shares for alpha stocks and 1,000 shares for beta stocks. Market makers are not obliged to deal with other market makers at their SEAQ quotes. In the alpha stocks, firm quotes are typically available for up to 100,000 shares. Approximately 75% of trades of between 100,000 and 1,000,000 shares are transacted at prices either at the quotes or better.

A market maker firm may commit itself to a better price and/or size than it is showing on SEAQ. For example, the firm may have an undesirably large long position in a stock but be unwilling to lower its SEAQ quotes because this might trigger a decline in competitors' quotes without eliciting any purchases. Or the market maker may wish to price-discriminate between a known group of final investors and the public. Market makers may also post better quotes on competing quote vendor systems or may be able to obtain better quotes using IDB.

SEAQ faces competition from a few proprietary quote systems that enable some market makers to post relatively unattractive quotes on the SEAQ screen and still capture order flow from their competitors.

Interdealer Broker (IDB) System

IDB is essentially a CATS-type order-driven market available to market makers only. (CATS is the Computer Assisted Trading System in place in the Toronto Stock Exchange; see Chapter 5 for further discussion.) Market makers can either post limit orders on the IDB screen or trade against the IDB quotes of other market makers. Either way, the orders are anonymous, and the quotes are firm and generally better than those shown on SEAQ. The IDB screen is seen only by market makers, and only market makers and brokers affiliated with them have access to the system. The system fulfills a valuable function within SEAQ by transmitting information about order flow, and thus tends to offset the fragmentation inherent in the multi–market maker system, although the diversion of orders impairs the transparency of the SEAQ market. However, some feel that the system makes market making less risky and thus contributes to the market's liquidity. The IDB network is provided free of fixed charges to market makers in return for commissions on trades brokered through it. Approximately 10% of total turnover on the Exchange is currently conducted through IDB.

SAEF

SEAQ's Automatic Execution Facility (SAEF) gives an on-line automatic execution for trades under 1,000 shares. Participation in SAEF is mandatory for market makers. SAEF orders are routed automatically to the market maker with the best price on SEAQ. When more than one market maker is on the yellow strip, orders are rotated beginning with the one with the quote for the largest size. However, as noted above, brokers can also designate the market maker firm that will get their business whether or not that market maker's SEAQ quote is on the yellow strip. Thus market makers who do not want to accept SAEF trades can consistently stay outside of the touch to "duck" these trades unless they are purposefully routed to them.

Trade Reporting

For alpha securities, there is on-line trade publication similar to the Consolidated Tape, known as TOPIC. Trades must be published within three minutes of their transaction. However, large trades are not individually shown on TOPIC. The occurrence of a large trade is signaled through a cumulative volume indicator, but the price only becomes known the following day with the publication of an "Official List" that gives a history of trades from the previous day.

Given that large trades account for 75% of the market value of all trading, the exemption from immediate publication impairs the relevance of the transaction record. Delaying price reporting for large transactions until the next day puts market makers with small market share at an even greater informational disadvantage because they see only a small fraction of the order flow in any case. Because the relevance of the transaction record is impaired, the transparency of the ISE market depends primarily on the publication of firm two-way quotes. This underscores the importance of good quotes. But the risks to the market maker firms of posting good quotes in size are substantial. This is why transaction prices are not being published immediately for large trades, why SEAQ quotes are not firm for inter–market maker trading, and why a public limit order facility currently under consideration may not be implemented. Unfortunately, these concessions to the market makers have restricted the system's flexibility to meet the disparate needs of different customers.

Market Opening

Market makers are free to put quotes on the screen from 7:30 A.M. to 6:00 P.M. with the mandatory quote period being from 9:00 A.M. to 5:00 P.M. No formal opening procedure exists on the ISE.

Block Trading

Institutional orders for alpha stocks are generally not negotiated in an upstairs market (as in the OTC), but are brought to the market makers and filled immediately. After taking a block, a market maker searches for counterparties or works off the inventory imbalance as market conditions and subsequent order flow permit. Market makers commonly negotiate with institutional customers by posting relatively wide spreads and then giving executions between their quotes. For very large blocks (over £1 million), a market maker may be unwilling to take the entire transaction at a reasonable price. The customer might then either use a broker to find suitable counterparties, or else divide the order into smaller pieces to be fed to the market piecemeal.

Limit Orders

No facility currently exists at ISE for customers to place limit orders. Customers who wish to do so must instruct their brokers to watch the screen and to place the orders with a market maker once their limits are reached. The only limit orders on the market are the orders that market makers put on the IDB screen. A trial limit order system, CLOSE (Central Limit Order Execution System), is currently being designed to accommodate the ISE's small retail customers.

Big Bang and Beyond

Before Big Bang, virtually all of the broking and jobbing firms were constituted as partnerships. Although incorporation had been permitted some years prior to Big Bang, outside ownership by any one shareholder was limited to 10%. Thus there was little incentive to forgo the tax benefits conferred by partnership to get the limited access to outside capital afforded by incorporation.

The jobbers provided the market with liquidity on a relatively small capital base (a base on the order of £60 million supported an annual turnover on the order of £180 billion). Jobbers were protected in a number of ways that do not now apply to present-day market makers:

- Entry was restricted. With only five significant jobbing firms (there are now 30 market makers), each saw a high proportion of the orders and was likely to know rapidly of any unusual order flow. There was no trade reporting, so jobbers had a far better view of the order flow than did brokers or investors.

- With the market being made on the floor of the Exchange, and with their continuous presence there, jobbers could see far more of what was happening. They could see brokers doing business with competitors, and they knew when a broker inspected their price and did not trade. With a screen-based telephone market, market makers' only advantage over other traders is their knowledge of the actual trades they themselves have made.

- Since the brokers had to deal on an ongoing basis with a small number of jobbers, brokers did not generally try to make a quick profit directly at the expense of the jobber. It was too easy for the jobbers to retaliate by giving that broker bad prices in the future.

- Performance measurement of institutional portfolios was not as tight or as frequent. Because of this, institutions were more willing than now to buy substantial blocks of stock that the jobber wanted to get rid of.
- Restrictions on insider dealing were far less stringent, so insiders and those with a privileged view of the order flow could make substantial profits.

Despite these advantages, jobbers had been facing declining profits over a number of years, and this had led to a reduction in the number of jobbing firms. Before Big Bang, there were only five substantial jobbing firms in operation, two of which were contemplating merger.

Big Bang

A number of elements came together to produce the radical change in the London Stock Market that is called Big Bang:

- The Office of Fair Trading had for some years been investigating the Stock Exchange under the competition laws. The Government finally agreed with the Exchange in 1983 to terminate the investigation on condition that the Exchange abolished brokers' minimum fixed commissions by the end of 1986.
- An increasing proportion of trades in U.K. securities between U.K. institutions was taking place off-Exchange through the medium of ADRs (American Depositary Receipts). Although this was in part due to investors seeking to avoid Stamp Duty, the cost of dealing through the Exchange was a contributory factor.
- The pressure on jobbers' profitability was leading to excessive concentration and reduced competition. There was concern that this might lead to wide spreads and high dealing costs.
- Strong pressures for change came from the international environment. The removal of currency exchange controls, the increased readiness of investors to place funds in foreign equity markets, and the aim of many banks and other financial institutions to create or extend their presence in the securities business meant that London either had to open up or see its business slip away.

Other changes became inevitable after the removal of fixed brokerage commissions. Brokers argued for the right to take on principal positions to allow them to offset the reduction in brokerage profits. Jobbers argued that they would have to be allowed to deal directly with clients if they were not to be put at a disadvantage relative to brokers. The single capacity approach underlying the old system thus had to be jettisoned. The developments that were collectively known as Big Bang (though some were introduced in the months prior to October 1986) were the following:

- *Opening up membership:* Membership was made corporate and open "to any body of fit, proper and adequately capitalised persons."[1]
- *Market makers:* Jobbers, or market makers as they were now called, were permitted to deal directly with customers. They were required to make continuous two-way prices in any stock in which they were registered to deal, in at least minimum size (currently 5,000 shares). In return, they received certain privileges, including the right/duty to post prices on SEAQ, relief from stamp duty, ability to borrow stock, and access to the interdealer/broker system.
- *Broker/dealers:* Brokers were freed to set their own commission charges and also to act as principals, if they could make their clients a better price than the market makers.
- The IDB network was established.
- SEAQ was established.
- Trade reporting was initiated.

The competing market maker system was thought to be best able to satisfy the needs of London's institutionally dominated order flow. It built on the existing skills of the jobbers who were accustomed to taking large principal positions on either side of the market. It also met the needs of institutional investors who were accustomed to being able to buy or to sell a substantial number of shares at a known price, without waiting for a final counterparty to be found.

Big Bang to the 1987 Crash

The most striking change following Big Bang was the abandonment of the Exchange floor. Within a matter of weeks, the exchange became a telephone market. The ISE was left with a relatively new trading floor, that is now only partially used by its options market.

Big Bang worked well in many ways. Thirty-three firms, many of which were part of well-capitalized financial companies, became registered market makers. The capital committed to market making increased enormously, from £60 million to over £1 billion.

In the alpha stocks, firm quotes were typically available for up to 100,000 shares (about $0.5 million by value), and the average touch at this size was 0.73%. But the SEAQ screen actually underestimated the depth of the market since, as noted, 75% of trades of between 100,000 and 1 million shares were transacted at prices on the screen or better. (Above 1 million shares there are no firms quotes; one of the early changes made to SEAQ was to raise the maximum quote size from 100,000 to 1 million shares.)

In the year after Big Bang, turnover on customer business virtually doubled to over £1.1 billion per day. By August 1987, the FT-SE index had risen by almost 50% above its level at the time of Big Bang. Since market makers generally held net long positions, their inventory profits, coupled with the increase in turnover, disguised the excess capacity and the underlying unprofitability of market making itself.

The problems associated with excess market making capacity did not surface until the bull market ended with the crash in October 1987. The crash itself weakened financial positions; then the steep decline in order flow that ensued generated substantial losses.

Over the period 12 to 30 October 1987, London prices fell 27% as compared with a fall of 23% in New York. The new system responded well to the test, however. The markets remained open at all times. Transactions took place at close to quoted prices except during two 15-minute intervals during the crash. Market makers were net buyers of £250 million in equities. The deviation between spot and index futures prices was far less pronounced than on the NYSE.

There were, however, accusations that market makers did not answer their phones, and certainly it was difficult to get through. But on October 19 and 20, the system handled more than twice the average number of daily transactions for 1987. There were inevitably capacity constraints, but no clear evidence has surfaced of any deliberate attempt to avoid the obligation to make a market.

Market makers were ill-positioned for the crash. They were long stock before it, and took on more shares as the market fell. Following the crash, spreads widened. The average touch for alpha stocks increased from 0.83% to 2.00% over the month. By the summer of 1988, the average touch had declined to 1.15%, but was still above its precrash level. The premium for large orders also rose sharply, and the size in which firm prices were quoted fell. And turnover declined sharply, almost to pre–Big Bang levels.

The integrated financial firms have continued to compete fiercely for order flow despite the losses. Synergies exist between market making operations and the provision of other financial services, and the firms believe that the future indirect rewards to market making for those that survive will be substantial.

The Price War

A price war started on 25 August 1988. Two of the largest market making firms [Barclays de Zoete Wedd (BZW) and Phillips and Drew (P&D)] reduced spreads and lowered the size in which they were prepared to make firm quotes to the minimum level of 5,000 shares. They made clear to their institutional customers that they were still prepared to deal with clients at the quoted price in large size, but that they did not wish to be forced to deal with competing market makers in this manner. BZW and P&D argued that they were in effect subsidizing their competitors who could take on large principal positions, knowing they could lay them off at good prices (with BZW and P&D). Some of the other market makers took up the challenge, and decided to attract business by quoting prices in still larger size than before. So the average touch in alphas fell from 1.15% to 0.80%, while the average largest quote size increased over the quarter to 140,000 shares from 70,000 shares.

Profitability was badly affected. Estimated annual losses by market makers collectively were running around £500 million in 1988. As one market maker noted, £350 million of revenue were offsetting £850 million of costs. There have been some retrenchments and a few outright withdrawals from the market, but there are still 30 registered market makers, with the top eight firms accounting for 80% of the business.

How long will the overcapacity last? What effect will its eventual elimination have on competitive pressures? If competition does weaken and appropriate structural changes are not made, will SEAQ spreads widen appreciably and depth decrease? If so, the screen will become more opaque, and fragmentation will become a problem.

The New Rules

The Elwes Committee

The price war, along with the emergence of possible defects in the system, led the ISE to establish the *Elwes Committee*. (The Chairman of the Committee, Nigel Elwes, is Director of S. G. Warburg Securities, London.) The committee's work resulted in two important interim rule changes: (1) market makers were allowed to refuse to trade with each other at their SEAQ quotes, and (2) the publication of price information on trades of £100,000 or more was delayed to the next day.

The first change was designed to meet the criticism that some market makers were avoiding their responsibility to provide liquidity by laying off positions with other market makers. The second change, the partial suspension of trade reporting, was motivated by the argument that immediate publication impeded the execution of large trades by allowing other traders to spoil the business, either by transacting or by moving their prices before the market maker who had received the order had the opportunity to make an offsetting trade. Large trades continue to be reported to the Exchange for control and surveillance reasons and are published the following day in the Daily Official List, but are no longer published electronically within three minutes of their taking place. The committee explored the possibility of delaying electronic reporting for only one or two hours, but this was rejected as technically unfeasible.

Some broker/dealers and market makers have spoken out sharply about the price war and rule changes, claiming that the market has been fragmented, that it is not transparent, that it is falling apart. David Walker, Chairman of the SIB, criticized the retreat from transparency. John Heimann of Merrill Lynch, charging that the rule changes are a blatantly unfair restraint on competition, saw them as an attempt to reestablish the old oligopoly that prevailed before Big Bang. Allowing market maker SEAQ quotes to be unfirm to other market makers, in particular, has been interpreted as disadvantaging foreign firms that cannot lay off unwanted inventory as readily as can domestic firms with large retail bases. Certainly, the changes have made life more difficult for those market makers with a small share of the order flow (who are therefore less likely to have direct knowledge of large orders) and for those who lack distribution capacity (and thus depend on other market makers for liquidity).

In addition to the practitioner-based Elwes Committee, the ISE commissioned an independent assessment of the system from the consultant firm, Touche Ross. The Touche Ross report argued that the system depends excessively on market makers and concluded that the dispersion of order flow between market makers is incompatible with a central market. The report proposed that a central order-processing system be set up to expose and match both market and limit orders. Market makers would have privileged access to the public order flow for a brief period (five to ten minutes). However, they would continue to be obliged to quote firm two-way prices, and other market maker privileges (relief from the stamp tax and stock borrowing concessions) would be made available to all members of the Exchange. These proposals represented a substantial shift from the philosophy behind the quote-driven market, toward a CATS-type system. With regard to some of the more immediate issues, the Touche Ross report endorsed the removal of the obligation on market makers to deal with each other, and recommended that the rule on delayed publication of large trades be reduced from one day to around 30 minutes.

The Elwes Committee's second report, which significantly modified its interim conclusions, was finished in May 1989. The committee endorsed the SEAQ philosophy and firmly rejected both the Toronto-type CATS and the NYSE-type specialist systems for the London market. The Committee's main recommendations were the following:

- Market makers should not be able to display worse prices on SEAQ than they display on other quote vendor systems. This was aimed particularly at market makers who offered better prices to institutional clients through closed user groups. Market makers could continue, however, to negotiate better prices than their quotes on individual trades.

- Brokers using either the ISE's own automatic execution system (SAEF) or an in-house system should only be able to route orders to a particular market maker if that market maker is committed on SEAQ to matching the touch for all public customers.

- Market makers should be evaluated to ensure that they honor their obligation to quote competitive prices and sizes. It also suggested that objective criteria should be devised to assess market maker performance (and, by inference, to deregister those who are not performing satisfactorily).

- Once effective evaluation of market makers is in place, it should be possible to reimpose the requirement that SEAQ quotes be firm to other market makers.

- The definition of a large trade that would not be subject to immediate publication should be refined to make it reflect more closely the liquidity in different stocks.

- Broker/dealers who are acting as agents in crossing two clients' orders should be required to expose the deal to the most competitive market maker to allow him or her to participate in the deal.

- An experimental limit order execution system (CLOSE) should be set up.

Following further consultation with member firms and discussion by the Stock Exchange Council, the Elwes Committee produced a third and final report in March 1990. This report largely built on the earlier findings. The new recommendations were that the following changes would occur:

- The classification of shares into alphas, betas, gammas, and deltas would be replaced by a uniform system based on the normal market size (NMS) in each security. The minimum quote size, the maximum size of trades subject to on-line reporting, and the size of trade that can be executed through the automatic execution system would all be tied to the NMS.

- Large trades would be published within 90 minutes rather than the following day. The introduction of the NMS would also have the effect of raising the threshold for delayed publication to transactions to £750,000 rather than £100,000.

- A "green strip" would be introduced to enable market makers to quote prices for small transactions on an anonymous basis. In this way, each market maker could quote one set of prices in small quantity, and another in institutional sizes.

The Stock Exchange Council will have to reach decisions on the report in light of both the comments from its members, and a report from the Office of Fair Trading that has criticized some of the rule changes concerning trade publication. The underlying issue, how to maintain a centralized market when the Exchange itself has very limited leverage, will likely remain.

Visibility of Market Information

As noted, equity trading in London is dominated by institutional investors. Order flow is low even in the most liquid stocks, most of the volume is in large trades, trading tends to be "one-way," and London's institutional investors put a high premium on immediacy—the ability to buy or to sell a large block of shares at short notice and at a good price. The institutions have been much less concerned about price continuity. In this environment, the quality of the quotes is of paramount importance.

The London equity market has traditionally lacked the investor protection offered by an open auction system or by trade publication. Pre–Big Bang, the main protection against bad prices was the fact that the jobber had to offer a firm two-way price without initially knowing which way the customer wanted to deal. Although London since Big Bang is far more open than it was, the transparency of the market continues to depend more heavily on the publication of firm two-way quotes than on trade publication.

The ISE has sought to maintain the integrity of the quotation system, and has been concerned about market makers posting poor prices on SEAQ and then giving better executions. Poor SEAQ prices impair market visibility and imply a certain amount of market fragmentation. (See Chapter 9.)

Trade Reporting

Following the February 1989 rule changes, trades of over £100,000 are only published the following day. Because these trades account for 75% of the value of customer business (7% by number of transactions), this change makes on-line trade reporting of marginal value. The Elwes Committee's final proposals would greatly raise the threshold for nonreporting, which is sensible. The current limits are, for most shares, well below the level where a market maker would need to lay off an inventory position immediately.

As discussed in Chapter 3, a significant difference exists between the informational signal transmitted by a quote and that transmitted by a transaction price. In the ISE market maker system, considerably more attention is given to the importance of good quote reporting, and less to transaction price reporting. The architectural strategy of Big Bang clearly hinges on screen transparency—that is, market makers putting on the screen the largest sizes and the best prices they are prepared to offer their customers.

The exemption of large trades from on-line reporting is based on the argument that there is a conflict between prompt and full trade reporting on the one hand, and high quality quotes on the other. Market makers will not be prepared to take large positions if they are required to publish their transactions before they can lay them off. In keeping with the basic philosophy of SEAQ, the Stock Exchange is prepared to sacrifice trade reporting in order to go all out for high quality quotes.

Nevertheless, the loss in transparency is risky for both traders and market makers. A trader contemplating a transaction will face the risk that a large trade has already taken place but is not yet public knowledge. Similarly, market makers have only a limited knowledge of the order flow unless it is their own quotes that are being hit. Delayed trade reporting further makes it easier for public traders to transact simultaneously with several different market makers. The restrictions on trade reporting have attracted a hostile response from the Office of Fair Trading for these reasons.

In short, a market maker benefits from keeping its own trades secret, but is hurt by not knowing other firms' trades. A consequence of delayed trade reporting is likely to be an improvement in the relative position of market makers with a large share of the order flow (large firms, because of their size, see a large part of the order flow and thus depend less on trade reporting). Thus, limited trade reporting may cause increased market concentration.

Preferencing

"Preferencing" refers to the means of diverting order flow to particular market makers who are not necessarily showing the best screen prices. In the retail market this occurs primarily with proprietary small order systems such as Kleinwort's BEST and BZW's TRADE. An order inputed by a broker through a terminal is executed in one of these proprietary systems at the best screen price, regardless of the price the market maker is showing on SEAQ at the time.

A preferencing issue also arises with respect to the ISE's own system, SAEF. As originally conceived, SAEF orders would have been routed automatically to the market maker with the best price on SEAQ. Brokers, however, successfully pressed for the right to designate the market maker firm that will get their business. This issue involves a conflict of interest for the ISE. The Exchange both sets market rules for others and wants its own automated execution system to be profitable. The ISE has promulgated but failed to confirm a decision that preferencing on SAEF should only be permitted when the market maker concerned is setting the best price on SEAQ.

Preferencing also exists with "Closed User Groups," where a market maker posts prices on a different screen system that is seen only by favored institutional clients. In general, these quotes are better than those displayed by the market maker firm on the SEAQ screen. The Elwes Committee has recommended that market makers should not be allowed to display quotes on any other system that are better than those they are showing in SEAQ. Furthermore, the Committee believes that if a market maker firm is committed to matching the touch for small trades on its proprietary system, then it must make a similar commitment to the public generally.

The solution proposed by the Elwes Committee is to enable market makers to quote prices for small order sizes, in addition to their existing quotes. The best prices in small size would be shown on a Green Strip. Market makers would only be allowed to execute trades with automatic execution facilities if they are on the Green Strip at that time.

Fair-Weather Market Making

The concept of *fair-weather market making* describes those firms that take the privileges associated with market making, but fail to meet the implicit obligations. The Elwes Committee uses the term to refer to a market maker firm that (1) will reduce its risk position at another market maker's expense, (2) will spoil another market maker's business when the latter is trying to place a large order, and/or (3) only wishes to deal with its own clients and affiliates.

Some of the concern about fair-weather market making may be due to the vigorous competition that has accompanied the rapid increase in capacity. From an economic point of view, the argument about privileges and obligations has little merit—with essentially unrestricted entry to market making, competition should ensure that the benefit of any subsidies would be passed on to customers in the form of narrower spreads. Further, it is difficult to see how any free market can prevent a market maker who has learned legitimately of a competitor's transactions from taking advantage of that knowledge. Nor is it reasonable to demand that a market maker hold a position rather than attempt to lay it off. Finally, the value of market maker privileges will be greatly reduced once stamp duty is abolished, which the Government has announced it intends to do.

The Elwes Committee has proposed that market makers performance be monitored and that fair-weather market makers be deregistered if they fail to make an active market. Specifying tight performance criteria for market makers would be a partial retreat from the philosophy of Big Bang. The membership of the Exchange was opened up at Big Bang. The intention was to establish a free environment where anybody who is prepared to abide by the rules may participate. Assessment has prompted two particular concerns in this setting. First, it seems to some to be an ad hoc measure that indicates a fundamental weakness in the design of the system. Second, it has raised the fear that the Exchange could use its discretion to register and deregister to protect unfairly the economic interests of some of its members.

Suggested Reading

Clemons, E., and Weber, B. "London's Big Bang: A Case Study of Information Technology, Competitive Impact and Organizational Change," *Journal of Management Information Systems*, Spring 1990.

The International Stock Exchange London, "Review of the Central Market in UK Equities," May 1989.

Jackson, P. "Management of UK Equity Portfolios." *Bank of England Quarterly Bulletin,* May 1987.

Jackson, P., and O'Donnell, T. "The Effects of Stamp Duty on Equity Transactions and Prices in the UK Stock Exchange." Bank of England discussion paper, October 1985.

Leach, J., and Madhavan, A. "Intertemporal Price Discovery by Market Makers: Active Versus Passive Learning." University of Pennsylvania working paper, November 1988.

Leach, J., and Madhavan, A. "Price Experimentation and Market Structure." University of Pennsylvania working paper, June 1989.

Neuberger, A., and Schwartz, R. "Current Developments in the London Equity Market." *Finanzmarkt und Portfolio Management*, 1990.

Pagano, M., and Roell, A. "Stock Markets." *Economic Policy,* April 1990.

Scott-Quinn, B. "A Strategy for the International Stock Exchange." *National Westminster Bank Quarterly Review,* February 1990.

Touche Ross, "Maintaining a Central Equities Market," May 1989.

Notes

1. "Review of Central Markets in U.K. Equities: A Consultative Document from the Council of the International Stock Exchange," The International Stock Exchange London, May 1989, p. 6.

5

From Toronto to Tokyo and Beyond: The Advent of Computerized Trading

The introduction of the computer has had major ramifications for the airline and retail banking industries, and it is playing a major role in the transformation of the world's equity markets. Market structure has been fundamentally challenged by increased competition from new electronic trading systems and intermarket linkages, and by the advent of sophisticated computer-based trading strategies.

Computerized trading did not have an easy beginning—the responses to the first proposals were emotional and pessimistic. For example, in the late 1970's, Paul Kolton, then Chairman of the Board of the Amex, commented that the introduction of an electronic system based on a consolidated limit order book (CLOB) "seems not an orderly step but a drastic departure; it is less a measured progression than a giant leap, with the landing place obscure."[1] More recently, Allen and Zarembo[2] have discussed the initial hesitancy on the part of NYSE specialist units to accept the Exchange's new automated display book (which is not an execution system).

An electronic display book was first introduced on the NYSE in June 1983 for one stock, Pan Am. On its first day, a news release concerning the company resulted in the stock trading at three times normal volume, making it the most active issue on the NYSE (over 1,000,000 shares changed hands). Because of the system's success with the heavy volume, it was called upon on 21 November 1983 to handle the anticipated order flow of nearly two billion newly listed shares when the seven Baby Bell Companies simultaneously started trading following the AT&T divestiture. The ease with which this extraordinary challenge was met resulted in widespread acceptance of the electronic display book by the NYSE specialists.

London's experience following the introduction of SEAQ, an electronic billboard, was also dramatic. The ISE had invested several million pounds to upgrade its floor in preparation for Big Bang in October 1986. By January 1987, equities trading had left the floor entirely, and it did so at a speed that was astonishing. Clemons and Webber[3] quote a trader as saying, "Within five minutes of Big Bang, on Monday morning, it was clear to me that the floor was dead." This shows why resistance to further technological change persists.

In this chapter we consider the use of the computer for the most critical trading function, trade execution. Our focus is mainly on stand alone trading systems where price discovery could be facilitated by the computer. Electronic systems such as the NASD's Small Order Execution System (SOES) and London's Interdealer Broker System (IDB) that are integrated with non-electronic markets, are discussed elsewhere (see Chapters 3 and 4).

Advantages of Computerized Trading

Whether newer technology is better is not determinable in an absolute sense, but depends on the relative costs of capital, labor, and other factors of production, as well as the nature of the tasks to be performed. It also depends on how the system is designed and the use to which it is put. For instance, a potential advantage of computerized trading is the rapidity with which orders can be electronically transmitted and executed. However, speed may also have undesirable consequences if it is not properly controlled. Each investor individually wants to be the first to trade on news. However, all investors, collectively, may be better off if the pace of events is slowed down.

The computer can fundamentally alter a trading arena. It is widely accepted that a specialist would not be expected to fulfill the affirmative obligation to make a fair and orderly market if all orders were electronically consolidated in a limit order book that was open to all traders. Of course a specialist could have a role to play in an electronic system, but his or her operations would doubtless change appreciably. The price discovery and stabilization services of this market maker may be needed less in a properly structured electronic market.

In recent years, computer technology has altered major international market centers, from Toronto to Tokyo to Europe. The advantages of computerized trading discussed below explain why.

Direct Access to Information

Mendelson and Peake[4] view an electronic market as a "visual crowd," as opposed to an "auditory crowd." The visual crowd has a significant informational advantage—it allows investors direct access to the information provided in the trading arena. That is, individuals away from the trading floor can see supply and demand on their own screens (not just the current bid and ask quotations). Using this information, investors can electronically transmit their orders to the trading arena via their brokerage firms' computers. Brokerage firm intervention may remain necessary, however, to protect traders from dealing with counterparties who have not been subjected to the financial scrutiny of a member firm.

Some information may, of course, be lost. The meeting of brokers in the auditory crowd on the trading floor may allow them to infer the traders who are behind large orders. Other nonquantifiable information—that which is transmitted by body language, tone of voice, and so on—is also lost. Clemons and Webber[5] quote a trader: "I thought all the information you needed was on the floor; eye contact, sweat, movement. You could always tell from the eyes of the junior trader whether his boss was long or short, and how badly they wanted to get out of their position."

However, information that is lost in a visual crowd would have been available only to those in the auditory crowd on the trading floor. Thus its absence in the visual crowd may make that system fairer for the wider community of traders.

Increased Market Scope and Liquidity

Participation by those away from the trading floor has traditionally been discouraged because of the relative informational disadvantage of outsiders vis-à-vis participants on the floor. Computerized systems that allow direct access offer all market participants an equal view of the market regardless of their geographic location. Orders can be entered and executed virtually instantaneously from remote locations, as has been pointed out by Lupien, a former specialist on the Pacific Stock Exchange and former President and Chairman of the Board of Instinet:

> In February 1984 I personally did some trades (for both listed and over-the-counter securities) on an IBM PC in Johannesburg, South Africa. . . . I pushed the button and, in 22 seconds, had a 400-share execution for an over-the-counter stock. . . . Opportunities of this kind are going to broaden what we think of as a great market today. They can bring in tremendous liquidity, for there is much latent demand out there.

Integration of Information

Electronic trading, linked to electronic information systems, may support a far greater flow of relevant information. The reason is that electronic systems let portfolio managers access merged data sets. Amihud and Mendelson[6] note that "One of the important advantages of automation results from the ability to integrate subsystems that were previously managed separately. Distributed database technology provides the ability to access geographically dispersed data systems as if they were stored on a single centralized database. The result is that system components that were treated as unrelated and independent may be integrated."

Computational Ability

Electronic trade execution can use the computer not just to transmit orders and information between traders and a market center, but also to match orders and to establish prices. The computational ability of the computer can be further exploited to allow the incorporation of complex orders. For example, the size of an investor's buy limit order for a security can be conditioned not only on that security's price, but also on the market breadth at that price and on the price of other issues (this is discussed further in Chapter 10).

Trade Negotiation

Trades can be negotiated privately and then brought to the computer for execution, as is currently done with block trading on the NYSE (see Chapter 6), or they can be negotiated electronically. To date, institutional traders have felt that simply entering orders into an electronic system may not provide sufficient control, and they have been reluctant to enter their orders in a black box system. But, as noted above, the computational capabilities of a computerized system can handle complex orders that will facilitate the negotiation of trades. The critical need is to design the orders and the trading system appropriately (the issue is considered further in Chapter 10).

Cost Savings

Automated trade execution economizes on the use of labor and space. Computerizing trade execution also allows order-handling and trade execution systems to be interfaced electronically with trade reporting and clearance systems. Errors are minimized and the settlement process expedited. The interface with market surveillance also reduces the cost of monitoring trading.

The First Electronic Trading Systems

Computerized systems generally mimic existing markets. Continuous markets are prevalent in North America and the Far East, and the computerized systems developed in these countries have largely been based on the principle of continuous trading. These include the Cincinnati Stock Exchange's NSTS, the Toronto Stock Exchange's CATS, the Tokyo Stock Exchange's CORES, and the Paris Bourse's CAC.

Peake, Mendelson, and Williams

The earliest comprehensive outline of an automated securities trading system is the National Book System proposed by Peake, Mendelson, and Williams (PMW). Mendelson[7] sets forth an automated trading system that subsequently was further advanced by Peake, Mendelson, and Williams. See Mendelson, Peake, and Williams[8] for a discussion of the PMW system. For a more recent discussion of the PMW system, especially in relation to the chaotic stock market conditions in October 1987, see Peake, Mendelson, and Williams.[9] The system was envisioned as a means of developing a consolidated limit order book (CLOB). Key features of the PMW proposal include the following:

1. All trading would be done through the electronic system. There would be no physical trading floor.
2. The limit order book would be open. Individual buy-sell orders would not be disclosed, but the aggregate quantities bid and offered at each price would be public information to all traders and investors.
3. Call market trading would be used to open each trading session.
4. Because of the capabilities of electronic communication systems, the scope of the market could be very wide—in principle, worldwide.
5. All crossing orders would be automatically executed.
6. Price (as the primary) and time (as the secondary) priority rules would be enforced.
7. There would be complete integration of order entry, trade execution, information reporting, monitoring-surveillance, and clearance-settlement systems.

While PMW's proposal was never implemented in its entirety, it has had considerable influence on the design of several automated trading systems discussed below that have been implemented.

The National Securities Trading System (NSTS)

The National Securities Trading System (NSTS), introduced in June 1978, was initially developed by Weeden and Co. NSTS is now owned and operated by the Cincinnati Stock Exchange. See Davis[10] for more information concerning NSTS. Brokers and dealers participating in NSTS enter market and limit orders via computer terminals. A central exchange computer automatically matches crossing orders and executes trades, in much the manner proposed by Peake, Mendelson, and Williams. NSTS is linked electronically to the Intermarket Trading System, through which much of its order flow is routed.

A major advantage of this system is that an NYSE member firm can function as a market maker in stocks in a manner that NYSE Rule 390 would otherwise prohibit. Merrill Lynch did this for several years, in effect becoming the major source of order flow for the Cincinnati Stock Exchange. But when Merrill stopped using NSTS for this purpose in April 1983, NSTS's share of consolidated volume for the stocks it handled fell from 2% to 0.6%.

There are two major reasons for the system's relative lack of success. First, NSTS never was the major trading arena for its issues, and hence it suffers from the disadvantages of a small market competing with a large market. Second, NSTS never attempted to meet the unique needs of upstairs traders who are reluctant to expose their orders in the open limit order book system used by NSTS.

The First National Electronic Exchanges

The Toronto Stock Exchange was the first major national exchange to institute electronic trading for its listed securities. The Tokyo and then Paris Stock Exchanges were the first to follow. Although they are all auction markets, these exchanges have in the past followed considerably different trading principals. In the next three sections, we describe the floor environments into which the new electronic systems have been introduced.

The Toronto Stock Exchange and CATS

The Toronto Stock Exchange is a nonprofit organization owned by brokerage firms and regulated by the Ontario Securities Commission. The operations of the Exchange are directed by a Board of Governors that is composed of the Exchange's president, elected exchange members, and public members.

Current Floor Trading Environment

Comprehensively viewed, Toronto's current floor system is an interesting combination of automated and nonelectronic procedures. The Exchange operates as an auction market, like the NYSE. It has the equivalent of NYSE's Rule 390; that is, all orders must be directed to it or to another recognized exchange. As in the United States, banks in Canada are not permitted to perform a brokerage function. Consequently, all trading is handled by brokerage firms that either act as agents or trade as principals for their own accounts.

The market-making function on the exchange is fulfilled by approximately 160 *designated market makers (DMMs),* professionals who resemble the NYSE specialists. DMMs set opening prices for their stocks and maintain bid and ask quotations throughout the trading day. Like specialists, the DMMs participate in stabilizing trades to ensure orderly price changes. Unlike NYSE specialists, they must also keep spreads acceptably tight for the stocks assigned to them.

Along with the DMMs, there are approximately 200 qualified floor traders who handle orders that require special attention. Both the DMMs and the floor traders must conform to the rules of conduct of the exchange.

The efficiency of Toronto's floor environment has been greatly increased with the introduction in 1983 of two electronic trading systems: the Market Order System of Trading (MOST) and the Limit Order Trading System (LOTS). MOST ensures guaranteed fills for client market orders of 599 shares or more on floor-traded stocks. Access to MOST is via CATS (Computer Assisted Trading System) terminals, members' order-routing systems, and terminals on the exchange floor.

LOTS handles priced orders at or outside the current market. LOTS is accessed the same way as MOST. Orders may be specified as day, open, GTC, and "Good till Certain Date." The system consolidates the orders in an electronic book that is open and accessible to traders on the floor and in members' offices. Book information for all TSE stocks is now available to investors, who may subscribe to the TSE's "Market by Price" feed that displays aggregate size and total number of orders at each of the five price levels.

Toronto's Pre-CATS Trading Floor

Before its modernization, Toronto's trading floor had been organized as a *board trading system*. Board trading operates in the following way. Orders at the market or one tick from the market are posted on a wall of the trading room (there is no limit order book in board trading). Order sizes are not revealed, and traders need honor only one board lot (100 shares for stocks selling between $1.00 and $100.00). Price, but not time, priority is observed. If two or more orders are announced at one price, the orders share the volume if they can do so in board lot amounts; otherwise the competing brokers toss a coin to determine who participates in the trade.

With board trading, if a broker wishes to buy shares of XYZ Corp., he or she goes to the part of the floor where the stock trades and announces the price at which the shares are being sought. If that price makes the market, the new bid for XYZ will be entered on the board by an exchange official as a price entry (without volume being disclosed), along with the broker's identification number. Any trader wanting to sell at that price will find the trader who posted the bid, and the buyer and seller will together determine the size of the trade.

Board trading uses minimal technology to display limited information (orders, with volume undisclosed, at the best and next-best bid/ask) to floor participants. Not surprisingly, the system has not endured. Toronto's floor environment was changed dramatically by the institution of its electronic systems (MOST, LOTS, and CATS). Concurrently, the role of the designated market makers (DMMs) was changed to resemble more closely that of the NYSE specialists.

Toronto's experience with continuous trading has enabled it to appreciate the value of the floor environment for handling orders that, because of their size, require special attention. For this reason, the trading floor has remained a vital part of the system. Currently, 600 stocks (out of 1,400 issues) and 80% of the trading activity remain on the floor.

The Computer Assisted Trading System (CATS)

In 1977, the Toronto Stock Exchange instituted its Computer Assisted Trading System (CATS), the world's first fully automated electronic trading system. The Exchange had turned to electronic trading in part because the growth of its options trading was creating a shortage of space on its trading floor. By the late 1960s, the Exchange had recognized the need to examine the feasibility of applying computer technology to the traditional trading process because (1) successively larger trading volumes were highlighting order and trade processing difficulties; (2) rapid technological advances were creating a trend toward more extensive dissemination of timely market information and trading data; and (3) international attention began focusing on the concept of electronic order routing and trading systems. The system initially met with much opposition from floor traders and was used only for issues with small average trading volume. Today, roughly half of the issues listed on the Toronto Exchange are traded exclusively on CATS.

CATS contains many of the features proposed by Peake, Mendelson, and Williams. The opening of each trading session (and reopening after any trading halt) is based on call market principles. After the opening, CATS is a continuous market that stores orders on an electronic book and displays them on CRT screens. Traders can post orders in the book or cross orders, thereby achieving execution at or between the current bid and offer, without interference. CATS also enables traders to monitor order status, to receive printed confirmation of orders and trades, and to access a broad spectrum of trading data and statistics.

Traders key their CATS orders into one of three markets: (1) the Board Lot Market, which handles round lot orders; (2) the Odd Lot Market, a separate book for odd lot trading, and (3) the Special Terms Market, which handles orders with special terms (minimum fill, all-or-none, and so on). Limit orders stay on the book for a duration (up to one year) specified by the trader. Several types of board lot orders can be entered into CATS. These include market orders, limit orders, on-stop (stop loss) orders, short sales, and minimum fill orders.

The complete limit-order book for each CATS stock is open and visible to all Exchange member firms via authorized trading terminals. The price and size of each individual order, as well as the broker number of the member firm that submitted it, are shown in the "Market by Order" display. Any trader may elect to conceal any portion of his or her order beyond 5,000 shares, but the cost of doing so is that the undisclosed portion of that order loses time priority after the disclosed portion is filled. Buy and sell orders are automatically matched and executed in price and time priority.

CATS has a $2\frac{1}{2}$ hour (7:00–9:30) preopening period, during which orders may be entered into the system. During this period, participants can enter limit orders, stop loss orders, or short sales. Unpriced orders within certain parameters are accepted and will participate at the opening price. A preopening indicated price is computed and displayed each time a new order is entered. The calculated opening price is established as the value that maximizes the total number of shares traded. Any excess demand or supply at the opening price is allocated as follows. All buy orders above, and sell orders below, the opening price execute in full. For orders at the opening price exactly, disclosed portions are given priority over undisclosed portions, and stock is distributed equally among orders that have parity.

The Tokyo Stock Exchange and CORES

The Tokyo Stock Exchange, where approximately 87% of all Japanese exchange trading is conducted, is an auction market, much like the NYSE. Unlike the Toronto experience, Tokyo's floor trading environment was not appreciably altered by the implementation of its electronic trading system.

Membership

Membership in the Tokyo Exchange is held by corporations (individuals and partnerships cannot become members) that are securities companies licensed by the Minister of Finance (MOF). Total membership is limited to ninety-three. The Exchange has two types of corporate members—regular members and saitori members. Regular members are agents (brokers) and principals (dealers) who engage in buying and selling securities, either for their own accounts or for their customers. The employees of regular member corporations are known as "trading clerks." The Saitoris, who are brokers' brokers, serve as middlemen in transactions among regular members. Employees of Saitori member corporations are known as "intermediary clerks." Unlike the NYSE specialists, the saitoris do not take positions in the securities they handle, and are prohibited from dealing directly with clients. The only exception to this rule is when a saitori member is required to "buy-in" to or to "sell-out" to rectify a member's loss that is due to the saitori's own error.

Trading clerks may trade between themselves without the go-between service of the intermediary clerks (as in crowd trading on the NYSE), but an intermediary clerk must be notified of a cross. Most transactions are made via intermediary clerks—it is more efficient for regular members to use their services, and saitori commissions are fixed on a per-share basis and charged, even if a trade is made without their service.

Auction Market

Transactions in listed securities are carried out during a morning session that runs from 9:00 A.M. to 11:00 A.M. and an afternoon session that runs from 1:00 P.M. to 3:00 P.M. For most domestic stocks, a trading unit is 1,000 shares for stocks with a par value under ¥500, and 100 shares for stocks with a par value over ¥500. The trading unit for foreign stocks ranges from 1 to 1,000 shares. Trades take place either on the Exchange's trading floor or through CORES. In a number of respects, CORES mimics the trading floor.

Transactions on the floor are made in one of two auction methods—the *Zaraba* method and the *Itayosa* method. The Zaraba method is employed during continuous trading. In continuous trading, the highest bid and the lowest offer for an issue are entitled to priority and, when there is price parity, time priority is enforced.

Opening trades for the largest stocks are executed under the *Itayosa* method, which batches orders in call market trading. In most opening situations, a disparity exists between the number of shares offered and bid at a given price. On the NYSE, this imbalance may be eliminated by the specialist trading for his or her own account. However, a saitori member is prohibited from taking a position and therefore cannot fill the gap between supply and demand and, unlike on the Toronto Stock Exchange, excess supply or demand is not rationed. Tokyo has four conditions that must be met to open a stock:

1. All market orders must be executed.
2. All limit orders to buy (sell) at prices higher (lower) than the price at which the opening trades will be made must be executed.
3. All limit orders to sell or to buy at the same price as the opening price must be executed.

4. Any member who placed limit orders to sell or to buy at the same price as the opening price, which must be executed as a result of condition (3) above, must place at least one trading unit on the other side of the market to ensure an exact cross.

The Trading Floor

Larger stocks are assigned to a "First Section" and smaller stocks to a "Second Section." The 150 most active First Section stocks are traded on the trading floor. The remaining 1,040 or so First Section stocks, all Second Section stocks, and all foreign stocks are traded through CORES, the Exchange's Computerized Order Routing and Execution System.

Orders on the trading floor are brought by a clerk to the appropriate trading post and placed with the intermediary clerk handling the security. Orders received by telephone are conveyed via hand gestures by telephone clerks to the intermediary clerks. The orders are entered into the clerk's order book and filled when crossed by counter orders. Trades entered on the order book are in effect for only one day. An unexecuted order must be placed again by the regular member if it is a week order, a month order, or Good 'Til Canceled.

Unlike the NYSE, the Tokyo Exchange has no rule that prohibits disclosure of the saitori's book. The trading clerks can see the books, which are on the counters of the trading posts, and know how many shares are being offered or bid, both at and away from the market. Prices and the identity of regular members are also shown.

The Computerized Order Routing and Execution System (CORES)

CORES, the Exchange's Computerized Order Routing and Execution System (a modified version of CATS), was instituted by the Tokyo Stock Exchange in 1982, and expanded in 1985 to include all 430 Second Section stocks and 780 of the over 1,000 First Section stocks. The system has led to substantial improvements in the Tokyo Exchange. Most notably, turn-around time has been shortened and erroneous trades have been greatly reduced.

To execute a trade through CORES, a regular member sends an order into CORES through an on-line terminal during regular trading hours. The order is accepted by the central processing unit (CPU) of CORES and is recorded on its order file. An order-acceptance notice is automatically sent to the regular member who placed the order. The orders are arranged in an order book in accordance with auction market principles—higher bids take priority over lower bids, lower offers take priority over higher offers, and in the event of price parity, the earlier order takes precedence. A saitori member instructs the CPU by keyboard to match a buy order and sell order in the electronic book shown on a display screen. (A saitori member may instruct CORES to execute matching orders automatically.) The details of the trade are immediately reported to the parties to the trade, and the transaction price is automatically transmitted from CORES to the market information system.

Market Information System

The Tokyo Exchange's computerized market information system was placed in service in September 1974 and upgraded in May 1985. The system supplies real-time information to the Exchange and to securities firms who subscribe to it. The prices of shares traded on CORES, as well as the prices of stocks traded face-to-face on the trading floor, are displayed on the *Stock Price Display Board* on the trading floor and on the *Stock Price Display Video and Quotation Board* at the securities companies. The previous day's closing price, current bid and asked quotations, and the last trade price of each listed issue are disseminated through this system.

The Paris Bourse and CAC

The capitalization of the French equity market places it among the largest in Europe. The major market center in France is, of course, the Paris Bourse. There are also six other exchanges—Bordeaux, Lille, Lyons, Marseilles, Nancy, and Nantes—that, together with Paris, form a single system operating under the same principles, rules, and regulations.

Current Trading Environment

Securities are traded on the Paris Bourse by member firms (called *Sociétés de Bourse*) in one of three centralized order-drive markets: (1) the official list includes large French and foreign companies; (2) the second market includes medium sized companies; and (3) the *hors-cote* market comprises small companies with low trading volume. The most actively traded French and foreign shares on the official list are traded in the monthly settlement market (*règlement mensuel,* RM). Settlement on the RM market is seven days before the end of each month. The least active French securities and foreign stocks on the official list and all second market and *hors-cote* stocks are traded in the cash market for immediate settlement.

The Paris Bourse has introduced sweeping changes in its system since the mid 1980s. Electronic trading and a continuous market were introduced in 1986; currently, all trading is conducted through the electronic system.

In 1988, Bourse membership, which was previously restricted to individuals, was transferred to firms. Bourse members had traditionally acted in a brokerage capacity; in 1988, the brokerage firms were for the first time allowed to deal as principals in the secondary market. These firms were also allowed to act as investment bankers in the primary market.

The Old Paris Call Market

Before electronic, continuous trading was introduced, the Bourse was a call market. In call market trading, orders do not transact immediately upon arrival but are batched for simultaneous, multilateral execution at a single price, at a specific point in time. In Paris, the call was verbal (*à la criée*) for the most active stocks and written for the less active stocks. Callbacks were permitted for *à la criée* issues.

The old system worked well for traders present at the verbal calls but had severe limitations for others. Perhaps the most critical problem was that participants away from the floor received no market information at all during the trading and price determination process.

By the early 1980s, major consideration was being given to changing the market's architecture. The CATS system was licensed from Toronto in October 1985, and trading with it began in June 1986 for a limited number of stocks. In Paris, the system is known as *cotation assistée en continu* (CAC). Acceptance of CAC by the financial community was accelerated when Paris started losing appreciable order flow to London following England's Big Bang in 1986.

The old call market procedure no longer exists. It has been replaced by the electronic market, which mimics a continuous trading system. All stocks are now on the new system.

Cotation Assistée en Continu (CAC)

Except for minor modifications, CAC is identical to CATS. The market's preopening phase extends from 9:00 A.M. to 10:00 A.M., and the continuous market extends from 10:00 A.M. to 5:00 P.M. CAC accepts the same orders as does CATS, and it similarly allows large traders to keep part of their orders hidden. The arrival of a new order immediately triggers a transaction if a matching order exists on the centralized book. Like Toronto's CATS, CAC gives traders an in-depth display of data that includes a security's symbol, cumulative number of shares traded since the market opening, and the price change from the previous day's close. The screen also displays, for the best five bids and offers, the number of orders placed, the total volume at the bid and the ask, and buyer/seller identification codes. The price, size, and time of the five most recent trades are also displayed.

Member firm order books are connected to the central computer by COCA (**Connection to CAC**). Along with linking order and information routing to trading functions, COCA monitors, sorts, and queues orders according to their times of arrival. The system also sends confirmations of order arrivals and trade executions to member firms. In addition, COCA sends updates on current market conditions to member firms.

Recent Developments in Electronic Markets

Institutional Networks, Inc. (Instinet)

Instinet is a profit-seeking corporation that was acquired by Reuters in 1987. The firm was founded in 1969 as an electronic block-trading system for institutions such as mutual funds, pension funds, and bank trust departments. To facilitate the negotiation of block trades between institutional investors, Instinet allows the counterparts to trade anonymously, concealing their negotiations from the market while they are being conducted electronically. The trades that result from these negotiations become public information only when they execute. This procedure provides an alternative to the direct human-to-human negotiation of orders in the upstairs market or on the trading floor.

For almost 15 years, Instinet handled a small volume of block trades. In 1983, it introduced a service that allowed specialists on certain regional exchanges and OTC market makers to guarantee trade execution at the best primary market quotes for orders up to 1,000 shares for approximately 5,000 exchange-listed and NASDAQ/NMS securities. The NYSE is the primary exchange market for exchange-listed securities; therefore, even if a regional exchange is posting a better quote, the order will be guaranteed at the NYSE quote. In 1987, the service was expanded to provide execution for trades in all U.S securities, ADRs, and alpha stocks on London's International Stock Exchange. Orders are now accepted from a minimum of 1,000 shares, up to a maximum of 500,000 shares.

This service, known as *Global Automatic Trade Execution Service (GATES)* has enabled Instinet to attract a large volume of limit orders to supplement its block trading. Brokerage firms found this feature attractive because they could offer their customers guaranteed execution (called "an automatic") for orders that were larger than those accepted at the time by the small-order execution systems of the exchanges and the NASD. In 1989, Instinet accounted for 3.09% of the volume of all the exchange and NASDAQ stocks combined. Commission costs are approximately one cent per share.

Instinet provides a limit order book for OTC securities where none had existed before. For exchange-listed securities, the Instinet screen also provides the inside quotes and depth at the quotes for the eight U.S. markets on which the stock might be traded, as well as the time that each quote was last updated. Instinet subscribers can respond either by matching displayed prices or by making a counter bid that is transmitted instantaneously to the user's terminal.

After Hours Trading on the NYSE

The NYSE recently announced its intention to begin after hours computerized trading. In the proposed system, buyers and sellers will be matched electronically by the Exchange or by brokers. Executions would be made at prices set at the Exchange's regular 4:00 P.M. close, and orders that are not matched in the crossing period will be returned to customers. The NYSE is also planning a special after hours session to handle program trades electronically.

The Exchange is responding to competition from other exchanges, from fourth-market crossing networks, and from London. The new system, which for the first time in modern history will allow trading off the floor and without the specialist's own involvement, will represent the most fundamental change in the Exchange's trading procedures since continuous trading was implemented in 1869.

Fourth Market Crossing Networks

Institutional investors are increasingly balking at the high costs of trading on organized exchanges and in the OTC market. Discontent with the expense of using intermediaries has contributed to the development of the electronic fourth market for crossing trades.

Trade crossing reduces commission costs for three reasons: (1) traders need not search for a counterparty, (2) middlemen (brokers and dealers) are eliminated, and (3) anonymity is preserved. The fourth market will continue to grow; it will become less of a sideshow and more of a main event. As noted, it is also forcing change at the NYSE.

The two most active facilities for crossing trades are Instinet's Crossing Network and POSIT (Portfolio System for Institutional Trading), which is owned jointly by Jefferies and BARRA.

In 1986, the Crossing Network began its equities trading service to match buyers and sellers anonymously after 4:00 P.M. Approximately 300 participants use personal computers to enter orders (or also, in the case of brokerage houses, to designate crosses). Computers pair buyers with sellers on a time priority basis. Trades are executed at the closing price for exchange-listed issues, and at the midpoint of the inside market (best bid and ask) for OTC issues. Commissions are 1 cent per share; minimum execution is 2,000 shares.

POSIT enables large investors, but not brokers and specialists, to trade baskets of at least 10 stocks among themselves. The orders are sent to a central computer where they are electronically matched with other orders. Unlike Instinet's Crossing Network, POSIT crosses are done during the trading day (from 7:00 A.M. to 7:00 P.M.). Similar to Instinet, the prices are obtained from those quoted on the exchanges, a practice known as "parasitic pricing." Commissions are one to two cents per share. In the spring of 1990, POSIT began international portfolio trading via a crossing network in London.

Single Price Auction Network (SPA*works*)

R. Steven Wunsch, founder of Wunsch Auction Systems, Inc., is currently implementing an electronic exchange, known as SPA*works*, that includes a price discovery feature based on call market trading principals.

Traders type their buy and sell limit orders directly into a network that links their workstations to a central computer. The central computer determines the single price that balances the buy and sell orders and maximizes the total number of shares that trade. That price is the auction price. All bids at that price and higher and all offers at that price and lower are executed. These auctions promote direct competition between buyers and sellers, with everyone getting the same view of the order flow and the same opportunity to trade at the same price.

Because SPA*works* concentrates trading at a single point in time, it draws liquidity-seeking customers to the market simultaneously, thereby providing them the opportunity to trade with natural counterparties rather than having to rely on the search facilities of brokers or the risk capital of dealers.

The Future of Electronic Trading

Computerized trade execution was first proposed in the 1970s. By the late 1980s, it had been adopted by major market centers including Toronto, Tokyo, and Paris. In the 1990s it is promising to become the predominant way in which business is done. Still, in the United States and London, although computers are being used extensively for order routing and information display, they are not yet being widely employed for trade execution. Nor is computerized trade execution being used for the largest securities on the Tokyo Stock Exchange.

The computer's success with trading smaller stocks is reflected in the extent to which CATS has been employed elsewhere. In addition to the modified version adopted by the Tokyo Stock Exchange in 1982, Toronto has licensed its CATS software to the Paris Bourse, where trading began in

1986, and to the Lyon Bourse, the Brussels Bourse, and the Spanish National Market of Madrid, Valencia, Bilbao, and Barcelona, where trading began in 1989. CATS software has also been licensed to the Sao Paulo Exchange, where trading on the system began in April 1990.

The problems and successes with electronic trade execution give insight into the direction electronic trading is likely to take in the future. CORES was more easily introduced on the Tokyo Stock Exchange than CATS had been in Toronto. There has been greater acceptance of fully automated trading in Japan than in the United States. Vis-à-vis Toronto, Tokyo floor trading was already a limit order book system, and call market trading was already being used to open the market for certain stocks. Vis-à-vis both Toronto and New York, because the saitori do not take principle positions in the shares assigned to them, CORES has not altered any professional's fundamental function in the trading arena.

The Paris experience was different. The new electronic system did not mimic the existing trading arrangements. Prior to the installation of France's modified version of CATS, the Bourse was a call market. CAC, like CATS, is a continuous trading system. This change would have been far more difficult to effect were it not for the fact that Paris was rapidly losing order flow to London, as competition intensified after Big Bang. The experience shows how quickly technological innovations can be made when a market center's competitive position is at risk.

Despite its successes, electronic trade execution still has not reached its full potential. A system has not yet been designed that can handle the negotiation of orders with an ease that will naturally attract institutional-sized orders. This largely explains why electronic trade execution does not currently exist in major market centers such as the NYSE and London's ISE, and why large trades generally bypass the electronic systems in Toronto and Tokyo. The development of a system that will accommodate the electronic negotiation of large trades is considered in Chapter 10.

Suggested Reading

Allen, A., and Zarembo, L. "The Displaybook: The NYSE Specialist's Electronic Workstation." In Lucas and Schwartz (1989).

Amihud, Y., Ho, T., and Schwartz, R. eds. *Market Making and the Changing Structure of the Securities Industry.* Lexington, MA: Lexington Books, 1985.

Amihud, Y., and Mendelson, H. "An Integrated Computerized Trading System." In Amihud, Ho, and Schwartz (1985).

———; "The Effects of Computer Based Trading on Volatility and Liquidity." In Lucas and Schwartz (1989).

Bloch, E., and Schwartz, R. eds. *Impending Changes for Securities Markets: What Role for the Exchange?* Greenwich, CT: JAI Press, 1979.

Bunting, J. "Moving from Today's to Tomorrow's Trading System." In Lucas and Schwartz (1989).

Clemons, E., and Webber, B. "London's Big Bang: A Case Study of Information Technology, Competitive Impact, and Organizational Change." *Journal of Management Information Systems,* Spring 1990.

Cohen, K., Maier, S., Schwartz, R. and Whitcomb, D. *The Microstructure of Securities Markets.* Englewood Cliffs, NJ: Prentice Hall, 1986.

Cohen, K., and Schwartz, R. "An Electronic Call Market: Its Design and Desirability." In Lucas and Schwartz (1989).

Davis, J. "The Intermarket Trading System and the Cincinnati Experiment." In Amihud, Ho, and Schwartz (1985).

Lucas, H., and Schwartz, R. eds. *The Challenge of Information Technology for the Securities Markets: Liquidity, Volatility, and Global Trading.* Homewood, IL: Dow Jones-Irwin, 1989.

Mendelson, H. "Market Behavior in a Clearing House." *Econometrica,* November 1982.

Mendelson, M. *From Automated Quotes to Automated Trading,* Bulletin No. 80–82, NYU Graduate School of Business Administration, Institute of Finance, March 1972.

Mendelson, M., and Peake, J. "The ABCs of Trading on a National Market System." *Financial Analysts Journal,* September–October, 1979.

Mendelson, M., Peake, J., and Williams, R. "Toward a Modern Exchange: The Peake-Mendelson-Williams Proposal for an Electronically Assisted Auction Market." In *Impending Changes for Securities Markets: What Role for the Exchange?* E. Bloch, and R. Schwartz, eds. Greenwich, CT: JAI Press, 1979.

Newman, M. "Quality of Markets: The London Experience." In Lucas and Schwartz (1989).

Peake, J., Mendelson, M., and Williams, R. "Black Monday: Market Structure and Market-Making." In Lucas and Schwartz (1989).

Wunsch, R. S. "Market Innovations." Paper delivered at Meetings of the Institute for Quantitative Research in Finance, Colorado Springs, October 1987.

Notes

1. See E. Bloch and R. Schwartz, eds. *Impending Changes for Securities Markets: What Role for the Exchange?* Greenwich, CT: JAI Press, 1979, p. 107.

2. A. Allen and L. Zarembo, "The Displaybook: The NYSE Specialist's Electronic Workstation," in H. Lucas and R. Schwartz, eds. *The Challenge of Information Technology for the Securities Markets: Liquidity, Volatility and Global Trading,* Homewood, IL: Dow Jones-Irwin, 1989.

3. E. Clemons and B. Webber, "London's Big Bang: A Case Study of Information Technology, Competitive Impact, and Organizational Change," *Journal of Management Information Systems,* Spring 1990.

4. M. Mendelson and J. Peake, "The ABCs of Trading on a National Market System." *Financial Analysts Journal,* September–October 1979.
5. Clemons and Webber, "London's Big Bang."
6. Y. Amihud and H. Mendelson, "An Integrated Computerized Trading System," in Y. Amihud, T. Ho, and R. Schwartz, eds. *Market Making and the Changing Structure of the Securities Industry.* Lexington, MA: Lexington Books, 1985.
7. M. Mendelson, *From Automated Quotes to Automated Trading.* Bulletin No. 80–82, NYU Graduate School of Business Administration, Institute of Finance, March 1972.
8. M. Mendelson, J. Peake, and R. Williams, "Toward a Modern Exchange: The Peake-Mendelson-Williams Proposal for an Electronically Assisted Auction Market." In E. Bloch and R. Schwartz, eds. *Impending Changes for Securities Markets: What Role for the Exchange?* Greenwich, CT: JAI Press, 1979.
9. J. Peake, M. Mendelson, and R. Williams, "Black Monday: Market Structure and Market Making," in H. Lucas, and R. Schwartz, eds. *The Challenge of Information Technology for the Securities Markets: Liquidity, Volatility, and Global Trading,* Homewood, IL: Dow Jones-Irwin, 1989.
10. J. Davis, "The Intermarket Trading System and the Cincinnati Experiment," in Y. Amihud, T. Ho, and R. Schwartz, eds. *Market Making and the Changing Structure of the Securities Industry.* Lexington, MA: Lexington Books, 1985.

6

New Share Issuance and Trading

Share issuance in the primary market and trading in the secondary market are two major, closely related services provided by investment banks, brokerage houses, and other securities firms. This chapter presents an overview of primary market activities and of two secondary trading activities of particular interest: negotiated block trading and program trading. It also considers payments for these services—spreads, commissions, and soft dollar rebates.

Share Issuance

An investment banker raising funds in the primary market is a market maker, similar to a dealer who operates in the secondary markets. The price paid to the issuing company for its shares is the investment banker's bid, and the offering price to the public is the investment banker's ask. As such, like any dealer, the investment banker hopes to earn the difference between the bid and the ask. Much like a dealer who bears the risk of committing capital to market making, an investment banker places capital at risk when underwriting an offering. Also like the dealer who plays a key role in the price discovery process, an investment banker determines the price at which new shares are sold to the public.

Funds may be raised through an initial public or private offering (IPO), or by selling additional shares of an existing issue.

Initial Public Offering

Going public broadens a firm's access to capital markets for raising funds and increases the marketability of the shares for owners. It also enables equity shares to be evaluated in the marketplace. This facilitates the assessment of a firm's cost of capital and, consequently, results in a more efficient distribution of funds across firms in the economy.

An investment bank operates as an appraiser in determining the price at which new shares are issued at an IPO. The appraisal involves an investigation of the financial, operational, and managerial capabilities of the firm; a forecast of future cash flows under various assumptions; and an assessment of the industry within which the firm operates. In addition, broad economic conditions are taken into consideration to determine the firm's current worth in the market and to assess the timing of an offering.

Along with valuing the firm, the investment banker markets the issue. Marketing efforts encompass four activities:

1. *Formation of a syndicate:* Most large issues are sold by syndicates formed by an investment banking firm that acts as the managing underwriter. The formation of a syndicate spreads the risk of any individual underwriter and enables the investment bankers to diversify their efforts and capital over a larger number of underwritings. The managing underwriter in a syndicate carries the largest single share of risk; risk to other members is distributed according to their participation and the underwriting agreement.

2. *Underwriting:* Underwriting a new issue is similar to underwriting insurance. The underwriter of an insurance policy assumes the risk of an adverse event's occurring (for instance, if the house on which an insurance policy has been written catches fire). The adverse event for new issue underwriting is that the issue will not be fully purchased by the public (because the offering price has been set too high).

3. *Placement of shares:* A sale of new issues in the open market is a *public offering;* a negotiated sale to a small number of individual and institutional investors is a *private placement.* Shares that are presold as a private placement reduce the underwriting risk incurred by the investment banking syndicate at the time of a public offering. After an offering, registered representatives of the syndicate firms join the marketing effort by calling the issue to the attention of their customers.

4. *Price stabilization:* After the offering is effective and during the flotation period, the syndicate manager supports price to facilitate acceptance of the issue in the secondary market. This stabilization against price decreases typically involves considerably more capital and control over price than is provided by stock exchange specialists in secondary markets. Issuing corporations themselves are prohibited from stabilizing their own shares (largely to prevent firms from manipulating their share price).

The following must be decided for an IPO:

1. The *share price,* which determines the firm's cost of capital, reflects the market's willingness to supply funds to it based upon the firm's

riskiness and the return required by investors. Thus, the offering price is set according to the market's receptivity to the issue. Setting this price is one of the most important and difficult steps in the offering process.

2. The *offering size* is determined by dividing the amount of capital to be raised by the share price. If, for example, the firm has decided it needs to raise $100 million and the initial offering price is determined to be $20 per share, the offering size would be set at about 5 million shares. A "Green Shoe" provision, so called because it was first used by The Green Shoe Company, allows the syndicate to purchase additional shares at the same price as the original offering to cover over allotment, which occurs when the syndicate has sold more shares than are available. With an over allotment provision, the syndicate eliminates the financial risk associated with short selling. The maximum over allotment is 15% of the original offering.

3. The *gross spread* is the difference between the per share offering price to the public and the per share proceeds to the company. The gross spread is paid to the investment banking firms participating in the offering and is comprised of: a management fee that covers syndicate expenses and a fee for the lead underwriter, and the underwriting discounts and commissions that are distributed to participants in relation to their participation.

4. The *timing* of an offering is crucial and difficult. It may take days for the SEC to give final approval (regulatory delay) and several days to float an issue (the flotation delay). Because the hoped-for offering price may have been established in advance of these delays, the issuers have in effect set their hopes on a future price, not a spot price.

5. The *amount of shares existing shareholders will sell* is important. Funds raised by an IPO can be used in part to purchase the equity holdings of current shareholders. However, the market may have a negative response if it perceives that the current owners are attempting to "bail out." For this reason, the current owners generally continue to hold an appreciable portion of the new financial package.

Because a future rather than a spot price is involved, the pricing of a new issue, as seen through the eyes of an investment banking firm, is similar to the pricing of a stock option.[1] The syndicate has effectively purchased the entire issue from the issuing firm at the offering price minus the gross spread, and has offered to sell the shares to the public at the offering price. Accordingly, the syndicate is long the stock and has extended (written) a call option to the public (the offering price of the issue is the exercise price of the call option, and the gross spread is the option premium received by the syndicate for writing the call option). The call option is costless to the public, however. If the issue is bought at the offering price, the syndicate earns the gross spread. At higher prices, the syndicate profits from its long position but loses dollar for dollar from having written the call. At lower prices, the syndicate loses, dollar for dollar.

Private Placement

Regulation A. Regulation A applies to a new issue of $1,500,000 or less. The shares may be offered for a period of up to, but not more than, 12 months. A *Reg A* offering is exempt from registration requirements.

Regulation D. A firm can save the cost of underwriting and, like a Reg A offering, avoid registration requirements by engaging in a private placement under Regulation D of the Securities and Exchange Act of 1933. Reg D exempts registration requirements for a security sale between the corporation and the buyer that is made by an offering statement to a "sophisticated investor" and to no more than 35 nonaccredited investors. Accredited investors are defined as financial institutions, large pension plans, insiders, or individuals with net worth of $1,000,000 or more, or gross income of $200,000 for each of the past two years.

Rule 144

SEC Rule 144 pertains to the secondary market. It permits the sale of unregistered securities in modest amounts, after a two-year holding period, without first registering them with the SEC. The size of the trades are limited to 1% of shares outstanding for shares traded over-the-counter, and to the greater of 1% of shares outstanding or the average weekly trading volume over the prior four-week period, for exchange-listed issues.

Rule 144a

SEC Rule 144a, enacted in August 1990, relaxes Rule 144 and thus liberalizes the private placement market. The rule allows large institutions (those holding stocks and/or bonds worth at least $100 million) to trade unregistered securities among themselves without first registering them with the SEC and without having held them for two years.

Because Rule 144a allows issues floated under Regs A and D to be more easily sold, investors are more willing to purchase the shares in the first place. Moreover, non-U.S. corporations will be more attracted to the U.S. market, as they had previously been discouraged by the strict disclosure laws associated with public issuance.

Removing the secondary market trading restrictions on privately issued securities held by institutions could ultimately position the U.S. in the center of a vast market for international equities if an efficient system is implemented to handle Rule 144a trading. Currently, the American Stock Exchange and the NASD are developing facilities to handle these trades.

Shelf Registration (SEC Rule 415)

In 1982, the SEC allowed further integration of the primary and secondary markets by passing Rule 415, which permits the shelf registration of both equity and debt issues. Specifically, a corporation can file for a security to be issued, at its discretion, at any time during a period of up to three years. The benefits of allowing 415 offerings include the following:

- *Transaction costs:* The transaction costs (legal fees, the underwriter's spread, and so on) may be lower for a 415 offering for two reasons: (1) the fixed cost can be distributed over a series of issuances and (2) competitive bidding between investment banks is more aggressive when shares are brought to the market with minimal delay.
- *Flexibility:* When shares are on the shelf, a corporation is free to decide during a three-year period just when they may be issued and can adjust the terms of an offering.
- *Market timing:* With shelf registration, an issuer can sell shares quickly after contacting an investment banker (often on the same day). Direct placement may also be facilitated when shares are sold from the shelf. In contrast, an issuer must wait at least 48 hours for SEC approval after filing a registration statement for a traditional sale.

The costs of allowing 415 offerings include the following:

- *Competition between investment banking firms:* Syndicates are smaller for 415 offerings; this favors the large investment banking firms, and can result in regional dealers being excluded from the market.
- *Market overhang:* Unissued shares on the shelf "hang over" the market exerting downward pressure on price. A number of studies have found evidence that the issuance of new shares exerts price pressure.[2]

Negotiated Block Trading

Along with raising new capital in the primary market, investment banks also handle large secondary market transactions. The transaction that most closely resembles a primary market flotation is a *registered secondary* offering used to facilitate a large sale. As with a new issue, a prospectus is required for a registered secondary, and the sale must be announced to the public in advance of the offering period.

Most large trades are not registered, but are negotiated away from the trading floor in the *upstairs market*. The upstairs market is a network of trading desks that communicate with each other and with institutional investors by means of computers and telephones.

Negotiation

To illustrate the negotiation process, let us consider an institutional investor who wishes to sell, at 35 ⅛ or better, 600,000 shares of XYZ common, a stock that has an average daily trading volume of 700,000 shares. The negotiation starts with the asset manager's trader contacting a block trader at a large brokerage firm.[3]

The institutional seller (or its agent) may contact a brokerage house that has revealed a sizable buying interest on the Autex screen. (Autex is an acronym that stands for "automated exchange." The firm displays buying and selling indications by broker/dealers to institutions.) Of course, quotes may have been placed on the Autex by a brokerage house that is simply "fishing" for customers, and several brokerage houses may be indicating an order that has originated from the same customer. Nevertheless, Autex does help sellers and buyers to find each other. In the present case, the seller calls the brokerage house and learns that an institutional buyer is behind a 200,000 share order on the Autex screen.

On this first contact, the seller reveals as little as possible to the block trader. The objective is to find out if the buy order does have sufficient size, while divulging minimum details about his or her own order. On the other hand, the block trader seeks to learn as much as possible about the seller's offer size and minimum acceptable price.

The relationship between the institutional trader and the block trader is crucial. These professionals must have trust and confidence in each other. Information has to be revealed, but the information could be used against the seller (the block trader could make a proprietary bid for some of the shares and then compete with the institutional trader as a seller). The block trader must strike a balance between seeking a better price for his or her customer, and pushing for an execution in order to get commission income.

In the first phase of the negotiation, the institutional trader indicates that the order is for 100,000 shares, and that "there is more behind it." The block trader conveys the impression that demand for the stock does exist, and understands that the institutional trader's offer is indeed very large. The block trader also determines that the institutional trader would sell at 35 ⅛ or better.

The next phase of the negotiation involves the block trader obtaining market information from the exchange floor, and contacting the trader who represents the buyer behind the 200,000 share order on Autex. The block trader finds out the size of the buy order and the highest price the buyer will pay. The buyer is in fact looking for 300,000 shares, and will pay a maximum of 35 ¼. The block trader also learns through the firm's floor broker that the exchange specialist knows another buyer is on the scene for 100,000 shares at the 35 level.

The block trader assembles the information to determine a reasonable price for the transaction. The seller will go down to 35 ⅛ for over 100,000 shares. One buyer will pay up to 35 ¼ for 300,000, and another (the one known by the exchange specialist) will probably go as high or higher than 35 ⅛ for 100,000. Another securities firm had recently shorted 50,000 at 35 ½ and would likely be a buyer at this level. The Instinet screen is showing a bid for 10,000 shares at 35 ¼, and a bid for 7,000 shares at 35 ⅛ (the buyers behind these bids, however, might be the ones behind some of the orders being worked on the exchange floor). The current market bid is for 1,200 shares at 35 ¼. Price has come down somewhat since last night's close at 35 ⅜, and the current market for a large seller initiated trade appears to be around 35 ¼ or less. The block trader senses that the seller's order is, indeed, very large. Therefore, putting the pieces together, he or she determines that 35 ⅛ is a fair price for the trade.

The block trader makes a bid to the institutional seller for 100,000 shares at 35 ⅛, and states that more could be sold at this price. The institutional trader reveals that the order is in fact for a total of 600,000 shares and that 35 ⅛ would be acceptable.

The block trader now has to put the deal together; 600,000 shares are on the sell side, and 460,000 shares are on the buy side: 300,000 from the institutional buyer behind the Autex message, 100,000 from the institutional buyer known by the specialist, 40,000 from another securities firm, and 20,000 from the book and floor traders.

Thus, 140,000 additional buy orders have to be lined up. The sales traders at the block trading desk place phone calls to institutional customers around the country, and inform them of a large two-sided transaction in XYZ at the 35 ⅛ level.

The phone calls attract three more buyers for another 100,000 shares in total. One buyer will participate "only on a print" (that is, only if all 600,000 shares actually do trade at 35 ⅛). This is a hedge fund that is attracted to the deal because of the temporary price pressure it is expected to exert on the market.

The block trader has now obtained a commitment to sell 600,000 shares at 35 ⅛, and commitments to buy 560,000 shares at 35 ⅛. At this point, the brokerage house decides to take a long position of 40,000 shares to facilitate the trade. The block trader's order, however, is to be reduced share-for-share if in the final moments any other buy orders appear on the NYSE floor.

The package assembled, the brokerage house transmits the buy and sell orders to the specialist post for execution on the exchange floor. The limit bids on the book at 35 ⅛ and better are protected (included in the transaction), and executed at 35 ⅛ under a cleanup price rule. The trade is executed, and the print crossing the Consolidated Transaction Tape shows that 600,000 shares of XYZ traded at 35 ⅛. The 40,000 shares the brokerage house has acquired are now given to its position trader to be worked off as quickly as possible.

A position trader is not a two-sided market maker but, as the name implies, a trader. As a trader, he or she submits sell orders (if the firm has acquired a long position) or buy orders (if the firm has acquired a short position). The position trader may also take an offsetting position in a related security to hedge a position that cannot be quickly unwound.

The brokerage house receives a commission for the 600,000 shares it bought (from the seller) and for the 560,000 shares it sold (to the buyers). Because it put its own capital at risk to facilitate the transaction (the position trader is long 40,000 shares that have to be worked off), the commission charged to the seller is greater than that charged to the buyer. The efforts of the block trader have resulted in a large number of shares transacting at a price that is reasonable in light of current market conditions. The transaction did put pressure on the market (the trade went through at 35 ⅛, while the current bid was 35 ¼). However, the negative price impact has been limited by the information gathering, selling, and risk-taking activities of the block trader.

Upstairs Traders Versus Exchange Specialists

The example points up several differences between the operations of a block trading desk and of a specialist:

- Block traders play an active role in searching for customers to take the contra side of a trade. Exchange specialists are required to be more passive in relation to the order flow.

- A brokerage house may act as both broker and dealer in the same block trade, can charge a commission on all shares traded, and may earn a spread while unwinding any position it took to facilitate the transaction. Exchange specialists act either as dealer or as broker in any particular trade; as dealers they expect to earn the spread, and as brokers (but only as brokers) they receive a commission.

- Exchange specialists (and OTC market makers) must continuously make two-sided markets for their stocks. The upstairs block trader, on the other hand, does not deal actively with a stock until contact has been established with another trader. At this point, the block trader makes the other side of the market, by finding other customers and/or by taking a contra position in the trade.

- Stock exchange specialists have an affirmative obligation to make a fair and orderly market. The brokerage house is under no obligation to stabilize a market (although it is in the house's own best interest to prevent its trades from being destabilized). Standard tick size rules do not apply to block transactions. Other rules do apply, however.

- The U.S. stock exchanges are continuous markets. The block trading desk requires time to put a deal together and, in the process of making a market, effectively batches orders for execution at a single price as in a call market. The batching interval is not fixed, but depends on how long the negotiation process lasts. After a transaction, the block positioner works off any long or short position in the continuous market.

- Much of the order flow does not, on its own, go to any single trading desk. However, block traders are free to seek customers on the contra side of a large deal. Consequently, upstairs traders have developed extensive networks that they use continuously. Every opportunity is taken by traders to contact their counterparts in other firms; every news bit that is hinted at is noted. Information networks are important for both exchange specialists and upstairs traders; the specialists, however, no longer have the only privileged view of the market.

Stock Arbitrage

Arbitrage involves buying an asset in one market at a lower price, and simultaneously selling that same asset in another market at a higher price. Stock arbitrage may be classified as either risky or riskless.

Riskless Arbitrage

A classic example of virtually riskless arbitrage involves certain stocks (mainly mining issues) that are cross-listed on the Toronto Stock Exchange (TSE) and the American Stock Exchange (Amex). Arbitrage firms have stationed agents at positions just off of, but in view of, the trading floors of the two exchanges. The TSE and Amex agents maintain telephone contact while continuously monitoring quotes for cross-listed stocks. When a price discrepancy appears, each agent communicates the appropriate buy or sell response to its representative on the trading floor. If the offsetting transactions can be made at the quoted prices, a virtually riskless arbitrage profit can be realized. The arb operation avoids currency risk by including the purchase or sale of a five day (the settlement period) forward contract for Canadian dollars.

Arbitrage is risky when a purchase and sale are not simultaneous and/or when opposing positions are taken on similar but not identical assets. With regard to the TSE/Amex arbitrage, price discrepancies may not be instantaneously found, the attention of the floor traders cannot always be caught (the floor traders are not involved exclusively in arbitrage trading), and thus the TSE and Amex transactions cannot be made at precisely the same moment. Hence, the operation is not totally without risk.

Risk Arbitrage

Risk arbitrage typically refers to possibilities created by corporate changes in capital structure. Risk arbitrage emerged as a consequence of the wave of corporate mergers in the 1960s and grew with the merger activity of the 1980s. Sizable premiums are commonly paid in takeover situations. Consequently, takeover bids generally increase the value of the target firm's stock and decrease the value of the acquiring firm's stock. Accordingly, arbitrageurs (arbs) take a long position in the target firm and a short position in the acquiring firm. The long/short combination allows exploitation of price movements caused by a takeover bid and hedges the arb's position: after acquisition, the short position in the acquiring company will be offset by the long position in the target company being converted into a long position in the acquiring company.

The arbitrageur has taken a position in the takeover deal, not in the target or acquiring companies per se. But the position must be taken before the takeover is a certainty—by the time a merger agreement between two companies is finalized, the arbitrage possibility will have long vanished. The risk to the arb is that the deal will fall through. When it does, the arbitrageur who is unable to unwind his or her positions quickly becomes an investor.[4]

Program Trading and Index Arbitrage

Program trading, either for their own accounts (proprietary) or for their customers' accounts, is another major activity of securities firms. A program may be run to keep a fund representative of a market index, to hedge a portfolio, or to engage in index arbitrage. Program trading accounted for 9.9% of the volume of the NYSE in 1989.

Basket Trading

A "basket" trade is defined as the simultaneous purchase or sale of 15 or more different stocks with a market value of one million dollars or more.

By holding a basket of stocks that is representative of an index, an investor can obtain the average market rate of return. As of December 1989, indexing had attracted $200 billion in stock investments, and the nation's 200 largest pension funds had tied 30% of their assets to one index or another.[5]

An investor can also buy or sell a futures contract written on a market index. The payment (settlement) on expiration of the contract depends upon how the index has changed between the contract date and the settlement date. As the index rises, traders with long positions are credited and traders with short positions pay the difference. As the index falls, traders with short positions are credited and traders with long positions pay the difference.

Standardized futures contracts on stock market indexes are traded on a number of exchanges:

- *S&P 500 Stock Price Index:* Futures contracts traded on the Chicago Mercantile Exchange (CME).

- *NYSE Composite Index:* Futures contracts traded on the New York Futures Exchange (NYFE).

- *Major Market Index (MMI):* Futures contracts traded on the Chicago Board of Trade (CBT). The MMI is comprised of 20 issues, 18 of which are DJIA stocks.

- *Value Line Index:* Futures contracts traded on the Kansas City Board of Trade (KCBT).

Portfolio Insurance

Portfolio insurance seeks to reduce the volatility of an equity portfolio by selling (buying) stock index futures contracts whenever the spot stock index falls (rises) beyond a trigger level. For example, the typical portfolio insurance model dictates a 20% reduction in equities assets, or the sale of futures contracts of an equivalent stock value, when the market declines by 10%.

The Brady Commission reserved some of its harshest criticism for the role portfolio insurance played in exacerbating the market decline of October 1987. During October 14–16, portfolio insurers sold the stock equivalent of $3.6 billion in the futures market. The futures market, however, could not supply sufficient liquidity to accommodate all indicated sales, and portfolio insurers had $8 billion on Monday that, according to their programs, should already have been sold.

As these sales were made on the 19th, the prices of the futures continued to fall, and the spread between the futures and spot markets widened. This activated index arbitrage sell programs, which transmitted the price decreases back to New York. The falling cash prices in turn triggered more portfolio insurance sell programs, and the vicious cycle continued.

The events of October 19th showed that the dynamic insurance programs did not immunize portfolios from falling prices, as the asset managers had anticipated they would. All shares could not be sold at the prices that triggered the programs, and the interaction of portfolio insurance with index arbitrage not only exacerbated the decline in both markets, but almost caused "meltdown." Consequently, this hedging strategy is not being widely used today.

Index Arbitrage

The most prominent type of program trading is index arbitrage. When the price of an index future is high relative to the underlying proxy portfolio, the portfolio is purchased and the future is simultaneously sold. When the price of the index future is low relative to the proxy portfolio, the future is purchased and the proxy portfolio is simultaneously sold. The implementation of such an arbitrage program is described in the Appendix to this chapter. Arbitrage programs are also run using options on market indexes. For simplicity, we discuss the index futures only.

Arbitrage opportunities between futures contracts on an index and the underlying stocks exist for the following reason. The price of each stock in an index is set in relation to the order flow and dealer pricing decisions for that particular stock. On the other hand, the price of futures contracts on the index reflect traders' anticipations concerning the value of the market in aggregate. The price of a contract for the market index should, of course, be related to the average price of the individual stocks that comprise the index, but there is no assurance that the established prices will be in alignment because the prices are set in different markets.

Index arbitrage trading has attracted much attention since the October 1987 crash and the October 1989 mini-crash. This trading strategy has appeared to many to cause extremely fast, sharp price movements. But little hard statistical evidence that would support a causal relationship has been found. The report of the NYSE's panel on *Market Volatility and Investor Confidence*[6] concluded that, "the observed correlation, however, does not necessarily mean that index arbitrage can be blamed for the price changes."

Index arbitrage should be desirable—it keeps pricing consistent across markets. As noted, the cash value of a market index reflects expectations concerning broad market conditions, as does the price of an index futures contract. These are valuable pricing guides for the individual stocks. If the average price of the individual stocks is out of alignment with the price of an index future, arbitrageurs step in, drive up the price of the undervalued asset(s), and drive down the price of the overvalued asset(s). In so doing, the arbitrageurs do not change the price level of both markets combined.

Nevertheless, prices can be destabilized by basket trading. Index trading in the cash market involves large orders that are transmitted directly to the NYSE without first being negotiated upstairs. Consequently, the programs may generate a market impact that is costly to the trader, but not easily controlled (because a large basket executes against a large number of considerably smaller contraside orders, it cannot be easily negotiated upstairs). The market impact effect causes excessive, short-run volatility.

The markets can also be destabilized when positions are unwound at expiration. Index futures contracts are satisfied by cash settlement rather than by the literal delivery of shares. Thus, an investor or securities firm with a long position in a portfolio of stocks and a short position in the corresponding index future, must sell the stocks to unwind the arbitrage position. This "forced" selling puts downward pressure on share prices. Similarly, a short position in the proxy portfolio and a long position in the index future puts upward pressure on share prices.

The NYSE has dampened expiration day affects appreciably by instituting a change in settlement procedures for the index futures. The settlement price of the index is now computed based on expiration day opening, rather than closing, prices. The procedure works as follows. All unwinding orders must be transmitted to the exchange before 9:00 A.M. Buy/sell imbalances are then reported on the Consolidated Tape so that contra-side orders may be attracted. Beginning at 9:30, the market for each stock is opened as soon as the specialist determines the opening price. The value of the index future on expiration is determined by averaging the opening prices of the stocks in the index.

Because orders in the cash market are executed at the opening and the settlement value of the index is computed using opening prices, the arb is unaffected by any price impact the unwinding trades might have. If the opening value of the index is pushed down by the sale of the individual stocks (or is pushed up by their purchase), the futures contract will itself be settled at a lower (or at a higher) price. Therefore, the destabilizing effects of their own unwinding trades is of no consequence to the arbs. However, because preopening imbalances are publicly disseminated, stabilizing orders are naturally attracted.

Initiatives Since the October 1987 Crash

Reacting to concerns that program trading, and particularly index arbitrage, might be contributing to excessive volatility, the NYSE enacted several measures to restrain program trading during periods of particular stress. As of 4 February 1988, the NYSE prohibited member firms from using SuperDOT, its electronic order delivery system, to execute program trades for index arbitrage for the remainder of any day, once the DJIA has moved by 50 points or more in either direction. This measure drew criticism because it can be circumvented by member firms with a large floor trader presence (manually executed program trades were not restricted). In July 1990, the SEC approved a new rule forcing traders to wait for an uptick (downtick) before buying (selling) the stock side of a transaction. Further, the Merc and the Chicago Board of Trade have raised margins on index futures trades. These policy changes may have unintended side affects—the linkage between the futures and equities markets may be weakened, and execution costs may be raised.

Since May 1988, the NYSE has required its member firms to submit daily reports of their program trading activity. The NYSE has been releasing monthly program trading reports since August 1988, and following the events of October 1989, program reports have been disseminated on a weekly basis.

On 26 October 1989, the NYSE initiated trading in its Exchange Stock Portfolio (ESP), a product that allows investors to buy or to sell all stocks in the S&P 500 Index with a single execution and to receive physical delivery. The basket, which costs approximately $5 million per unit, is designed to relieve some of the pressure these large transactions place on the NYSE specialists. The high unit price has limited the market to large institutional investors, and the product has not been successful. On most days no trades are reported.

Commissions and Soft Dollar Payments

The Elimination of Fixed Commissions

The most significant change in the securities industry in the U.S. since its early development, was the elimination of the fixed commission structure on 1 May 1975. The Securities Exchange Act of 1934 had exempted the NYSE from certain statutes in the U.S. antitrust legislation and, until the 1975 Amendments, the Exchange had been free, subject to permission from the SEC, to set minimum commission rates on stock transactions.

Commission income accounted for roughly half of the gross income of member firms of the NYSE in the period 1971–1974.[7] As one might expect, broker/dealer firms competed fiercely for this income. Brokerage firms offered a package—order handling, record keeping, custodial services, advisory services, dividend collection, and research. In the era of fixed commissions, commission dollars alone typically paid for the entire package. The components other than order handling were in essence a rebate to customers in the form of services, rather than in hard dollars.

Three undesirable consequences of the fixed commission structure had become increasingly apparent with the growth of institutional trading:

1. The level of the minimum rates was excessively high (purportedly, the excess portion of commissions relative to the cost of order handling ranged as high as 90% for large orders).[8]

2. The market was being fragmented by large traders turning to regional exchanges and the third market to escape the fixed commission structure.

3. Related services (research, and so on) were being oversupplied.

We have now had almost two decades of experience with negotiated commissions, and few would argue that the deregulation was not justified. In the early 1970s, however, three concerns in particular were raised, and the issues remain relevant today.

Competition in the Brokerage Industry.   The NYSE argued that because of economies of scale in brokerage, more efficient brokerage houses would drive less efficient houses out of business in a fully competitive environment. The elimination of fixed (high) rates would therefore lead to increased concentration in the brokerage industry. According to the Exchange, the price of brokerage services would then actually be higher for customers because of the enhanced market power of the large firms.

Might commission rates ultimately be higher if big firms are allowed to drive weaker firms out of business and then impose noncompetitive prices? This could indeed occur if average costs for a securities firm are negatively related to volume because of economies of scale in brokerage. The efficient regulatory solution in such a case would be to allow only a few firms (the biggest and the best) to be the providers of the service, and then to regulate those firms. That is, rather than establishing a *minimum* commission at a high price to ensure the existence of inefficient firms, a *maximum* commission should be stipulated at a low value to keep the price of brokerage in line with the cost of providing the service.

The Exchange's empirical findings with regard to economies of scale have been challenged by a number of subsequent studies and, in fact, an alarming increase of concentration did not occur in the brokerage industry in the years following the deregulation in 1975.[9] Firms of varying size have coexisted, and specialty firms have found their niche in the industry. According to Tinic and West[10], there is no evidence that the elimination of fixed rates has enabled larger brokerage firms to improve their relative position in the industry.

Other Brokerage Services.   Some have felt that fixed minimum commissions are required to ensure that certain essential services other than order handling be provided by the brokerage houses. The primary concern is that the quantity and quality of research might be impaired if competition is allowed to drive commissions to a level that just covers the cost of order handling.

Whether bundled or not, other services would in theory be optimally provided in a competitive environment as long as no market failure is operative. A market failure argument is possible, however, particularly with regard to research. Would a sufficient amount of information be produced as a private good in a free market? Was information being overproduced when commission rates were fixed?

All told, there is little indication that either the quantity or the quality of research has diminished appreciably with the introduction of negotiated rates. Furthermore, investors now have the freedom not to obtain, and not to pay for, research that is not desired. As Tinic and West [11] note, "Under fixed rates and the bundling of services, many investors 'consumed' research for which they would not have paid hard cash. If they were now unwilling to buy these services outright, who would want to say that this was bad?"

Soft Dollars and Directed Commissions*

Soft dollars are credits investment managers receive from brokerage firms (much like frequent flier miles) in exchange for direct trading commissions to certain brokers. (Soft dollar payments are still not allowed by the SEC on trades done through principals, that is, where the brokerage firm trades for its own account.) Soft dollar credits can be used to purchase services such as research or products such as Quotron machines. On 22 April 1986, the SEC lifted the restriction against the products brokers can commercially provide, broadening the range of products and services that investment managers can accept from brokerage firms. Partly as a result of the difficulty inherent in pricing these services, they are not paid for with cash, but with "soft dollars."

In 1989, the estimated cash value of soft dollar credits ranged from $500 to $800 million, out of institutional commissions of $2.5 billion. [12] Currently, about 25% of annual institutional commissions are believed to be directed by investment managers so as to obtain soft dollar rebates. [13]

Allocation of Trading Costs.   Under conventional payment schemes, a plan sponsor pays an investment management company its explicit trading costs such as commissions, plus a percentage of capital managed. Indirect costs

---

* Material in the remainder of this section draws on R. Schwartz and D. Whitcomb, *Transaction Costs and Institutional Investor Trading Strategies*. Monograph Series in Finance and Economics, No. 1988-2/3, Salomon Brothers Center for the Study of Financial Institutions, New York University Graduate School of Business Administration, 1988, used with permission.

such as staff salaries are not included. Therefore, an investment management company can lower its out-of-pocket operating costs by directing its commissions so as to substitute outside research for in-house research. The plan sponsor or fund may be paying heavily, however—the broker to whom the commissions are directed might not be obtaining the best executions for its client.

Excessive directing can hinder a trader's ability to obtain best execution for difficult trades, and most plan sponsors limit the proportion of a fund's brokerage that their investment managers can direct. Moreover, a brokerage firm seeking investment management clients has an incentive to assure plan sponsors that investment management firms will not be given soft dollars that are inefficient to the plan sponsors. And the investment managers may themselves limit their receipt of soft dollars to attract plan sponsors' accounts. Nevertheless, soft dollars may still be excessive in competitive equilibrium because monitoring agreements with investment managers to limit their use are costly. For instance, if the plan sponsor pays for research, monitoring is difficult because research obtained for one client of the money management firm can easily be used for other clients as well.

Agreements may require the investment management firm to fund the research itself and recover the cost through its management fee. More plan sponsors are now directing investment managers to give a share of their business to brokers who give cash rebates. Plan sponsors also direct traders to take some of their business to discount brokers that do not provide research services.

Unbundling Research.   Research has been called "the cheapest commodity on the street." There are several reasons why:

1. A brokerage firm trading for its own account, is likely to undertake technical and/or fundamental analysis for its own use. Providing the research to clients then becomes a joint product with trading, where each can be produced separately in varied proportions, but where some of both will always be produced.

2. Research reports are a form of advertising and an excuse for a broker to telephone a potential client.

3. The soft dollars are a discount that is disguised to minimize commission rate competition among full-service brokers.

With complete unbundling, the question arises as to whether or not producers of research will be able to charge enough to a large enough number of users to justify producing it. They will, as long as producers can keep users from reselling it or from acquiring it without charge. Since investment managers clearly do not wish to share information with competitors, there is reason to believe that research can be marketed as a private good and that enough will be produced. Thus, while soft dollars are currently popular, many believe that discounting and unbundling (that is, paying directly for, and only for, each service one gets) will ultimately prevail. Who would provide the research, and how much would be provided if all brokers were discount brokers, remains to be seen.

Trading Performance Measurement

Saving on commission costs is inadvisable if doing so results in losing more on the spread and market impact. Thus, plan sponsors and investment managers are increasingly spending soft dollars to obtain trading performance measurements. The choice of a broker can affect the spread paid and market impact. A broker can do several things for a difficult block trade that requires expertise, judgment, and/or the commitment of risk capital. First, the broker can use his or her feel for the market to determine proper market timing. Second, a good institutional broker has a network of counterparts that aid in finding the best contra block. The institution may avoid market impact this way and even save the spread. If a good contra block cannot be found quickly and quietly, the broker may break up the order and feed it to the market, or take all or part of the contra side itself. The growing interest in best execution and the evidence that not all brokers can deliver it, has also led plan sponsors and investment managers to experiment with various pricing systems that are logical complements to unbundling, in that they reflect a desire to pay for the amount and quality of a service that is actually rendered.

In a tiered commission rate system, an institutional trader classifies a potential transaction according to its prospective difficulty and is allowed to pay a higher commission for more difficult trades. The definition of a difficult trade has been the subject of debate. Some firms distinguish loosely between "no brainers," discretionary trades, and capital commitment trades.

If one can measure the execution costs of a trade, why not give brokers an incentive by letting them share in the gains of trading at lower execution costs, and help pay for losses on trades where execution costs get out of control? On investment management firm, Batterymarch, does this. The commission cost differences between "successful" and "unsuccessful" trades are small (one to three cents per share), and it remains to be seen whether this scheme will attract the best brokers and improve execution.

Performance Incentive Fees. Some plan sponsors have considered using performance incentive fees for their investment management firms. The SEC ruled in November 1985 that large investors can negotiate incentive fees with their investment advisors based on performance over at least one year. Instead of basing fees on a straight percent of assets, these schemes pay investment managers a smaller percent of assets plus a share of any return exceeding a benchmark such as the return on the S&P 500. This gives investment management firms an incentive to choose brokers with the lowest overall transaction costs, and to obtain research in the most cost-effective way.

Performance incentive fees, however, may create an incentive to increase the riskiness of a portfolio. This problem may be resolved if a plan sponsor sets a benchmark return consistent with the riskiness desired. Another distortion is caused if the scheme rewards returns above the benchmark, but does not penalize returns below. This defect can be corrected by making the performance fee symmetrical. Risk of investment manager bankruptcy, however, destroys the symmetry of the incentive fee. This suggests that performance incentive fees will work best with large, well-capitalized investment management firms.

Appendix—Implementing an Index Arbitrage Program

To illustrate arbitrage between a representative basket of stocks and a stock index future, we define the following variables:

F = the price of the index future

S = the cash or "spot" price of the index (the average price of the stocks in the index)

m = the number of days until the futures contract matures

T = the percentage transaction cost of running a program (the dollar transaction cost divided by the current value of the index)

r = the annualized risk-free rate of interest over the m-day period

d = the annualized dividend yield for a portfolio that proxies the index, for the m-day period (d is negative for a short position in the proxy portfolio)

The percentage differential between the price of the future and the cash price, $(F-S)/S$, is *the basis*. At maturity, F equals S and hence the basis is zero. Because the cash price must equal the futures price by the end of the m-day period, the basis represents a return that is realized over the m-day period. The annualized value of this return is $[(F-S)/S][365/m]$. If the basis is positive, an investor may obtain the return by a *long arbitrage* (buying the stocks in the index portfolio and shorting the index future). If the basis is negative, the return may be obtained by a *short arbitrage* (shorting the stocks and buying the future).

Both the long arbitrage and the short arbitrage eliminate all risk associated with change in the level of prices (that is, the arb's profits are not affected by proportionate change in F and in S). If, for example, prices increase, profits realized from a long position in the stocks would be offset, dollar-for-dollar, by losses realized from the short position in the index future. Similarly, losses from a short position in the stocks would be offset, dollar-for-dollar, by profits from the long position in the index future. The hedged position also establishes an equivalent offsetting of profits and losses if prices decrease over the m-day interval. Therefore, because F must equal S when the futures contract matures, the basis is a riskless (gross) return for an investor with the appropriate long or short arbitrage position.

The total gross return (expressed as a rate per annum) is the annualized basis plus the dividend yield (d). The dividend yield is an additional return for an investor with a long arbitrage, but is subtracted out as a cost for an investor with a short arbitrage. If the arbitrage is riskless, the total gross return must, in the absence of transaction costs, equal the risk-free rate, r. Therefore,

$$[(F - S)/S] [365/m] + d = r \qquad (A6.1)$$

For the riskless arbitrage, the equilibrium value of the annualized basis is

$$[(F - S)/S] [365/m] = r - d \qquad (A6.2)$$

Because d is generally less than r, we must generally have F greater than S.

If the basis differs form the value given by equation (A6.2), an arbitrage opportunity exists. The difference, however, must be large enough to cover transaction costs (T). For a positive basis, a long arbitrage is profitable if

$$[(F - S)/S] [365/m] - T[365/m] > r - d \qquad (A6.3)$$

For a negative basis, a short arbitrage is profitable if*

$$-[(F - S)/S] [365/m] - T[365/m] > r - d \qquad (A6.4)$$

Index arbitrage is not riskless, and a program will not be run unless the inequalities shown in equations (A6.3) and (A6.4) are sufficiently large. A premium of from 200 to 250 basis points is commonly required to compensate for risk. The risks involved include the following:

1. Transaction costs may vary because the cost of achieving rapid executions cannot be known with certainty.

2. The realized dividend yield may differ from the expected dividend yield.

---

* Recall that d in equation (A6.4) is negative because the arb has shorted the stock. Hence for a short arbitrage to be profitable, the positive return form the negative basis, minus transaction costs, must exceed the risk-free rate of interest *plus* the dividend yield declared on the proxy portfolio, r−(−d).

3. The proxy portfolio may not track the market index perfectly; hence at the close of day m, the futures price may not exactly equal the average cash price for the basket of stocks that comprise the proxy portfolio.

An arbitrage opportunity is best exploited by keeping transaction costs at a minimum and by achieving rapid execution of the program via SuperDot. As a back-up, large brokerage firms also maintain the capability of delivering orders manually to the specialist posts. Market orders are generally used because the window of opportunity is never open for long, and speed is essential.

A number of decisions must be made to set up a program. These entail the following:

1. Selection of the specific market index to use for the arbitrage (the S&P 500 is commonly used).

2. Selection of the specific stocks to include in the proxy portfolio used for the arbitrage (purchasing all 500 shares in the S&P 500 would be unnecessary and too cumbersome; baskets typically contain from 100 to 400 stocks).

3. Choice of the appropriate risk-free rate of return (r) (a short-term borrowing or lending rate is commonly used).

4. Computation of the expected dividend yield.

5. Determination of the critical value the basis must attain for a program to be activated: the determination of this value involves an assessment of transaction costs, T, and of r and d, and of the premium that must be added to compensate for risk.

6. Specification of the size of the program. Programs are generally as large as possible. A constraint on size, however, is that larger programs are more apt to result in adverse price effects.

Suggested Reading

Amihud, Y., Ho, T., and Schwartz, R. eds. *Market Making and the Changing Structure of the Securities Industry.* Lexington, MA: Lexington Books, 1985.

Asquith, P., and Mullins, D., Jr., "Equity Issues and Offering Dilution." *Journal of Financial Economics,* January-February 1986.

Bhagat, S., Marr, M. W., and Thompson, G. R. "The Rule 415 Experiment: Equity Markets." *Journal of Finance,* December 1985.

Bloch, E. *Inside Investment Banking.* Homewood, IL: Dow Jones-Irwin, 2nd edition, 1989.

Bloch, E., and Schwartz, R. (eds.). *Impending Changes for Securities Markets: What Role for the Exchanges?* Greenwich, CT: JAI Press, 1979.

Copeland, T., and Galai, D. "Information Effects on the Bid-Ask Spread." *Journal of Finance,* December 1983.

Dann, L., and Mikkelson, W. "Convertible Debt Issuance, Capital Structure Change and Financing-Related Information." *Journal of Financial Economics,* June 1984.

Grossman, S. "Program Trading and Market Volatility: A Report on Interday Relationships." *Financial Analysts Journal,* July-August 1988.

Hess, A., and Frost, P. "Tests for Price Effects of New Issues of Seasoned Securities." *Journal of Finance,* March 1982.

Mikkelson, W., and Partch, M. "Stock Price Effects and Costs of Secondary Distributions." *Journal of Financial Economics,* June 1985.

Schwartz, R., and Whitcomb, D. *Transaction Costs and Institutional Investor Trading Strategies.* Monograph Series in Finance and Economics, No. 1988-2/3, Salomon Brothers Center for the Study of Financial Institutions, New York University Graduate School of Business Administration, 1988.

Stoll, H., and Whaley, R. *Expiration Day Effects of Index Options and Futures.* Monograph Series in Finance and Economics, No. 1986-3, Salomon Brothers Center for the Study of Financial Institutions, New York University Graduate School of Business Administration, 1986.

Summer, A., Jr., "Comments on Professors Bloch, Lorie and The Future." In Bloch and Schwartz (1979).

Tinic, S. "Anatomy of Initial Public Offerings of Common Stock." *Journal of Finance,* September 1988.

Tinic, S., and West, R. "The Securities Industry Under Negotiated Brokerage Commissions: Changes in the Structure and Performance of New York Stock Exchange Member Firms." *Bell Journal of Economics and Management Science,* Spring 1980.

West, R., and Tinic, S. "Minimum Commission Rates on New York Stock Exchange Transactions." *Bell Journal of Economics and Management Science,* Autumn 1971.

Wyser-Pratte, G. *Risk Arbitrage II.* Monograph Series in Finance and Economics, No. 1982-314, Salomon Brothers Center for the Study of Financial Institutions, New York University Graduate School of Business Administration, 1982.

Notes

1. E. Bloch, *Inside Investment Banking,* Homewood, IL: Dow Jones-Irwin, 2nd edition, 1989.

2. P. Asquith and D. Mullins, Jr., "Equity Issues and Offering Dilution," *Journal of Financial Economics,* January-February 1986; L. Dann, and W. Mikkelson, "Convertible Debt Issuance, Capital Structure Change and Financing-Related Information," *Journal of Financial Economics,* June 1989. A. Hess, and P. Frost, "Tests for Price Effects of New Issues of Seasoned Securities," *Journal of Finance,* March 1982; P. Marsh, "Equity Rights Issues and the Efficiency of the U.K. Stock Market," *Journal of Finance,* March 1982; W. Mikkelson and

M. Partch, "Stock Price Effects and Costs of Secondary Distributions," *Journal of Financial Economics,* June 1985.

3. My thanks to Bart Breakstone and Theresa Woolverton for providing source material upon which this example is largely based.

4. For additional details concerning the risks involved see G. Wyser-Pratte, *Risk Arbitrage II.* Monograph Series in Finance and Economics, No. 1982-314, Salomon Brothers Center for the Study of Financial Institutions, New York University Graduate School of Business Administration, 1982.

5. *The Wall Street Journal,* 26 December 1989.

6. New York Stock Exchange, Inc. NYSE Panel Report, *Market Volatility and Investor Confidence.* New York: New York Stock Exchange, Inc. 1990, p. 18.

7. NYSE *Fact Book 1974,* 1976.

8. A. Summer, Jr. "Comments on Professors Bloch, Lorie, and The Future," in E. Bloch, and R. Schwartz, eds. *Impending Changes for Securities Markets: What Role for the Exchanges?* Greenwich, CT: JAI Press, 1979.

9. For analysis and further references, see R. West, and S. Tinic, "Minimum Commission Rates on New York Stock Exchange Transactions," *Bell Journal of Economics and Management Science,* Autumn 1971.

10. S. Tinic and R. West, "The Securities Industry Under Negotiated Brokerage Commissions: Changes in the Structure and Performance of New York Stock Exchange Member Firms," *Bell Journal of Economics and Management Science,* Spring 1980.

11. Tinic and West, "Securities Industry under Negotiated Brokerage Commissions," pp. 39–40.

12. *The Wall Street Journal,* 14 April 1989, p. C-1.

13. R. Schwartz and D. Whitcomb, *Transaction Costs and Institutional Investor Trading Strategies.* Monograph Series in Finance and Economics, No. 1988–2/3, Salomon Brothers Center for the Study of Financial Institutions, New York University Graduate School of Business Administration, 1988.

PART II

Market Architecture

7

Issues in Market Operations

The objectives of a trading system are twofold: fair, cost-effective trade execution and accurate price determination. The achievement of these objectives depends on a market's architecture—the procedures, rules, and protocols that determine how orders are handled and translated into trades. The link between market architecture and price determination is important because trading is a costly activity.

Much standard economic analysis is based on the assumption of frictionless (costless) trading in a perfectly competitive environment. Perfect competition means that, for a homogeneous resource, the number of buyers and sellers is sufficiently great so that no trader is large enough relative to the market to affect the resource's price. Price takers make only one decision with respect to the resource: the quantity to buy (demand) or to sell (supply) at a price that is determined by market forces. "Market forces" is an abstract concept meaning that if demand exceeds supply, competition among buyers will cause prices to rise or, if supply exceeds demand, competition among sellers will cause prices to fall. Problems concerning market operations do not exist in this environment.

A market center such as the New York Stock Exchange (NYSE) is sometimes cited as an example of a perfectly competitive environment: standardized units are bought and sold (any share of IBM common is like any other share of IBM common), and a large number of investors own and trade shares of IBM (as of 31 July 1990, over 574 million IBM shares were outstanding, owned by over 793,000 shareholders). Therefore, one might expect the price of IBM shares to be determined by market forces. So it is, but more is involved, because the NYSE is not a frictionless market.

Transaction Costs

Trading is impeded by taxes and commissions; order handling and clearance costs; trading halts, blockages, and other trading restrictions; and the

123

adverse price impact a trader's order might have in a relatively thin market. Transaction costs are classified as either *explicit costs* or as *execution costs* (which are by their nature, implicit). The explicit costs are visible and easily measured; they include, for example, commissions and taxes. Execution costs, on the other hand, are not easily measured; they exist because orders may, as a result of their size and/or the sparsity of counterpart orders on the market, execute at relatively high prices (if they are buy orders) or at relatively low prices (if they are sell orders).

Trading costs reduce returns for investors. They also cause investors to adjust their portfolios less frequently and, accordingly, to hold portfolios that would not be optimal in a frictionless environment. Pent-up demand increases the eagerness with which investors seek to transact when they eventually do come to the market. The more eager the trader, the more likely he or she is to place a market order (demand immediacy) rather than a limit order (supply liquidity).

Moreover, when trading is costly, traders do not generally reveal the number of shares they would buy or sell at the market clearing price. This is because, when they establish their orders (typically one quantity, at a single price), traders are uncertain as to the prices at which orders might execute. Consequently, as is not the case in the standard competitive model, investors use trading strategies. Understand the existence, nature, and impact of the strategic trading decisions sheds much light on the behavior of the secondary markets and on the operations of its participants.

Execution Costs

Active Versus Passive Trading

To understand execution costs, it is helpful to distinguish between active and passive trading. In an exchange market with continuous trading, an execution is realized when two counterpart orders cross. This happens if one or more of the following cases occur:

1. One public trader posts a limit order, and another public trader submits a market order that executes against the limit order.

2. An exchange specialist or over-the-counter market maker sets the quote, and a public market order executes against the specialist's or dealer's quote.

3. Two or more public traders negotiate a trade. The negotiation may take place on the floor of the exchange, in the upstairs market, or in the fourth market.

In each case, one party to the trade may be viewed as an active trader, and the other party as a passive trader. The one who is seeking to trade without delay is an active trader. Active traders are the public market order traders (cases 1 and 2 above) and the trader who initiates the negotiation process (case 3). Passive traders include the limit order trader (case 1), the specialist or dealer (case 2), and the trader who does not initiate the negotiation process (case 3). Active traders generally incur execution costs; these payments are a positive return for passive traders.

The Bid-Ask Spread

Because matched or crossed orders trigger transactions that eliminate the orders from the market, bid-ask spreads must be positive and, with discrete prices, must be at least as large as the smallest allowable price variation ($\frac{1}{8}$ point for most issues on the NYSE). The spread is the execution cost of a round-trip. Consequently, half of the spread is the execution cost of either a purchase or a sale.

Market Impact

Market impact refers to the additional cost (over and above the spread) that a trader may incur to have a large order execute quickly. It is the higher price that must be paid for a large purchase or the reduction in price that must be accepted for a large sale. Market impact is a "sweetener" paid to induce the market to absorb the large order. Because of it, the effective spread is wider on average for a large order than for a small order.

The Measurement of Execution Costs

Attempts have been made to measure and assess execution costs. Hasbrouck and Schwartz[1] report average execution costs that range from 2.5 cents a share (0.12% of value) for Amex and NYSE issues to 9.0 cents a share (0.44% of value) for NASDAQ/NMS issues. Berkowitz, Logue and Noser[2] report an average execution cost of 2.0 cents a share (0.05% of value) for block trades of several thousand shares in NYSE stocks. Wilshire Associates[3] report an average execution cost of 7.5 cents a share (0.23% of value) for their own trades. Beebower, Kamath and Surz[4] of SEI Corp. report that capital commitment brokers reduce execution costs relative to other brokers (full-service and discount) and that the reduction is not offset by the higher commission rates that they charge.

These results, though based on different methodologies and assumptions, are quite consistent. Nevertheless, the estimates are broad averages and should be accepted with caution. Particularly difficult has been measuring the execution costs of large trades and determining how these costs depend on the size of a trade, the difficulty of a trade, and the market center in which the trade is made. Another problem in measuring execution costs is distinguishing between active and passive trades so as to obtain a measure of execution costs for the active traders. Since trading is a zero sum game for all participants, execution costs are underestimated if active and passive orders are not properly identified.

Execution Costs and Market Thinness

Large numbers of individuals invest in companies whose shares are traded in the major market centers, but the markets for these companies' shares are thin (even for the largest companies). This is because, during any trading session, only a small number of individuals actually seeks to trade. The problem can be particularly striking within the trading day: at any specific moment in time, only a handful of individuals (if any) may be actively looking to buy or to sell shares.

Markets are thin because investors seek to trade only when they are sufficiently dissatisfied with their portfolio holdings to incur the costs of a transaction. This is in contrast with the markets for most goods and services, where an individual must periodically make purchases in order to consume a resource (someone who drinks ten cans of beer a week must on average buy ten cans of beer a week).

Thinness is not directly measurable, but may be proxied by inverse measures, such as the number or value of shares outstanding, the number or value of shares traded during any time interval (for example, trading day), or the number of shareholders. Bid-ask spreads are wider and prices are more volatile for thinner issues. Smaller issues generally trade less frequently, which means that trading and price adjustment delays are lengthier. Additionally, price adjustments to changing market conditions are typically less accurate for thinner issues.

The importance of thinness as a determinant of the trading characteristics of individual securities has been documented empirically, and professional traders are well aware that one of the most important influences on a stock's price behavior is its size. This would not be the case in the absence of transactions costs; in a frictionless environment, thinness would not matter.

Liquidity

Three characteristics of assets and portfolios are relevant to a portfolio manager: return, risk, and liquidity. Return is easily defined and measured, and risk, although more difficult to measure, is also an operational concept. But how might one define and measure liquidity? How is the liquidity of individual assets related to the liquidity of a portfolio? To what extent is liquidity affected by the characteristics of an asset, and to what extent by the marketplace where the asset is traded? Difficulties in defining and measuring liquidity largely explain why this attribute of financial assets and markets has not been incorporated in formal stock evaluation and selection models.

Definition of Liquidity

Liquidity refers to the ability of individuals to trade quickly at prices that are reasonable in light of underlying demand/supply conditions. One approach to measuring liquidity involves assessing the depth, breadth, and resiliency of the market for an asset:

Depth: A market is deep if orders exist at an array of prices in the close neighborhood above and below the price at which shares are currently trading. Bid-ask spreads are tighter when a market has depth.

Breadth: A market is broad if the best buy and sell orders exist in substantial volume (that is, if the orders are sufficiently large). Market impact is slight when a market has breadth.

Resiliency: A market is resilient if temporary price changes due to temporary order imbalances quickly attract new orders to the market that restore reasonable share values. Trades are less apt to be made at inappropriate prices when a market is resilient.

The liquidity of a market may also be proxied by the frequency with which an asset trades and by the magnitude of an asset's short period price instability.

This set of attributes, viewed comprehensively, can lead to conflicting assessments (for example, a market may be deep but lack breadth). Thus we do not have an unambiguous, operational definition of liquidity. Nevertheless, measures such as an asset's average bid-ask spread or short-period price volatility may be used as proxies in statistical analyses.

The cost of illiquidity is that, because a price concession must be paid to execute orders quickly, buyers incur higher prices, and sellers receive lower prices when they initiate trades. No concession would be necessary in a frictionless environment in which all markets and assets are equally and perfectly liquid. In other words, execution costs are attributable to illiquidity.

Misconceptions Concerning Liquidity

The Liquidity Ratio. A common measure of liquidity relates the number or value of shares traded during a short time interval to the absolute value of the percentage price change over the interval. The larger the ratio of shares traded to the percentage price change, the more liquid the market is presumed to be. This view underlies various measures of specialist performance that have been used by the stock exchanges, and characterizes the approach taken by some researchers to measure and to contrast the liquidity of different market centers.[5,6]

The liquidity ratio may not be meaningful because the advent of news also causes prices to change. If the separable impact of news is not taken into account, a large trading volume associated with small price changes need not be evidence of a liquid market. On the contrary, it could suggest that prices have adjusted inefficiently to informational change. This is because a bid that is too high attracts market orders to sell, and an ask that is too low attracts market orders to buy. Thus the slower the adjustment of the quotes after news, the larger is the number of shares that will trade during the price adjustment process. Consequently, to the extent that trading is triggered by informational change rather than by changing investor liquidity needs, the liquidity ratio is smaller (not larger) in a more efficient market.

Market Power.   Another common misconception about liquidity concerns the market power of large traders. *Market power* is generally attributed to a seller who faces a downward sloping long-run demand curve or to a buyer who faces an upward sloping long-run supply curve. Institutional and other investors who are large enough to have a long-run effect on the price of a security may consider the market for that security to be illiquid for them. This is a misuse of the term: a market is illiquid only if, because of trading costs, orders execute at disequilibrium prices in the *short run*. If a 20% shareholder (or a subset of shareholders who in aggregate hold 20% of shares outstanding) decides to sell, the equilibrium price of a stock may change, regardless of the efficiency of the marketplace. Such a price change is not a manifestation of illiquidity.

Price Uncertainty.   A further misconception about illiquidity concerns uncertainty. Traders may consider the market for a security to be illiquid if they do not know the price at which shares of the asset may be transformed into cash at some future date. This view confuses illiquidity with uncertainty. Price uncertainty may be an attribute of a frictionless market; illiquidity is a property only of a nonfrictionless market. The concept of *illiquidity* is distinct from the concept of risk, and an investor's distaste for illiquidity is distinguishable from an investor's distaste for risk.

Price Discovery

A Price Discovery Error*

That prices set in reasonably competitive markets may not reflect desired values can be illustrated by solving for an equilibrium and demonstrating that the realized price can in fact deviate from it. Consider a market for

* The discussion in this subsection draws on material from Schwartz (1990), used with permission.

TABLE 7.1 *Traders Grouped by Initial Shareholdings*

	Trader Designation					
	BH	BM	BL	SL	SM	SH
Initial Share Holdings (thousands):	100	650	675	725	750	1300
Buy (Sell) Order at $50.25 (thousands):	+600	+50	+25	−25	−50	−600
Number of Traders in Group:	7	6	0	48	6	5

a financial asset that is comprised of 72 investors (a large enough number for it to be competitive). Abstracting from the usual complexities, assume that all of the investors, without their knowing it, happen to have identical investment intentions and identical expectations about the asset's current transaction price. Thus, trading is motivated only by differences in initial shareholdings. Assume orders are batched for execution at the same time and at the same price. Not knowing one another's investment plans, the traders do not know the price of shares until it is set in the market.

Group the 72 investors according to their initial shareholders and the number of shares they want to buy or to sell at $50.25, as shown in Table 7.1, where B and S identify the buyers and sellers respectively, and H, M, and L identify relatively high, medium, and low desires to trade at $50.25.

If all traders were to submit an order at $50.25, the market would clear exactly. This is because the total number of shares sought for purchase and offered for sale at $50.25 are, respectively,

$$B = 7 \times 600 + 6 \times 50 = 4500$$

$$S = 5 \times 600 + 6 \times 50 + 48 \times 25 = 4500$$

Furthermore, $50.25 is the only price which, if it were announced in advance, would equilibrate the market.

But, when the transaction price is uncertain, no investor will write an order at $50.25. Rather, the optimal orders with transaction price uncertainty can be shown to be the following:[7]

Trader Designation	BH	BM	BL	SL	SM	SH
Price	51.00	50.12	50.00	50.50	50.37	49.50
Buy or sell (thousands)	+600	+200	+250	−250	−200	−600

TABLE 7.2   *Market Clearing*

Price	Cumulated Buys (thousands)	Cumulated Sells (thousands)	Imbalance (thousands)
$50.500	4200	16200	−12000
→$50.375[a]	4200	4200	0
*$50.250[b]	4200	3000	+1200
$50.125	5400	3000	+2400
$50.000	5400	3000	+2400

[a] The arrow denotes the clearing price.
[b] The star denotes the desired equilibrium price.

The clearing price is found by cumulating these orders and taking the value at which the buy/sell imbalance is zero, as shown in Table 7.2. For the given distribution of investors, the clearing price is shown to be $50.375, $\frac{1}{8}$ of a point greater than the equilibrium value of $50.25. Even though perfectly competitive and comprised of rational agents, the market has found the "wrong" price.

Price Discovery Errors Are an Execution Cost

The price discovery error just illustrated can be considered an execution cost. The market clearing price was pushed above its equilibrium value because "eager" buyers raised their prices to assure receiving a transaction, and "patient" sellers raised their prices because of the possibility (but not the expectation) of the clearing price being higher. Thus, the price discrepancy can be viewed as a market impact effect caused by traders collectively (market impact in the standard interpretation is caused by one trader).

Misconceptions Concerning Price Discovery

Only in recent years has awareness of the price discovery function of a securities market emerged, and efficient price discovery still remains an essentially unarticulated objective. This is due to several reasons. Some observers of the market believe that orders simply reflect what traders individually believe shares of an asset are worth. If this were correct, it would imply that the equilibrium market price would be between the highest bid and the lowest ask in a continuous market or where the market buy and sell order functions cross in a call market. However, the orders investors submit to the market are written in relation to their demand curves, their expectations concerning the clearing price, and their knowledge of how orders are handled in the market. When these factors are taken into account, it is apparent that market clearing prices will deviate from desired equilibrium values, as shown in Table 7.2.

Price discovery may not have been explored as an issue because of the literature that has confirmed the Efficient Market Hypothesis (see Chapter 16 for a discussion of the EMH). Inaccurate price discovery does not necessarily imply a violation of the EMH, however. EMH refers to *informational efficiency* not to *design efficiency*. Consequently, the EMH is not violated if errors in price discovery cause price changes that are correlated over time, but the patterns are too diffuse to be profitably exploited.

The Securities and Exchange Commission (SEC) has not taken much account of price discovery in the equity markets, although the Commodities Futures Trading Commission (CFTC) has recognized price discovery as an important function of the futures markets. A reason for the difference in regulatory focus is that, for the equity markets, it has not been clear how to assess observed prices because base prices (against which a contrast can be made) do not exist. Nevertheless, price swings recently observed in the market suggest the importance of taking price discovery into account as a regulatory objective, particularly with regard to market design.

Price Instability

The aspect of price instability that relates to market structure is the excessive short-period volatility attributable to execution costs and illiquidity, and to errors in price discovery. The exaggerated price changes are a very short run phenomenon; consequently, returns must be analyzed over very brief intervals to observe them. Execution costs directly contribute to price volatility as transaction prices bounce between the higher values paid by eager buyers, and the lower values received by eager sellers. Inaccurate price discovery can be destabilizing because, if investors do not have confidence that a price level is reasonable, their sell orders may cause prices to drop precipitously, or their buy orders may cause prices to rise sharply. These adjustments may explain the bouts of extreme instability that have occurred in recent years.

If prices are more volatile because of execution costs, insufficient liquidity, and the complexity of price discovery, then volatility can be reduced by improving the systems used for handling orders and translating them into trades. Two possibilities for bringing additional liquidity to the market and strengthening the accuracy of price discovery are the institution of an electronic call market (see Chapter 10) and the establishment of a stabilization fund (see Chapter 11).

Market Structure Matters

Transaction costs not only lower returns but, because they affect order placement (limit orders may be discouraged, for instance), can increase price volatility. Thus, lowering transaction costs is of paramount importance.

Transaction Costs and Returns

We can conservatively assess the impact of trading costs on returns for the active trader by assuming a commission rate of 5 cents a share and a minimum bid-ask spread of ⅛ of a point. Assume a portfolio manager is considering investing in an asset that is currently trading at $50, that the manager has forecasted a price of $55 one year hence, and that the stock does not pay a dividend. With costless trading, the expected return for the one year holding period is $5/50 = 10\%$.

Introducing the 5 cent commission and the ⅛ point spread, the current quotes are 50 bid and 50 ⅛ ask, and the expected quotes one year hence are 55 bid and 55 ⅛ ask. Shares currently cost $50.175 (50 + .125 + .05) and the expected net price one year hence is $54.95 (55 − .05). This gives an expected return of 9.517%. The (minimal) transaction costs have reduced the expected return for an investor by roughly 5%.

The average NYSE issue trades at the $30 level. For a $30 dollar stock, the 5 cent commission and 12.5 cent spread together turn a 10% expected return (3/30) into a 9.196% return (2.775/30.175). Thus a cost that is .583% of the asset's price (.175/30), lowers the expected return on the asset by 8.04%. The example is conservative: commissions exceed 5 cents a share for many investors (they range above 50 cents per share for retail orders), spreads are commonly larger than ⅛ of a point, and market impact is an additional cost for a large investor. Inaccurate price discovery may introduce even larger transaction costs for the active traders.

The Trade-Off Between Explicit and Implicit Costs

Transaction costs can be reduced for all traders by improving the operational efficiency of the market centers through appropriate architectural design. However, focusing excessively on some components of cost can lead to undesirable results. For instance, commissions are currently being driven way down for institutional trades, and market makers, becoming increasingly dependent on trading profits, may widen spreads and not provide the capital that dampens market impact. But large investors do not necessarily respond optimally to the trade-off because commission costs are explicit, while execution costs are hidden.

The desirability of restoring commission income should be assessed. It is far better for an institutional trader to pay ten cents or more in commissions and to trade at appropriate prices, than to save pennies on commissions and pay dollars because trades are made at "bad" prices.

Suggested Reading

Amihud, Y., and Mendelson, H. "Liquidity and Asset Prices: Financial Management Implications." *Financial Management,* 1988.

Beebower, G., Kamath, V., and Surz, R. "Commission and Transaction Costs of Stock Market Trading." Working paper, SEI Corporation, July 1985.

Berkowitz, S., Logue, D., and Noser, E., Jr. "The Total Cost of Transactions on the NYSE." *Journal of Finance,* March 1988.

Bernstein, P. "Liquidity, Stock Markets, and Market Makers." *Financial Management,* Summer 1987.

Campbell, J., and Kyle, A. "Smart Money, Noise, Trading, and Stock Price Behavior." Working paper, Princeton University, 1986.

Cohen, K., Hawawini, G., Maier, S., Schwartz, R., and Whitcomb, D. "Friction in the Trading Process and the Estimation of Systematic Risk." *Journal of Financial Economics,* August 1983b.

Cohen, K., Maier, S., Schwartz, R., and Whitcomb, D. *The Microstructure of Securities Markets.* Englewood Cliffs, NJ: Prentice Hall, 1986.

Cooper, K., Groth, J., and Avera, W. "Liquidity, Exchange Listing, and Common Stock Performance." *Journal of Economics and Business,* February 1985.

Dann, L., Mayers, D., and Raab, R. "Trading Rules, Large Blocks and the Speed of Price Adjustment." *Journal of Financial Economics,* January 1977.

Dimson, E. "Risk Management When Shares Are Subject to Infrequent Trading." *Journal of Financial Economics,* June 1979.

Economides, N. and Siow, A. "The Division of Markets Is Limited by the Extent of Liquidity." *American Economic Review,* March 1988.

Gammill, J., and Perold, A. "The Changing Character of Stock Market Liquidity." *Journal of Portfolio Management,* Spring 1989.

Gilster, J. "Intertemporal Cross-Covariances Among Securities Which Trade Daily." Working paper, Michigan State University, 1987.

Grossman, S., and Miller, M. "Liquidity and Market Structure." *Journal of Finance,* July 1988.

Harris, L. *Liquidity, Trading Rules, and Electronic Trading Systems.* New York University Salomon Center Monograph Series in Finance and Economics, No. 1990-4, Leonard N. Stern School of Business, New York University, 1990.

Harris, L., Sofianos, G., and Shapiro, J. "Program Trading and Intraday Volatility." New York Stock Exchange working paper, February 1990.

Hasbrouck, J., and Ho, T. "Order Arrival, Quote Behavior, and the Return Generating Process." *Journal of Finance,* September 1987.

Hasbrouck, J., and Schwartz, R. "Liquidity and Execution Costs in Equity Markets." *Journal of Portfolio Management,* Spring 1988.

Hawawini, G. *European Equity Markets: Price Behavior and Efficiency,* Monograph Series in Finance and Economics, Salomon Brothers Center for the Study of Financial Institutions, No. 1984-4/5, New York University Graduate School of Business Administration, 1984.

Hui, B., and Heubel, B. "Comparative Liquidity Advantages Among Major U.S. Stock Markets." DRI Financial Information Group Study Series no. 84081, 1984.

Kraus, A., and Stoll, H. "Price Impacts of Block Trading on the New York Stock Exchange." *Journal of Finance,* June 1972.

Lippman, S., and McCall, J. "An Operational Measure of Liquidity." *American Economic Review,* March 1986.

Marsh, T., and Rock, K. "Exchange Listing and Liquidity: A Comparison of the American Stock Exchange with the NASDAQ National Market System." American Stock Exchange Transactions Data Research Project Report Number 2, January 1986.

McInish T., and Wood, R. "Adjusting for Beta Bias: An Assessment of Alternate Techniques: A Note." *Journal of Finance,* March 1986.

Pagano, M. "Trading Volume and Asset Liquidity." *Quarterly Journal of Economics,* 1989.

Roll, R. "A Simple Implicit Measure of the Effective Bid-Ask Spread in an Efficient Market." *Journal of Finance,* September 1984.

Schwartz, R. "Price Discovery, Instability, and Market Structure." Appendix G of Report of *The Panel on Market Volatility and Investor Confidence.* New York: New York Stock Exchange, Inc., 1990.

Schwartz, R., and Whitcomb, D. *Trading Strategies for Institutional Investors.* Monograph Series in Finance and Economics, Salomon Brothers Center for the Study of Financial Institutions, No. 1988-2/3, New York University Graduate School of Business Administration, 1988.

Schwert, G. W. "Stock Market Volatility." In Appendix C of Report of the New York Stock Exchange's *Panel on Market Volatility and Investor Confidence.* New York: New York Stock Exchange, Inc., 1990.

Stoll, H., and Whaley, R. "Stock Market Structure and Volatility." *Review of Financial Studies,* Spring 1990.

Subrahmanyam, A. "A New Rational for Markets in Baskets of Stocks." UCLA working paper, April 1989.

Wagner, W. *The Complete Guide to Securities Transactions.* New York: Wiley, 1989.

Wilshire Associates, "Transitional Management," Research Report, 1986.

Wood, R., McInish, T., and Ord, J. "An Investigation of Transaction Data for NYSE Stocks." *Journal of Finance,* July 1985.

Notes

1. J. Hasbrouck and T. Ho, "Order Arrival, Quote Behavior, and the Return Generating Process." *Journal of Finance,* September, 1987.
2. S. Berkowitz, D. Logue, and E. Noser, Jr. "The Total Cost of Transactions on the NYSE." *Journal of Finance,* March 1988.

3. Wilshire Associates, "Transitional Management," Research Report, 1986.

4. G. Beebower, V. Kamath, and R. Surz, "Commission and Transaction Costs of Stock Market Trading," Working paper, SEI Corporation, July 1985.

5. K. Cooper, J. Groth, and W. Avera, "Liquidity, Exchange Listing, and Common Stock Performance," *Journal of Economics and Business,* February 1985.

6. B. Hui and B. Heubel, "Comparative Liquidity Advantages Among Major U.S. Stock Markets," DRI Financial Information Group Study Series no. 84081, 1984.

7. The analytics are from C. Bronfman and R. Schwartz, "Order Placement and Price Discovery in a Securities Market." Paper delivered at the meetings of the American Finance Association, Washington, DC, December 1990. They assume each investor has a downward sloping demand curve to hold shares and use a specific probability distribution for the current clearing price to solve for the best order for each investor.

8

The Role of Market Makers

Market makers play a key role in the U.S. equity markets. The dealers are center stage in the OTC markets, as are the specialists in the exchange markets.

Dealers are common in many markets, but the operations of securities dealers are unique. This is because of the function they perform regarding price determination and because of the nature of the costs they incur. A major input into the provision of marketability services is the willingness of the dealer firm to commit capital to service a public sell order when the firm has a long position or to service a public buy order when the firm is short the stock. Willingness of a dealer to make a market is expressed by the magnitude of the inventory fluctuations it will accept.

Services Provided

All market makers provide immediacy in the sense that they enable buyers and sellers to meet each other in time and in space. The quotes that dealers post on the market further help to stabilize prices and to keep prices in tune with the market's underlying demand propensities. Furthermore, OTC dealers and exchange specialists enforce various trading rules that bring order and fairness to a market.

The Supply of Immediacy

The dealer is most easily understood as a supplier of immediacy. *Immediacy* denotes the ability of buyers and sellers to transact promptly.

As discussed in Chapters 2 through 4, an important structural difference between trading systems for the equity markets is whether middlemen act as brokers/agents or as dealers/principals. The OTC market makers are dealers; the exchange market makers (specialists) are both dealers and brokers. The exchange specialists can be brokers because of a design feature of the exchange market: the public limit order book, where buy and sell orders are stored. Public traders on the NYSE have a choice: they can transact with the specialist, against the book at a stated price, or they can leave their own limit orders with the specialist.

To analyze a dealer's supply of immediacy, assume that there are a large number of traders in the market for a security, assume that there is a monopoly dealer, and assume that buyers and sellers meet each other by trading through this dealer. Consider what happens when the dealer knows the buy/sell propensities of the traders, sets prices accordingly, and intermediates in the trades. The curves labeled B and S in Figure 8.1 show, respectively, the traders' aggregate buy and sell propensities. At P* the number of shares traders in aggregate would wish to buy equals the number they wish to sell. In a frictionless market, Q* shares would trade at the price P*.

It is not a simple matter, however, for buyers and sellers to find each other in time. The dealer provides a solution by continuously standing ready to buy and to sell. But the service is not free; the dealer sells to buyers at higher ask prices and buys from sellers at lower bid prices. The spread is the dealer's compensation. The curves labeled S' and B' in Figure 8.1 reflect this reality. S' is the supply curve of immediately available shares; B' is the demand curve for shares that can be immediately bought. Hence S' and B' reflect the dealer's sale of immediacy.

FIGURE 8.1   *Market Buy and Sell Curves With and Without the Provision of Immediacy*

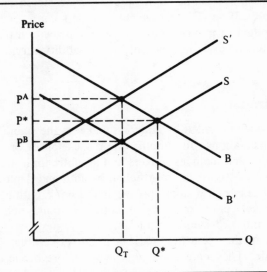

At each quantity, the vertical distance between S and S' and between B and B' shows the charge imposed by the dealer. For simplicity, let this distance be the same at all Q and for both sets of curves. Equilibrium is given by the intersection of S' and B and, equivalently, by the intersection of S and B'. The intersection of S' and B establishes the market ask (P^A), and the intersection of B' and S establishes the market bid (P^B). The transaction volume at both the bid and the ask is Q_T.

Because buyers and sellers arrive sporadically at the market, they generally do not find each other "in time." We assume that traders cannot leave orders on the market because no mechanism exists for handling the orders. Therefore, despite the fact that the market should clear at P* with Q* shares transacting, the market, by itself, cannot operate. The market forms because the dealer posts an ask of P^A and, at this price, sells Q_T shares to the market (given the buy curve labeled "B," Q_T is the number of shares the market wishes to purchase at P^A). The dealer also posts a bid of P^B, and at this price buys Q_T shares from the market (given the sell curve labeled "S," this is the number of shares the market wishes to sell at P^B). Accordingly, Q_T shares pass via the dealer, from public sellers to public buyers. The dealer has accommodated the public's demand for immediacy by selling from inventory and buying for inventory. As discussed, the dealer is compensated for providing this service by buying at a relatively low price (the bid), and by selling at a relatively high price (the ask). Note that, because transacting in the market is not costless, the actual number of transactions, Q_T, is less than the frictionless market number, Q*.

The existence of a dealer is not necessary for immediacy to be provided to a market: (1) middlemen may be brokers and they can be compensated by a commission, (2) public limit orders can be stored on a public limit order book, and (3) newly arriving public orders can execute immediately by transacting against public orders previously placed on the book. On the other hand, immediacy is not the only marketability service provided by a dealer.

Price Stabilization

The second service provided by a market maker is the stabilization of short-period price fluctuations. To simplify the discussion of price stabilization, assume a system that includes brokers and a public limit order book. If the book is "thick," that is, there is sufficient breadth and depth, market orders can execute at reasonably stable prices; if the book is thin, market orders may have a sizable price impact. Consequently, transaction prices are less volatile if the limit order book is thicker.

Participants in the securities markets prefer prices that, all else equal, are less volatile. They care about this as investors because investors are generally assumed to be risk averse. They care about this as traders because they are averse to transaction price uncertainty. Therefore, it is desirable to have thicker limit order books and the greater price stability that such books imply.

Public limit order traders are not separately compensated for the stability their orders provide. In this regard, price stability is an "externality" that attends the placement of limit orders.[1] Like any other externality, it is not separately charged for in the free market, and therefore is not supplied in optimal amounts by market participants.

Because stabilization is undersupplied in a market composed of public traders alone, inclusion of a professional market maker can improve the market. The improved quality of the market will in turn increase trader participation in the market (this is because traders tend to avoid operationally inefficient, volatile markets). The increased order flow will increase the dealer's returns because, for a given size of the spread and commissions, gross revenues are larger the greater the transaction rate.

When a stock's price is low, market makers buy; when the price is high, they sell. In so doing, they narrow the bid-ask spread and attract investors to the market. The more market makers transact by buying low and selling high with the idiosyncratic arrival of orders, the more profitable their operations are. Accordingly, of their own free will, dealers will supply a certain amount of stability to the market.

Professional market makers, however, may not supply the socially optimal amount of stability. *Competitive market makers* will supply less than the socially optimal amount because the increased order flow that results from any one market makers' stabilization activities is shared by them all. Thus externalities are involved, market makers can free-ride on each other's efforts, and individual dealers only take their private benefits into account. A *monopoly market maker* internalizes the benefits that are external to the competitive dealers but, like any monopolist, realizes greater profits by restricting supply and raising price.

In an attempt to achieve the socially optimal provision of stabilization services, NYSE regulations include the specialist's "affirmative obligation" to maintain a "fair and orderly market," which requires specialists to stabilize prices more than they would on their own. The specialist provides additional stability by entering quotes and transacting when transaction-to-transaction price changes would otherwise be unacceptably large. (Transaction-to-transaction price changes could be unacceptably large if the book is sparse, if the equilibrium spread is not sufficiently tight, and if the advent of large orders exerts undue pressure on the market.) When the market is moving down, the affirmative obligation forces the market maker to buy; when the market is moving up, the specialist must sell. These transactions that serve to counter market trends may not be profitable. Rather than buying low and selling high, the specialist might buy low and subsequently sell lower, or sell high and subsequently buy higher.

Specialists, however, have a privileged position vis-à-vis the market. Each stock is assigned to just one specialist unit on the floor of an exchange, and the flow of orders to the exchange, for that stock, is all directed to the particular specialist's post. No other single trader has an equivalent view of, or power over, the order flow. Successful specialists realize profits from this privileged position. This is how the system compensates the specialist for taking positions that serve more nearly to achieve a socially optimal amount of stabilization.

No market maker can have an appreciable impact on price movements over long periods of time. If, for instance, a stock goes from $32 to $132 in a year, it will do so regardless of the specialist's intervention, which is as it should be. Price changes of this magnitude reflect informational change, and there is no reason to perturb the market's assessment of the change. Specialists do not even try; rather, their intervention is intended only to make the movements of price from one level to another more orderly.

Specialists can reduce price volatility without affecting the eventual adjustment of prices to new equilibrium levels because short-period price movements typically show excessive volatility relative to the volatility of longer period movements. (Refer to Chapter 16 for further discussion on the relationship between long-period and short-period price volatility and empirical evidence thereon.) Thus, satisfaction of the specialist's affirmative obligation need not interfere with longer run adjustments.

Price Discovery

Another function of the market maker is to facilitate the market process of finding reasonably accurate prices. Market makers do not have a perfect view of the market—they have a *better* view than most traders because of their privileged position vis-à-vis the order flow. As discussed, specialists alone know the orders on the books, have a sense of the orders being held in the crowd by their trading posts and are in frequent communication with the upstairs traders. This feel for the market enables them to improve the quality of prices established on the market.

Market makers affect the quality of price formation in three ways. First, their own quotes directly set market prices. Second, the quotes specialists/dealers post on the market are signals that public traders react to in writing their own orders; therefore, market makers indirectly affect market prices by influencing the public order flow. Third, exchange specialists search for market clearing prices at the start of the trading day and during trading halts caused by the advent of news.

Accurate price discovery may help to stabilize short-period price movements. Furthermore, price stabilization and price discovery are both consistent with the provision of immediacy. This is because "immediacy" refers not only to the ability to trade promptly, but also to the ability to trade at prices that are reasonable in light of current market conditions. Smidt's[2] analysis of the market maker emphasizes the supply of liquidity *in depth*, namely the ability of investors to trade quickly and in size, at the market maker's quotes. Consequently immediacy, reasonable price stability, and accurate price discovery are all attributes of prices that are "fair and orderly."

The Market Maker as Auctioneer

As an auctioneer, the market maker organizes and oversees trading, and participates in trades to facilitate the market process. Exchange specialists organize trading by maintaining the limit order books and by assuring that trading priority rules (price, time, and size) are honored. Exchange officials in call market trading, tabulate the buy and sell orders, and announce clearing prices. These functions are primarily clerical, and their burden is increasingly being reduced by automated order handling procedures. Exchange specialists also oversee trading to ensure that various exchange rules are not violated. In particular, destabilizing trades are not allowed; for instance, short sales (with exceptions) may only be executed on plus ticks or on zero plus ticks. In this capacity, the specialist is supported by the surveillance and stock watch systems of the exchanges. On some exchanges (such as the Tokyo Stock Exchange), market makers act only in the clerical bookkeeping and regulatory oversight capacities and are not allowed to trade the stocks assigned to them.

The Costs of Market Making

Labor Costs

Skilled Labor. In the U.S. continuous trading systems:

- Each order that arrives at the market and each trade that is made conveys information to the market maker.
- If the market maker participates in the trade, his or her inventories of cash and of stock are affected.

Consequently, dealers/specialists frequently adjust their quotes while they trade. For the dealer houses, this means that trained personnel must continuously monitor CRT screens and telephones for the stocks for which they are responsible. Likewise, the exchange specialists must stand by their posts and respond to orders as they arrive.

Trading is complex, and mistakes may be extremely costly. A year of training is generally required before a new trader is allowed to handle anything but a "no brainer" (the term used for an order that does not require special handling). The emotional, intellectual, and even physical requirements of trading are demanding. Consequently, the supply of skilled traders is limited, and labor costs are high.

Unskilled Labor.   Market making also entails a considerable amount of paper handling and record keeping. This is done in part by clerks who assist the specialists, dealers, and floor traders, and in part by the market makers themselves. Many of the more clerical aspects of market making are now computerized, as physical capital has been substituted for relatively unskilled labor throughout the industry.

Capital Costs

Physical Capital.   Along with the standard need for buildings and equipment, computer technology has substantially increased the investment in physical capital needed for market making.

Electronic equipment is being used for information display, record keeping, and, increasingly, for decision making and trade execution. Electronic display systems, communication systems, and touch screen technology are turning market maker posts into fully automated workstations.

The new technology has increased the number of trading decisions each trader can make, and, in so doing, has created a greater demand for highly sophisticated traders. Consequently, taking both the quality and the quantity of the labor input into account, trading has remained labor intensive, despite the increase of physical capital.

Financial Capital.   The second capital cost of market making is the financial capital required for the dealership function. Electronic equipment itself has not reduced the financial commitment needed to provide a market in depth, although better intermarket linkages have made it easier for some market makers to rebalance their inventories by interdealer trading. More importantly, the new technology has spurred the growth of markets in futures and options; these instruments are now used by market makers to hedge positions and thereby to reduce the amount of capital at risk. Nevertheless, for both the dealer-oriented OTC markets and the specialist-oriented exchange markets, the requisite financial capital remains a major cost of market making in the U.S. continuous trading environment.

The Cost of Bearing Risk

Risk bearing is central to the dealership function. Dealers, unlike brokers, acquire ownership in the shares they trade. The dealer, however, trades to make a market rather than for his or her own investment motives. As a result, he or she will generally acquire an unbalanced portfolio with respect to his or her trading account. Securities dealers maintain separate investment and trading accounts. The desired portfolio weight for the investment account is determined in the same way as for any investor (see Chapter 12). The desired portfolio weight for the trading account is close to zero. However, market makers must allow their trading accounts to vary from zero. If buyers come along, they must be willing to assume a short position; if sellers appear, they must be willing to assume a long position.

A dealer is subject to uncertainty concerning the future price and the future transactions volume in the asset. Not knowing when future transactions will be made, the dealer does not know how long an unbalanced inventory position will have to be maintained.

Ho and Stoll[3] have shown that diversifiable risk is relevant to a dealer. The intuitive explanation is that, in performing the dealership function, the market maker acquires inventory that is not in and of itself desired and as a byproduct accepts risk that could have (but has not) been diversified away. The market maker must therefore be compensated for the cost of bearing this risk.

The Cost of Ignorance

The cost of ignorance is the cost to the dealer of trading with better informed investors. Dealers and specialists may have an advantage over many public traders; they do not, however, have an advantage over *all* traders. Some public traders receive news and transmit orders to the market before the dealer has learned of the informational change. When this happens, the public trader profits at the dealer's expense.[4]

The dealer controls the cost of ignorance by adjusting his or her quotes. To see how, we first assume that all trading is motivated by idiosyncratic liquidity reasons, and that the dealer is never at a disadvantage because of an asymmetric distribution of information. In such a situation, the dealer profits from the random occurrence of liquidity transactions at the bid and the ask.

What happens when traders who are better informed than the dealer enter the market? When an order to buy or to sell arrives, the dealer does not know whether it is from an informed trader or from a liquidity trader. If it is from an informed trader, the transaction will not be profitable from the dealer's point of view. The dealer will therefore take the defensive action of increasing the ask quote and lowering the bid. To see the protection this widening of the spread offers, consider the ask and the possibility that bullish news will trigger the arrival of a buy order. The higher the dealer's ask, the more reasonable the quote may be, after the fact, vis-à-vis an informationally motivated order. Therefore, by selling to the buyer at the higher ask, the dealer will not lose as much because of his or her relative ignorance.

The dealer cannot, however, achieve total protection by sufficiently widening the spread. Regardless of how much the ask is raised and the bid is lowered, any informationally motivated trade, if it occurs, will be at the dealer's expense because an informed public investor will not seek to trade unless he or she profits from the transactions.

Furthermore, the dealer's defensive maneuver is not costless—in the process of increasing the ask and lowering the bid to guard against informational traders, the dealer loses other customers, the liquidity traders. That is, by widening the spread, the dealer transmits some of the cost of ignorance to the liquidity traders, and the liquidity traders transact at lower rates when the cost of transacting is greater. Therefore, the extent to which the spread can be widened is limited.

The dealer, in other words, faces a trade-off. A tighter spread will encourage more liquidity trading (which increases the dealer's revenue), but also results in the dealer being exploited more often by information traders (which increases the dealer's costs). As the spread is widened, the dealer gains more protection against informational traders, but increasingly loses revenue from transacting with liquidity traders. The trade-off is resolved by setting a spread that is optimal (it balances the marginal cost of accommodating more informational traders, with the marginal revenue realized by servicing more liquidity traders). Because the dealer always loses when trading with better informed investors, some investors must trade for non-informational reasons if the dealer is to survive as a supplier of marketability services. Alternatively stated, the dealer faces an adverse selection problem vis-a-vis the informational traders. This is because the only time these traders seek to trade with the dealer is when they have superior information. Accordingly, the dealer cannot operate profitably by dealing with these traders alone. Without liquidity traders, a dealer market would collapse.

Market Maker Spreads

Demsetz[5] estimated the relationship between a stock's spread and its transaction volume and observed that these two variables are negatively correlated for a sample of NYSE stocks. The finding has subsequently been substantiated by many other studies. Transactions volume has generally been taken as the output measure for the quantity of dealer services produced. The value of shares outstanding for an issue, which is highly correlated with transactions volume, has also been used as an alternative measure of the size of a market. Demsetz interpreted his observation as evidence of economies of scale in market making.

The existence of scale economies is important for one reason in particular: if average production costs decrease as a firm becomes ever larger, the largest firm in an industry will have a cost advantage over its competitors that will eventually drive the other firms out of business. Sufficient economies of scale in market making would therefore mean that market making is a natural monopoly. Such a finding would have major implications for the industrial structure of the equity markets.

We find however, that on the OTC, multiple dealers typically make markets in a stock. Where we observe a single dealer on the stock exchanges, it is the affirmative obligation of that dealer to provide a "fair and orderly market" that makes it uneconomical for the exchanges to assign listed issues to more than one specialist unit. As discussed, the stabilization activities of one market maker benefit all. Accordingly, individual market makers have little incentive to supply stability to the market in a competitive environment (rather, each would prefer to free ride on the stabilization provided by others). In addition, the exchange, in its surveillance and regulation of specialists, would find it impossible in a competitive environment to assess and to regulate specialist responsibility for the provision of stabilization services beyond that which they would freely provide. And stock exchange specialists are not, strictly speaking, monopolists—as noted above, they face competition from the limit order book, from floor traders, from upstairs market makers, and for cross-listed stocks, from competing market centers.

Various hypotheses have been advanced concerning the cause of pervasive empirical evidence that spreads are tighter for thicker issues. Two lines of approach are particularly interesting: (1) the *price* received by the market maker for supplying his or her services (the bid-ask spread) is not exactly equal to the cost of providing the service, and (2) dealer spreads are not the same as market spreads.

The Spread-Cost Relationship

Spreads would clearly differ from the cost of supplying dealer services if market making were a natural monopoly, because positive profits are realized when average revenue (price) is greater than average cost. (A monopolist maximizes profits by equating marginal revenue and marginal cost, not average revenue and average cost.) With price not equal to average cost, observing that spreads are less for stocks with larger transactions volume does not necessarily imply that the cost of supplying marketability services is less for these stocks.

Smidt[6] has hypothesized that the negative price/volume relationship is due to competition being greater for larger issues. With regard to exchange-listed securities, Smidt notes that "specialists face more competition in high-volume issues than in low-volume issues, and that they therefore quote more nearly competitive bid-ask spreads in these issues." Smidt,[7] as does Logue,[8] further differentiates spreads from the cost of providing immediacy by suggesting that the cost of immediacy is, more precisely, the difference between actual transaction prices and frictionless (theoretical) market equilibrium prices. This view has subsequently been incorporated in various formal models of the pricing of dealer services (see, for instance, Ho and Stoll).[9]

In long-run competitive equilibrium with zero economic profits, price does equal average cost. Allowing for this, Benston and Hagerman[10] and Hamilton[11] consider another factor that can keep spreads equal to the cost of market making and still generate a negative spread/transactions volume relationship: industry economies of scale that are external to individual dealer/specialist firms. With external economies, average costs for an individual dealer firm can rise with the firm's own transaction volume, but the *height* of the firm's cost curve will be lower when the total transactions volume in the market is greater.

Economies of scale may be realized as trading increases for a security because (1) a superior information flow attends a larger aggregate order flow (even if it is divided across dealer firms), (2) an enhanced opportunity for interdealer trading makes it easier for individual dealers to rebalance their portfolios (and so reduce the cost of risk), and (3) an increased proportion of idiosyncratic orders relative to informationally motivated orders may characterize a larger market.

Dealer Spreads Versus Market Spreads

A number of studies of the spread/trading volume relationship have used market spreads, not individual dealer spreads in empirical tests. These include the studies of Demsetz,[12] Tinic,[13] Tinic and West,[14] Barnea and Logue,[15] and Branch and Freed.[16] In the absence of monopoly dealers, market spreads generally differ from individual dealer spreads. Demsetz[17] pointed out that on the NYSE, "the spread is determined by persons acting individually, by specialists, by floor traders, or by outsiders submitting market or limit orders." Tinic and West[18] were among the first to recognize explicitly that in the Toronto Stock Exchange (TSE), "bid-ask prices are not necessarily those quoted by a dealer: the reported prices in the TSE simply represent the highest bid and the lowest ask prices that are available at any point in time; it is quite possible that at any given moment, neither will have originated from the floor of the Exchange."

Consider the relationship between the market spread and individual spreads in an OTC-type market composed of many dealers who post quotes that, in general, vary from dealer to dealer. The discussion below follows Cohen,

FIGURE 8.2 *Dealer Bid and Ask Quotes*

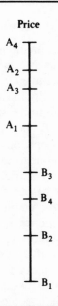

Maier, Schwartz, and Whitcomb.[19] Figure 8.2 shows the bid and ask quotes of four dealers. Dealer 1 has the lowest of the asks (A_1) and dealer 3 has the highest of the bids (B_3). Accordingly, dealers 1 and 3 between them set the market spread ($A_1 - B_3$). Consider the spread that would be set by any other dealer or pairing of dealers (for instance, $A_3 - B_3$, the spread of dealer 3, or $A_1 - B_4$, the spread that would be set by dealers 1 and 4). Among all these alternative spreads, the market spread ($A_1 - B_3$) is the smallest. Therefore, we can identify the market spread more generally as follows. Let

$$S_{ij} = Min(A_i, A_j) - Max(B_i, B_j) \qquad (8.1)$$

be the spread which would be given by a pairing of the ith and j^{th} dealers. The market spread will equal the smallest element in the set of all S_{ij}, namely $Min(S_{ij})$. Let us therefore consider how $Min(S_{ij})$ behaves as the number of dealers (N) in a market increases.

We must have S_{ij} positive for all i,j because crossing-quotes trigger trades (which eliminate the crossing-quotes). However, if we ignore the interaction between dealers in the setting of quotes (that is, suppose that each dealer firm sets its own quotes myopically without reference to the quotes of others), it would seem that there is no lower bound on S_{ij} other than zero. For simplicity, suppose the S_{ij} are distributed uniformly in the interval 0 to Max (S_i).* Then the expected value of the market spread is given by

$$E[\text{Min } S_{ij}] = [\text{Max } S_i]/C^{N,2} \tag{8.2}$$

where $C^{N,2}$ is the number of combinations of N items taken two at a time. $E[\text{Min}S_{ij}]$ clearly goes to zero as N, and hence $C^{N,2}$ increases. We thus see that, other things being equal, market spreads will be tighter in markets where more dealers post quotes on the market. Similar proofs could be constructed for any other probability distribution on S_{ij} that satisfies the condition that the probability of S_{ij} being less than any value, epsilon, is positive for all positive values of epsilon.

This demonstration might lead one to expect that the market spread would vanish if the number of dealers were sufficiently large. The above discussion, however, has not taken account of the interaction between dealers in the setting of quotes. The spread will endure in very large markets because, with nonfrictionless trading and hence sporadic order arrival, no trader or dealer will post a quote infinitesimally close to a counterpart quote already established on the market. Rather, if the price at which a dealer is willing to trade is close enough to a counterpart market quote, the dealer will "jump" his or her price and transact with another dealer at that dealer's quote. Therefore, the lower bound of S_{ij} is some value greater than zero.

The Dynamic Behavior of Dealer Spreads

Dealers in many industries do not adjust their quotes as they trade, but only when they believe market conditions have changed sufficiently. This is not the case with securities dealers, because for them trading and price determination are concomitant processes. Traders in the securities markets are continually searching for a clearing price that continuously changes with news, with shifts in investor expectations, and with change in investor liquidity needs. Consequently, securities dealers generally alter their quotes as they trade in order to reduce their cost of risk bearing and of ignorance.

Consider the relationship between a dealer's quotes (A and B) and the underlying market clearing price (W), as depicted in Figure 8.3. The smaller $A - W$ is relative to $W - B$, the more likely it is that the next transaction will be at the ask. The higher the quotes are relative to W, the more likely it is that the next transaction will be at the bid. A public purchase at the dealer's ask lowers the dealer's inventory, and a public sale at the dealer's bid increases the dealer's inventory. Therefore, the dealer firm can control its inventory and hence its inventory costs by properly adjusting its quotes

---

* S_i is the spread for $i = j$ (i.e., it is the ith dealer's individual spread), and Max (S_i), the largest individual dealer spread, equals Max (S_{ij}).

FIGURE 8.3 *Relationship Between a Dealer's Quotes and the Market Clearing Price*

(A and B) in relation to the underlying clearing price (W). In Ho and Stoll's[20] model (which assumes the maximization of the expected utility of profits as the objective function), dealers primarily adjust the position of A and B relative to W, rather than the size of the spread (A − B) itself. In contrast, in Amihud and Mendelson's[21] model (which assumes the maximization of expected profits), the size of the spread also changes in response to the dealer's inventory fluctuations. Recognizing this control mechanism, we can now see that dealers will generally increase their quotes after a sale and lower their quotes after a purchase.

Assume the firm starts a trading session with a flat (zero) position. Then, following a public purchase at the ask, the dealer will be short the stock. This negative inventory can be worked off by raising both the bid and the ask (the increase in A − W will discourage further public purchases; the decrease in W − B will encourage public sales to the dealer). Alternatively, after starting with a zero inventory position and realizing a public sale at the bid, the dealer will have a long position in the stock; this inventory can be worked off by lowering the bid (which will discourage further public sales) and by lowering the ask (which will encourage public purchases).

A dynamic pricing policy also decreases the cost of ignorance. To see this, let a public order arrive to buy at the dealer's ask. The dealer, as we have noted, does not know if the order has been motivated by idiosyncratic reasons unique to the trader or by news. The arrival of a *second* buy in succession would strengthen the signal. Accordingly, the dealer's optimal sales price (ask) for the second buy order is higher than for the first. Therefore, given the possibility of a second buy order arriving in succession, the dealer increases the ask, and so maintains optimal protection against the better informed traders.[22]

Therefore, in relation to both the cost of risk bearing and of ignorance, the dealer will increase the quotes after a sale and decrease the quotes after a purchase. This dynamic pricing policy has been modeled in the dealer pricing literature.[23] The approach taken is to assume that the arrival of orders and the behavior of an underlying clearing price can be described by statistical processes, and that the dealer makes pricing decisions in relation to the anticipated order flow in a multiperiod context. That is, rather than setting quotes at the start of a single decision period and maintaining them until the end of the period, the dealer makes a sequence of decisions through time. The dealer firm accordingly sets its quotes in the current period in relation to the pricing paths that might subsequently be followed.

The future path that the price will follow depends in part on the current quotes. The current quotes determine the next trade, which affects the next inventory position and the quotes that will be set in the following period. The quotes set in the next period in turn affect future trades, future inventory positions, and hence future quotes. Therefore, the dealer firm's final wealth position depends in part upon where the initial bid and ask quotes are set.

The dealer accordingly sets the current quotes and sees what happens. As trading actually occurs with the passage of time, the dealer firm remakes its decisions, always considering how the situation might look as of the last point in time and then working backward to the current moment.

Spread Adjustments and Inventory Control

The dynamic pricing policy is largely motivated by a desire to maintain reasonable bounds on inventory fluctuations. As a means of illustrating, assume the dealer starts with a desired inventory position of zero, and sets bid and ask quotes so that the rate at which sell orders are expected to arrive equals the rate at which buy orders are expected to arrive. Assume the expected time rates of order arrival remain constant over time if the bid and ask quotations remain constant. As buy orders actually arrive, the dealer firm sells shares and its inventory of shares is depleted; as sell orders arrive, the dealer firm buys shares and its inventory of shares grows. If the bid and ask quotes are maintained (and if the expected order arrival rates remain constant), the dealer's inventory will, by the law of large numbers, fluctuate between ever increasing bounds. The inventory fluctuations will eventually result in a portfolio imbalance either long or short that forces the dealer firm into bankruptcy.

The dealer firm therefore controls its inventory by placing a bound on the long position and on the short position that it will accept. When the maximum long position is reached, the dealer ceases to buy; when the maximum short position is reached, the dealer ceases to sell. Furthermore, as the bounds are approached, the firm adjusts its quotes to reduce the probability

FIGURE 8.4 *Relationship Between a Dealer Firm's Quotes and Its Inventory Position*

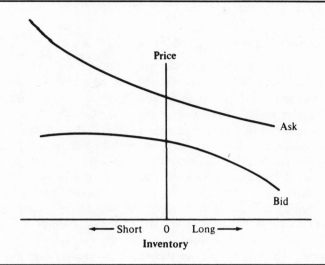

that moves further from the desired inventory position will occur. These associated price adjustments and inventory fluctuations have been modeled by Amihud and Mendelson.[24,25]

Amihud and Mendelson[26] show how the dealer firm controls its inventory by using an inventory-based pricing policy. The policy is illustrated by Figure 8.4, where price is shown on the vertical axis and the dealer's inventory position is shown on the horizontal axis. The negatively inclined curve labeled "Ask" in the figure shows how the dealer's asking price changes with the inventory position; the negatively inclined curve labeled "Bid" shows how the dealer's bid price changes with the inventory position. Note that the ask and the bid decrease as the dealer's inventory increases above the preferred value (which we have assumed to be zero) and that the ask and the bid increase as the inventory falls below the preferred value (that is, when the dealer has a short position). Note also that the spread widens as the inventory moves further (in either direction) from zero.

The tighter the bounds placed on allowable inventory fluctuations, the steeper the ask and bid curves in Figure 8.4, and the larger the spread at each inventory level. Tighter (looser) inventory bounds imply less (more) willingness on the part of the dealer firm to supply marketability services. Therefore, the willingness of the dealer firm to make a market in a stock is reflected by the slope of the two curves, and by the vertical distance between them. Flatter curves and smaller spreads result in less volatile transaction prices. Therefore, a dealer firm that is willing to commit more capital to market making will make a better, more orderly market.

Quoted Spread Versus Realized Spreads

Stoll[27] has noted that the continual changing of quotes following transactions differentiates the *realized spread* from the quoted spread and thus changes the price of dealer services. As discussed above, a dealer's quotes tend to fall after a dealer purchase and to rise after a dealer sale. Therefore, rather than buying at a bid quotation and then selling at the ask, the dealer will sell at some *lower* ask. Similarly, rather than selling at an ask quotation and then buying at the bid, the dealer will buy at some *higher* bid. Adjusting the quotes in this manner reduces the size of what Stoll calls "the realized spread." That is, the dynamic behavior of the quotes implies that dealers will generally buy and sell at prices that are closer to one another than the bid and ask quotations posted on the market at any one point in time.

The dealer's revenue is derived from the realized spread, not from the quoted spread. Therefore, because the realized spread is smaller than the quoted spread, the dealer's defensive actions in response to inventory risk and ignorance are not costless for the dealer. Stoll[28] estimates that the realized spread (expressed as a percentage of the bid price) is roughly 50% of quoted spreads for NYSE stocks. The magnitude of the percentage reduction may be somewhat overstated, however, because floor traders commonly transact within the quotes and because specialists do give transactions "between the quotes" when the arrival of a market order would otherwise cause a transaction-to-transaction price change that is unacceptably large (given the affirmative obligation of the specialist).

The Effect of Interdealer Competition on Spreads*

We now consider the effect of interdealer competition on the size of dealer spreads. Assume a set of competitive dealers who are identical in all respects (wealth, risk aversion, expectations, ability, and so on) except for their inventory positions. Being identical, they would generally set identical spreads; only different inventory positions will cause differences in their quotes.

Further, following Amihud and Mendelson,[31] assume that the dealers each adhere to an inventory policy that sets limits on the long and short positions they will assume. As discussed above, when a dealer firm hits an inventory constraint, it will cease to post an ask (if the maximum short position has

---

* The discussion in this subsection draws upon Ho and Stoll[29] and Ho and Macris.[30]

been reached) or a bid (if the maximum long position has been reached). To see most simply what this implies for the dealer's average revenue, let the inventory constraints be plus and minus one round lot.

At each inventory position, each dealer firm can determine (1) the profit maximizing quotes that would be set if it had a monopoly position, and (2) the quotes that would leave the firm as well off as it would have been had it not traded. This second set of values is "the reservation quotes" of the dealer.

Assume all dealers start with a zero inventory and thus post both bids and asks. Customers shop around to find the dealers with the best quotes. The dealer firms compete with each other by bettering their quotes until no incentive exists to better them further. This interdealer competition forces all dealers to their reservation quotes. The reason is that each dealer would profit by servicing the first transaction at a wider spread and so will compete to get it. Since all dealers are identical (and start with identical inventory positions), the process drives the quotes to the reservation values.

Once trading begins, since all dealers have identical quotes, orders will arrive randomly at the different dealer houses. After each transaction, the dealer that serviced it will either be long one round lot or short one round lot. As trading progresses, a situation will occasionally arise where all dealers but one have a long position, or where all but one have a short position. These occurrences generate an interesting result: all dealers but one will have reached an identical inventory constraint (either long or short), and thus all but one will cease posting a quote on one side of the market. When this occurs, the one remaining dealer has a temporary monopoly position. The dealer firm with the monopoly position will not be driven to post a reservation quote, but instead will post the quote of a monopolist and will realize a monopoly profit if an execution is achieved at the quote.

Interdealer competition will, of course, prevent dealers from enjoying monopoly profits in the long run. However, the dynamic process of competition in a competitive dealer industry affects the average spread realized by the dealers. For simplicity, assume the spreads between the reservation quotes and between the monopoly quotes are constant over time. Then the expected spread (the price of dealer services) is

$$E(P) = pr^A(A^M - B^R) + pr^B(A^R - B^M) + (1 - pr^A - pr^B)(A^R - B^R) \quad (8.3)$$

where A^R and B^R are the reservation ask and bid quotations, A^M and B^M are the monopoly ask and bid quotations, pr^A is the proportion of round trips that are made with the dealer firm being the only firm to post an ask, pr^B is the proportion of round trips that are made with the dealer firm being the only firm to post a bid, and $(1 - pr^A - pr^B)$ is the proportion of round trips that are made under competitive conditions.[32]

The Determinants of Dealer Bid-Ask Spreads

Our analysis highlights four classes of variables as determinants of dealer spreads: (1) an activity variable, (2) a risk variable, (3) an information variable, and (4) a measure of interdealer competition. In analyses of these variables, researchers have generally considered the spread as a percent of the bid price, rather than in absolute value. Percentage spreads are more meaningful because they should, aside from the effect of price discontinuity, be independent of the price level (that is, the percentage spread for a $120 stock should be roughly the same as the percentage spread for a $15 stock.) Price discontinuity, however, will increase the average percentage spread for the $15 dollar stock. This is because with ⅛ pricing, the minimum absolute price change of ⅛ is a more substantial percent of $15 than of $120.

Activity.   All else equal, the greater the trading activity in a stock, the lower the spread a market maker will quote. The reason follows from the existence of economies of scale on the dealer level in market making. An increased order flow reduces the time between transactions and hence the inventory risk of the dealer. That is, with more frequent order arrival, a dealer can more quickly redress any inventory imbalance with any given change in the quotes. The common measure of trading activity is the average number or value of shares traded per period. The empirical evidence is that, all else constant, the percentage spread is less when the normal trading activity in a stock is greater.

Risk.   The normal transaction volume for a stock is related to the length of time a dealer will expect to hold any unwanted inventory position. The variance of returns measures the risk to the dealer of holding the inventory over this period. The relevant measure of risk with regard to market making is unsystematic risk, rather than total risk or the market model beta. The empirical evidence is that, all else constant, the percentage spread is greater for riskier securities. Furthermore, residual risk does appear to be a major factor in the relationship.

Information.   Allowing that the market maker may not feel secure about being the first to receive news in all its details, it is likely that the spread will widen at times of substantial informational change. One way to test this by regression analysis would be to consider the effect of current trading volume on the spread, while taking separate account of the stock's normal trading volume, as suggested above. Unfortunately, a thorough empirical test along these lines has not yet been performed.

Competition. Competition brings spreads in line with costs. The standard measure used in the literature has been the number of market makers. The empirical evidence has clearly shown that percentage dealer spreads are narrower when the number of dealers making a market in the stock is greater.

The activity variable and interdealer competition should further effect market spreads. That is, the inside spread should be smaller as the average trading activity in a stock and the number of dealers making a market in a stock gets larger. This is attributable in part to the natural effect of aggregation to reduce the inside spread relative to the individual dealer spreads. Further, it is accounted for by the fact that the thickness of a market stabilizes price, and results in traders being willing to post quotes closer to quotes already established on the market.

Short run variations in trading activity, however, should be positively related to the size of the market spread. This is because these variations cause the spread to fluctuate around its equilibrium value—temporary increases in transactions volume can clear limit orders off the book, thereby widening the spread; temporary decreases in transactions volume can result in more orders accumulating on the book, thereby narrowing the spread.

The Monopoly Dealer Model

Garman[33] presented the first formal model of the determination of a monopoly dealer's quotes. Like Demsetz,[34] Garman structured the dealer function in relation to the sporadic arrival of orders for a stock in a continuous market where trades can be made at any time that two counterpart orders cross. Buyers and sellers meet in this market through Garman's monopoly dealer. By assuming that all orders are for one round lot, the buy and sell propensities of traders can be described by the number of 100 share orders that arrive at the market over an interval of time.

Let R_B and R_S be the arrival rates for, respectively, the buy and sell orders. Figure 8.5 shows that R_B and R_S are both functions of the stock's share price, P. The negatively inclined curve labeled R_B reflects the fact that, as the share price is lowered, more investors want to buy one round lot; the positively inclined curve labeled R_S reflects the fact that, as the share price is raised, more investors want to sell one round lot. Figure 8.5 shows that at a price of P^*, arrival rates for buy and sell orders both equal R^*.

The time rates show the number of orders that are *expected* to arrive over some period of time (for example, a trading day); the actual order arrival is an uncertain (stochastic) process. Garman[35] assumes a Poisson order arrival process, and R_S and R_B are arrival rate parameters for the process. Garman's analysis goes beyond Demsetz's[36] in taking account of the stochastic

FIGURE 8.5   *Relationship Between Share Price and the Arrival Rates of Buy and Sell Orders*

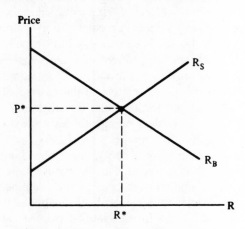

variation in the number of orders which will be placed in any interval of time. Because of the sporadic nature of order arrival, the counterpart buys and sells generally do not meet each other in time. Therefore, in the absence of any other market mechanism, the dealer firm must exist to make the market.

Garman's[37] dealer firm sets quotes to maximize its expected profits from trading per period of time. Since "quantity" is measured by the *expected* rates of order arrival, at a price of P, the dollar volume of both sales and purchases is uncertain. Because all investors trade with the single dealer, the dealer is a monopolist vis-à-vis the buy curve, and a monopsonist vis-à-vis the sell curve. Accordingly, the dealer firm achieves maximum (expected) profits by equating the marginal cost of buying shares with the marginal revenue obtained from selling shares. Garman's model is simplified by the assumption that the market maker has no transaction costs of doing business (that is, the only cost of selling shares is the cost of buying shares). In Figure 8.6, the marginal cost function is the upward sloping straight line labeled R'_S, and the marginal revenue function is the downward sloping straight line labeled R'_B. The intersection of these two lines establishes R^{*M} as the equilibrium expected rate of transactions for the monopoly dealer. Accordingly the dealer firm's optimal ask is given by P^A, and its optimal bid is given by P^B. These prices and the associated quantity (R^{*M}) identify the expected profit maximizing supply of dealer services in the monopoly dealer market.

FIGURE 8.6 *Determination of the Optimal Supply of Dealer Services in a Monopoly Dealer Market*

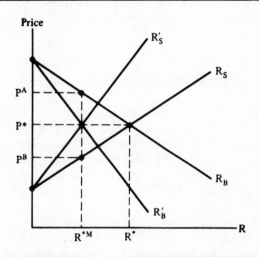

The role of dealer inventories can be reviewed in the context of Garman's[38] model. As with the Demsetz[39] market maker, the Garman dealer has to accept nonzero inventory positions as trading progresses. In part, this is because of the *asynchronous pattern* in which buy and sell orders arrive. If the dealer starts with a zero inventory position in the stock and the first order to arrive is a sell, the dealer will have to accept a long position in the stock; if two or more buy orders happen to arrive next, the dealer will then have to accept a short position in the stock. Therefore, the dealer's inventory fluctuations depend, after the fact, on the specific sequence in which the buy and sell orders happen to have arrived on the market during the trading day. But, unlike the Demsetz model, there is a second factor in the Garman model that also accounts for inventory fluctuations: the order flow is *stochastic*, and R^{*M} is the *expected* rate of buy and sell arrivals. After the fact, it might turn out, for the trading session, that more buy orders in total have arrived at the dealer's ask (P^A) than sell orders have arrived at the dealer's bid (P^B). In such an event, the dealer firm will, on net, have reduced its inventory of the stock. Or perhaps more sell orders have arrived given the dealer's bid than buy orders have arrived given the dealer's ask; in this event, the dealer will, on net, have added to its inventory.

The dynamic dealer pricing models have extended Garman's model[40] by showing how the dealer firm will change its quotes over time so as to keep its inventory within reasonable bounds. The wider the allowable inventory bounds, the smaller will be the spread and the more stable will be the quotes. We see again that the dealer firm's willingness to supply marketability services is an expression of its willingness to accept an unbalanced inventory position.

The Competitive Dealer Model

On average, there were 10.6 market makers per security in the NASDAQ market in 1989.[41] Is this number too small to suggest the empirical realism of the perfectly competitive model of standard microeconomic theory?

In 1989, 458 market makers in total made markets for 4,963 securities in the NASDAQ system. The provision of marketability services for one stock is a close substitute in production for the provision of marketability services for other stocks. Dealers are free to pick the stocks they make markets in virtually at will. The elasticity of supply for these services is, therefore, large for all stocks, and the potential entry of additional dealer firms in each of the markets keeps prices competitive. If excess profits are being made in some stocks, additional dealers will appear to compete the profits away.

The costs of the dealer firm were considered above. We now show how these interact to give the expected profit-maximizing output solution for the competitive dealer firm, and an equilibrium output for the market in aggregate. The analysis yields insight into two empirical observations of particular interest: (1) the number of dealers making markets in most individual stocks is relatively small, and (2) the number of dealer firms increases less than proportionately with the size of the aggregate market for a stock.

Analytical Context

1. We consider long-run analysis only (and therefore avoid the need to distinguish between fixed and variable cost).

2. Although each dealer makes markets in many different securities, we simplify the analysis by considering the cost curve of the dealer firm as it applies to one market alone.

3. Although the realized bid-ask spread of individual dealer firms varies over time, we simplify the analysis by assuming that, at all times, the dealer makes decisions in relation to an expected price of dealer services given by: $E(P) = (1 - pr^A - pr^B)(A^R - B^R) + pr^A(A^M - B^R) + pr^B(A^R - B^M)$, as discussed. The competitive dealer firm is, strictly speaking, a price taker with respect to $E(P)$. Ho and Stoll[42] show that the *size* of the dealer spread is only weakly dependent upon the dealer's inventory (although the *location* of the spread vis-à-vis

the frictionless market clearing price is dependent on the inventory position).

4. The dealer firm's objective is to maximize expected profits.

Long-Run Solution

Figure 8.7 shows the long-run profit-maximizing solution for the competitive dealer firm. The output of the firm is measured by the expected number of transactions the dealer participates in. The figure shows that, at an expected price of $E(P_1)$, the optimal expected output per trading session is $E(T_1)$. We first consider what this means and then explain how the solution was obtained.

Expected Number of Transactions.   Because order arrival is stochastic, the dealer firm does not know in advance how many transactions per trading session it will actually participate in at the price $E(P_1)$. Rather, given $E(P_1)$, the firm will adopt an inventory policy that implies an expected number of transactions equal to $E(T_1)$. That is, the dealer firm places bounds on the magnitude of the inventory fluctuations it will accept, and when the maximum long or short inventory position is reached the dealer firm does not service additional public sell or buy orders. Given these bounds and the expected arrival rate of orders, the firm expects to participate in $E(T_1)$ transactions.

After the fact, the dealer firm will realize a particular transaction rate, and will have experienced a specific pattern of inventory adjustments. If,

FIGURE 8.7 *Long-Run Profit-maximizing Solution for the Competitive Dealer Firm*

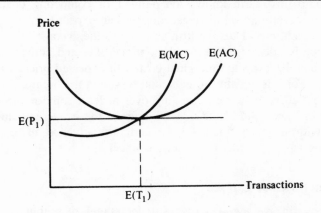

by chance, buy and sell orders happen to have arrived in a well interspersed pattern, the inventory fluctuations required to service the order flow will have been small and the dealer will participate in more than $E(T_1)$ transactions. Or if, by chance, the buy and sell orders happen to have arrived in clusters (either because of the vagaries of order arrival or because of the pattern of adjustment to informational change), the inventory fluctuations required to service the order flow will have been large, the inventory bounds will have been hit more frequently than anticipated, and the dealer will have participated in fewer than $E(T_1)$ transactions. Nevertheless, the firm sets the maximum inventory limits in advance and, having set these limits, anticipates that it will participate in $E(T_1)$ transactions during the next trading session.

Expected Average Revenue.   Along with being uncertain as to what its actual transaction volume will be, the dealer firm is also uncertain as to what its average revenue will be. Price uncertainty exists because the firm does not know in advance the number of times it will be alone on one side of the market and hence will charge the monopoly price for the next transaction. The dealer firm's output decision, however, is not affected per se by the frequency with which it will realize the monopoly price (excess profits are in any event eliminated by competition). If the dealer firm realizes the monopoly price more often (that is, if there are fewer competing dealers), then it will be willing to supply market maker services with a tighter spread in the reservation quotes. Dealer firms cannot enjoy the occasional receipt of the monopoly price unless they continually post quotes in the market, because they will not receive order flow unless they do so. Therefore, they are willing to sustain a slight loss from the competitive quotes if they are occasionally compensated by the realization of a monopoly return. The uncertain mix between the two prices, however, keeps the average price uncertain.

The competitive firm knows the number of competing dealers in the market and the proportion of transactions it can expect to make under monopolistic conditions. Thus the firm also knows the average price to expect. The competitive dealer solves for the optimal expected number of transactions by equating expected marginal cost with expected price, as shown in Figure 8.7. For this equality to exist and to give a maximum, the expected average cost curve must be increasing over at least some range of output, as shown in Figure 8.7. Note that we refer to the *expected* value of costs because, with inventory fluctuations uncertain in advance, the exact cost of maintaining any given trading volume is uncertain.

The Dealer's Cost Curve

The decrease in average cost over smaller ranges of output is reasonable for the dealer firm. Regardless of the transaction volume it might sustain, a firm can make the market in a stock only if it is willing to commit at least a minimum amount of labor and financial capital to posting quotes (so as to be known as a market maker), to staying informed about the company in question (to control the cost of ignorance), and to gain some understanding of the behavior of the order flow for the security. This expenditure does not increase proportionately as the firm expands its market making activities in the stock. Therefore, economies of scale are expected over relatively small values of output.

As the firm's market making activities in a stock continue to increase, however, the firm must accept ever greater inventory fluctuations in its trading portfolio (as discussed above). These fluctuations become increasingly costly as they become larger. Thus diseconomies of scale are expected beyond a certain transaction volume, and average costs will rise.

The Equilibrium Number of Dealer Firms

Having identified the optimal output solution for the competitive dealer firm, we next consider the aggregate output for all firms making a market in the stock. Figure 8.8 illustrates the output equilibrium that exists when the demand for marketability services is given by the negatively inclined curve labeled "D" in Panel A, and when all dealer firms have the same average cost curve labeled "$E[AC_i]$" in Panel B. The assumption that all firms have identical cost curves simplifies the exposition. Most importantly, the height of the average cost curves is typically taken by theoretical economists to be the same in competitive markets.[43]

FIGURE 8.8 *Determination of the Optimal Supply of Dealer Services in a Competitive Dealer Market. (a) Industry Equilibrium. (b) Equilibrium for the ith Dealer Firm*

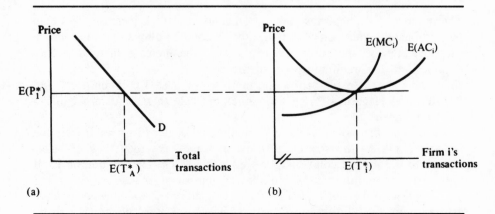

The value of average cost at the minimum point on the firm's average cost curve establishes $E(P_1^*)$ as the no-profit, long-run, competitive equilibrium price of marketability services. Given the demand curve, D, the aggregate expected transactions volume at $E[P_1^*]$ is $E[T_A^*]$. Given $E[T_A^*]$ and the optimal expected transaction volume for each firm (shown to be $E[T_i^*]$ in Panel B of Figure 8.8), the equilibrium number of dealer firms, N^*, is given by

$$N^* = E(T_A^*)/E(T_i^*). \qquad (8.4)$$

Given N^*, the expected price $E(P_1^*)$ is the appropriately weighted average of the competitive spread (namely, the spread of the reservation quotes) and of the noncompetitive spread that is realized when the dealer firm is isolated on one side of the market. $E(P^*)$ is given by the height of the average cost curve. N^* is given by the equation (8.4) and the monopoly quotes can be separately determined; therefore, the competitive quotes can be obtained from equation (8.3).

As noted above, relatively few dealer firms make a market for most OTC stocks, which implies that the optimal transaction volume for a firm, $E(T_i^*)$, is large relative to the total transaction volume for the issue, $E(T_A^*)$. The optimal value of $E(T_i^*)$ is given by the dealer firm's cost curve, while the demand for marketability services is related to the size of the company whose stock is being traded. There are substantial costs to dealers of making a market in a stock, of remaining informed about a company, and of staying attuned to the trading characteristics of the company's stock. If demand is too small relative to the cost of making a market, the asset will not be publicly traded. When the stock does meet the minimum requirements for public issue, its relatively small trading volume will attract the interest of only a few dealer firms. Then, if the stock's trading volume increases, more dealer firms will start to make a market in the stock.

External Economies of Scale

The number of dealer firms making a market in a stock increases less than proportionately with increases in the stock's trading volume. This is because each dealer's average cost curve shifts with the increase in total trading volume, and the minimum point of the curve is lower and further to the right. This shift is explained, along the lines suggested by Hamilton[44] and Benston and Hagerman,[45] by economies of scale that are external to the individual dealer firms.

Economies that are external to the individual dealer firms result from the following: (1) As the size of an issue increases, the total flow of information to the market concerning the issue increases (the corporation itself will release more information and a larger number of financial analysts will pay attention to the stock). (2) As the aggregate order flow increases, dealers can more quickly work off an unbalanced inventory position, both by trading with the public at an increased rate, and by trading with each other. (3) As the aggregate market for a stock increases (all else equal), the amount of liquidity trading may increase relative to informational trading, which reduces the risk associated with any given inventory imbalance (inducing the dealer firm to devote more financial capital to making a market in the stock).

The Long-Run Supply Curve of Dealer Services

Figure 8.9 shows the long-run supply curve of dealer services (the curve labeled "S" in Panel a) with economies of scale that are external to the individual dealer firm. When the market demand for dealer services is given by the curve labeled "D_1" in Panel a, N_1^* firms make a market in the stock, each firm receives the expected price $E(P_1^*)$, each expects to transact at rate $E[T_1^*]$, and the expected aggregate number of market transactions is $E[T_{A1}^*]$. Underlying this solution is the fact that, when the expected aggregate number of market transactions is $E[T_{A1}^*]$, the expected average cost curve for each firm is the curve labeled $E(AC_{i1})$.

When the market demand shifts to the curve labeled "D_2" in Panel a, equilibrium is again achieved for the industry and for each of the individual dealer firms which comprise it. This new solution gives an expected aggregate transaction rate $E(T_{A2}^*) > E(T_{A1}^*)$. Because the expected transaction rate is greater (and recalling the economies of scale that are external to the individual dealer firms), the expected average cost curve for each firm is lower, with its minimum point further to the right (as shown in Figure

FIGURE 8.9 *Derivation of the Long-run Supply Curve of Dealer Services. (a) Market Demand and Supply. (b) Equilibria for the* i[th] *Dealer Firm*

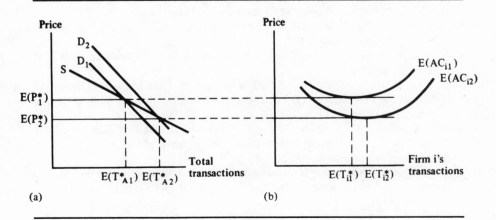

8.9, Panel b by the relationship between $E(AC_{i1})$ and $E(AC_{i2})$). Because the $E(AC)$ curve is lower in the second situation, the market clearing price is also lower—$E(P_2^*) < E(P_1^*)$. Because the minimum point on the firm's average cost curve is further to the right, $E(T_{i2}^*) > E(T_{i1}^*)$. Because the output of each firm has increased, the number of firms in the market has increased less than proportionately with the aggregate transactions volume $[N_2^*/N_1^* < E(T_{A2}^*)/E(T_{A1}^*)]$.

Note the following about the long-run solution just attained. The individual dealer firms realize no excess expected profits from their market making operations—free entry into an industry ensures that, in the long run, the price of the service will just equal its minimum average cost of production. The external economies of scale, nevertheless, produce a result of major import: the long-run supply curve of dealer services to the market for a stock is negatively inclined. Therefore, we should expect to observe smaller dealer spreads in larger markets (recall that $E(P)$ is the size of the average dealer spread in a competitive market), and we do.

Suggested Reading

Amihud, Y., Ho, T., and Schwartz, R., eds. *Market Making and the Changing Structure of the Securities Industry.* Lexington, MA: Lexington Books, 1985.

Amihud, Y., and Mendelson, H. "Dealership Market: Market-Making with Inventory." *Journal of Financial Economics,* March 1980.

Amihud, Y., and Mendelson, H. "Asset Price Behavior in a Dealership Market." *Financial Analysts Journal,* May/June 1982.

Bagehot, W. "The Only Game in Town." *Financial Analysts Journal,* March/April 1971.

Barnea, A., and Logue, D. "The Effect of Risk on the Market Maker's Spread," *Financial Analysts Journal,* November/December 1975.

Benston, G., and Hagerman, R. "Determinants of Bid-Asked Spreads in the Over-the-Counter Market." *Journal of Financial Economics,* December 1974.

Branch, B., and Freed, W. "Bid-Ask Spreads on the Amex and the Big Board." *Journal of Finance,* March 1977.

Cohen, K., and Cyert, R. *Theory of the Firm,* 2nd edition. Englewood Cliffs, NJ: Prentice Hall, 1975.

Cohen, K., Maier, S., Schwartz, R., and Whitcomb, D. "The Impact of Designated Market Makers on Security Prices: II. Policy Proposals." *Journal of Banking and Finance,* November 1977.

Cohen, K., Maier, S., Schwartz, R., and Whitcomb, D. "Market Makers and the Market Spread: A Review of Recent Literature," *Journal of Financial and Quantitative Analysis,* November 1979.

Conroy, R., and Winkler, R. "Informational Differences Between Limit and Market Orders for a Market Maker." *Journal of Financial and Quantitative Analysis,* December 1981.

Copeland, T., and Galai, D. "Information Effects on the Bid-Ask Spread." *Journal of Finance*, December 1983.

Demsetz, H. "The Cost of Transacting." *Quarterly Journal of Economics*, February 1968.

Garman, M. "Market Microstructure." *Journal of Financial Economics*, June 1976.

Glosten, L. "Components of the Bid-Ask Spread and the Statistical Properties of Transaction Prices." *Journal of Finance*, December 1987.

Glosten, L., and Harris, L. "Estimating the Components of the Bid/Ask Spread." *Journal of Financial Economics*, May 1988.

Glosten, L., and Milgrom, P. "Bid, Ask, and Transaction Prices in a Specialist Market with Heterogeneously Informed Traders." *Journal of Financial Economics*, March 1985.

Hakansson, N., Beja, A., and Kale, J. "On the Feasibility of Automated Market Making by a Programmed Specialist." *Journal of Finance*, March 1985.

Hamilton, J. "Competition, Scale Economies, and Transaction Costs in the Stock Market." *Journal of Financial and Quantitative Analysis*, December 1976.

Hasbrouck, J. "Inferring the Extent of Informational Asymmetries from Trades and the Variance of Efficient Prices: An Econometric Analysis." Paper presented at the Western Finance Association Conference, Santa Barbara, California, June 1990.

Hasbrouck, J. "The Information Content of Stock Trades." *Journal of Finance*, March 1991.

Hasbrouck, J. "The Pricing Errors Implied by the Autocovariances in Short-Term Stock Returns." New York University Stern School of Business working paper, February 1988.

Hasbrouck, J. "Trades, Quotes, Inventories, and Information." *Journal of Financial Economics*, December 1988.

Ho, T. "Dealer Market Structure: A Dynamic Competitive Equilibrium Model." Working Paper, New York University Graduate School of Business Administration, March 1984.

Ho, T., and Macris, R. "Dealer Market Structure and Performance." In Amihud, Ho, and Schwartz, (1985).

Ho, T., and Stoll, H. "On Dealer Markets Under Competition." *Journal of Finance*, May 1980.

Ho, T., and Stoll, H. "Optimal Dealer Pricing Under Transaction and Return Uncertainty." *Journal of Financial Economics*, March 1981.

Ho, T., and Stoll, H. "The Dynamics of Dealer Markets Under Competition." *Journal of Finance*, September 1983.

Logue, D. "Market Making and the Assessment of Market Efficiency." *Journal of Finance*, March 1975.

Mildenstein, E., and Schleef, H. "The Optimal Pricing Policy of a Monopolistic Marketmaker in the Equity Market." *Journal of Finance*, March 1983.

O'Hara, M., and Oldfield, G. "The Microeconomics of Market Making." *The Journal of Financial and Quantitative Analysis*, December 1986.

Seppi, D. "Equilibrium Block Trading and Asymmetric Information." *Journal of Finance*, March 1990.

Sirri, E. "Bid/Ask Spread, Price, and Volume in a Specialist Market." Paper presented at the Western Finance Association Conference, Santa Barbara, California, June 1990.

Smidt, S. "Which Road to an Efficient Stock Market: Free Competition or Regulated Monopoly?" *Financial Analysts Journal,* September/October 1971.

Stigler, G. "Public Regulation of the Securities Markets." *Journal of Business,* April 1964.

Stoll, H. "The Supply of Dealer Services in Security Markets." *Journal of Finance,* September 1978.

Stoll, H. "The Pricing of Security Dealer Services: An Empirical Study of NASDAQ Stocks." *Journal of Finance,* September 1978.

Stoll, H. "Alternative Views of Market Making." In Amihud, Ho, and Schwartz, (1985).

Stoll, H. *The New York Stock Exchange Specialist System.* Monograph Series in Finance and Economics, Salomon Brothers Center for the Study of Financial Institutions, New York University Graduate School of Business Administration, 1985.

Stoll, H. "Inferring the Components of the Bid-Ask Spread: Theory and Empirical Tests." *Journal of Finance,* March 1989.

Tinic, S. "The Economics of Liquidity Services." *Quarterly Journal of Economics,* February 1972.

Tinic, S., and West, R. "Competition and the Pricing of Dealer Services in the Over-the-Counter Stock Market." *Journal of Financial and Quantitative Analysis,* June 1972.

Tinic, S., and West, R. "Marketability of Common Stocks in Canada and the USA: A Comparison of Agent Versus Dealer Dominated Markets." *Journal of Finance,* June 1974.

Venkatesh, P., and Chiang, R. "Information Asymmetry and the Dealer's Bid-Ask Spread: A Case Study of Earnings and Dividend Announcements." *Journal of Finance,* December 1986.

Notes

1. For further discussion, see K. Cohen, S. Maier, R. Schwartz, and D. Whitcomb, "The Impact of Designated Market Makers on Security Prices. II. Policy Proposals," *Journal of Banking and Finance,* December 1977.
2. S. Smidt, "Which Road to an Efficient Stock Market: Free Competition or Regulated Monopoly?" *Financial Analysts Journal,* September/October 1971.
3. T. Ho and H. Stoll, "Optimal Dealer Pricing Under Transaction and Return Uncertainty," *Journal of Financial Economics,* March 1981.
4. For further discussion, see W. Bagehot, "The Only Game in Town," *Financial Analysts Journal,* March/April 1971, and T. Copeland and D. Gala, "Information Effects on the Bid-Ask Spread," *Journal of Finance,* December 1983.

5. H. Demsetz, "The Cost of Transacting," *Quarterly Journal of Economics,* February 1968.
6. Smidt, "Which Road?"
7. Ibid.
8. D. Logue, "Market Making and the Assessment of Market Efficiency," *Journal of Finance,* March 1975.
9. Ho and Stoll, "Optimal Dealer Pricing."
10. G. Benston and R. Hagerman, "Determinants of Bid-Asked Spreads in the Over-the-Counter Market," *Journal of Financial Economics,* December 1974.
11. J. Hamilton, "Competition, Scale Economies, and Transaction Costs in the Stock Market," *Journal of Financial and Quantitative Analysis,* December 1976.
12. Demsetz, "Cost of Transacting."
13. S. Tinic, "The Economics of Liquidity Services." *Quarterly Journal of Economics,* February 1972.
14. S. Tinic and R. West, "Marketability of Common Stocks in Canada and the USA: A Comparison of Agent Versus Dealer Dominated Markets." *Journal of Finance,* June 1974.
15. Barnea and Logue (1975).
16. Branch and Freed "Bid-Ask Spreads on the Amex and the Big Board," *Journal of Finance,* March 1977.
17. Demsetz, "Cost of Transacting." p. 39.
18. Tinic and West, "Marketability," pp. 732–733.
19. K. Cohen, S. Maier, R. Schwartz, and D. Whitcomb, "Market Makers and the Market Spread: A Review of Recent Literature," *Journal of Financial and Quantitative Analysis,* November 1979.
20. T. Ho and H. Stoll, "On Dealer Markets Under Competition," *Journal of Finance,* May 1980.
21. Y. Amihud and H. Mendelson, "Dealership Market: Market Making with Inventory," *Journal of Financial Economics,* March 1980.
22. Ibid. Amihud and Mendelson also consider how a market maker can infer shifts in the market's buy/sell order functions (due to informational change) from change in the rates at which new orders arrive at old prices.
23. See Amihud and Mendelson, "Dealership Market"; Ho and Stoll, "On Dealer Markets"; and E. Mildenstein and H. Schleef. "The Optimal Pricing Policy of a Monopolistic Marketmaker in the Equity Market," *Journal of Finance,* March 1983.
24. Amihud and Mendelson, "Dealership Markets."
25. For a clear assessment and interpretation of the model, also see Amihud and Mendelson (1982).
26. Amihud and Mendelson, "Asset Price Behavior in a Dealership Market," *Financial Analysts Journal,* May/June 1982.
27. H. Stoll, "Alternative Views of Market Making," in Y. Amihud, T. Ho, and R. Schwartz, eds. *Market Making and the Changing Structure of the Securities Industry,* Lexington, MA: Lexington Books, 1985.
28. H. Stoll, "Dealer Inventory Behavior: An Empirical Investigation of NASDAQ Stocks," *Journal of Financial and Quantitative Analysis,* September 1976.

29. T. Ho and H. Stoll, "The Dynamics of Dealer Markets Under Competition," *Journal of Finance,* September 1983.
30. T. Ho and R. Macris, "Dealer Market Structure and Performance," in Y. Amihud, T. Ho, and R. Schwartz, eds. *Market Making and the Changing Structure of the Securities Industry.* Lexington, MA: Lexington Books, 1985.
31. Amihud and Mendelson, "Dealership Market."
32. See T. Ho,"Dealer Market Structure: A Dynamic Competitive Equilibrium Model," working paper, New York University Graduate School of Business Administration, March 1984, for further discussion.
33. M. Garman, "Market Microstructure," *Journal of Financial Economics,* June 1976.
34. Demsetz, "Cost of Transacting."
35. Ho and Stoll, "Dealer Market Structure and Performance."
36. Demsetz, "Cost of Transacting."
37. Ho and Stoll, "Dealer Market Structure and Performance."
38. Ibid.
39. Demsetz, "Cost of Transacting."
40. Amihud and Mendelson, "Dealership Market"; Ho and Stoll, "Dealer Markets Under Competition"; and Mildenstein and Schleef, "Optimal Pricing."
41. NASDAQ 1990 *Fact Book,* National Association of Security Dealers.
42. Ho and Stoll, "Dealer Markets Under Competition."
43. Cohen and Cyert, *Theory of the Firm,* 2nd edition, Englewood Cliffs, NJ: Prentice Hall, 1975.
44. Hamilton, "Competition."
45. Benston and Hagerman, "Determinants of Bid-Asked Spreads."

9

Consolidation of the Order Flow

Orders are consolidated in two ways: in space (spatially) and in time (temporally). Trading is spatially consolidated if orders are routed to one market. Trading is temporally consolidated if orders are batched together for execution at a single price. In the United States, much attention has been given to spatial consolidation versus fragmentation; recently, increasing attention is also being given to the desirability of temporally consolidating orders in call market trading.

Spatial Consolidation in an Agency/Auction Market

Off-Board Trading Restrictions—NYSE Rule 390

Through the mid-1970s, the NYSE was considered by many an exclusive club that only the privileged could join, and the Exchange's fixed commission structure had been found to be anticompetitive and unjustified. In this context, the NYSE's off-board trading restriction, Rule 394, appeared to be another anticompetitive barrier that the Exchange had erected to protect its narrow self-interest. The off-board trading restriction and minimum fixed commissions both date back to 17 May 1792 when, in response to emerging competition, 24 brokers signed an accord known as the "Buttonwood Agreement" in honor of a tree on Wall Street under which the document was signed. Rule 394 prohibited both agency and principal executions away from the Exchange, requiring member firms to bring all orders for listed securities to the floor of an exchange for execution. The Amex has a similar rule, known as Rule 5.

Following the Securities Acts Amendments of 1975, Rule 394 was modified (and its number changed to 390) to allow agency transactions away from the Exchange floor. Member firms, however, were still prohibited from participating as principals in off-board trading. This prevented brokerage houses from assuming a dealership function and thereby kept them from making their own markets in listed stocks.

In July 1980 the SEC instituted Rule 19c.3 on an experimental basis, freeing Exchange members to make off-board markets for issues that were listed on the Exchange after 26 April 1979. The day before this rule became effective, *The Wall Street Journal*[1] reported that "Most major broker-dealers say they will begin trading listed [19c.3] stocks if competitive pressures make such a move advisable." At that time, it appeared that substantial order flow might be diverted from the exchanges.

But in-house market making in the newly listed 19c.3 stocks proved to be a short-lived experiment. The operation was not as profitable as it would have been for established volume leaders. Moreover, the brokerage houses that competed with the specialists by making markets in 19c.3 stocks reportedly received unfavorable treatment by the specialists when trying to rebalance their inventory positions. For these reasons, by mid-1983, Merrill Lynch, Morgan Stanley, PaineWebber, Goldman Sachs, and virtually all other large firms had stopped making markets in 19c.3 stocks. Although the experiment did not succeed, the debate concerning the total removal of off-board trading restrictions has continued. The U.S. General Accounting Office's report of March 1990 focused largely on off-board trading restrictions, but did not come to any conclusions.[2]

Degrees of Spatial Consolidation

Spatial consolidation is not an all-or-nothing feature of an exchange-based system; a continuum of possibilities exists. At one extreme, a highly consolidated system might be based on a single limit order book to which all orders must be directed. At the other extreme, a highly fragmented system might consist of a number of separate market centers linked only by the profit motivated behavior of arbitrageurs. The U.S. equity markets lie between the two:

- *The First Market*   An order transmitted to an exchange is directed to the post of the specialist firm to which the stock has been assigned. The order might be placed on the book, execute against the book, or execute against the specialist's own quotes. The order might execute against a counterpart order held by a floor trader in the crowd by the specialist's post or it might be directed to a specialist's post on another exchange if the stock is cross-listed.

- *The Third Market*   The order could be executed in the third market by a dealer firm that is not a member of a stock exchange or, for a 19c.3 stock, by a member firm.

- *The Fourth Market* The orders of two institutional investors may be crossed without the services of an intermediary in the fourth market.
- *The Upstairs Market* A large order might be negotiated off-board in the "upstairs market" and then brought to the trading floor as a "put-through."

Spatially fragmented markets may be (and typically are) interlinked, both by telephone communication and by computer. For example, ITS displays quotes posted in different markets to market makers on the national exchanges, regional exchanges, and OTC markets. ITS also provides an electronic linkage for intermarket executions. The Consolidated Quotations System (CQS) gives public traders floor information for Exchange-listed issues that are traded in different markets.

These electronic linkages enable arbitrageurs to keep prices set in different market centers "in tune" with each other and, if orders are adequately exposed to the market, to preserve price priorities. Electronic linkages, however, do not transform a fragmented market into a consolidated market. For example, in a fully consolidated market, orders can be executed according to a secondary priority rule as well as the primary rule that the best-priced orders execute first. This is not possible in a fragmented system.

Interdealer Versus Intermarket Competition

The term *interdealer competition* applies when the order flow for a stock is split among market centers (a national and/or regional exchange, the in-house market of a broker/dealer firm, an electronic fourth market trading system, and so on). The term *intermarket competition* applies to the broader competition between market centers for listing, for trading in different products, and so on.

Two Markets—Stocks and Market Makers

Most people favor competition both in the provision of dealer services and between the buyers and sellers of a stock. Unfortunately, the two types of competition are, to an appreciable extent, incompatible: if all orders for a stock are consolidated in one market to maximize the competitive interaction of traders, competition between dealers in the provision of marketability services must be sacrificed. Alternatively, with adequate interdealer competition, the order flow must to some extent be fragmented.

The problem is that there is not one market, but two—the market for the stock that is traded, and the market for the provision of dealer services. Consequently, two different prices are of concern—the price of the stock that is traded and the price of marketability services. A trade-off exists because enhancing the competitive interaction of participants in one of these markets necessarily weakens the competitive interaction of participants in the other.

Competition Among the Market Centers

The typical progression of a public corporation in the past had been for it first to trade OTC when it went public, then for it to list on the Amex as it gained greater strength and visibility, and finally for it to list on the NYSE as it attained full stature and acceptability.

Some firms now remain on the OTC as they grow and mature, in the belief that the competitive dealer market is better for their stocks and that the services provided by the exchanges are not worth the listing costs involved. The NASD has confronted the exchange markets by both improving the quality of its NASDAQ system and increasing the visibility of the stocks on its NASDAQ/NMS list. As the quality of the NASDAQ/NMS stocks has become more widely recognized, the relative luster of an exchange listing has dimmed somewhat.

The exchanges have reacted by developing new products and new trading technologies. They also opened their doors to new members, lengthened trading hours, tightened their regulation of the specialists, and greatly improved the intermarket trading system. In short, the quality of the exchange markets has also improved.

The exchanges now face a broader competitive challenge than that provided by the OTC alone. The regional and national exchanges compete with each other, with new systems such as Instinet's Crossing Network and Jeffries' Posit, and with foreign market centers such as London's International Stock Exchange. This competition has had a profound impact on the provision of marketability services and has also motivated tremendous technological change and innovation in recent years.

In the past, the fragmentation/consolidation debate has primarily focused on the desirability of having multiple dealers make markets for a single security. But, interdealer competition may not be the only way or even the best way of improving the equity market system. Intermarket competition will keep the supply of dealer services competitive. This alternative avoids fragmenting the order flow for individual securities and provides a stronger incentive for technological development.

The Effects of Spatially Consolidating the Order Flow

Order Exposure and Price Priority.   Order exposure and price priority are desirable for both efficiency and fairness. The major concern about a fragmented order flow has been that orders will not be fully exposed to the market and that price priority will be violated (called "overreaching").

Overreaching may occur because a new order might not find the *best* counterpart order against which to execute. Overreaching might also occur if brokers/dealers provide in-house executions at inferior prices without their customers knowing what the best prices are. The violation of price priority in a fragmented system will increase the thinness of the market, and hence result in greater price volatility and wider bid-ask spreads.[3] The exposure of orders in the market not only prevents overreaching, but also encourages competing dealers to improve their quotes.

Secondary Priority Rules.   A secondary priority trading rule specifies the sequence in which orders written at the same price will execute. The most common secondary priority rule is time priority (the order that has been placed first, executes first). Other rules include partial execution according to time priority (for example, after 1,000 shares of an order have executed, the remainder of the order goes to the end of the queue), size priority (the largest order executes first), and random selection (the order that transacts next is selected by chance).

When quotes are posted at the same price in more than one market center, the next order to execute depends on the market center to which the next counterpart order happens to be transmitted. If it is not possible to predict which the next market will be, then the secondary priority rule implicitly imposed is one of random selection. If the market center can be predicted, then some other secondary priority rule is implicit in the prediction rule. An advantage of a consolidated trading system is that it enables the secondary priority rule to be specified explicitly.

The most widely used secondary rule is time priority. Because there are advantages in a gaming situation to letting other players go first, the use of time priority can help to counteract the undesirable tendency of traders to hold back their orders. Another incentive to trade quickly, of course, is when the order is motivated by informational change that the trader believes has not yet been fully reflected in market prices. Also, because of the secondary rule, a trader might try to beat the queue of orders at a price by increasing the order's bid price (or by decreasing its ask price). Without a time priority rule, the trader might be less apt to better the order's price and instead simply hope to get a lucky draw in the random selection when the next order arrives.

Computer simulation has shown that a time priority rule, vis-à-vis random selection, causes a reduction of the bid-ask spread and an increase in the probability that a limit order will execute within a given period of time.[4] Thus adoption of a time priority rule should improve the thickness and quality of a market.

Information Consolidation.   The physical gathering of orders in a market center and the congregation of traders on a trading floor contribute to the consolidation of information. Geographic proximity helps traders sense trading interest in the crowd around the specialist's post. The floor environment may also enable some traders to infer who the customers are behind the large orders. For example, a trader seeing that a certain brokerage house is using a particular two-dollar broker (rather than their own commission house broker) to work an order, may infer that a certain informed institutional investor is behind the order.

When information is consolidated, traders receive more accurate signals on which to base their orders. Thus, fragmentation of the order flow to bolster interdealer competition could impair the quality of the market by obscuring the informational content of the order flow.

The Diverse Needs of Different Traders.   A market may have to be fragmented to some extent because different traders operate differently in the marketplace. Size is the primary distinction among investors and traders in this regard. For example,

- Small retail customers are most likely to leave their limit orders on the order book or to have their market orders executed as quickly and inexpensively as possible through electronic order-routing systems such as SuperDOT.

- Intermediate-sized orders are commonly worked by traders on the exchange floor.

- Very large orders are typically negotiated off the floor in the "upstairs" market.

Market fragmentation is a cost that, to some extent, must be incurred to obtain the operational flexibility a system should have. At present, achieving an effective integration of the diverse needs of traders is a challenge the designers of a trading system must continue to face.

Fairness.   A trading system must be fair for reasons of both equity and efficiency, but the importance of the issue extends further. Traders who believe that others consistently obtain superior executions might shy away from a market. As a consequence, trading volume would be reduced, the price of shares would be depressed, and the manifestations of a thin market would become more apparent (wider spreads, more volatile prices, and less accurate price discovery). These effects could then cause other traders to reduce their participation in the market, and a decline in the quality of the marketplace would be perpetuated.

Consolidating orders can result in a fairer, more orderly system for several reasons: (1) rules may be enforced in a consolidated system that cannot be imposed in a fragmented system, (2) market surveillance is more effective (and less costly) in a consolidated system, and (3) consolidation of the order flow facilitates the access of all participants to market information and ensures the broad market exposure of all orders.

The Public Goods Aspect of Marketability Services. The marketability services of an exchange-based trading system include both a private and a public aspect. A public good is a good or service for which the quantity available for one person is available for all. Consumption of a public good by one person does not preclude others from consuming it. Further, a public good is available to an individual, regardless of the individual's willingness to pay for it. Goods are public goods because the market technology does not exist (or else is too expensive to use) to prevent people who do not pay for a good from consuming it. Public goods are undersupplied in a free market because demand for them is underrevealed in the private sector.

Immediacy is a private good; the trader (and only that trader) who demands immediacy obtains it and pays for it by buying at the higher ask price or by selling at the lower bid price. On the other hand, price stabilization, price discovery, and protection against exploitation, fraud, manipulation and other violations of the rules of the game are public goods. If prices are stabilized, they are stabilized for all traders; if prices closer to equilibrium values are found by the system, all traders benefit from the greater accuracy of the information that is thereby conveyed; and market surveillance protects investors as a group. The fragmentation of a market can impair the provision of these public goods.

Consolidation/Fragmentation in a Competitive Dealer Market

Order flow is necessarily fragmented in a competitive dealer market. However, a secondary priority rule is not meaningful in a dealer market (public orders execute immediately against a dealer's quotes), information transmission occurs largely by telephone (OTC dealers in the U.S. are free to talk directly with their customers), and public goods services can be optimally supplied (NASD is a self-regulatory organization). Fragmentation in a competitive dealer market specifically denotes trades taking place at different prices at the same time. The potential for a competitive dealer market to fragment in this manner has been most clearly recognized in relation to London's equity market. The reason is that trades are commonly made within the quotes in the ISE's screen-based SEAQ system. (The London equity market is described more broadly in Chapter 4.) Much of the concern in the U.K. about fragmentation has involved developments that could worsen the prices shown on SEAQ and thus lead to fragmentation in the future. Currently, fragmentation is not serious.

The ISE has no rule equivalent to NYSE Rule 390, and thus integration depends on the attractiveness of dealing through the central market, rather than on regulation. Nonmembers are free to deal directly with each other. Members can also bypass market makers and deal directly with each other. The fact that virtually all trades in London in U.K. equities are done through the ISE, and that 85% of the trading is with market makers, testifies to the quality of the service being offered. Nevertheless, market fragmentation manifests itself in various ways.

Within-the-Spread Transactions

London's SEAQ system would seem to have a high degree of transparency, with competing quotes in large size being displayed to all those interested and with speedy (within three minutes) reporting of the price and size of each trade taking place in the market. Transparency is impaired, however, by the following:

1. Market makers are generally prepared to deal within their quotes, particularly when they are not on the touch, and will normally deal at quoted prices in much larger size. The more this happens, the less will the screen represent best prices available to customers.

2. Large trades are only published the following day. The fact that a large trade has taken place is made publicly known through the cumulative volume indicator, but the price only becomes known the following day with the publication of the Daily Official List. If the Elwes Committee's recommendations in its Final Report are accepted, only the very largest trades will be subject to delayed publication, and the value of the transaction record will be at least partially restored.

3. The system allows each market maker to put up only one set of quotes (a bid and ask in a size he or she chooses). In principle, a system that allows the market maker to display an entire price schedule would be more transparent. The Elwes Committee has now gone some way to meeting this point by proposing a Green Strip system that will enable market makers to quote different prices for large and small trades.

Market makers have an incentive, of course, to announce good quotes and large size: the advertising attracts order flow, especially for the market maker who has a quote in the yellow strip. This incentive is limited, however, because favored relationships and customer loyalty exist between various market maker firms and institutional customers, and market makers will typically match or even better the touch for favored customers.

An individual market maker might not wish to quote the price and size at which he or she is really prepared to deal for a number of reasons. Essentially, stating wider spreads and then giving transactions between the quotes adds flexibility to screen-based trading. It gives market makers time to alter their quotes on the screen following informational change, and it enables them to service customer orders without constantly adjusting their screen quotes in a way that would signal their inventory positions.

Quoting poor prices and/or small size on the screen, and then making better prices over the phone, also enables market makers to price-discriminate between customers. If a market maker gives its own customers good prices, other parts of the company are rewarded with profitable business. Conversely, the firm may wish to avoid trading with, or else offer poorer prices to, customers who are known to be slow payers or who have poorly run back offices. And, most importantly, the fact that a particular customer is in the market wanting to trade in a certain way carries information that the market maker firm might wish to reflect in the prices it quotes over the phone.

For example, if a broker/dealer firm that does a large amount of principal trading with its own customers wishes to sell stock to a market maker firm, it is likely that this broker/dealer has tried and failed to place the shares with its own customers. The market maker firm would thus offer a lower price because little buying interest exists for the stock, and because others now know that the shares are overhanging the market. The firm will also discriminate between a trader who always seems to buy ahead of a price move and one who follows a mechanical strategy such as running an index fund.

Price discrimination and poor screen prices go together. If visibility is to be upheld, then price discrimination must be severely curtailed. Curtailing price discrimination, however, will benefit the informed trader and the broker/dealer, at the expense of the uninformed trader who has not hawked a transaction around the market. If the relatively "informationless" traders are sufficiently disadvantaged, they could bypass the market and deal with each other directly (as some traders are now doing in the United States, via systems such as Barra/Jeffries' Posit and Instinet's crossing network). The market makers would then see a declining proportion of the order flow and would be disadvantaged by increasingly trading with better-informed customers. If carried to its logical conclusion, the market could fragment, and the market maker system could cease to be viable.

There is no evidence that this is happening at present. Competition is so fierce that screen prices are good, and there is little incentive to bypass the market makers. But if spreads were to widen enough to give market makers an economic return on their capital, it is possible for the threat to become real.

Fragmentation of the ISE's Order Flow

Off-Board Trading. Virtually all trades in London in U.K. equities are reported to the Exchange and are subject to its surveillance and reporting rules. The ISE, however, has no monopoly on securities trading. As the Elwes Committee has stated, "In the U.K. there is no obligation for clients to execute their securities business on an Exchange, nor for dealers in securities to join an Exchange. That being so, business will only continue to be attracted to the ISE if the prices at which investors can buy and sell securities 'on market' are more competitive than can be obtained elsewhere."[5]

Trades that Bypass Market Makers.   The fact that a trade is carried out on-exchange does not guarantee that it will be channeled through a market maker, however. Currently, some 10 to 15% of trades bypass the market makers, a similar proportion to that which existed prior to Big Bang. Brokers and dealers can act as principals or cross customer orders without reference to market makers.

A worsening of screen prices widens the scope for trades to bypass the market makers. This is a potentially serious threat to market makers who must see the order flow to establish good prices. The Elwes Committee has proposed that a cross be exposed to a market maker firm, and that the firm be able to participate in the cross if it so desires. The market makers, however, still will not know of trades between broker/dealers and clients.

Fragmentation Between Market Makers.   On a marketwide basis, 25% of the market making firms handle 80% of trading volume. Over 90% of the alpha stocks have at least ten registered market makers. Thus, most market makers have only an incomplete view of the order flow. They depend heavily on the SEAQ screen (which is public), on the IDB screen (which is available only to other market makers), and on those orders and requests for quotes that they themselves receive.

Two major rule changes introduced in 1989 and currently under discussion hurt a market maker with a small share of the order flow: (1) delayed publication of large trades suppresses important information about order flow, which keeps smaller market makers relatively uninformed; and (2) restricting the obligation of market makers to trade with each other impedes inter–market maker trading and, in so doing, hurts the smaller firms in particular. Inter–market maker trading is a particularly important means of information transfer in the absence of immediate trade reporting. However, without firm quotes, this market may function less efficiently, and an incentive is created for market makers to club together.

Market makers with a small market share or who are otherwise relatively powerless, would likely be excluded from the club. Thus for various reasons, the rule changes disadvantage the small market makers. The rule changes have been partially reversed (the threshold for nonpublication was raised, the delay in trade reporting limited to 90 minutes, and the obligation to deal in at least normal market size reinstated); nevertheless, taken as a whole they might encourage concentration in the industry.

Because market maker firms give executions within the spread, dispersal of the order flow across them has caused concern that different customers can realize different execution prices under identical market conditions. The differential price enhancements for within-the-spread transactions are bound to make both quotes and transaction prices noisier reflections of underlying economic conditions. This must, to some extent, impair price discovery and raise questions of fairness.

The point of entry of an order into a system should not matter in a truly consolidated market. In the U.K., the execution realized by a public customer depends on the market-making firm to which the order has been submitted, and the system is, indeed, fragmented. With tight spreads and good depth at the quotes, the fragmentation that presently exists is not of major concern. This might change if spreads were to widen with a diminution of excess capacity and a weakening of inter–market maker competition.

Quote Vendor Systems and Closed User Groups. Three automated execution systems—the ISE's SAEF, Barclays de Zoete Wedd's TRADE, and Kleinwort Benson's BEST—are estimated to have captured approximately 10% of trading volume.[6] Of primary concern is the order flow being diverted to the two private systems, TRADE and BEST. The uneasiness concerning these systems is that a market maker could post relatively unattractive quotes on the SEAQ screen and still capture order flow from its competitors. A market maker firm may in fact commit itself to a better price and/or size than it is showing on SEAQ.

The Elwes Committee report to the ISE (1988) has rightly seen this as a threat to the integrity of the market. Straightforward fragmentation exists if the prices being quoted are better than the SEAQ touch. Accordingly, the Committee has recommended that market makers not be allowed to quote better prices (or the same price in larger size) on some other system, apart from IDB, than they quote on SEAQ. But the ISE cannot regulate the activities of nonmembers, and if an economic function is fulfilled by these alternative markets, they will be set up. The issue underscores the limits of the ISE's ability to prevent the market from fragmenting.

The Interdealer Broker System. Fragmentation is also thought by some to exist because of the interdealer broker (IDB) system. 10% of total turnover on the Exchange is currently being conducted through IDBs. A recent report by the consulting firm Touche Ross, states that "the reason why access to the IDB system has become an issue is because it is a form of limit order system that would be attractive to other traders."[7] The suggestion is made in the report that the system be opened to all principal traders. Doing so would no doubt decrease the importance of market makers as more public orders would be directly crossed with each other. This would be a major step toward a central order-processing system.

Any competitive dealer market is fragmented in ways that need not characterize an agency/auction system such as the NYSE. Public orders are not consolidated in a single file with secondary trading priority rules enforced (for example, the first or largest public orders at a price execute first). Indeed, secondary priority rules have little relevance when public orders are routinely executed immediately against a market maker's quotes. A secondary priority rule is used, however, with respect to the display of market maker quotes. The quote of the most competitive market maker on each side of the market for a security is displayed on the yellow strip; when two or more market makers are tied in setting the best quote, the market maker with the largest size is given priority on the yellow strip. Moreover, an OTC dealer's affirmative obligation to make a two-sided market is not comparable to an NYSE specialist's affirmative obligation to make a "fair and orderly" market. This means that orders and executions need not be consolidated so as to ensure price continuity or other measures of market quality that are more characteristic of the NYSE.*

Temporal Consolidation—Call Market Trading

Call Market Versus Continuous Market Trading

One of the most basic design features of a trading system is whether it is structured as a call or as a continuous market. A continuous market allows trades to be made at any time that public orders cross with each other or with a dealer's quotes. In a call market, orders are batched for simultaneous execution at a single price when the market is "called." For this reason, the call market is sometimes referred to as a "single price auction." Calls are typically held once or twice per day for a stock.

The U.S. financial markets (both the securities exchanges and the OTC markets) are continuous trading systems. Major call markets include the stock exchanges in Austria, Belgium, Germany, and Israel. Until recently, the Paris Bourse was also a call market.

Continuous trading has long been favored in North America and the Far East and is currently being adopted more widely by market centers in Europe. This is in part because existing call markets have not allowed the dissemination of price indications to participants away from a trading floor and have not provided continuous access to the market. These limitations may be overcome, however, by appropriate use of electronic technology and by incorporating a call market alternative into a continuous trading environment (as discussed in Chapter 10).

---

* Material in this section is adapted from A. Neuberger, and R. Schwartz, "London Equity Market," *Finanzmarkt und Portfolio Management,* 4th issue number 3, 1990.

A call market operates very differently from a continuous market, and traders write their orders differently in the two systems. (See the Appendix to this chapter and the Appendix to Chapter 13 for further discussion.) With a continuous market, traders can observe the behavior of bid and ask quotations, transaction prices, and trading volume over the course of a trading day. This information on current market conditions, called *floor information,* is valuable to traders in writing their orders. The essence of a call is that orders that have accumulated over a period of time are batched for simultaneous execution, and all crossing orders are executed at the same price. Because public orders interact directly with other public orders in the batching process, a dealer need not participate in trading as a middleman.

Call Market Trading

Written/Oral. Trading in a call market can be either by written auction or by verbal auction. The Paris Bourse, for example, used a verbal auction for actively traded issues, and a written auction for smaller issues. The verbal auction is more expensive to operate, but also more desirable for floor traders who can adjust their orders as the call searches for a clearing price. Traders in the written auction must, in ignorance of current market conditions, specify the price and size of their orders before trading begins (as must traders who are not present on the floor in the verbal auction).

Whether written or verbal, the orders for an issue are revealed to an auctioneer (an exchange official) when the market is called. Buy and sell orders are matched at the price that most closely equates the aggregate number of shares offered for sale (at that price and below) with the aggregate number of shares sought for purchase (at that price and above). Then, all market orders to buy and all buy limit orders at the clearing price or higher are executed, as are all market orders to sell and all sell limit orders at the clearing price or lower.

The price priority rule is necessarily adhered to in call market trading. A secondary priority rule is also required because with discrete order size and minimum allowable price changes, no price may exist at which the total number of buy orders precisely equals the total number of sell orders. (The minimum allowable price change is $1/8$ of a point for most issues traded in the U.S. equity markets.) Therefore, orders on the "heavy" side of the market must either be rationed or absorbed. The excess of buys over sells (or of sells over buys) is typically rationed by random selection or by *pro rata* execution. Some call markets assure than an execution will be realized by all market order traders and limit order traders with prices better than the clearing price, and therefore ration only those limit orders with prices equal to the clearing price. Alternatively, the excess may be absorbed by professional traders acting in a dealer capacity. A time priority rule is not possible if orders are not posted in the market until the market is called;

with an electronic call, orders can be posted early and time priority can be used.

Order Types. Both limit and market orders can be submitted to a call. As with continuous trading, the limit orders specify a maximum price for buy orders and a minimum price for sell orders. Market orders transact at whatever price is established at the call. Compared with continuous trading, however, market order traders are far less certain about the prices at which their orders will transact: advanced indications are generally not posted in currently existing call markets, and bid/ask quotations are not revealed until the market is called.

In fact, market order traders may not even be assured a transaction: call markets generally have a provision that no trading will be allowed if the price established at a call differs by more than a maximum allowable amount from the price established at the previous call. Consequently, a market order submitted to a call market does not resemble a market order submitted to a continuous market; rather, it is equivalent to a limit order written at the highest allowable call price (for a buy order) or at the lowest allowable call price (for a sell order).

More complex orders can be submitted to an electronic call market, however, because of the computational power of the computer. In fact, a major aspect of an electronic call market's architecture is the design of the types of orders that can be submitted to it. This issue is discussed further in Chapter 10.

Mixed Systems

Temporal consolidation, like spatial consolidation, is not an all-or-nothing feature of a trading system. Call markets such as the German and Austrian exchanges allow for continuous trading, referred to as a "call back period," after call market trading has been completed for certain larger issues. On the Geneva and Zurich Stock Exchanges, traders standing around an oval counter announce their buy and sell orders as an exchange official sequentially calls the market for listed securities. Any trader can, however, interrupt the list whenever desired and reactivate trading in any issue for which the market has already been called.

Some continuous exchange markets operate as a call at one particularly critical moment during the trading day—at the market opening. The opening bell rings at 9:30 A.M. on the NYSE and Amex, but the market for individual stocks does not open until the specialist has found an opening price. In the opening procedure, orders that have been placed before the start of the trading session are batched together, tentative price indications may be given out to the "crowd" of brokers and floor traders, and the buy/sell desires of floor traders are assessed. Much like the call market auctioneer in a batched trading regime, the specialist starts trading at a price that best balances the buy and sell desires expressed when the market opens.

The Tokyo Stock Exchange (TSE) is a continuous trading system. However, for a small number of the most heavily traded securities on the TSE, both a morning and an afternoon session are opened and closed with a formal market call.

The Benefits of Temporal Consolidation

Operating Costs. Substantial economies are realized from batching orders and clearing them out at the same price:

- The call process takes less time. The clearing price can typically be found for a stock in a matter of minutes, after which traders turn their attention to the next stock. In contrast, trading continues for a stock as long as the market is open in a continuous system.

- All orders are executed simultaneously at a single price in call market trading, and the cost of doing so is not appreciably affected by the size of the order flow per se. In continuous trading, counterpart orders are executed as they cross, and operating costs do increase with the size of the order flow.

- All trades are made at the same price at a call, and a specific counterparty to each trade does not exist. Brokerage houses, therefore, need only clear net transactions, not gross transactions on a trade-by-trade basis.

- Because all trades are at the same price, fewer errors are made, which facilitates subsequent clearing and settlement processes.

Immediacy. Time batching orders naturally provides immediacy to the market. Because the time of each call is predetermined, the orders of counterpart traders can meet in time without the services of a dealer or the posting of limit orders. Consequently, traders need not pay the spread to transact with immediacy. In fact, the bid-ask spread does not exist in call market trading.

Market Impact. Time batching reduces the market impact of individual orders because an order of any given size is less significant when it is temporally consolidated with other orders. Furthermore, trading at predetermined points in time reduces the need for participants to search for the contra side of a trade, a process that can disclose their intentions and cause adverse price affects.

Anonymity. Multilateral trading at predetermined points in time generally affords participants greater privacy.

The "Bagging" of Limit Orders.   While limit orders in a continuous market execute at the prices at which they are placed, all orders in a call market execute at a single clearing price in one multilateral trade. Thus traders who have posted priced orders gain protection from being exploited by better informed agents when share values suddenly jump. In other words, the call market allows traders to place limit orders without giving others an option to trade against them to their detriment in a fast-moving market. Consequently, a single price environment encourages traders to place limit orders and thus to supply liquidity as well as to demand it.

Insurance Against Transaction Price Uncertainty.   Consolidating the order flow intertemporally allows investors to obtain protection from transaction price uncertainty by submitting reservation prices to the market. (A reservation price is the highest (lowest) price at which a trader will buy (sell) in an all-or-nothing situation. See Chapter 13, Appendix A for further discussion.) The higher reservation buy prices and lower reservation sell prices give investors more assurance that their orders will indeed execute; but because each investor transacts at the call price, not at the price of his or her own order, the assurance is obtained at minimal personal cost.

Price Discovery.   The call market arrangement most closely approximates the theoretical Walrasian auction, and it is likely that desired Walrasian prices would be most successfully found in actual markets if the order flow were to be temporally consolidated. This is because market conditions can best be assessed by aggregating all orders rather than by dealing with them one at a time as they arrive on the market. (For further discussion, see "Structuring an Electronic Market, in Chapter 10.)

The most difficult part of trading is finding the price at which to open a market after it has been closed for a period of time. It is generally easier to track the price as trading progresses and new quotes and transaction prices are recorded. This is what the continuous market does: it finds an opening price using a call market opening procedure and then allows trading to continue. Traders have to shoot at a moving target, however, and under stressful conditions, prices in the continuous market might not track equilibrium values appropriately. In such an environment, trading should be halted to switch into a call market mode so that appropriate values can be rediscovered.

One Price for All.   Share prices should reflect broad market conditions that are the same for all traders. Therefore, given the information set, price should be the same for all traders. The only justification for price differing among different traders as their orders execute sequentially in a continuous trading regime, is if the process itself enables more accurate prices to be discovered. But this is not necessarily the case.

Price Stabilization. Time batching stabilizes price for a given order flow. Assume a set of traders write their orders before the start of a trading session. If the orders are executed sequentially as they arrive in a continuous market regime, the transaction price will fluctuate according to the sequence in which the orders happen to arrive. If a series of buys happen to arrive in succession, the prices of the last trades in the sequence will be relatively high. Alternatively, if a series of sells happen to arrive in succession, the prices of the last trades will be relatively low. Consequently, the price realized by any trader depends not only on the underlying market conditions, but also on when in the sequence of orders the trader's order happens to arrive. Sequencing risk, as a source of price instability, is eliminated in call market trading.

Fairness. Because all orders execute at the same time, at the same price, and under the same conditions, the procedure is fairer to all participants, regardless of their size or position vis-à-vis information flows.

For example, if trading is not halted in a continuous market following the advent of substantial news, the early recipients of the information have an opportunity to profit at the expense of the uninformed. To protect themselves from being exploited by informed traders, dealers and specialists set wider quotes than they otherwise would. These costs (exploitation of the uninformed and wider bid-ask spreads) are avoided in a call market.

The Disadvantages of Temporal Consolidation in a Nonelectronic Environment

Accessibility. In a call market, investors can trade only at those times when the market is called (typically once or twice per day). Therefore, access to the call market is limited. "Accessibility" is different from "immediacy." Traders do not always have access to a continuous trading system (the market is closed overnight, on weekends, and for holidays). Immediacy refers to the ability of buyers and sellers to meet quickly when the market is open. Time is of the essence when an investor's trading decision depends on the execution that has been or might be realized for another order. Arbitrage between securities is not riskless when transactions cannot be made instantaneously and, with limited access to the market, transactions cannot be made in quick succession in different stocks. Because arbitrage transactions between securities improve the quality of pricing in the markets, the extent to which these transactions are curtailed by limited accessibility in call market trading is a disadvantage of the system. The short-period price movements that are arbitraged, however, underscore the inefficiency of continuous trading, which argues in favor of order batching.

Limited accessibility to the market is costly with regard to other interdependent trading decisions. Call markets typically trade the list of stocks sequentially (typically in alphabetical order). Therefore, it may not be possible for a buy or a sell decision to be based on the result of trading another stock. For example, if an investor wants to sell Xerox common and buy American Airlines common, and the market for American Airlines is called first, the size of the investor's purchase cannot be related to the price realized from the sale in the same trading session.

The Dissemination of Floor Information.   In call markets, traders present on the floor of an exchange hear prices called out and have an opportunity to state the specific number of shares they wish to transact at each price. Consequently, they can buy or sell the precise number of shares desired at a price. For such traders, call markets imply no informational disadvantage vis-à-vis continuous trading. This is not the case for traders who, not being present on the exchange floor, have no advance indication of what the next price will be. To date, this has remained one of the most fundamental limitations of a call market system. The problem can be overcome, however, with electronic technology (see Chapter 10).

Transaction Uncertainty.   The posted quotes of some traders give other traders an option in continuous trading that does not exist in call market trading: trades can be made with a high degree of certainty at the market quotes. Of course, order transmission is not instantaneous, and with continuous trading the quotes can change while the investor is communicating his or her market order to the exchange. However, the change is not likely to be large because order transmission is fast, and the affirmative obligation of the specialists keeps prices relatively stable for brief periods of time.

Reservation Price Effect.   The submission of reservation prices to a call market has an aggregate effect that no individual trader will take into account: this order placement strategy may itself contribute to the volatility of the transaction price. This effect is analyzed in the Appendix to this Chapter.

Why the Order Flow May Fragment

As discussed above, traders benefit from a market where orders are consolidated, trading priority rules are enforced, prices are set with reasonable accuracy, price movements are orderly, and trading is closely monitored. The superiority of such a market may not guarantee its existence, however. The reason is that traders individually may have an incentive to turn to off-board (satellite) markets.

Order flow may divert from a primary market because individuals do not take the public goods aspects of marketability services into account when they make their private trading decisions. If an individual believes his or her order will receive a better execution in market "B" than in another market "A," the order will be transmitted to market B even if provision of the public goods–type services is superior in market A. This can lead to problems: if enough orders are transmitted to market B instead of A, the quality of the public goods–type services provided by A will deteriorate, to the detriment of all.

Some alternative trading systems (we will refer to them generically as market B) currently extend the following guarantee to traders: "an order will execute in market B at the best price established in market A." Because market B's price is based only on the price set in market A, this policy is referred to as *parasitic pricing*. The customer who directs an order to market B benefits from the accuracy of the price established in market A and from the protection offered by the surveillance systems of market A. In addition, the limit order trader in market B has the opportunity for faster execution because the queue of orders may be shorter than in market A. All traders, of course, cannot receive a faster execution by switching to market B. Yogi Berra is quoted as having once said, "no one goes there anymore, it's too crowded." A corollary to Berra's law is of equivalent validity: everyone is now on the new queue, it's shorter.

Because market B does not provide the public goods-type services that A provides, it can operate at lower cost and can accordingly charge lower commissions than market A. Individuals thus have a private incentive to send their orders to market B. Collectively, however, they can all lose. Market A will provide less of the public good because it will receive less revenue due to its reduced order flow. Therefore, a rule that forces spatial consolidation is socially desirable.

The situation described above can occur if both market A and market B are continuous trading systems or if market A is continuous and market B is a call market without a price discovery mechanism (such as Instinet's Crossing Network). This situation will not arise if market A is a call market with a price discovery mechanism and market B is a continuous market, if prices in B are allowed to change as trading progresses.

A trader who selects the continuous market rather than the call when both are available demands immediacy/accessibility and is willing to pay the price (the bid-ask spread and more volatile, less accurate prices). Participants in the call are knowingly giving up accessibility for more accurate price discovery, anonymity, and lower trading costs. Thus, with both systems in place, a socially optimal amount of temporal consolidation may be achieved.

Therefore, reducing or eliminating the undesirable effects of currently existing call markets through proper system design will strengthen the competitive efficiency of the markets. Modern electronic technology in particular may contribute significantly to the efficiency of call market trading. This possibility is considered further in the next chapter.

Appendix—The Effect of Temporal Consolidation on the Prices of Orders and Trades

Order Determination

The downward sloping curves labeled B^N and B^R in Panel A of Figure 9A.1 show, respectively, the normal buy curve and the reservation buy curve of the investor. (Refer to Appendix A of Chapter 13 for the economic analysis pertaining to the normal and reservation curves.) The normal curve shows that if the investor knows the market clearing price will be P_1, he or she will want to buy Q_1 shares. The reservation curve shows that the reservation price of Q_1 shares is P^R. That is, P^R is the highest price the trader will pay rather than not obtain Q shares at all. To structure the call and continuous systems so as to obtain a meaningful *ceteris paribus* comparison under transaction price uncertainty:

1. Assume that the individual's buy curves and the clearing price he or she expects is the same for the two market regimes.

FIGURE 9A.1 *Contrast of an Investor's Order Placement Decision in Call Market and Continuous Market Environments. (a) At the Price P_1 the Investor Wants to Buy Q_1 Shares: the Reservation Price for Q_1 Shares Is P^R. (b) The Optimal Limit Order to Submit to a Call Market Is Illustrated by Point C; the Optimal Limit Order to Submit to a Continuous Market Is Illustrated by Point B*

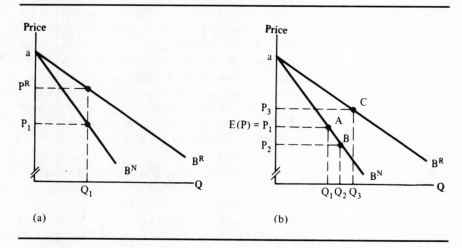

(a)   (b)

2. Let the expected price be $E(P)$ with $E(P) = P_1$, and allow for a small variance of price around $E(P)$.

3. Assume that the order submitted to the continuous market is placed on a limit order book. (See Chapter 13 for further discussion).

4. Transaction price uncertainty is the same in the two trading regimes in the sense that the probability of the clearing price achieving any particular value or better in the call market, equals the probability of a limit order executing at that price in the continuous market. (Recall that the investor in the continuous market will realize an execution if price falls enough in the market for his or her order to set the market quote, and if a counterpart market order then arrives.)

For this scenario, a point such as B on the normal buy curve represents an optimal order to submit to the continuous market, and a point such as C on the reservation buy curve represents an optimal order to submit to the call market.

Contrasting points A and B, we see that transaction price uncertainty in the continuous market has caused the investor to increase the size of the order, and to lower the order's price somewhat. This is because with transaction price uncertainty, the investor may submit an order to buy at a lower price solely on the chance that price will be less than $E(P)$ and that a desirable execution will be realized. Or, in continuous trading, the investor might under different conditions decrease the order size and increase its price. That is, changing the relationship between the expected price, the variance of price, and the intercept "a" of the investor's buy curve, could cause the price of the order to be higher and the size to be smaller than the price and size identified by point A. If the intercept parameter is sufficiently above $E(P)$, the investor will be eager to trade. In this case, rather than gambling on the price being better than expected, he or she will raise the price of the order (and decrease the order's size) to increase the probability that the order will indeed execute.

Contrasting points A and C, we see that transaction price uncertainty in a call market has caused the investor to increase both the size and the price of the order. Unlike the continuous market, this is always the case. The price increase is attributable to the order being picked from the reservation buy curve rather than from the normal buy curve. The intuitive explanation for the increased size of the order is the following. The protection the investor gains against transaction price uncertainty by placing the order at the (higher) reservation price allows the order to be moved down the reservation buy curve (price is lowered somewhat and the share size increased), so as to yield more consumer surplus if the clearing price turns out to be lower than expected.[8]

Market Buy and Sell Curves

Having contrasted the orders an individual would alternatively submit to a continuous market and to a call market, we can now show how temporally consolidating the order flow will affect the market's aggregate buy and sell order curves.

The process of aggregating orders to obtain the market buy curve is illustrated in Figure 9A.2 with reference to the normal buy curve. The individual orders, of course, execute sequentially as they arrive at the continuous market, and for that reason aggregating these orders is not of interest in and of itself. The aggregation shows the price and transaction volume that would be established in a call market if the change in the trading system had no effect on the order flow. Panel A shows the normal buy order curves for three different traders. The point identified on each of the curves shows

FIGURE 9A.2 *Aggregation of Individual Orders to Obtain the Market Buy Curve. (a) Individual Buy Order Curves and Order Points. (b) Aggregation of Individual Order Points*

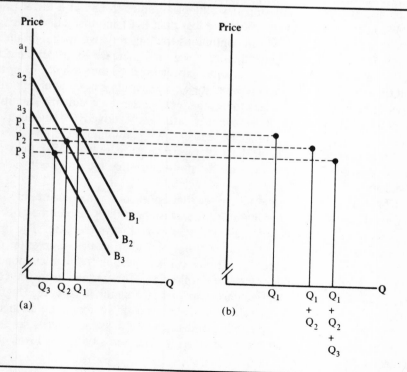

the order that each individual would write given the expected clearing price, the variance around the price, and a continuous market regime. Panel B shows the aggregation of these orders. At P_1, only the first trader submits an order, and the size of that order is Q_1. At P_2, the second trader also submits an order, and the aggregate order quantity is $Q_1 + Q_2$. At P_3, the third trader also submits an order, and the aggregate order quantity is $Q_1 + Q_2 + Q_3$. Individual sell orders are aggregated by a similar process. When the aggregation is done for a large number of traders, the process results in a set of market buy and sell order curves.

Now consider the aggregation of buy orders submitted to the call regime. To highlight the effect of the system, we accentuate the impact it has on the order flow by taking the variance of the transaction price about its mean to be very small. The aggregation process is the same, but the buy orders themselves are different. Specifically: (1) the buy prices will be greater than $E(P)$, and (2) orders written at prices in the neighborhood immediately above $E(P)$ will be for only a small number of shares.

The Inelasticity of Order Functions

Buy orders will not be submitted to the call market at a price less than $E(P)$ because we have assumed the transaction price is distributed tightly around $E(P)$. An order will be submitted at a price close to $E(P)$, only if the vertical difference between B^N and B^R is small at $E(P)$. Visual inspection of Figure 9A.1 shows that this vertical distance is less, the closer $E(P)$ is to the price intercept "a" of the demand curves. Consequently, an investor who submits an order at a reservation price only slightly above $E(P)$ will submit an order for a small number of shares. (This assumes that the buy curves are not highly elastic.)

Now assume a large (but bounded) set of buyers, all of whom view the same mean and variance of the transaction price. Let the buyers be distributed according to the price intercept parameter, "a," of their buy curves. (For simplicity, assume the slope of the buy order curve is the same for all buyers.) Let each buyer submit one order. Buyers for whom $a - E(P)$ is large will write an order at a relatively high price and for a relatively large number of shares; buyers for whom $a - E(P)$ is small will write an order at a price close to $E(P)$, and the order will be for a relatively small number of shares. Aggregating these buy orders according to the procedure depicted by Figure 9A.2 gives the buy order function for the call market. This is the curve labeled "Buy" in Figure 9A.3.

The important characteristic of the market buy curve is that it becomes increasingly inelastic as price decreases in the neighborhood immediately above $E(P)$. As the price is lowered, more investor orders are included in the aggregate demand for shares but, as we have seen, the share size of

FIGURE 9A.3 *Buy Order Function for a Call Market*

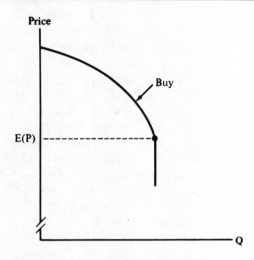

the marginal orders becomes very small. With a *bounded* distribution of investors, the number of investors submitting buy orders as price falls in the range above $E(P)$ cannot increase rapidly enough to reverse the effect of the size of each trader's order becoming smaller.[9]

The Market Clearing Price

Assume that the distribution of sellers is symmetric with the distribution of buyers. That is, for every i^{th} buyer with a specific $a_i - E(P)$, there exists a jth seller with an $E(P) - a_j$ of identical magnitude. The resulting market buy and sell curves are labeled "Buy" and "Sell" in Figure 9A.4.

The sell curve is a mirror image of the buy curve around the line at $E(P)$. This is because in this example the distributions of buyers and sellers are symmetrical. For the symmetrical distributions, the market clearing price, P^*, equals $E(P)$, as shown in Figure 9A.4. There is, however, no reason for the distributions of buyers and sellers to be symmetrical.

Figure 9A.5 shows an alternative configuration where the buy orders more than offset the comparable sell orders [because the values of $a_i - E(P)$ tend to be larger than the counterpart values of $E(P) - a_j$]. In Figure 9A.5, the clearing price, P^*, is greater than $E(P)$. If buyers and sellers are alternatively distributed so that the sell orders more than offset the buy orders, then P^* is less than $E(P)$.

FIGURE 9A.4 *For Symmetrical Distributions of Buy and Sell Orders, the Call Market Clearing Price P* Equals the Expected Clearing Price E(P)*

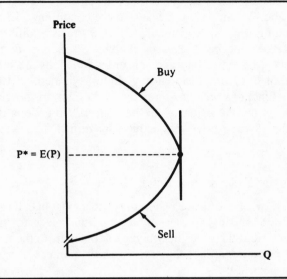

FIGURE 9A.5 *For Asymmetrical Distributions of Buy and Sell Orders, the Call Market Clearing Price P* Does Not Equal the Expected Clearing Price E(P)*

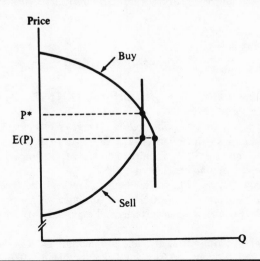

The call market system will affect the individual orders, but not the clearing price if buyers and sellers are symmetrically distributed (with regard to the intercept parameter of their buy/sell curves) and if the traders have homogeneous and unbiased expectations of the clearing price (that is, if E(P) is indeed the equilibrium price). Because these conditions will not generally hold, the clearing price will generally differ from its equilibrium value in the call market, as indeed it does in continuous trading. Further, the fact that the market's aggregate buy and sell order functions are inelastic in the neighborhood of E(P), implies that any slight asymmetry between the buy and sell order functions will have a magnified effect on the clearing price. Therefore, as the configuration of the buy and sell functions changes from call to call, the clearing price may exhibit magnified fluctuations from call to call.

Eliminating the Reservation Price Effect

A nonnegligible amount of price uncertainty must exist in call market trading when traders submit single orders at reservation prices to the call. This volatility results from the order flow being endogenous to the trading system and from the particular effect that existing call market arrangements have on the trading decision.

The volatility results from the submission of reservation prices and can be eliminated by inducing traders to submit orders from their ordinary demand curves. An investor submits a point from his or her reservation curve when submitting *just one* order to a specific call. If multiple orders are submitted (or if an order's size is adjusted as a call proceeds), prices closer to the investor's ordinary buy or sell curve will be selected. Therefore, the reservation price effect on volatility is dampened if investors submit multiple (scaled) orders.

Suggested Reading

Bloch, E., and Schwartz, R. "The Great Debate over NYSE Rule 390." *Journal of Portfolio Management,* Fall 1978.

Bloch, E., and Schwartz, R., eds. *Impending Changes for Securities Markets: What Role for the Exchange?* Greenwich, CT: JAI Press, 1979.

Cohen, K., and Conroy, R. "An Empirical Study of the Impact of Rule 19c-3." *Journal of Law and Economics,* April 1990.

Cohen, K., Conroy, R., and Maier, S. "Order Flow and the Quality of the Market." In *Market Making and the Changing Structure of the Securities Industry,* Y. Amihud, T. Ho, and R. Schwartz, eds. Lexington, MA: Lexington Books, 1985.

Cohen, K., Maier, S., Schwartz, R., and Whitcomb, D. *The Microstructure of Securities Markets.* Englewood Cliffs, NJ: Prentice Hall, 1986.

Freund, W. "Electronic Trading and Linkages in International Equity Markets." Paper given at the American Economic Association Meetings, New York, December, 1988.

Garbade, K., and Silber, W. "Structural Organization of Secondary Markets: Clearing Frequency, Dealer Activity and Liquidity Risk." *Journal of Finance*, June 1979.

Garbade, K., and Silber, W. "Dominant and Satellite Markets: A Study of Dually-Traded Securities." *Review of Economics and Statistics*, August 1979.

Hamilton, J. "Electronic Market Linkages and the Distribution of Order Flow: The Case of Off-Board Trading of NYSE-listed Stocks." In *The Challenge of Information Technology for the Securities Markets*, H. Lucas and R. Schwartz, eds. Homewood, IL: Dow Jones-Irwin, 1989.

Ho, T., Schwartz, R., and Whitcomb, D. "The Trading Decision and Market Clearing under Transaction Price Uncertainty." *Journal of Finance*, March 1985.

Mendelson, H. "Consolidation, Fragmentation, and Market Performance." *Journal of Financial and Quantitative Analysis*, June 1987.

Seligman, J. "The Future of the National Market System." *Journal of Corporation Law*, Fall 1984.

Notes

1. *The Wall Street Journal,* 17 July 1980, p. 3.
2. U.S. General Accounting Office, *Securities Trading,* March 1990, (GAO/GDD-90-52).
3. See K. Cohen, R. Conroy, and S. Maier, "Order Flow and the Quality of the Market," in Y. Amihud, T. Ho, and R. Schwartz, eds. *Market Making and the Changing Structure of the Securities Industry.* Lexington, MA: Lexington Books, 1985.
4. Ibid.
5. *Elwes Committee Report,* May 1989, p. 14.
6. Touche Ross Report, "Maintaining a Central Equities Market," report to International Stock Exchange, London, May 1989, p. 23.
7. Touche Ross Report, "Maintaining a Central Equities Market," p. 26, May 1989.
8. For further discussion, see T. Ho, R. Schwartz, and D. Whitcomb, "The Trading Decision and Market Clearing Under Transaction Price Uncertainty," *Journal of Finance,* March 1985.
9. Ibid.

10

Electronic Call Market
Trading: A Proposal

An electronic system can mimic one, or a combination of, three trading modes: a continuous order-driven market, a continuous quote-driven market, or an order-driven call market. (Examples of used and proposed equity trading systems are described in Chapter 5.) Selection among these modes must be made with reference to the major users of the system and to their particular needs. For this reason, the chapter first considers the growing domination in the marketplace of institutional investors.

We propose an electronic call market as the appropriate facility for handling the institutional order flow. Call market trading is discussed in the section called "Temporal Consolidation: Call Market Trading" in Chapter 9. In brief, the advantages are as follows. Knowing when a market will be called helps buyers and sellers to meet in time, and consolidating orders makes large traders less dominant in the market. A variety of contingent orders can be used most effectively in an electronic call to accommodate the negotiation of block trades and to minimize market impact. In general, order handling and trade execution costs are lower in a call market, and the bid-ask spread is eliminated.

Moreover, price discovery is facilitated and price stability can be enhanced. Because all orders execute at the same time, at the same price, and under the same conditions, the procedure is fairer to all participants. And, because all orders that execute do so at a single price, traders who have posted priced orders gain protection from being exploited by better-informed agents when share values suddenly jump. Consequently, a single-price environment encourages traders to place limit orders, and thus to supply liquidity as well as to demand it.

To date, however, call market trading has suffered from two major limitations: access to the market has been limited (to one or two calls a day), and participants away from the trading floor have received no indications about current market prices while the call is taking place. Both of these can be ameliorated with the use of electronic technology. Calls can be held more frequently when computerized, and information can be widely distributed to participants regardless of geographic location. And fortuitously, some of the disadvantages of electronic trading can be overcome by mimicking a call market rather than a continuous market.

Further, it is not suggested that continuous trading be eliminated, but that electronic call market trading be integrated with continuous trading, so that traders may be free to select the environment that best fits their personal needs.

Catering to the Institutional Market

The major customers today are the institutional investors and, to be success-ful, an electronic system must cater to their needs. Total assets of domestic institutional investors rose from $89.6 billion or 31% of GNP in 1950, to $4,937.1 billion or 94.3% of GNP in 1989. The proportion of these assets that are held in equities has increased from 10% in 1950 to nearly 30% in 1989. At year-end 1989, domestic institutions held equity assets equal to roughly 50% of total NYSE capitalization. Institutions and member firms together now account for over 70% of the share volume on the NYSE. Block trades (10,000 shares or more), a widely accepted proxy for institutional ac-tivity, have grown from 3.1% of NYSE share volume in 1965, to 51.5% in 1989.

Similar changes have occurred in Tokyo and London. On the Tokyo Stock Exchange, share ownership by domestic financial institutions has risen from 18.2% of outstanding shares in 1952 to 45.6% in 1989. Financial institu-tions together with member firms and nonfinancial businesses accounted for 76.7% of total share volume in Japan in 1989, while on London's Inter-national Stock Exchange, domestic and foreign institutions accounted for 73.3% of trading by value in June 1989 (see Table 10.1).

Institutionalization has fundamentally altered the way in which orders are written, submitted to the market, and translated into trades. The suit-ability of systems such as the NYSE and the OTC market, both of which were designed to handle a retail order flow, needs to be reconsidered. The importance of three changes in particular that have been brought about by institutionalization must be underscored: (1) the growth of average trade size, (2) indexation, and (3) the growth of the upstairs market.

Trade Size

The portfolios held by major institutional investors are enormous. In 1989, the top 200 defined benefit pension funds together had equity assets of

TABLE 10.1   *Trading Activity in New York (NYSE), Tokyo (TSE), and London (ISE), 1989 (by type of investor; % of volume for NYSE and TSE; % of value for ISE)*

	Nonmember Institutions	Member Firms	Retail/Other
NYSE	46.2	25.7	28.1
TSE	53.4[a]	23.3	23.3
ISE[b]	73.3[c]	n.a.	23.6[d]

[a] Includes shares traded by foreigners and nonfinancial businesses.
[b] June 1989 only.
[c] Includes shares traded by domestic and foreign institutions.
[d] Includes domestic and foreign individuals.
Sources: "Investor Activity Report," Securities Industry Association, May 1990; TSE Fact Book, 1990; and "Market Structure: Transaction Survey Results," International Stock Exchange, July–September 1989.

$542.4 billion. Thus, on average, these funds each managed $2.7 billion worth of equity.[1] Even if a $2.7 billion portfolio is diversified equally across 100 issues, substantial positions must be held in the individual stocks: 540,000 shares of each issue, at an average price of $50 per share.

The large positions give rise to large orders that are "worked" on the trading floor or negotiated in the upstairs market. If automated trade execution is to be successful, it must handle the negotiations with at least the same facility that characterizes direct human interaction, either face-to-face or by telephone.

Indexation

The difficulty portfolio managers have had outperforming benchmark market averages is one of several factors contributing to increased indexing or passive investment on the part of institutions. Such investment strategies now account for a substantial portion of institutionally managed assets. A *Pensions and Investments* survey of the top 50 index fund managers located $277.7 billion in indexed funds as of May 1990.[2] Salomon Brothers estimated that, as of December 1988, $177.8 billion, or 25% of pension fund (ERISA) assets were indexed to the S&P.[3] Current estimates are that up to 30% of total institutional equity portfolios are indexed.[4]

Indexation leads to commoditization. *Commoditization* means that equity issues are selected with reference to statistical estimates of their risk and return attributes, and without regard to other "fundamental" information related to the future value of each stock. Stocks with similar risk-return measures are treated as perfect substitutes for one another, just as agricultural commodities of a particular variety sell at the same price, regardless of the particular farms on which they are grown. With commoditization, it is risk that is priced in the marketplace, and all issues with the same risk sell at the same price, as is the case under the assumptions of the Capital Asset Pricing Model. A consequence of commoditization is that institutional investors typically trade baskets of stocks, for which they have downward-sloping demand.

With downward-sloping demand, asset prices must be determined in the marketplace by the interaction of the buy and sell orders of traders. An electronic system, to be socially desirable, must be able to establish prices that are as accurate, given underlying buy and sell desires, as those found in our current, nonelectronic trading markets.

The Growth of the Upstairs Market

Trade negotiation in the upstairs market is described in Chapter 6 in the section called "Negotiated Block Trading." The discussion illustrates the extent to which institutional traders need to receive market information from others, but seek to transmit only minimal information themselves. Providing an arena where adequate information may be obtained is a primary objective of the system set forth below.*

Structuring an Electronic Market

Order Handling in an Electronic Call Market

Institutional orders must be carefully handled because (a) prices signal information, (b) transaction volume signals information, and (c) large orders generate adverse price effects simply because of their size. Traders, seeking floor information before placing their orders and not wishing their own orders to signal information to others, generally do not enter orders into an electronic system until just before trading begins. This is clearly the case for an electronic continuous market such as CATS that provides a "warm up" period before trading starts with an opening call.

Three types of orders can easily be used in an electronic call to facilitate an environment where (a) sufficient information can be transmitted to traders, (b) traders will not hold back their orders because of informational signaling

---

* Portions of this section, "Catering to the Institutional Market," have been adapted from Schwartz and Shapiro (1990), used with permission.

and market power effects, and (c) traders can be induced to enter their orders earlier in the "warm up" period that precedes the market call. These types of orders are *scaled orders, percentage orders,* and *cross-price contingent orders*.

Scaled Orders.   Scaled orders are orders written at multiple prices. They are desirable because transaction prices are uncertain. The trader simply specifies the alternative number of shares he or she wishes to buy or to sell at alternative prices, conditioning the quantity at each price on the information that would be signaled if that price were to be the clearing price.

Scaled orders are not without cost in continuous trading. For example, assume a stock has last traded at 50 ⅛, and that an investor would like to buy 1,000 shares at 50, or 1,100 at 49⅞, or 1,200 at 49¾, and so on down to 1,800 shares at 49. To focus on the extremes, the investor could submit a fully scaled order (1,000 at 50, 100 at 49⅞, 100 at 49¾, . . . , 100 at 49) or a single order to buy 1,800 at 49. The cost of selecting the fully scaled order is the higher amount paid for intramarginal purchases if price actually does fall to 49 in the continuous market. Thus, if the possibility of the price decrease is deemed large enough by the investor, the single order point (buy 1,800 at 49) should be submitted and the intermediate order points should not be disclosed.

In a call market, on the other hand, the intramarginal orders all execute at the common clearing price. Consequently, the intramarginal cost does not exist in call market trading.

Percentage Orders.   A percentage order states how much of an order will be activated based upon trading volume in the issue. For example, with a 50% percentage order of 100,000 shares, 10,000 shares of the order are activated if total trading volume, including the part of the percentage order that executes, equals or exceeds 20,000. Percentage orders are currently used in the NYSE's continuous market environment. They are particularly suitable for use in an electronic call market.

To simplify the operations of an electronic call, let us assume that the minimum size of a percentage order is 10,000 shares (a block), and that percentage orders can only be entered in integer multiples of 10,000. Thus any "odd lot" portion of a block order (for example, 6,000 shares of a 26,000 share block) must be entered as a regular limit order. Additionally, each percentage order is interpreted as a maximum percent; actual percentages may be below the maximum specified because orders are only executed in integer multiples of 10,000 shares.

Use of a percentage order mitigates the impact an order might have on a market clearing price simply because of its size. Percentage orders also cope with the informational signaling problem. For one thing, the order is not activated (and thus is not revealed to the market) unless it is sufficiently small relative to the market. Secondly, the trader who wishes to buy or to sell more at a price when volume is heavy because of any informational signal that volume conveys, can do so automatically with the use of a percentage order. Thus, like a scaled order, a percentage order reduces the trader's need for prior information while suppressing the informational signal that his or her own order might convey. Specifying a percentage parameter, like scaling an order, effectively puts order handling on automatic pilot.

Cross-Price Contingent Orders.   A cross-price contingent order also puts order handling on automatic pilot by relating the size of an order for one stock to the price of another stock or basket of stocks such as a market index. For example, the order might state, "buy 10,000 shares of XYZ common at $50 or less if the S&P 500 index is at 320 or higher." Orders contingent on the prices of other securities are useful for a trader seeking to rebalance a portfolio, where the price at which one issue is to be bought depends on the price at which another issue is sold. Or, orders conditioned on a market index are useful for an individual who wishes to trade by limit order on company specific fundamentals without being exposed to adverse marketwide informational change.[5]

Cross-price contingent orders can be used to create what Beja and Hakansson[6] call "joint orders." Beja and Hakansson note that joint orders may enable an economically efficient allocation of shares (across investors for a set of securities) to be realized in a single round of trading. They also write

. . . suppose an investor considers two assets to be essentially equivalent for his portfolio purposes, and wishes to buy the cheaper of the two. If limit orders for each asset are allowed to depend only on the price of that asset and not on the price of the other, there is no combination of limit orders that will achieve the desired objective in one round. . . . This gives a tremendous advantage to 'the man on the spot,' who does not have to rely on limit orders and can react personally to prices immediately as they become effective.

Cross-price contingent orders as well as percentage orders can in principle be handled in both continuous and call market environments. However, their advantage in a call environment is that they facilitate the achievement of simultaneous, general equilibrium solutions.

Price Discovery in an Electronic Call Market

A call market is an explicit price discovery mechanism that allows the batching and execution of all eligible orders at a single point in time. At the time of an auction, prices for the array of submitted orders (both market and limit) are compared electronically to determine the single price that balances buys and sells. All higher bids and lower offers are filled at the auction price. This price is the desired price, given the submitted orders.

The call market procedure further enhances price discovery by encouraging "better" orders. Because orders execute at the clearing price rather than at their own price limits, the placement of limit orders and scaled limit orders is encouraged. This is because limit order traders do not risk being "bagged" by informational traders as they do in continuous trading, and because all trades are executed at the common clearing price. The use of scaled orders is particularly desirable for the operations of a call market: multipoint orders are in closer alignment with the investor's demand curve, whereas single point orders are more apt to be at reservation prices, and the submission of reservation prices can cause the clearing price to be more volatile, as discussed in the Appendix to Chapter 9.

Taking Account of Percentage Orders

The procedure used for determining the clearing price at an electronic call can be illustrated with the use of a numerical example. Assume the computer is assessing the balance between buy and sell orders for XYZ shares at the price of 50. The total number of buy orders at 50 and higher can be calculated and then contrasted with the total number of sell orders at 50 and lower. If the total number of buy orders exceeds the total number of sell orders, the procedure is repeated at the next higher price. If the total number of buy orders is less than the total number of sell orders, the procedure is repeated at the next lower price. The search is continued until the price is found that best balances the total number of shares sought for purchase and the total number offered for sale.

We can illustrate the calculation of order size when percentage orders are used with the following example. Let 50 be the first price assessed at a call, and assume the following buy orders:

	Shares
Market buy orders	20,000
Limit buy orders at 50 and higher	30,000
Individual percentage buy orders at 50 and higher:	
40% order	40,000
25% order	100,000
10% order	50,000
10% order	20,000
10% order	10,000

A simple computational procedure can be used to determine that, if 50 is indeed the clearing price, the total buy volume is 150,000 shares. The breakdown is as follows:

	Shares	Percent of Total Buy Volume @ 50
Market orders	20,000	
Regular limit orders	30,000	
40% limit order	40,000	26.6 < 40
25% limit order	30,000	20.0 < 25
10% limit order	10,000	6.7 < 10
10% limit order	10,000	6.7 < 10
10% limit order	10,000	6.7 < 10
Total buy volume @ 50	150,000	

All 40,000 shares of the 40% order execute because the block is less than 40% of the total buy volume at 50 (150,000 shares). Only 30,000 shares of the 25% order execute (the next largest execution, 40,000 shares, would be 26.6% of the total, which would violate the percentage parameter for the order). 10,000 shares of each of the three 10% limit orders execute (20,000 shares is 13.3% of the total, which would violate the percentage parameters for the first two orders, and the last order is for only 10,000 shares).

The computer would similarly determine the total sell volume at 50. If 50 is indeed the clearing price, then total sells would equal total buys and the percentage parameters on the individual orders would be satisfied. If buys exceed sells or if sells exceed buys, the next higher or the next lower price would be assessed until the clearing price is found.

The procedure regarding percentage orders can be understood intuitively. Institutional investors are concerned about adversely affecting market prices because of the size of their orders. The standard response to this problem has been to negotiate the price of an order given its size. When traders on both sides of the market submit percentage orders, they are effectively negotiating the size of their orders at a given price. That is, buy orders at a price are increasingly activated as the number of shares offered for sale at that price increases, and the sell orders at that price are increasingly activated as the number of shares sought for purchase increases. In practice, the computational demands made by this iterative process make it difficult to program directly. Fortunately, a simpler computational procedure can be used, because the buy and sell sides of the market may first be assessed separately and then matched. Discontinuities in share volume may create a minor problem that can be handled as follows. If due to discontinuities exact clearing is not possible, transaction volume is set equal to the light side of the market and the number of orders on the heavy side of the market is reduced as follows. All percentage orders on the heavy side of the market are reduced if their percentage constraints relative to the light side of the market are violated. Any additional required reduction is achieved through pro rata allocation of orders at the clearing price exactly (all intramarginal orders execute in full).

Taking Account of Cross-Price Contingent Orders

The computational requirements to process orders that are contingent on the prices of different assets would make extremely heavy demands on a trading system's central computer. Fortunately, an alternative exists. If some traders submit their orders before a market is called, then other traders are able to observe the *indicated* clearing prices for the set of securities. In addition, the trading system should display an index of the indicated clearing prices of shares in the system during the precall period. Programs run by the individual trading desks can then be used to indicate the specific cross-price contingent orders. Although the results would only approximate an ideal one-trading-round solution, the approximation would be adequate if the number of cross-price contingent orders is small, and if other orders are submitted sufficiently in advance.

Any trader using a scaled and percentage order, but not a cross-price contingent order, should not be reluctant to submit an order early. This is because that trader need not receive an informational signal (the order is on automatic pilot) and need not fear transmitting an informational signal (the percentage feature keeps enough of the order hidden). Nevertheless, an inducement for early order submission may be required. This can be achieved by making the commission smaller, the earlier an order is placed. Traders using cross-price contingent orders would then pay a higher commission and receive the price information they seek, while others are compensated for making that information available by being charged a lower commission. One proposed trading system, SPA*works,* will in fact charge a commission that increases exponentially as a call is approached.

Resolving the Disadvantages of Call Market Trading

Certain disadvantages of traditional call market trading are identified in Chapter 9. These are largely resolved by computerizing the call market.

Accessibility. Electronic calls can be held as frequently as desired. Additionally, continuous trading can be preserved and integrated with the electronic call.

Dissemination of Floor Information. This is an advantage of the electronic call market. Moreover, it gives all players equal access to the market and so establishes a level playing field.

Transaction Uncertainty. This uncertainty can be mitigated by displaying indicated clearing prices before the call is held. Moreover, the risk of buying (selling) at a relatively high (low) price during a trading session is eliminated because all crossing orders execute at the same price.

Reservation Price Effect. This effect is mitigated by encouraging the placement of scaled orders in the electronic call.

Integration of Call and Continuous Trading

The electronic call market should be integrated with a continuous auction market. The electronic call should be used at least three or four times during a trading day: to open the market, at twelve noon, to close the market, and once during the overnight period for globally traded issues.

The Opening Call

The NYSE currently opens the market in each of its listed securities with a multilateral trade that is a form of call market trading. However, participants away from the floor do not see the book as it fills up during the preopening period, and many of the large orders are entered by floor traders rather than electronically (see Chapter 2). Consequently, the NYSE's call market is not as efficient as it might be, and many professional traders choose to wait for the market to open and then submit their orders (typically within the first half hour of trading). We propose that the NYSE's opening call be improved, along the lines discussed in this chapter.

The Twelve Noon Call

The belief is common that, once a market has opened, the competitive flow of buy and sell orders enables market clearing prices to track theoretically desirable, equilibrium values. This may not be the case, however. Orders are strategically placed, they are responsive to the signals clearing prices convey, and price discovery in the continuous market can be perturbed, particularly at times of stress. In view of this, we propose that trading be halted in the continuous market at 11:55 A.M., and then reactivated at twelve noon using the electronic call market. The five-minute halt would provide an automatic, time-triggered circuit breaker that would activate the price discovery mechanism and restore orderliness to the market under stressful conditions. But the five-minute pause would be brief enough not to impair access to the market unduly, even under normal conditions.

The Closing Call

Closing prices have particular importance because of their use for various assessment and other legal purposes. We propose that trading switch from a continuous to a call market mode at the end of each trading day to facilitate the discovery of more accurate closing prices. To achieve this, the continuous market should halt operations at 3:55 P.M., orders should be batched for five minutes, and then the closing call should be held. Along with facilitating price discovery, the closing call would enable market-on-close orders to execute at the close exactly.

The Overnight Call

The overnight call would facilitate trading in the less liquid overnight market and would economize on the use of labor during the after-hours period. As noted in Chapter 5, the NYSE is in fact planning to use the call market mode for its after-hours trading.

Overall Benefits

Instituting these four calls while retaining continuous trading will give traders the alternatives they need to handle their orders properly. Those who do not demand immediacy can avoid the costs by waiting and trading in one of the four market calls. Those who do demand immediacy can obtain it by paying the necessary price. And for the broader community, more accurate and stable prices will be established. We turn to the stabilization of prices in a call market environment in Chapter 11.

Suggested Reading

Amihud, Y., Ho, T., and Schwartz, R., eds. *Market Making and the Changing Structure of the Securities Industry.* Lexington, MA: Lexington Books, 1985.

Amihud, Y., and Mendelson, H. "An Integrated Computerized Trading System." In Amihud, Ho, and Schwartz (1985). Lexington, MA: Lexington Books, 1985.

Bloch, E., and Schwartz, R. eds. *Impending Changes for Securities Markets: What Role for the Exchange?* Greenwich, CT: JAI Press, 1979.

Cohen, K., Maier, S., Schwartz, R., and Whitcomb, D. *The Microstructure of Securities Markets,* Englewood Cliffs, NJ: Prentice Hall, 1986.

Cohen, K., and Schwartz, R. "An Electronic Call Market: Its Design and Desirability." In Lucas and Schwartz (1989). Homewood, IL: Dow Jones-Irwin, 1989.

Lucas, H., and Schwartz, R. eds. *The Challenge of Information Technology for the Securities Markets: Liquidity, Volatility, and Global Trading.* Homewood, IL: Dow Jones-Irwin, 1989.

Mendelson, M. *From Automated Quotes to Automated Trading.* Bulletin No. 80–82, NYU Graduate School of Business Administration, Institute of Finance, March 1972.

Mendelson, M., and Peake, J. "The ABCs of Trading on a National Market System." *Financial Analysts Journal,* September–October 1979.

Mendelson, M., Peake, J., and Williams, R. "Toward a Modern Exchange: The Peake-Mendelson-Williams Proposal for an Electronically Assisted Auction Market." In Bloch and Schwartz (1979). Greenwich, CT: JAI Press, 1979.

Miller, M. "Index Arbitrage and Volatility." In the NYSE Panel Report, *Market Volatility and Investor Confidence.* New York Stock Exchange, Inc. June 1990.

Peake, J., Mendelson, M., and Williams, R. "Black Monday: Market Structure and Market-Making." In Lucas and Schwartz (1989). Homewood, IL: Dow Jones-Irwin, 1989.

Schwartz, R., and Shapiro, J. "The Challenge of Institutionalization for the Equity Markets." In *Institutional Investors: Challenges and Responsibilities,* Arnold W. Sametz, ed. Homewood, IL: Dow Jones-Irwin, 1991, forthcoming.

Sheeline, W. "Who Needs the Stock Exchange?" *Fortune,* 9 November 1990.

Wunsch, R. S. "Market Innovations." Paper delivered at meetings of the Institute for Quantitative Research in Finance, Colorado Springs, October 1987.

Notes

1. *Pensions & Investments,* 22 January 1990.
2. *Pensions and Investments,* August 6, 1990.
3. "Global Equity Market Review and Outlook: 1988–1989," Salomon Brothers, Inc.
4. W. Sheeline, "Who Needs the Stock Exchange?" *Fortune,* 9 November 1990.
5. Also see M. Miller, "Index Arbitrage and Volatility," in the NYSE Panel Report, *Market Volatility and Investor Confidence.* New York Stock Exchange, Inc., June 1990.
6. A. Beja and N. Hakansson, "From Orders to Trades: Some Alternative Market Mechanisms," in *Impending Changes for Securities Markets: What Role for the Exchanges?* E. Bloch and R. Schwartz, eds. Greenwich, CT: JAI Press, 1979, p. 148.

11

Stabilization of Stock Prices

The inherent short-term instability of stock market prices makes the systems, procedures, and protocols instituted to facilitate trading and to provide a fair and orderly market of paramount importance.* In recent years, the need for a mechanism to stabilize stock prices, both at times of particular stress and under normal trading conditions, has been widely recognized. Such a mechanism would alleviate public concern about excess volatility and could lower the cost of capital for listed companies.

The only effective way to stabilize a market is to commit capital to market making. The commitment must be substantial, and funds injected into the market to keep prices from plummeting should not be subject to rapid withdrawal at a later date if market makers are threatened with a shortage of capital and/or seek to rebalance their portfolios. With regard to the crash in 1987, the Brady report notes that 13 specialist firms "without buying power on October 19 appear to have increased their positions slightly more than average through October 19, and decreased their positions slightly more rapidly than average thereafter."[1]

The capital required for an adequate provision of liquidity is beyond that which most specialist and dealer firms currently command. Nevertheless, a stabilization fund that is established for a company may be small relative to the total value of the company's shares. This is because asset markets are thin on the margin. That is, there are not a lot of orders on the book or on the trading floor. Therefore, a relatively small purchase or sale could reduce short-run price fluctuations appreciably. We recommend that a fund be established. The chapter first describes the fund, and then proposes that they be established by the listed corporations.

---

* This chapter is adapted from R. Schwartz, "A Proposal to Stabilize Stock Prices," *The Journal of Portfolio Management*, Fall 1988, and R. Schwartz, Reply to Comment by G. Jarrell and P. Seguin on "A Proposal to Stabilize Stock Prices," *The Journal of Portfolio Management*, Winter 1990; used with permission.

The Economic Framework

The chapter first considers how institutions may stabilize prices by buying shares in a falling market and by selling them in a rising market. These stabilization transactions require the establishment of a fund for a company. We recommend that the intensity of the stabilization effort be determined by the issuing company and that the company supply the required capital.

Demand and Supply of Shares

Consider a stabilization fund that has been established for a listed company, for example, the XYZ Corp. The fund would buy XYZ shares in a falling market and would issue XYZ shares in a rising market to soften the impact of any change in market demand. With reference to Figure 11.1, we can see how this will dampen the price swings for XYZ shares.

If the market's demand to hold XYZ shares is the curve labeled D_1 and if N_1 shares are outstanding, the market-determined price per share is P_1. If market demand is the curve labeled D_2 and if the number of shares is fixed at N_1, share price is P_3. However, if the number of shares outstanding is N_2, when demand is given by D_2, share price is the intermediate value, P_2.

By appropriately buying and selling shares as price falls and rises, the stabilization fund is effectively adjusting the number of shares that are publicly held. In Figure 11.1, points 1 and 2 lie on an upward sloping curve labeled N. This curve shows how the number of shares outstanding is

FIGURE 11.1 *Price Determination for Shares of XYZ Corp*

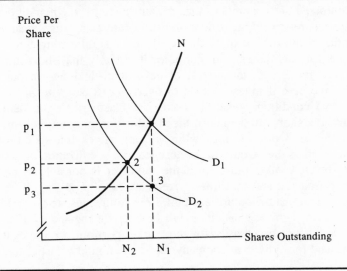

adjusted by the fund as the price of shares changes. The equation we use to describe the curve is the following:

$$N = gP^S \qquad (11.1)$$

where P is the price per share, g is a location parameter that depends on the initial share price and number of shares outstanding, and S is a parameter that expresses the intensity of the stabilization effort. The parameter g may be simply adjusted for stock dividends, splits, reverse splits, and share repurchase or new share issuance for non-stabilization purposes.

The Price Elasticity of Demand

The success of a stabilization program depends on the demand response of the market. If changing the number of shares outstanding would not, in and of itself, affect the total value of shares, the program will stabilize share prices while leaving the total value of shares to be determined entirely by the location of the market's demand curve to hold shares.

The issuance or purchase of shares by a stabilization fund is not equivalent to a stock split or reverse split, however, and hence might not cause a proportional price change. As shares are purchased or issued in the marketplace, the resulting price change will reflect the market's willingness to relinquish or to absorb these shares. The less price-responsive the market's demand for a company's stock, the more price must change for additional shares to be absorbed or relinquished by the market. Therefore, the procedure will be more effective (and less costly) when the market's demand is less responsive. (See the Chapter 11 appendix for further discussion.)

Because of the relative paucity of orders on the book and on the trading floor (compared to the number of shares outstanding), the market demand to hold shares is relatively inelastic in the short-run. Long-run demand curves, on the other hand, may be quite elastic (shares of similar companies are good substitutes for each other). Furthermore, it is likely that short run demand curves shift more with the arrival of news than do long-run curves (this would be the case if investors tend to overreact to news in the short run). If these two conditions generally hold (less elastic short-run demand and more unstable short-run demand), the stabilization program will on average dampen short-run price swings while leaving prices free to adjust in the long run much as they would in the absence of a stabilization program. This desirable result would hold even if the stabilizer is not able to distinguish between permanent and transitory price changes.

To the extent that the securities of different companies are good substitutes for each other, demand elasticities will be high for the shares of individual companies but not necessarily for the market portfolio in aggregate. Even if the demand for individual company shares is infinitely elastic, the demand for the market portfolio is downward sloping (see Chapter 12). Thus, the market in aggregate can be stabilized if stabilization funds are widely adopted for the individual securities.

The Stabilization Procedure

The Stabilization Formula

The parameter S is an elasticity that describes the supply responsiveness of the number of shares outstanding to change in the market price per share. The parameter S can be shown to be an elasticity by taking the derivative of N in Equation 11.1 with respect to P, multiplying both sides by P, and then dividing both sides by N. Thus we can write

$$S = \frac{\text{Order size}}{\text{Shares outstanding}} \bigg/ \frac{\text{Price change}}{\text{Price}} \qquad (11.2)$$

Equation 11.2 shows that the stabilization parameter is the ratio of two other ratios: (1) order size relative to issue size, and (2) the size of a price change relative to an issue's share price. This relationship expresses the relative intensity of a stabilization effort. For example, if S is set at 0.02, the fund always stands prepared to buy 0.1% of the shares outstanding if the share price decreases by 5%, or to increase the number of shares outstanding by 0.1% if the share price increases by 5%.

Solving Equation 11.2 for order size gives the stabilization formula,

$$\text{Order size} = S \times \frac{\text{Price change}}{\text{Price}} \times \text{Shares outstanding} \qquad (11.3)$$

Equation 11.3 shows that the larger S is, the greater the intensity of the stabilization effort. Because S is positive, a price decrease gives a *negative* order size, which is interpreted as a buy order because it signals a reduction in the number of shares outstanding. Conversely, a price increase gives a *positive* order size, which is interpreted as a sell order because it signals an increase in the number of shares outstanding. Thus, the formula calls for entering buy orders in a declining market and for entering sell orders in a rising market.

Setting the Value of S

An example illustrates how S may be set. Let the XYZ Corp. have 100 million shares outstanding, an average daily trading volume of 200,000 shares, and a current share price of 52½. Assume that a 100,000 share sell order placed at 55 would be substantial relative to the market and would provide

desired stability to the market. No decisions other than the size of the orders
to be placed *given the current price of shares,* and the price increments at
which these orders are placed, need be made. Let the price increments for
the stabilization orders be $2.50. The stabilization parameter is obtained by
substituting the appropriate numerical values into Equation 11.3:

$$S = \frac{100,000}{100,000,000 \times 0.05} = 0.02 \qquad (11.4)$$

The value of S, once determined, is used to establish the size of all stabilization orders. Fixing S in this manner ensures that the relative intensity
of the stabilization effort remains constant as the level of the company's
share price changes with the receipt of news, and as its number of shares
outstanding changes with share purchases and sales. The appendix to this
chapter presents a further assessment of the stabilization formula.

Fund Versus Market Maker Stabilization

OTC market makers have no affirmative obligation to stabilize a market and
NYSE specialists have only a limited obligation, as is recognized in the
Brady report:[2]

> The NYSE rules do not state the maximum or minimum amounts of liquidity,
> depth and continuity required to be provided by a specialist in the execution of
> his function of maintaining, as far as reasonably practicable, a fair and orderly
> market. This lack of precision is understandable given the vague nature of the
> concept of a "fair and orderly market." Insofar as the maximum obligation of a
> specialist in a down market is concerned, a specialist is not expected to exhaust
> his capital by purchasing stock in the face of a flood of sell orders.

The fund as a stabilizer differs appreciably from a traditional third party
market maker. Unlike a specialist or dealer, the fund would never rebalance
its cash/inventory portfolio after making stabilization trades. Another difference is that specialist stabilization is local demand smoothing, while the
proposed stabilization procedure is global demand smoothing. That is, the
fund is designed to inject or to withdraw substantial capital from the market,
particularly at periods of stress. The global demand smoothing should enable specialists in turn to supply more local demand smoothing—specialists
would be able to lay off some of their inventory imbalances on the stabilization fund.

The Maximum Cost of the Procedure

The maximum cost of a stabilization program is the maximum possible cost
of buying shares in accordance with the stabilization formula, if share price

were to decrease without reversal from its current level to zero. It is shown in the appendix that the dollar cost of the purchase relative to the total value of equity shares outstanding is given by Equation 11.5:

$$\text{Maximum Percentage Cost} = \frac{S}{S + 1} \qquad (11.5)$$

Equation 11.5 shows that, for S sufficiently less than unity, the maximum percentage cost is approximately equal to S. In our numerical illustration, S is .02; therefore the maximum cost relative to the value of shares outstanding is approximately 2.0%.

Rules and Procedures for Operating the Stabilization Fund

This subsection sets forth certain rules and procedures that further define the stabilization procedure.

1. Stabilization orders are placed only at market openings and reopenings following halts during the trading day, as part of an exchange's automated opening procedure. All or part of an unexecuted stabilization order may be canceled after any opening or reopening.

2. The stock exchange specialist for an issue may, with the permission of a floor official, call a halt during the trading day. The halt would allow trading to switch into a call market mode and would activate the stabilization procedure.

3. Stabilization transactions are made only when the market price rises to or falls to a trigger price. Trigger prices are set by the exchange at discrete intervals (for example, at every $2.50 increment).

4. The number of shares purchased or sold in a stabilization transaction is determined using the stabilization parameter (S) and number of shares outstanding (N). The values of S and N are publicly known; thus, market participants could easily determine in advance what the share issuance or purchase would be, given the price established at the next opening or reopening.

5. The fund selects the value of S; it must give advance notice before reducing any commitment to stabilize.

6. The fund is large enough to make all required purchases if price were to decrease by a specified amount (for example, 40%). The size of the fund is adjusted whenever the firm issues new shares or repurchases shares for nonstabilization purposes.

7. The firm whose shares are stabilized must supply the fund with shares if needed in accordance with the stabilization formula as its share price

rises. The cash generated by newly issued shares can be passed on to the issuing company if the fund is large enough to satisfy Rule 6.

8. The fund may purchase shares only on a downtick (where a negative change in N is called for), in an amount equal to or greater than that given by S. This provision enables a firm to reduce its equity base for reasons other than stabilization, while ensuring that such share repurchase is stabilizing. Similarly, a firm may issue more shares through a Rule 415 offering (the shelf registration rule) only on an uptick (where a positive change in N is called for), in an amount equal to or greater than that given by S.

9. Cash contributions to the stabilization fund are invested in Treasury bills to the fullest extent possible.

Rules 1, 3–6, and 9 require further explanation.

Stabilization at the Opening Only.   As stated in Rule 1, the procedure calls for stabilization orders to be submitted only at market openings and at reopenings after halts during the trading day. The restriction simplifies the procedure. In periods of particular stress, the specialist for an issue can activate the procedure by calling a halt (the circuit breaker concept) and reopening the market using the call market mode.

Under more normal conditions, widespread knowledge of the stabilization orders that will be forthcoming at the next opening will help to stabilize the market during any given day. For example, assume that on a particular trading day, the market for XYZ shares opens at 50 ½ and then decreases to 47 ½. Sell orders at even lower prices would be discouraged by public knowledge that the fund will stand ready to buy 100,000 shares at 47 ½ at the next opening. Furthermore, if sell orders are discouraged, additional buy orders will be encouraged because of the reduced probability of price dropping further in the short run.

Stabilization rules cannot be reasonably enforced in a continuous market if price changes are discontinuous. The advantage of having the stabilization orders entered only at market openings and reopenings is that at these times the exchange's order execution procedure resembles a call market. The call market best approximates an auction where the price that is struck is indeed an equilibrium value. The stabilization fund would submit its full set of order points to the call and then transact appropriately at the price that clears all crossing orders.

Prices set in both call and continuous markets reflect a multiplicity of factors: informationally motivated orders, liquidity-motivated orders, anticipations of short-run price movements, and various strategic trading decisions. The price set in a call market could also, simultaneously, reflect the liquidity supplied to the market by the corporate stabilization procedure. This need not reduce the speed with which prices reflect underlying equilibrium values, as might occur if the stabilization orders were entered in a continuous market.

Discreteness of the Trigger Prices. Rule 3 calls for transactions to be made only when opening prices reach certain trigger values that are set by the exchange. This allows the procedure to be profitable for the fund. That is, discreteness in the trigger prices creates a spread. Hence, like a traditional market maker, the fund may profit from price reversals by buying at lower prices and then selling at discretely higher prices.

Commitment to Stabilize. A stabilization plan can become destabilizing (or extremely costly) if traders believe that the stabilizer will back down in the face of a large order imbalance. Rules 4, 5, and 6 should prevent the procedure from suffering from this vulnerability. The stabilizer would never rebalance its cash/shares inventory as it purchases or issues shares in accordance with the stabilization formula (Equation 11.3). The stabilizer would purchase only limited, predetermined numbers of shares, and only if price were to decline to lower values; consequently, the stabilizer need never exhaust its resources in an attempt to support an unrealistic price level. Financing would be prearranged; hence, the public need never be uncertain about a fund's ability to carry out an announced stabilization program.

Liquidity of Last Resort. Rule 9 calls for the stabilization fund to invest in Treasury bills. In the advent of a broad market decrease such as occurred on 19 October 1987, many stabilization funds would sell Treasury bills to pay for share purchases. The federal government could provide liquidity to the system by repurchasing the Treasury bills as they are sold by the stabilization funds. The stabilization procedure, therefore, provides the means by which the federal government can be a liquidity provider of last resort.

Neutrality of the Procedure

The stabilization program attempts to manipulate neither price nor the total value of a company's equity shares. It imposes no artificial support or resistance levels, trading restrictions, or other trading blockages. The procedure simply calls for varying the number of shares outstanding as price changes. Varying the number of shares alleviates pressure for price to change in response to demand shifts. Consequently, as demand fluctuates, price will fluctuate less.

There is no informational signal in the stabilization program. Market participants will understand that any share issuance or purchase is determined by a formula based on price movements and the stock's stabilization parameter. The parameters are publicly known, and the company's participation at the next market opening is completely predictable.

Numerical Illustration

A numerical example illustrates how the stabilization program would work. Assume the XYZ Corp has 100,000,000 shares outstanding, that the last transaction at a trigger price was at 52 ½, and that the stabilization parameter (S) is .02.

Share Repurchase Schedule

Table 11.1 shows the trigger prices at which additional purchases are to be made, along with the size and dollar cost of the purchases. The first row in the table shows that if the opening price were to decrease to 50, the fund would be committed to purchase up to 96,000 shares at the opening at a price of 50. The order size is determined using Equation 11.3.

The table shows all additional purchases that would be made at subsequent openings if the price were to decrease without reversal from 50 to 2 ½ with each trigger price being hit. In the example shown, 5,206,000 shares in total would be bought at a total cost of $86,384,000. The fund would be obligated to incur this cost, if necessary. However, if 30 is the minimum price the fund must be prepared to buy down to if shares are currently trading at 52 ½, then only $42,448,000 would have to be carried in the stabilization account. The size of the fund is 0.84% of the total value of outstanding shares; this is consistent with Equation 11.4, since S is .02 and only 40% of the maximum total cost is put in the fund.

Table 11.2 illustrates the implementation of the stabilization procedure in relation to various possible clearing prices that could be established at the next opening or reopening:

1. No shares are purchased if the market clearing price is 50 ⅛ or higher.

2. If the clearing price equals the trigger price of $50, 96,000 shares would be purchased and $4,800,000 would be drawn from the stabilization account to pay for the purchase. The fund would then be committed to stabilize down to a price of 27 ½ and must be augmented by $4,510,000 to satisfy the obligation.

3. At clearing prices from $47 ⅝ through $50, the fund would purchase 96,000 shares. However, if the clearing price set at the next opening is $49 ⅞, the fund would buy at $49 ⅞; if the price is set at $49 ¾, the fund would buy at $49 ¾, and so on.

TABLE 11.1 *Stabilization Commitment of the XYZ Fund (Repurchases)*

(1)	(2)	(3)	(4)	(5)
	Percentage Price Change	Shares	Additional Shares Repurchased (thousands)	Maximum Cost of Additional Repurchase (thousands)
Trigger Price	from Previous Trigger	Outstanding (thousands)	$(2) \times (3) \times (S = .02)$	$(1) \times (4)$
50	4.8	100,000	96	$ 4,800
47½	5.0	99,904	100	4,770
45	5.3	99,804	106	4,770
42½	5.6	99,698	112	4,760
40	5.9	99,586	118	4,720
37½	6.3	99,468	126	4,724
35	6.7	99,342	134	4,690
32½	7.1	99,208	142	4,614
30	7.7	99,066	154	4,620
27½	8.3	98,921	164	4,510
25	9.1	98,748	180	4,500
22½	10.0	98,568	197	4,432
20	11.1	98,371	218	4,360
17½	12.5	98,153	245	4,287
15	14.3	97,908	280	4,200
12½	16.7	97,628	362	4,525
10	20.0	97,266	389	3,890
7½	25.0	96,875	484	3,630
5	33.3	96,391	642	3,210
2½	50.0	95,749	957	2,392
Total to Price = 30			1,088	$42,448
Total to Price = 2½			5,206	$86,384

4. At clearing prices from $45 ⅛ through $47 ½, the fund would purchase 196,000 shares (96,000 + 100,000) at the price set in the market, as described above.

5. At clearing prices from $42 ⅝ through $45, the fund would purchase 302,000 shares (196,000 + 106,000). And so on.

Share Issuance

Share issuance is based on the purchase schedule shown in Table 11.1: the number of shares purchased at any trigger price gives the number that would be sold at the next higher trigger. Assume that a stabilization purchase at

TABLE 11.2 *Implementation of Stabilization Commitment (Repurchases)*

Market Clearing Price	Shares Repurchased (thousands)	Cost of Repurchase (thousands)
50 ⅛	–0–	–0–
50	96	4,800
49 ⅞	96	4,788
49 ¾	96	4,776
.	.	.
.	.	.
.	.	.
47 ⅝	96	4,572
47 ½	196	9,310
47 ⅜	196	9,285
.	.	.
.	.	.
.	.	.
45 ⅛	196	8,844
45	302	13,590
44 ⅞	302	13,552
.	.	.
.	.	.
.	.	.
42 ⅝	302	12,872

a trigger of $52 ½ is followed by the price series, 50, 47 ½, 50, 52 ½, 50. The associated sequence of stabilization transactions is given in Table 11.3. The example shows that each time price descends to a trigger (for example $50), the number of shares outstanding before the transaction is the same (namely, 100,000,000) and the number of shares purchased by the fund is the same (that is, 96,000). Note that the company would not transact at a trigger price (for example, repurchase at 50) unless it had realized a sale at the next higher trigger price (for example, the company does not make a repurchase at 50 unless price increases as far as $52 ½ before again falling to 50). Therefore, fluctuating prices will not cause the number of shares outstanding to change (drift up or down) in the long run.

The Profitability of Price Reversals

The example shows why the dollar figures given in Table 11.1 are maximum amounts. If the clearing price at the opening jumps directly to a lower trigger

TABLE 11.3 *Repurchase Example*

Price	Transaction (thousands)	Shares Outstanding Before Transaction (thousands)	Shares Outstanding After Transaction (thousands)
50	Buy 96	100,000	99,904
47½	Buy 100	99,904	99,804
50	Sell 100	99,804	99,904
52½	Sell 96	99,904	100,000
50	Buy 96	100,000	99,904

price (for example, $47½ rather than $50), the fund purchases all required shares at the lower trigger price; if the clearing price is below a trigger price, the firm purchases all shares at the lower value, not at the trigger price. Additionally, if reversals occur as price decreases over a range of trigger prices, the firm realizes gross revenues by alternately buying at lower prices and selling at higher prices.

Consider a stabilization purchase of 100,000 shares at the trigger price of $47½ (the second row in Table 11.3). The higher price of $50 (the third row of the table) then becomes a trigger price for a sale. When the higher trigger has been hit, the stabilization fund sells 100,000 shares at 50 and realizes $250,000 from the round trip.

Excessive short-term volatility is associated with an excessive frequency of price reversals in the short run. Even in the absence of excessive short-term volatility, reversals occur simply by chance. The revenue generated by the reversals offsets part of the cost of maintaining the fund. In addition, the stabilization fund receives interest on its holdings of Treasury bills.

Ask the Issuing Companies to Join the Party

The most appropriate sources of funds on the requisite level are the listed companies themselves.

- The listed companies might in any event be prepared to issue additional shares in a rising market to the stabilization fund.
- The companies are financially capable of providing substantial capital to market making.
- Stabilization will reduce the return required by shareholders and thus increase the price of shares and lower their cost of equity capital. Allowing a corporation to determine and pay for the stabilization it desires

would internalize this benefit and thus enable an optimal provision of the service.

- Turning to the listed companies instead of the large broker/dealer firms may avoid a further increase in the concentration of power in the securities industry.

In any event, a mechanism should be provided to facilitate price stabilization by corporations if companies on their own accord would freely elect to use it. The important consideration is that the result be price stabilization, not manipulation. Other factors have to be considered as well.

The Effect of Stabilization on Leverage

One concern is that the corporate stabilization program will increase a company's debt/equity ratio. For a number of reasons, this concern may not be well founded:

1. The stabilization program does not call for a substantial change in the number of shares outstanding; hence, any direct impact on financial aggregates should be small.
2. Share issuance in a rising market finances subsequent purchases in a falling market.
3. The stabilization program will itself generate income from price reversals that will help to preserve the equity base.
4. Formalizing share issuance and purchase is an investment decision, not a financing decision. As is true for any other investment, it need not result in an increased debt/equity ratio.
5. The negative effect on share price of any increase of risk attributable to a possible increase in leverage may be more than offset by the positive effect on share price due to the increased liquidity that corporate stabilization brings to the market. A higher share price implies a lower cost of equity capital for the stabilizing company, thus a substitution of equity for debt, and hence a decrease in the company's debt/equity ratio.

Risk of Bankruptcy

Another potential concern is that a commitment to price-stabilize could force an increasingly unprofitable company to expend capital on share repurchase as its stock price drops and that the expenditure could increase the probability of bankruptcy. Obviously, any negative cash outflow could trigger bankruptcy, once a sufficiently critical level is reached. Nonetheless, this concern may not be well founded. Nothing distinguishes stabilization expenditures from other cash outlays that are desirable on their own merit. A company should be no more reluctant to curtail its stabilization efforts than, for instance, to cancel an insurance contract on its plant and equipment if the expenditures are, in and of themselves, profitable. If the stabilization program is indeed profitable on balance because it generates trading profits and interest income and lowers the cost of capital, the program should lower, not raise, the probability of bankruptcy. In any event, a company is always free to change its stabilization parameter (to zero if desired), provided sufficient advance notice is given.

The Effect of Informational Change on the Program

Inconsistent Trades.   Trades that are inconsistent with corporate strategy may be forced following certain events. For example, a firm that wishes to purchase shares to defend against a hostile takeover attempt would be forced to sell shares in accordance with the stabilization formula as the takeover attempt drives the price of shares up. Note, however, that the number of shares that must be issued by the stabilizing company at each price increment ($2.50) is small relative to the number of shares outstanding; therefore, the cost to a predator of acquiring shares in this manner becomes enormous as the price increments mount. Furthermore, after any downtick, the company would be free to repurchase as many shares as the market will supply.

Manipulation of Share Price Through Information Release.   The main concern about extending to corporations the freedom to stabilize is that it might allow them to manipulate the prices of their shares. Because the stabilization program is a fully articulated, transparent procedure, a corporation would not be able to manipulate its share prices directly. However, it might do so through the manipulation of information. A stabilizing company that can control the release of news so as to alternate between favorable and unfavorable announcements could generate profitable price reversals for its stabilization program.

Two factors should prevent companies from generating price reversals through news release: (1) meaningful company-specific news releases are infrequent, which makes the opportunities limited, and (2) the action would be illegal and involve stiff penalties.

Appendix—Effect of Supply Response on the Market Clearing Price

In this appendix we model the effect of a supply response on the percentage change of a clearing price caused by a demand shift. The market's demand curve expresses investor desires to hold shares of a firm's stock; assume this curve to be of constant elasticity. The supply curve of shares is set by the company; it could by design be given constant elasticity (as discussed in the section, "The Economic Framework"). Therefore, let the demand and supply relations be described by

$$N = aP^{-B} \qquad a, B > 0 \qquad\qquad (11.A1)$$

$$N = gP^{S} \qquad g, S > 0 \qquad\qquad (11.A2)$$

where a and g are quantity-dimensioned location parameters and B and S are the elasticities of demand and supply, respectively. From Equations 11.A1 and 11.A2 we obtain

$$P^{c} = [a/g]^{1/(S+B)} \qquad\qquad (11.A3)$$

where P^{c} is the clearing price of the company's stock.

Change in the demand for the asset can be represented by change in the location parameter a. Totally differentiating Equation 11.A3, treating P^{c} and a as variables, and rearranging, we get

$$dP^{c} = \frac{1}{S + B} \ (a/g)^{1/(S+B)}(da/a) \qquad\qquad (11.A4)$$

Dividing by P^{c} gives

$$dP^{c}/P^{c} = [1/(S + B)][da/a] \qquad\qquad (11.A5)$$

The percentage change da/a, which is quantity dimensioned, can be transformed into a change that is price dimensioned. Taking logs of Equation 11.A1, differentiating totally, setting dN = 0, and rearranging, we obtain

$$da/a = B(dP/P) \qquad\qquad (11.A6)$$

where dP/P is the vertical shift of the demand function. Substituting Equation 11.A6 into 11.A5 we have

$$dP^{c}/P^{c} = [dP/P][B/(S + B)] \qquad\qquad (11.A7)$$

Assessment of the Stabilization Effect

Equation 11.A7 is our key result. Setting the supply response parameter (S) equal to zero shows that the percentage change of the clearing price is dP/P if the number of shares remains fixed as the demand curve shifts. However, when the number of shares changes (S>0), the percentage change in the clearing price is dampened for any finite value of B. Equation 11.A7 shows that dP^{c}/P^{c} becomes smaller (in absolute value) as S gets larger for any given value of dP/P and B. For $S = B$, $dP^{c}/P^{c} = (\frac{1}{2})(dP/P)$; hence, matching the supply elasticity to the demand elasticity cuts the returns variance by 4.

The intensity of a firm's stabilization efforts is measured by the stabilization parameter, S. Differentiating Equation 11.A2 with respect to P and rearranging enables us to specify the corporate share issuance or repurchase (dN) to be associated with any percentage price change as

$$dN = (dP^c/P^c)NS \qquad (11.A8)$$

which is consistent with Equation 11.3.

The effect of the firm's stabilization efforts depends on the demand response. It is clear from Equation 11.A7 that dP^c/P^c goes to zero as B decreases without bound (stabilization is almost total even for small dN when the demand elasticity is arbitrarily small) and that dP^c/P^c goes to dP/P as B increases without bound (stabilization is totally ineffective even for large dN when demand elasticity is infinite).

Equation 11.A7 has an interesting interpretation for the case where B = 1. With unitary demand elasticity, the market's assessment of the total value of shares outstanding ($V = P^cN$) is not affected by a supply response. For this case, the percentage change in the total value of shares outstanding due to a demand shift equals dP/P (the vertical shift in the demand curve). Setting B = 1, rearranging Equation 11.A7, and recognizing that dV/V = dP/P if B = 1, we have

$$\frac{dV}{V} = \frac{dN}{N} + \frac{dP^c}{P^c} \qquad (11.A9)$$

Thus with unitary demand elasticity, the percentage change in the total value of shares equals the percentage change in the number of shares outstanding plus the percentage change in the price per share. This special case makes it easy to visualize how a firm can substitute a percentage change in N for a percentage change in P^c so as to dampen its price volatility.

Cost of the Program

The maximum cost of the stabilization program is the dollar expenditure that would be incurred to repurchase continuously all shares currently outstanding (N) if price were to decline continuously and monotonically to zero. Let C be this cost. We obtain C by rearranging Equation 11.A2 to express P as a function of N, and then integrating with respect to N. This gives

$$C = \int_0^N (N/g)^{1/S}dN = [gS/(S + 1)][N/g]^{(S+1)/S} \qquad (11.A10)$$

To express C as a percentage of the total value of equity shares currently outstanding, we divide Equation 11.A10 by PN, which gives the following equation:

$$C/PN = S/(S + 1) \qquad (11.A11)$$

This is Equation 11.5 in the text. It is clear from Equation 11.A11 that the percentage cost goes to unity as S increases without bound, equals $\frac{1}{2}$ for $S = 1$, and is approximately equal to S for S sufficiently below unity.

Suggested Reading

De Long, B., Shleifer, A., Summers, L., and Waldman, R. "Positive Feedback Investment Strategies and Destabilizing Rational Speculation." *Journal of Finance,* June 1990.

Greenwald, B., and Stein, J. "Transactional Risk, Market Crashes, and the Role of Circuit Breakers." Paper presented at the Western Finance Association Conference, Santa Barbara, California, June 1990.

Jarrell, G., and Seguin, P. "A Proposal to Stabilize Stock Prices: Comment." *The Journal of Portfolio Management,* Winter 1990.

Mann, R., Shapiro, J., and Sosebee, D. "Recent Episodes of Extreme Volatility." In the NYSE Panel Report, *Market Volatility and Investor Confidence* (Appendix D). New York Stock Exchange, Inc., June 1990.

Poterba, J., and Summers, L. "Mean Reversion in Stock Prices." *Journal of Financial Economics,* October 1988.

Schiller, R. "Do Stock Prices Move Too Much to be Justified by Subsequent Changes in Dividends?" *American Economic Review,* June 1981.

Schwert, G. "Stock Market Volatility." In the NYSE Panel Report, *Market Volatility and Investor Confidence* (Appendix C). New York Stock Exchange, Inc., June 1990.

Schwert, G. "Why Does Stock Market Volatility Change Over Time?" *Journal of Finance,* December 1990.

Schwert, G., and Pagan, A. "Alternative Models for Conditional Stock Volatility." *Journal of Econometrics,* 1990.

Stein, J. "Overreactions in the Options Market." *Journal of Finance,* September 1989.

Notes

1. *Report of the Presidential Task Force on Markets Mechanisms,* Washington, DC: U.S. GPO, 1988, p. VI-46.
2. Ibid., p. VI-8.

PART III

Price Determination

12

Share Evaluation

This chapter shows how equity shares are evaluated according to their risk and return characteristics. To do this, we first consider an investor's optimal portfolio selection.

Portfolio Selection

The Objective

Let three points in time, $T = 0, 1, 2$, identify two time periods: (1) the period from 0 to 1 is a brief trading period (for example, one day), and (2) the period from 1 to 2 is an individual's holding period (for instance, one year). The individual seeks to maximize the expected utility of wealth that will be realized at the end of the holding period, $T = 2$. That person's utility function for wealth can be written as the following equation:

$$U = U(W_2)$$

where the subscript 2 denotes wealth at $T = 2$. For a discussion of utility functions and other microeconomic concepts used in this chapter, see the appendix to Chapter 13.

The decision maker's portfolio at the start of the investment period, $T = 1$, is described by the share holdings N_{i1}, $i = 1, \ldots, M$ assets. Assume a single period analysis. Thus for each ith asset, $N_{i1} = N_{i2}$. Therefore we can suppress the time identification on share holdings and write

$$W_2 = \sum_{i=1}^{M} P_{i2}N_i$$

where P_{i2} is the price of the ith asset at time $T = 2$.

The investor controls the value of W_2 by his or her selection of the N_i. However, because the change of share value for each security is subject to variation, the investor does not have total control over the future value of the portfolio, but rather is faced with a set of uncertain outcomes. For this reason, the investor is not able simply to maximize utility. Rather, decisions are made with reference to *expected* utility.

Following the standard Von Neumann-Morgenstern approach, we take the investor's objective to be the maximization of the expected utility of wealth. This objective is not directly assumed in the Von Neumann-Morgenstern formulation, but rather is implied by a more basic set of assumptions. See Baumol for further discussion.[1] Specifically, the investor seeks to

$$\underset{N_i}{\text{Max}} \, E[U(W_2)] = \underset{N_i}{\text{Max}} \int U(W)f(W) \, dW \qquad (12.1)$$

where E is the *expectations operator* and $f(W)$ is a *probability density function*. The maximization is with respect to the specification of the N_i. There are alternatives to the maximization of expected utility: the maximization of the geometric mean return and various safety first criteria. For further discussion, see Elton and Gruber.[2]

By optimally combining assets according to their risk and return characteristics, the investor obtains the N_i, $i = 1, \ldots, M$, that maximize the expected utility of W_2. Accordingly, we will consider how the risk/return characteristics of individual stocks are related to the risk/return characteristics of a portfolio.

Given W_0, we can rewrite $U(W_2)$ as $v(r_P)$. (It is straightforward to show that, W_0 given, r is a linear transformation of W_2.) The advantage of dealing with r_P rather than with W_2 is that the parameters of the returns distribution relate to a portfolio's composition and are independent of an individual decision maker's own wealth position.

For theoretical analysis, we assume r_P, the return on the portfolio, to be normally distributed. This enables two parameters alone, mean and variance, to describe the returns distribution. (A third moment of the returns distribution, *skewness,* has also been considered in some portfolio selection models. For further discussion, see Elton and Gruber.[3]) Therefore, for normally distributed returns, we rewrite $v(r_P)$ as

$$U(W_2) = f[E(r_P), \text{Var}(r_P)] \qquad (12.2)$$

where $E(r_P)$ is the *mean return* and $\text{Var}(r_P)$ is the *variance of returns* over the investment period. There are two other conditions under which utility can be written as a function of mean and variance: (1) quadratic utility and (2) lognormally distributed returns. Economists differ in their willingness to assume quadratic utility. The empirical evidence suggests that returns distributions are approximately lognormal, however, and the assumption of

FIGURE 12.1 *Risk Averse Investors Realize Higher Expected Utility with a Greater Expected Return (Variance Constant), or with a Lower Variance of Returns (Expected Return Constant)*

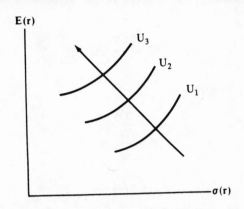

lognormality is widely accepted. To simplify the discussion here, we assume that returns are distributed normally.

From Equation 12.2, it can be shown (and it is easy to accept intuitively) that risk averse investors realize higher expected utility with a greater expected return (variance constant) or with a lower variance of returns (expected return constant). This is shown in Figure 12.1, where we display a family of mean-variance indifference curves. The investor maximizes expected utility by attaining the highest possible indifference curve in mean-variance (of returns) space. The arrow pointing to the northwest in Figure 12.1 shows the direction of increasing utility.

The Mean and Variance of Portfolio Returns

Optimal portfolio selection is a constrained maximization problem where the constraint is given by the set of risk/return combinations available in the marketplace. To derive this constraint, it is necessary to compute portfolio mean and variance from the means, variances, and covariances of individual assets. This is done as follows:

Any dividend paid during the period is assumed to be paid at time $T = 2$, and P_{i2} is the actual price plus the dividend per share. The return on the ith asset in the portfolio is

$$R_i = \frac{P_{i2}}{P_{i1}} = \frac{P_{i1} + \Delta P_i}{P_{i1}} = 1 + r_i \qquad (12.3)$$

where R_i is a *price relative;* $\Delta P_i = P_{i2} - P_{i1}$; and r_i has the standard returns dimension with which most people are more accustomed. R is used in some places in the text and r in others, depending on which is simpler in context to treat mathematically. The change in the value of a portfolio over the investment period is

$$\Delta W = \sum_{i=1}^{M} \Delta P_i N_i \tag{12.4}$$

The return on the portfolio is

$$r_P = \frac{\Delta W}{W_1}$$

$$= \frac{\sum_{i=1}^{M} \Delta P_i N_i}{W_1} \tag{12.5}$$

Equation 12.5 can be rewritten as

$$r_P = \sum_{i=1}^{M} \left(\frac{P_{i1} N_i}{W_1}\right)\left(\frac{\Delta P_i}{P_{i1}}\right) \tag{12.6}$$

The dollar weight of the ith stock in the portfolio is

$$w_i = \frac{P_{i1} N_i}{W_1} \tag{12.7}$$

Substituting Equation 12.7 into 12.6 and using the definition of r_i gives

$$r_P = \sum_{i=1}^{M} w_i r_i \tag{12.8}$$

Taking expectations of Equation 12.8 gives the expected mean return,

$$E[r_P] = \sum_{i=1}^{M} w_i E[r_i] \tag{12.9}$$

Taking variances gives

$$\text{Var}\,(r_P) = \sum_{i=1}^{M}\sum_{j=1}^{M} w_i w_j \sigma_i \sigma_j \rho_{ij} \tag{12.10}$$

where σ_i is the standard deviation of returns on the ith asset, and ρ_{ij} is the correlation between the return on the ith and the jth assets. Equations 12.9 and

12.10 show how the means, variances, and covariances for a set of stocks combined in a specific way (that is, a specific set of portfolio weights) result in specific values for the mean and variance of the portfolio's return.

The Var(r_P) equation (12.10) follows the rule that the *variance* of a sum is equal to the sum of the variances plus twice the sum of the covariances. To see this, consider the case where there are only two assets (asset 1 and asset 2):

$$\sigma_1\sigma_1\rho_{11} = \sigma_1^2 \qquad \text{for i, j} = 1, \text{ since } \rho_{11} = 1$$

$$\sigma_2\sigma_2\rho_{22} = \sigma_2^2 \qquad \text{for i, j} = 2, \text{ since } \rho_{22} = 1$$

$$\sigma_1\sigma_2\rho_{12} = \sigma_2\sigma_1\rho_{21} \quad \text{for i} = 1, \text{j} = 2 \text{ and i} = 2, \text{j} = 1$$

Substituting into the variance equation gives

$$\sigma_p^2 = w_1^2\sigma_1^2$$
$$+ w_2^2\sigma_2^2$$
$$+ 2w_1w_2\sigma_1\sigma_2\rho_{12}$$

where $\sigma_1\sigma_2\rho_{12} = \text{Cov}_{12}$

The Constraint

Different assets can be combined in a portfolio in many different ways, thus a feasible set of alternative portfolios is available to the decision maker. The decision maker adjusts the portfolio weights so as to obtain the one portfolio in the feasible set that maximizes his or her expected utility.

Equation 12.9 shows that the portfolio's expected return is an average of the individual stock returns, with each return weighted by the stock's dollar importance in the portfolio. Equation 12.10 shows that the relationship between the returns variance for the portfolio and the returns variances for the stocks is more complicated. To analyze the stock/portfolio variance relationship, write Equation 12.10 for two stocks (A and B):

$$\text{Var } (r_P) = w_A^2 \text{ Var } (r_A) + w_B^2 \text{ Var } (r_B) + 2w_Aw_B\sigma_A\sigma_B\rho_{AB} \qquad (12.11)$$

If the returns on the two stocks are perfectly correlated ($\rho_{AB} = 1$), Equation 12.11 is a perfect square. Thus we have

$$\text{Var } (r_P) = (w_A\sigma_A + w_B\sigma_B)^2 \quad \text{for } \rho_{AB} = 1 \qquad (12.12a)$$

$$\text{Var } (r_P) < (w_A\sigma_A + w_B\sigma_B)^2 \quad \text{for } \rho_{AB} < 1 \qquad (12.12b)$$

Taking square roots of (12.12) gives

$$\sigma_P = w_A\sigma_A + w_B\sigma_B \quad \text{for } \rho_{AB} = 1 \qquad (12.13a)$$

$$\sigma_P < w_A\sigma_A + w_B\sigma_B \quad \text{for } \rho_{AB} < 1 \qquad (12.13b)$$

We see that the portfolio return's *standard deviation* is the weighted average of the *standard deviations* of the individual stock returns if the stock returns are perfectly correlated with each other. Thus we generally deal with means and standard deviations, even though the term *mean-variance analysis* is commonly used. Notice that the horizontal axis of Figure 12.1 is labeled $\sigma(r)$. Mean-standard deviation indifference curves are also simpler to deal with on the utility side of the analysis, although here too the term *mean-variance* is commonly used.

For the moment assume a universe of two stocks (A and B) whose returns are perfectly (positively) correlated. The mean and standard deviation parameters for these stocks are shown in Figure 12.2 by the coordinates of the points labeled A and B. In addition, the mean and standard deviation parameters for a *portfolio combination* of the two stocks are given by the coordinates of a point that lies on the straight line between A and B (this follows from Equations 12.9 and 12.13a). We have illustrated such a point by the one labeled P in Figure 12.2. For simplicity, we have taken $w_A = w_B$. Accordingly, P is halfway between A and B, $E(r_P)$ is halfway between $E(r_A)$ and $E(r_B)$, and σ_P is halfway between σ_A and σ_B.

FIGURE 12.2   *Mean and Standard Deviation Parameters for a Two Stock (A and B) Portfolio,* $P_{AB} = 1$

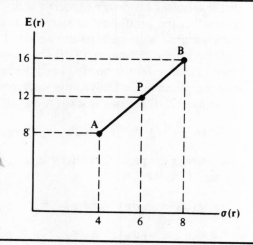

Next consider the standard deviation of portfolio returns for the more typical case of $\rho_{AB} < 1$. It is clear from Equation 12.11 that a reduction in ρ (all else constant) reduces $\text{Var}(r_P)$. Therefore, since Equation 12.13a holds for $\rho = 1$, for $\rho < 1$ we must have

$$\sigma_P < w_A\sigma_A + w_B\sigma_B \tag{12.14}$$

the result shown by Equation 12.13b. For a given set of weights (w_A, w_B), the difference between σ_P and the weighted average of the standard deviations of the individual stocks depends on how far the correlation coefficient, ρ, is below unity. At the lower limit $(\rho = -1)$, $\text{Var}(r_P) = (w_A\sigma_A - w_B\sigma_B)^2$, from which it follows that $\text{Var}(r_P)$ will be zero if $w_A/w_B = \sigma_B/\sigma_A$.

Note the direction of the inequality in Equation 12.14. The effect of this inequality is shown graphically in Figure 12.3. For the particular case where $w_A = 0.5$, $w_B = 0.5$, we have $E(r_P) = 12$ and $\sigma_P = 4.5 < 6$. More generally, the locus of all $E(r_P)$, σ_P points (for differing values of w_A and w_B) is a concave arc from A to B. The concavity of the arc reflects the fact that, for $\rho < 1$, portfolio diversification reduces the variance of portfolio returns.

Let a third stock (C) be introduced. As shown in Figure 12.4, we now have a positively inclined concave arc between A and B and a second such arc between B and C. The point labeled AB on the first arc shows the mean-variance parameters of a two-stock portfolio defined by $w_A = 0.5$, $w_B = 0.5$.

FIGURE 12.3 *Mean and Standard Deviation Parameters for a Two Stock (A and B) Portfolio,* $P_{AB} < 1$

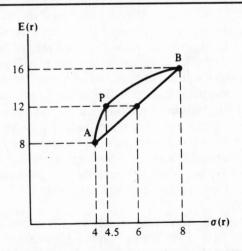

FIGURE 12.4   *Mean and Standard Deviation Parameters for a Three Stock (A, B, and C) Portfolio*

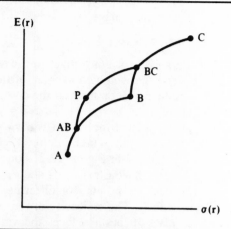

The point labeled BC on the second arc shows the mean-variance parameters of a two-stock portfolio defined by $w_B = 0.5, w_C = 0.5$. What if the decision maker's wealth were divided between an AB-type portfolio and a BC-type portfolio?

Replication of the preceding discussion would show that the mean-variance parameters of this three-stock portfolio are given by the coordinates of a point on the concave arc from AB to BC. For instance, the weights $w_{AB} = 0.5, w_{BC} = 0.5$ (which are equivalent to $w_A = 0.25, w_B = 0.5, w_C = 0.25$) would identify a point such as the one labeled P in Figure 12.4.

The *positively* inclined mean-variance indifference curves in Figure 12.1 reflect the fact that risk averters value expected returns but dislike returns variance. Therefore, given the existence of point P in Figure 12.4, the risk averse decision maker would not place all of his or her wealth in asset B. The reason is that the point labeled B lies below and to the right of the arc between AB and BC and thus is dominated by multistock portfolios such as P, which give a higher expected return and/or a lower returns variance. (Stock B, of course, is not dominated out. B enters the multistock portfolios: it is only dominated out as a single-stock portfolio.) Less than perfect returns correlation explains the variance reduction associated with portfolio diversification, and this in turn explains why risk averters generally hold diversified portfolios.

The feasible set and the constraint can now be identified. These are illustrated in Figure 12.5. Each dot in Figure 12.5 shows the mean–standard deviation parameters for each asset the decision maker considers for

FIGURE 12.5 *Feasible Set and Constraint*

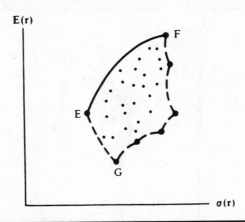

inclusion in his or her portfolio. The dashed and solid lines on the outer border delimit the set of all feasible mean–standard deviation combinations, given the means, variances, and covariances for the individual stocks. For the most part, multiple-stock portfolios lie along the left-hand segment that passes through points G, E, and F, for reasons discussed in relation to Figure 12.4. The constraint itself is the positively inclined, solid line segment between E and F. This is because, when the investor has achieved a portfolio along the EF arc, greater expected returns can be obtained only at the cost of higher variance, and lower variance can be realized only at the expense of lower expected returns. Accordingly, this arc is called the *efficient frontier.* The efficient frontier is the constraint. Note that the investor is an efficient decision maker only if he or she has achieved a position where a trade-off is necessary to get more of a "good" or less of a "bad." Alternatively stated, the ability to improve one's position at no cost indicates a suboptimal solution, and hence inefficiency.

The Optimal Portfolio Decision

The optimal portfolio is given by the point of tangency between the efficient frontier and the highest indifference curve the investor can reach. The tangency solution identifies the optimal mean-variance combination given the alternatives that are available and the investor's utility function. The solution is illustrated in Figure 12.6 by the point labeled P*. When portfolio P* is selected, the decision maker achieves an expected return of E(r)*, a standard deviation of $\sigma*$, and an indifference curve labeled U*.

FIGURE 12.6 *Tangency Solution Identifying Optimal Mean-Variance Combination*

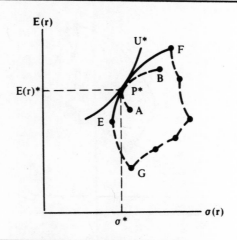

In Figure 12.6, the optimal portfolio lies on the arc between point A and point B. Assume that point A is associated with a single stock. Point B may represent either a single stock or a multistock portfolio; if the latter, assume that stock A does not enter portfolio B. We can consider the specific equation that shows how A and B are combined to get portfolio P* and may thereby determine stock A's weight (w_A^*) in P*. In a similar fashion, we can obtain the weight (w_i^*) for any other i^{th} stock in the portfolio. The weights express the investment decision.

Note the following about the optimal investment decision:

- Because for each ith asset $w_i = (P_i N_i)/W_1$, and since W_1 is given, determining optimal weights is equivalent to determining optimal dollar holdings in each asset. Therefore, for given market prices (the P_i), the individual's investment decision reduces to determining how many shares to hold of each stock (the N_i).

- The investment decision is implemented by buying or selling the appropriate number of shares of each asset, given the solution for the optimal weights, initial portfolio holdings, and share prices.

- Just as the portfolio decision is *stock dimensioned*, so too is the trading decision. That is, if the decision maker wants to hold N_i^* shares of the ith asset and currently holds N_0 shares, then he or she will seek to trade $N_i^* - N_0$ shares. (See Chapter 13, Appendix A, for a discussion of stock vs. flow dimensions.)

- There is no fundamental distinction between buyers and sellers in the securities market. Any trader is either a buyer or a seller, depending on his or her desired portfolio adjustment. $N_i^* - N_0 > 0$ indicates a buy decision, and $N_i^* - N_0 < 0$ indicates a sell decision.

- The desired share holding for an asset depends upon the price at which shares of the asset can be bought or sold. There are two reasons for this: (1) Expected returns, variances, and covariances all depend on the relationship between initial prices (the P_{i1}) and end of period prices (the P_{i2}); hence the optimal investment decision also depends on the initial prices. (2) The decision concerning the total dollar investment in a security is translated into the number of shares to hold (N_i^*) *given* the price per share (P_i).

The Capital Asset Pricing Model

This section shows how the portfolio selection model may be extended to obtain an equilibrium pricing model for risky assets. The formulation is the *Capital Asset Pricing Model* (CAPM). The CAPM was first developed by Sharpe,[4] Lintner,[5] and Mossin.[6] A recent alternative to explaining asset prices is arbitrage pricing theory (APT). See Ross,[7] and Elton and Gruber[8] for further discussion. Assume the following:

- Each investor has a single investment period, from T_1 to T_2.

- Each investor makes his or her portfolio decision with regard to the mean and variance of portfolio returns.

- Investors agree on the mean, variance, and covariance characteristics of individual securities; that is, investors have *homogeneous expectations*.

- Each investor can borrow or lend unlimited amounts of a risk-free asset at a risk-free rate of interest r_f.

- There are no taxes, transaction costs, short selling restrictions, or other frictions in the market.

- Price and quantity (of share holdings) are continuous variables.

- No individual has the economic power to affect any price by his or her trading (that is, the market is perfectly competitive).

The Capital Market Line

Introduction of a risk-free asset changes the efficient frontier (the arc from E to F in Figures 12.5 and 12.6). To see how, select a point on the EF arc, such as the point labeled X in Figure 12.7(a). The risk/return parameters for combinations of the risky portfolio X, and the risk-free asset, are given by

FIGURE 12.7 *Introduction of a Risk-Free Asset Changes the Efficient Frontier. (a) The Efficient Frontier. (b) The Capital Market Line and an Investor's Indifference Curve*

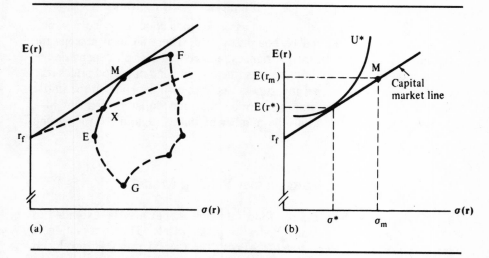

the dashed line from r_f through X.* The dashed line is above the EF arc in the region to the left of X. Hence, over this region, higher mean returns and/or lower returns variance can be obtained by combining the risky portfolio X and the risk-free asset.

Next consider the point labeled M along the EF arc. The risk/return parameters for combinations of the risky portfolio M, and the risk-free asset, are given by the solid line from r_f through M. Because the solid line is above the dashed line, the portfolio combinations it describes dominate the portfolio combinations described by the dashed line. That is, higher expected returns and/or lower returns variance can be obtained from portfolios on the solid line, than on the dashed line. Because the solid line through M is tangent to the EF arc, no other line from r_f to any other point along the EF arc lies above the solid line through point M. Therefore, the efficient frontier with unlimited borrowing and lending at the riskless rate is the straight line that passes from r_f through M. This line is called the *capital market line*.

---

* Return variance for the risk-free asset is zero, and there is no covariance of return between the risk-free and the risky assets. Therefore, the locus of mean, standard deviation values for the combined portfolio is a straight line, with the standard deviation for the combined portfolio being equal to $w_x \sigma_x$, where w_x is the weight of the risky portfolio in the combined portfolio.

Because investors have homogeneous expectations, they all make decisions with respect to this capital market line.

Each investor selects the specific risk/return combination given by the point of tangency between the capital market line and the highest indifference curve he or she can attain, as illustrated in Figure 12.7(b). For each investor, the specific combination of the risky portfolio (M) and the riskless asset depends on the tastes of the individual. If (with reference to Figure 12.7) the point of tangency is to the right of M, the investor borrows the risk-free asset and pays the rate r_f; if the point of tangency is to the left of M, the investor lends the risk-free asset and receives the rate r_f [as shown by the tangency solution depicted in Figure 12.7(b)]. The combination of risky stocks, however, is the same for all investors—it is the portfolio M.

When the market is in equilibrium, all shares of all issues must be held by investors; accordingly, M must be the market portfolio of all stocks. The capital asset pricing model shows how equilibrium share prices are determined for each security in the market portfolio. To obtain the equilibrium pricing relationships, first write the equation for the capital market line. From Figure 12.7(b), it is clear that the intercept parameter is r_f, and that the slope parameter is $[E(r_m) - r_f]/\sigma_m$. Accordingly, the equation for the capital market line is

$$E(r) = r_f + \left[\frac{E(r_m) - r_f}{\sigma_m}\right]\sigma \qquad (12.15)$$

Equation 12.15 shows that the return on an equilibrium portfolio can be decomposed into two parts: (1) r_f compensates the investor for postponing the receipt of income (waiting), and (2) $\{[E(r_m) - r_f]/\sigma_m\}\sigma$ compensates the investor for risk. $[E(r_m) - r_f]$ may be viewed as the price of risk (that is, what the market will pay the investor for accepting risk). In Equation 12.15, the total compensation for risk taking is, therefore, the price per standard deviation of the market portfolio, which is $[(E(r_m) - r_f]/\sigma_m$, times the amount of risk accepted, which is σ.

The Security Market Line

The capital market line shows the risk/return relationship to which an equilibrium portfolio must conform, given the assumptions of CAPM. Individual securities, however, are not generally equilibrium portfolios, and thus they do not generally lie on the capital market line. An equation equivalent to Equation 12.15, to which the risky securities must conform, is obtained by identifying the relevant measure of risk for each asset in the market portfolio.

The relevant measure of risk for the ith asset is the increase in the risk of the market portfolio caused by a small increase in the ith asset's weight in the market portfolio. That is, in keeping with the standard microeconomic pricing model, the compensation for risk bearing with regard to the ith asset equals the price of risk times the marginal increase in portfolio risk attributable to an increased investment in the ith asset. The change in portfolio risk is therefore obtained by differentiating the standard deviation of the market portfolio with respect to the portfolio weight of the ith asset. The derivation is shown in the appendix to this chapter; the derivative equals σ_{im}/σ_m.

Replacing σ in Equation 12.15 with σ_{im}/σ_m, the measure of the ith stock's contribution *on the margin* to overall market risk, gives

$$E(r_i) = r_f + \left[\frac{E(r_m) - r_f}{\sigma_m}\right]\left(\frac{\sigma_{im}}{\sigma_m}\right). \tag{12.16}$$

Equation 12.16 can be rewritten as

$$E(r_i) = r_f + \beta_i[E(r_m) - r_f] \tag{12.17}$$

where

$$\beta_i = \frac{\sigma_{im}}{\sigma_m^2}$$

Equation 12.17 is the equation for the *security market line,* shown graphically in Figure 12.8. The expected return/beta (β) characteristics of all efficiently priced securities (and portfolio combinations of securities) must lie on the security market line, given the CAPM assumptions. Consequently,

FIGURE 12.8   *The Security Market Line*

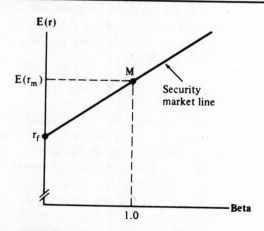

the market portfolio must also lie on the security market line, as shown in Figure 12.8 by the point labeled M, with coordinates $E(r) = E(r_m)$ and $\beta = 1.0$.

The Characteristic Line

The equation for a security's *characteristic line* is

$$r_i = r_f(1 - \beta_i) + \beta_i(r_m) \qquad (12.18)$$

This equation is shown graphically in Figure 12.9. The line can be estimated by regressing the returns for the ith security on the returns for the market portfolio.[*] The regression line passes through the *point of means* [the point in Figure 12.9 with coordinates $E(r_i)$ and $E(r_m)$], and the slope parameter of the regression equation equals the security's returns covariance with the market return, divided by the variance of the market return.[†] Therefore, Equation 12.18 assessed at the point of means can be rewritten as Equation 12.17.

---

[*] Tests for the CAPM typically regress excess returns for the stock on excess returns for the market, using an equation of the form

$$r_i - r_f = a + b[E(r_m) - r_f]$$

where the parameter a is expected to be zero, and the parameter b is the estimate of beta.
[†] The slope parameter, b, of any regression equation $y = a + bx$ is equal to $Cov(y, x)/Var(x)$.

FIGURE 12.9   *The Characteristic Line*

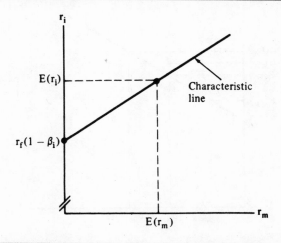

Equilibrium Prices for Individual Assets

Equation 12.17 can also be written as

$$\frac{E(r_i) - r_f}{E(r_m) - r_f} = \beta_i \qquad (12.19)$$

The numerator of the left-hand side of Equation 12.19 is the excess expected return (over the risk-free rate) for the ith security, and the denominator is the excess expected return for the market portfolio. Equation 12.19 shows that, in equilibrium, the excess return for the asset in relation to the excess return to the market must be proportionate to the systematic risk of the stock.

The *equilibrium price* for the ith asset in the market portfolio is the value that equates the expected return for the asset with the expected return shown by the security market line, given the value of the asset's beta coefficient. As is next discussed, an arbitrage argument supports this equilibrium condition.

Figure 12.10 restates the *security market line* as a relationship between the expected return on an asset (or portfolio) and the asset's covariance, $Cov(r_i, r_m)$. That is, the horizontal axis in Figure 12.10 is beta (β), the horizontal axis in Figure 12.8, times $Var(r_m)$. Figure 12.10 also shows the expected return, covariance relationship for two different assets (A and B) and for two different portfolios, the market portfolio (M) and a portfolio C. Portfolio C is selected so that $Cov(r_C, r_m)$ equals $Cov(r_A, r_m)$.

FIGURE 12.10   *The Relationship Between the Expected Return on an Asset or Portfolio and Its Covariance with the Market*

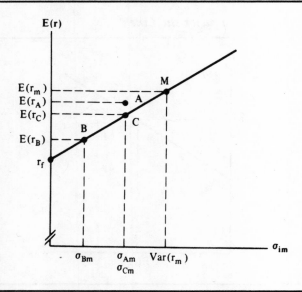

Given asset B and the market portfolio, a portfolio such as C must exist. The reason is that portfolio C can be formed by combining asset B and the market portfolio in proportions w_B and w_m that satisfy

$$\text{Cov}(r_C, r_m) = w_B\text{Cov}(r_B, r_m) + w_m\ \text{Var}(r_m)$$
$$= \text{Cov}(r_A, r_m) \tag{12.20}$$

with

$$E(r_C) = w_B E(r_B) + w_m E(r_m) \tag{12.21}$$

The simultaneous existence of asset A and portfolio C presents an attractive investment opportunity. By simultaneously obtaining a long position in asset A and an offsetting short position in portfolio C, an investor can receive an expected return of $E(r_A) - E(r_C) > 0$. This is because, for any return on the market, the return for the long position (using Equation 12.18 and adjusting the intercept parameter to reflect the additional expected return) is

$$r_{+A} = [r_f(1 - \beta) + E(r_A) - E(r_C)] + \beta(r_m) \tag{12.22}$$

The return on the short position is

$$r_{-C} = -r_f(1 - \beta) - \beta(r_m) \tag{12.23}$$

Hence, adding Equations 12.22 and 12.23 we have that, whatever the return on the market, the expected return to the hedged position is $E(r_A) - E(r_C)$, and the beta for the hedged position is equal to zero. Because unrestricted short selling and zero transactions costs have been assumed, the investor can attain the hedged position by using the proceeds from selling C short to finance the long position in A. Hence, the return r_f is not required to compensate for the delayed receipt of income and, given the market price of risk, the hedged position would be taken by the investor.

If, alternatively, asset A were to map directly below point C in Figure 12.10, a long position in portfolio C and an offsetting short position in asset A would yield a positive expected return of $E(r_C) - E(r_A)$. Again beta for the position would be zero, the return r_f would not be required, and the hedged position would be taken by the investor.

In general, if the expected return/beta characteristics of a risky asset do not describe a point on the security market line, a profitable arbitrage opportunity exists. This is because any point off the line implies the simultaneous existence of two investments with identical risk (beta), but different expected returns. Arbitrage trading will lead investors to acquire a long position in the underpriced asset and a short position in the overpriced asset.

Arbitrage is the process by which the prices of otherwise identical resources are brought into alignment with each other. The increased demand for a security with an expected return that is too high (given its beta) increases the asset's share price and lowers its expected return. Short selling a security with an expected return that is too low (given its beta) decreases the asset's share price and raises its expected return. The price changes brought about by the arbitrage trading continue until the expected return for each asset, given its beta coefficient, is brought into harmony with the relationship described by the security market line.

For the capital asset pricing model, the market demand curve to hold shares of each risky asset is infinitely elastic at the equilibrium price. The reason is that the different assets and/or portfolios are perfect substitutes for one another, and being perfect substitutes, they must trade at the same price. Thus the price of each asset is determined, given its market risk (beta), the risk-free rate of interest, and the market price of risk.

The Market Model

The Market Model Equation

The return on a risky asset is a linear function of the return on the market under the strict assumptions of the capital asset pricing model. The intercept parameter of the linear equation equals the risk-free rate of interest times one minus the asset's beta coefficient (see Equation 12.18 for the asset's characteristic line).

The *market model* also relates the return on a risky asset to the return on the market portfolio. The equation for the market model is

$$r_{it} = a_i + b_i r_{mt} + e_{it} \tag{12.24}$$

where b_i is the stock's beta coefficient as in equation (12.18), and e_{it} is the market model residual. The *residual* is that part of the price change for the stock that is not related to the return on the market. If the strict form of CAPM is satisfied, a_i in Equation 12.24 will equal $r_f(1 - b_i)$.

Informational Change

The capital asset pricing model provides a theoretical foundation for the market model. The relationship between the stock return and the return on the market portfolio described by Equation 12.24 may also be attributable to informational change that affects a broad spectrum of stocks and to portfolio rebalancing.

Informational change that affects many assets generates price changes that are cross-sectionally correlated. This is clearly true for changes in aggregate economic indicators (such as unemployment or inflation), because these indicators have a pervasive impact on the market.

Informational change need not and indeed does not affect the price of all assets identically. Rather, it differs across assets according to the market model parameters. Stocks with high beta coefficients have percentage price changes that on average are greater than the market; stocks with beta coefficients between zero and unity have percentage price changes that on average are less than the market; and negative beta stocks have price changes that on average counter broad market movements.

Portfolio Rebalancing

Portfolio rebalancing is the readjustment of portfolio weights by investors that occurs when price changes in the market cause the weights to stray from their optimal values. Assume, for instance, that Liquidity Inc. strikes oil, and that the price of the stock rises. *Ceteris paribus,* four changes will occur as the new equilibrium value of price is attained: (1) the weight of Liquidity Inc. in investor portfolios will be greater; (2) the expected return on the stock will be greater (to compensate for the larger portfolio weight); (3) investors will be wealthier (because of the increased value of this asset); and (4) the equilibrium price of other stocks will be higher.

One reason for the increased price of other shares is the increased demand due to greater investor wealth. But there is a more important reason: if the relative portfolio weight for Liquidity Inc. is to be greater, other weights must be less; the inducement for the other weights to be less is a reduction in the expected returns for the other assets, and this reduction occurs as *ceteris paribus,* the share prices of the other assets rise.

The realignment of share prices is the effect of portfolio rebalancing. As can be seen from the preceding discussion, after the process is complete, the price of Liquidity Inc. and of all other stocks will be higher. The increased average value of equities can, of course, be supported only by additional funds being committed to the market. In the context of the CAPM, this would be attributable to a decreased demand to hold the risk-free asset. Because portfolio rebalancing causes the prices of different assets to move in harmony with one another, it generates systematic market movements. Of course, the broader market movements will not be apparent when an issue as small as Liquidity Inc. is the sole recipient of informational change. Nevertheless, the relationship is there. Moreover, the relationship is important when the informational change relates to a significant proportion of firms.

Because of portfolio rebalancing, informational change need not affect all stocks for all stocks to exhibit reasonably consistent, cross-sectionally correlated price movements.

Systematic (Undiversifiable) Versus Unsystematic (Diversifiable) Risk

The market model can be used to distinguish two types of risk: *systematic risk* and *unsystematic risk*. To see this, take variances of Equation 12.24:

$$\text{Var}(r_{it}) = b_i^2 \, \text{Var}(r_{mt}) + \text{Var}(e_{it}) \tag{12.25}$$

Because the return on the stock is partially explained by the return on the market index, part of the riskiness of the stock is explained by the underlying riskiness of all stocks. The first term on the right-hand side of Equation 12.25 is the stock's *systematic risk*. Because the market related component of a stock's return is perfectly correlated with the market, the systematic variance cannot be reduced by portfolio diversification. For this reason, systematic variance is often called *undiversifiable risk*. It is clear from Equation 12.25 that if a stock's beta coefficient is greater than unity, the systematic variability of the stock's return is greater than that of the market. On the other hand, the systematic component of the stock's return is more stable than the return on the market portfolio if the stock's beta coefficient is positive but less than unity.

The second term on the right-hand side of Equation 12.25 is the stock's *unsystematic risk*. Because the price movements for the stock are in part independent of general market movements, part of the riskiness of the stock is independent of the riskiness of the market. Because the residual return for one stock is uncorrelated with (1) the residual return on other stocks and (2) the return on the market index, unsystematic risk can be reduced by portfolio diversification. For this reason, it is often called *diversifiable risk*. In a frictionless environment, the risk averse decision maker will hold a well diversified portfolio so as to eliminate diversifiable risk.

The Market Portfolio

The Investor's Demand Curve

This section shows how the value of the market portfolio is determined. Assuming the market portfolio is traded as if it were a single risky asset, we first show how an individual investor's demand curve to hold shares of the market portfolio can be derived from his or her utility (of wealth) function. We restate the utility function to make explicit the price at which shares of the market portfolio may currently be traded, and the mean and variance of future share prices. The manipulation of the utility function involves a procedure called Taylor expansion. See, for example, R. G. D. Allen for a discussion of the Taylor procedure.[9]

The demand curve to hold shares of the market portfolio may be obtained directly from the utility function, as shown in Appendix A to Chapter 13. The derivation of the demand curve follows Ho, Schwartz, and Whitcomb.[10] Assume the following:

- The investor's portfolio comprises a risk-free asset and one risky asset (shares of the market portfolio).
- Share price and share holdings are continuous variables.
- Short selling is unrestricted.

- The existence of a brief trading period, T_0 to T_1, that is followed by a single investment period, T_1 to T_2.
- All transactions made during the trading period are settled at point in time T_1.
- The investor seeks a portfolio at the beginning of the investment period (at time T_1) that will maximize the expected utility of wealth to be realized at the end of the investment period (at time T_2).
- Investor expectations with respect to the share price at the end of the investment period (at time T_2) are exogenously determined (expectations are independent of the current price of shares).
- All investors are risk averse.

The following variables are used:

C_0 = holdings of the risk-free asset at the beginning of the trading period (T_0)

C_1 = holdings of the risk-free asset at the beginning of the investment period (T_1)

N_0 = number of shares of the market portfolio held at the beginning of the trading period (T_0)

N_1 = number of shares of the market portfolio held at the beginning of the investment period (T_1)

$R_0 - 1$ = risk-free rate of interest over the trading period

$R_1 - 1$ = risk-free rate of interest over the investment period

P_1 = price at which shares of the market portfolio are purchased or sold during the trading period

P_2 = price at which shares of the market portfolio can be sold at the end of the investment period (T_2)

Q = number of shares traded by the investor at the beginning of the investment period (T_1); $Q > 0$ indicates a purchase; $Q < 0$ indicates a sale

The Model. The decision maker starts the *investment period* with C_1 dollars of the risk-free asset and N_1 shares of the market portfolio (the risky asset). Therefore, wealth at T_2 is given by $C_1 R_1 + N_1 P_2$. As of T_1, this wealth is uncertain because P_2 is uncertain. As of T_1, the expected utility of end of period wealth can be written as

$$EU(C_1 R_1 + N_1 P_2) \qquad (12.26)$$

The decision maker starts the *trading period* with C_0 dollars of the risk-free asset and N_0 shares of the risky asset. If during the trading period the decision maker were to exchange holdings of the risk-free asset for Q shares of the risky asset at a price of P_1, the *expected utility of end of period wealth,* written as a function of P_1 and Q, given N_0 and C_0, would be*

$$h(P_1, Q|N_0, C_0) = EU[(C_0R_0 - QP_1)R_1 + (N_0 + Q)P_2] \quad (12.27)$$

where $C_0R_0 - QP_1 = C_1$ and $N_0 + Q = N_1$. Equation 12.27 can be rewritten as

$$h(P_1, Q|N_0, C_0) = c + gQ(a - bQ - P_1) \quad (12.28)$$

where $\quad c = U(W) - \pi N_0^2 \, U'(W)/R_1$
$\qquad g = U'(W)R_1$
$\qquad a = [E(P_2) - 2\pi N_0]/R_1$
$\qquad b = \pi/R_1$
$\qquad \pi = -\frac{1}{2}[U''(W)/U'(W)] \, \text{Var}(P)$

The step from Equation 12.27 to Equation 12.28 involves expanding (Taylor expansion) the investor's utility around the expected value of wealth if the investor does not trade. The procedure is a convenient way of introducing the variance term into the utility function. Two further assumptions are required to obtain Equation 12.28: (1) the third derivative of utility with respect to wealth is small enough to ignore; and (2) the squared deviation of the expected rate of return on the risky asset from the risk-free rate is small enough to ignore.

Measures of Risk Aversion.   Before analyzing Equation 12.28, we first identify two measures of an investor's risk aversion and define an investor's risk premium. The two measures of risk aversion are: (1) $R_A = -U''(W)/U'(W)$ is a measure of absolute risk aversion; and (2) $R_R = WR_A$ is a measure of relative risk aversion. Because we have $U'' < 0$ for a risk averse decision maker, we have $R_A, R_R > 0$ for risk aversion. Larger values of R_A and R_R indicate higher degrees of risk aversion. R_A is a measure of *absolute* risk aversion because it reflects the decision maker's reaction to uncertainty in relation to the *absolute* (dollar) gains/losses in an uncertain situation. R_R is a measure of *relative* risk aversion because it reflects the decision maker's reaction to uncertainty in relation to the *percentage* gains/losses in an uncertain situation. For further discussion, see Pratt.[11]

Risk Premiums.   A *risk premium* is the minimum dollar compensation a decision maker would require to hold a risky asset in place of an alternative that involves no risk. Specifically, a decision maker would be indifferent between a riskless investment with a certain return of D dollars, and

---

* The vertical line in the parenthesized expression on the left-hand side of Equation 12.27 means "given."

a risky investment with an expected dollar return of $E(Z)$ equal to D plus the investor's risk premium. In general, the investor's risk premium depends upon his or her utility function and initial wealth, and upon the distribution of Z.

Pi (π) in Equation 12.28 is a risk premium: π equals one-half of R_A (the measure of the investor's absolute risk aversion) times $Var(P_2)$, which measures the absolute (dollar) risk attributable to holding one share of the market portfolio. The uncertainty associated with holding N shares of the risky asset is $Var(NP_2) = N^2 Var(P_2)$; thus the total risk premium for holding N shares is

$$\pi_T = \pi N_1^2 \tag{12.29}$$

Dividing Equation 12.29 by $N_1 (= N_0 + Q)$ gives the risk premium per share (the average risk premium):

$$\pi_A = \pi N_1 \tag{12.30}$$

Differentiating Equation 12.29 with respect to N_1 gives the risk premium for a marginal share (the *marginal risk premium*):

$$\pi_M = 2\pi N_1 \tag{12.31}$$

Dividing Equation 12.31 by P_1 expresses the marginal risk premium as a percentage of current price:

$$\pi_{M\%} = \frac{\pi_M}{P_1} = \frac{2\pi N_1}{P_1} \tag{12.32}$$

The return on the combined portfolio of N_1 shares of the market portfolio and C_1 dollars of the risk-free asset is

$$r_P = \left(\frac{P_2}{P_1} - 1\right)\left(\frac{P_1 N_1}{W}\right) + \left(1 - \frac{P_1 N_1}{W}\right) r_f \tag{12.33}$$

and the variance of the return on the combined portfolio is

$$Var\left[\left(\frac{P_2}{P_1}\right)\left(\frac{P_1 N_1}{W}\right)\right] = \left(\frac{N_1}{W}\right)^2 Var(P_2) \tag{12.34}$$

Thus the investor's risk premium associated with the uncertain return realized from the combined portfolio is

$$\pi_{rp} = \left(\frac{N_1}{W}\right)^2 \pi \tag{12.35}$$

The various risk premiums identified here are used in the subsection "Interpretation" that follows.

The Reservation Demand Curve. Equation 12.28 can be used to obtain both a reservation price demand curve and an ordinary demand curve. We consider the *reservation demand curve* first. The maximum price at which the decision maker would be willing to buy any given number of shares, $Q > 0$, or the minimum price at which the decision maker would be willing to sell any given number of shares, $Q < 0$, is the *reservation price* for the purchase or sale. Equation 12.28 shows that, if no trade is made (that is, if $Q = 0$), the decision maker's expected utility is equal to c. The reservation price for any value of Q is the price that equates the expected utility $[h(P_1, Q|N_0, C_0)]$ if the trade were made, with the expected utility (c) if no trade were made. Thus the reservation price for any value of Q is given by

$$h(P^R, Q|N_0, C_0) = c \qquad (12.36)$$

where P^R is the reservation price associated with the trade of Q shares. For Equation 12.36 to be satisfied, we must have a $-bQ - P_1 = 0$. Hence the reservation price demand curve is

$$P^R = a - bQ \qquad (12.37)$$

The Ordinary Demand Curve.   Using Equation 12.28, we can also obtain the ordinary demand curve. At any value of P_1, the decision maker selects the value of Q that maximizes expected utility. Hence, the ordinary price demand curve is given by

$$\frac{\partial h}{\partial Q}(P^o, Q|N_0, C_0) = 0 \qquad (12.38)$$

where P^o is the "ordinary" price associated with the trade of Q shares. Therefore, differentiating h in Equation 12.28 with respect to Q, setting the derivative equal to zero, and rearranging gives

$$P^o = a - 2bQ \qquad (12.39)$$

D^R, the reservation curve given by Equation 12.37, and D^o, the ordinary curve given by Equation 12.39, are shown graphically in Figure 12.11. Note the following about the two curves:

- For both curves, the parameter a shows the price at which Q is zero, and hence the price at which the initial number of shares (N_0) will be held.

- The price intercept for the reservation and ordinary demand curves can be obtained by substituting $Q = -N_0$ into Equations 12.37 and 12.39, respectively. The intercept for the ordinary demand curve is $E(P_2)/R_1$, the present value (at the risk-free rate) of the price expected for point in time T_2. The intercept for the reservation demand curve is $[E(P_2) - N_0]/R_1$.

FIGURE 12.11 D^R, *the Reservation Curve in Equation 12.37,* *and* D^o, *the Ordinary Curve in Equation 12.39*

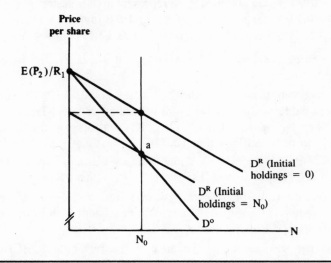

- The location of D^R depends on initial share holdings; the location of D^o does not.

- Both curves are linear. Linearity is a consequence of an assumption made to simplify the derivation: the squared deviation of the expected rate of return on the risky asset from the risk-free rate is small enough to be ignored. The assumption is reasonable for the neighborhood of $E(P_2)/R_1$, but is not acceptable for prices sufficiently different from $E(P_2)/R_1$. Consequently, linearity is a reasonable approximation only as long as the price (P_1) of the risky asset does not deviate too far from the present value of the expected future price. One might expect the demand curve to hold shares of the market portfolio to be convex from below, such that it does not intersect the quantity axis. This is because, with zero storage cost, the investor would hold an unlimited number of shares at a sufficiently low price per share.

- The slope (dP/dQ) of the reservation demand curve given by Equation 12.37 is half that of the ordinary demand curve given by Equation 12.39.

- The slope of the demand curve would be zero (the price elasticity of demand would be infinite) if the risk premium were zero (that is, if the investor were risk neutral), in which case the market portfolio and the risk-free asset would be perfect substitutes.

Interpretation

The previous subsection shows how the demand curve to hold shares of the market portfolio can be obtained for a representative investor, given the risk-free rate of interest, expectations of P_2, and the investor's utility function. Figure 12.12, which reproduces part of Figure 12.11, shows that:

- If the price per share of the market portfolio is P_1, the investor will hold N_1 shares.

- The reservation price for the N_1 shares equals $E(P_2)/R_1$ minus the present value of the risk premium per share, $\pi A/R_1$. The equation for D^R when $N_0 = 0$ is $[E(P_2)/R_1] - bN_1$, and $bN_1 = \pi A/R_1$ (from the definition of b and Equation 12.30).

- Because the slope (dP/dN) of the ordinary demand curve is twice that of the reservation curve, $[E(P_2)/R_1] - P_1 = 2\pi A/R_1$.

- The present value of the total risk premium π_T/R_1 equals the area of the rectangle $[E(P_2)/R_1]ABP^R$, which, consistent with Equation 12.29, equals $\pi(N_1)^2/R_1$.

- Consumer surplus equals the area of the rectangle $P^R BCP_1$, which equals the area of the triangle $[E(P_2)/R_1]CP_1$.

FIGURE 12.12   *The Relationship Between the Reservation Curve, Ordinary Curve, Total and Average Risk Premium, and Consumer Surplus*

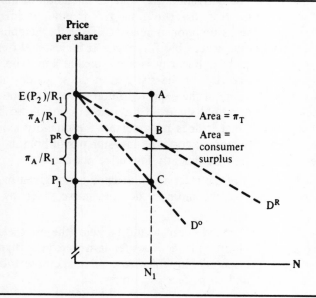

The Risk Premium and the Market Price of Risk. When the investor has traded the optimal number of shares of the market portfolio at the market determined price per share, his or her risk premium can be related to the market price of risk. To see how, assess the ordinary demand curve at $P^o = P_1$:

$$P_1 = \frac{E(P_2)}{R_1} - \frac{2\pi N_1}{R_1} \qquad (12.40)$$

Multiplying by R_1/P_1, rearranging, and recognizing that $[E(P_2)/P_1] - 1 = E(r_m)$ and $R_1 - 1 = r_f$, we get

$$\frac{2\pi N_1}{P_1} = E(r_m) - r_f \qquad (12.41)$$

Therefore, using Equation 12.32 we have

$$\pi_{M\%} = E(r_m) - r_f \qquad (12.42)$$

As discussed in the previous section, the right-hand side of Equation 12.42 is the price of risk. We thus see that the investor achieves an optimal holding of the risky asset by obtaining the number of shares that equates the marginal risk premium with the market price of risk. This result is consistent with the consumer choice model: price is equated with marginal value. Here, the price is the additional expected return the investor receives as compensation for accepting risk, and the marginal value is the marginal risk premium required by the investor.

It is apparent from Equation 12.31 that the marginal risk premium increases with N. For a given price of risk, if the investor holds fewer shares than the value given by the ordinary demand curve, the marginal risk premium will be less than $E(r_m) - r_f$; consequently, the investor will *increase* his or her share holdings until his or her marginal risk premium has risen to equality with the market determined price of risk. Alternatively, if the investor holds more shares than the value given by the ordinary demand curve, the marginal risk premium will be greater than $E(r_m) - r_f$; consequently, the investor will *reduce* his or her share holdings until the marginal risk premium has fallen to equality with the market determined price of risk.

The Investor's Optimal Point on the Capital Market Line. The demand model can be assessed to show the determination of the investor's optimal point on the capital market line (Equation 12.15). From Equation 12.35 we have

$$\pi = \pi_{rp} \left(\frac{W}{N_1} \right)^2$$

which, using $R_A = -U''(W)/U'(W)$, the measure of absolute risk aversion, can be written as

$$\pi = \tfrac{1}{2}R_A \operatorname{Var}(r_p)\left(\frac{W}{N_1}\right)^2 \qquad (12.43)$$

Because $\sigma_p = (NP/W)\sigma_m$, we have $\operatorname{Var}(r_p) = \sigma_p(NP/W)\sigma_m$ and can write Equation 12.43 as

$$\pi = \tfrac{1}{2}R_A \sigma_p\left(\frac{PW}{N_1}\right)\sigma_m \qquad (12.44)$$

Substituting 12.44 into 12.41 and simplifying gives

$$R_R\sigma_p = \frac{E(r_m) - r_f}{\sigma_m} \qquad (12.45)$$

where $R_R(= WR_A)$ is the measure of relative risk aversion.

Equation 12.45 shows that for the investor to hold an optimal portfolio, the market price of risk per standard deviation of the market portfolio must be equal to the investor's coefficient of relative risk aversion times the standard deviation of the combined portfolio's return.

Letting $w = N_1P_1/W$, substituting $w\sigma_m = \sigma_p$ into Equation 12.45, and rearranging gives

$$w = \frac{E(r_m) - r_f}{\operatorname{Var}(r_m)R_R} \qquad (12.46)$$

Equation 12.46 shows that the percentage of wealth that the risk averse investor invests in the market portfolio is positively related to the expected return $E(r_m)$, and negatively related to r_f, $\operatorname{Var}(r_m)$, and R_R. Investors all face the same values of $E(r_m)$, $\operatorname{Var}(r_m)$, and r_f; the investors are assumed to differ, however, according to their degree of risk aversion. More risk averse investors (larger R_R) have smaller optimal values of w and hence are more apt to lend at the risk-free rate (which implies $w < 1$); less risk averse investors (smaller R_R) have larger optimal values of w and hence are more likely to borrow at the risk-free rate (which implies $w > 1$).

The right-hand side of Equation 12.45 is the market price of risk per standard deviation of the market portfolio. As discussed in the section on the capital asset pricing model, the total compensation for risk taking is the price of risk times the number of standard deviations the investor accepts (here, the standard deviation of the combined portfolio). Thus, multiplying both sides of Equation 12.45 by σ_p, we obtain

$$R_R \operatorname{Var}(r_p) = \left[\frac{E(r_m) - r_f}{\sigma_m}\right]\sigma_p \qquad (12.47)$$

Adding r_f to both sides of Equation 12.47 gives the investor's total compensation for waiting and for risk taking:

$$E(r_p) = r_f + R_R \text{ Var}(r_p)$$

$$= r_f + \left[\frac{E(r_m) - r_f}{\sigma_m} \right] \sigma_p \qquad (12.48)$$

Equation 12.48 shows that the location of the investor's optimal point on the capital market line (Equation 12.15) depends on his or her measure of relative risk aversion (R_R).

The ith Risky Asset's Point on the Security Market Line. The demand model can also be assessed to show the location of a risky asset on the security market line (Equation 12.17). Equation 12.42 shows that the marginal risk premium for each investor, as a percentage of P_1, will equal $E(r_m) - r_f$. Therefore, for each investor,

$$\frac{R_A \text{ Var}(P_2)N_1}{P_1} = E(r_m) - r_f \qquad (12.49)$$

It follows from the equation for the ordinary demand curve (Equation 12.39) that investors with lower values of R_A hold a larger number of shares, such that the product $R_A N_1$ is the same for all investors. Because $r_m = (P_2/P_1) - 1$, $\text{Var}(r_m) = \text{Var}(P_2)/P_1^2$. Substituting $\text{Var}(r_m)P_1^2 = \text{Var}(P_2)$ into Equation 12.49 and simplifying gives

$$R_A \text{ Var}(r_m)P_1 N_1 = E(r_m) - r_f \qquad (12.50)$$

Using $P_1 N_1 = wW$ we obtain

$$w R_R \text{ Var}(r_m) = E(r_m) - r_f \qquad (12.51)$$

Equation 12.51 can be interpreted as an equilibrium condition for each investor. Because $R_R w = R_A N_1 P_1$, and because the product $R_A N_1$ is constant across investors, $R_R w$ is constant across all investors. [It is also clear from Equation 12.46 that the product $R_R w$ must be constant across all investors, because $E(r_m)$, r_f, and $\text{Var}(r_m)$ are the same for all.]

The equilibrium condition for each investor with respect to the market portfolio implies an equilibrium condition for each investor with respect to any i^{th} risky asset in the market portfolio. The CAPM showed that the relevant measure of risk for the ith risky asset is $\beta_i = \sigma_{im}/\text{Var}(r_m)$. Therefore, writing $\text{Var}(r_m) = \sigma_{im}/\beta_i$, substituting into Equation 12.51, and multiplying both sides by β_i we get

$$w R_R \sigma_{im} = \beta_i [E(r_m) - r_f] \qquad (12.52)$$

Adding r_f to both sides of Equation 12.52 gives

$$E(r_i) = r_f + wR_R\sigma_{im}$$

$$= r_f + \beta_i[E(r_m) - r_f] \qquad (12.53)$$

Equation 12.53, assessed at $w = 1$, shows that the expected return for the ith risky asset depends on its covariance with the market return, and on the measure of relative risk aversion for an investor whose optimal combined portfolio contains the market portfolio only. The equation also shows that the ith risky asset's specific location on the security market line (Equation 12.17) depends on the covariance of the asset's return with the return on the market portfolio, as discussed in the section about the CAPM.

Market Equilibrium

Determination of the *equilibrium market price* of risk can be visualized as follows. Arbitrarily select a value of $E(r_m) - r_f$ and consider the number of shares of the market portfolio that investors in aggregate will seek to hold, as each attempts to obtain the specific number of shares given by his or her ordinary demand curve at the particular value of $E(r_m) - r_f$. If the total number of shares demanded exceeds the total number of shares available, excessive buying pressure will increase the price of a share of the market portfolio, and $E(r_m) - r_f$ will decrease. Alternatively, if the total number of shares demanded is less than the total number of shares available, excessive selling pressure will decrease the price of a share of the market portfolio, and $E(r_m) - r_f$ will increase. The equilibrium value of the price of risk, $[E(r_m) - r_f]^*$, is the price that equates the aggregate desire to hold shares of the market portfolio with the total number of shares available to be held.

For the capital markets to achieve equilibrium, an equilibrium value for the risk-free rate, r_f, must also be attained. If r_f is below its equilibrium value, investors in aggregate will seek to borrow more of the risk-free asset than they are willing to lend, thus putting upward pressure on r_f. Alternatively, if r_f is above its equilibrium value, investors in aggregate will seek to lend more of the risk-free asset than they are willing to borrow, putting downward pressure on r_f. The equilibrium value of the risk-free rate, r_f^*, is the rate that equates the aggregate desire to borrow the risk-free asset and the aggregate desire to lend the risk-free asset.

Therefore, when the capital markets are in equilibrium: (1) the number of shares investors in aggregate wish to hold of the market portfolio equals the number of shares available, and (2) the amount of the risk-free asset they wish in aggregate to lend equals the amount they wish in aggregate to borrow. When the market has achieved this equilibrium, each investor will hold the specific number of shares that equates his or her own marginal risk premium with the equilibrium market price of risk, $E(r_m)^* - r_f^*$.

FIGURE 12.13 *Capital Market Equilibrium*

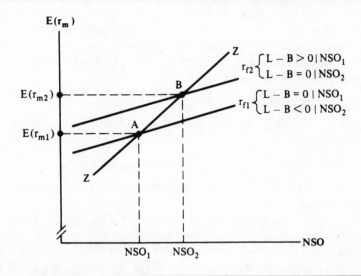

The capital market equilibrium is described graphically by Figure 12.13. The expected return on the market portfolio is shown on the vertical axis, and the *number of shares outstanding* (NSO) of the market portfolio is shown on the horizontal axis. Each of the upward sloping r_f-curves shows the relationship between the expected return on the market portfolio and NSO, for the associated value of r_f. $E(r_m)$ is determined given NSO and r_f because (1) the marginal risk premium is established by the aggregate demand curve evaluated at NSO, and (2) the marginal risk premium equals $E(r_m) - r_f$. For a given value of r_f, $E(r_m)$ is an increasing function of NSO because the marginal risk premium is an increasing function of NSO.

Let r_{f2} be greater than r_{f1}. The upward sloping line labeled r_{f2} is above the line labeled r_{f1} because (1) the equilibrium value of the risk premium is determined for a given value of NSO, and (2) the higher the risk-free rate, the higher must be the expected return on the market portfolio for the risk premium to equal its equilibrium value.

Let $L - B$ (aggregate lending minus aggregate borrowing) stand for investors' net aggregate desire to lend at the risk-free rate. For a given value of NSO, the higher the risk-free rate, the larger $L - B$ is. Information concerning the net desire to lend is given in Figure 12.13 by the labels shown for the two r_f curves. The upper curve shows, for the rate r_{f2}, that $L - B > 0$ when the number of shares outstanding is NSO_1, and that $L - B = 0$ when the number of shares outstanding is NSO_2. The lower curve shows, for the rate r_{f1}, that $L - B = 0$ for $NSO = NSO_1$, and $L - B < 0$ for $NSO = NSO_2$.

Given a value for NSO, the capital market is in equilibrium if $L - B = 0$, and if the market price of risk equals each investor's marginal risk premium. Such an equilibrium is shown in Figure 12.13 by point A for $NSO = NSO_1$, and by point B for $NSO = NSO_2$.

$$\text{At point A :} \qquad L - B = 0 \quad \text{with } r_f = r_{f1}$$

Given that $r_f = r_{f1}$, the marginal risk premium for NSO_1 equals the price of risk with $E(r_m) = E(r_{m1})$.

$$\text{At point B :} \qquad L - B = 0 \quad \text{with } r_f = r_{f2}$$

Given that $r_f = r_{f2}$, the marginal risk premium for NSO_2 equals the price of risk with $E(r_m) = E(r_{m2})$.

Notice that the equilibrium value for the risk-free rate is shown to be higher if the number of shares of the market portfolio is $NSO_2 > NSO_1$. This is because (1) as NSO increases, the risk premium increases; (2) r_f constant, the risk premium increases by $E(r_m)$ increasing; but (3) if $E(r_m)$ were to increase r_f constant, $L - B$ would become negative; and hence (4) r_f must also increase to maintain $L - B = 0$.

Because r_f increases with NSO, capital market equilibrium will lie on the more steeply inclined line labeled ZZ that passes through points A and B. The intersection of ZZ and the vertical line at the exogenously determined value of NSO identifies the equilibrium values of the expected return to the market portfolio and the risk-free rate of interest. For example, if $NSO = NSO_1$, $E(r_m)^* = E(r_{m1})$, and $r_f^* = r_{f1}$. Alternatively, if $NSO = NSO_2$, $E(r_m)^* = E(r_{m2})$ and $r_f^* = r_{f2}$.

The Discounted Cash Flow Model

The chapter has thus far shown that the riskiness of a stock (or portfolio) can be measured by the stock's beta coefficient and that the expected return for the stock is a function of beta (β). We now use a simple discounted cash flow (DCF) model to show how the stock's price is set by discounting future dividends at an appropriate discount rate (k).

The Model

Assume a company's earnings are expected to grow at a steady rate of g per year for the unlimited future. At the end of each year a constant percentage of earnings is paid out as dividends to investors, and the remainder is retained so that the firm's assets can grow at the rate g. The investor who buys a share of the firm's stock can be thought of as purchasing an infinite stream of dividend payments that also grows at the rate g. The price of a share can be determined by assessing the dividend stream using a risk-appropriate discount rate to obtain a present value.

If, for simplicity, we evaluate a stock that has just gone ex-dividend, we can write*

$$P_0 = D_0(1 + g)/(1 + k) + \cdots + D_0[(1 + g)/(1 + k)]^\infty \qquad (12.54)$$

which, being the sum of an infinite geometric progression, can be rewritten as

$$P_0 = D_1/(k - g) \qquad (12.55)$$

Similarly, we expect share price one year hence to be

$$P_1 = D_2/(k - g) \qquad (12.56)$$

Substituting $D_1(1 + g)$ for D_2 in Equation 12.56 and dividing by Equation 12.55 gives

$$P_1/P_0 = (1 + g) \qquad (12.57)$$

Thus g is also the rate at which the stock's price appreciates.

Solving (12.55) for k we have

$$k = D_1/P_0 + g \qquad (12.58)$$

Equation 12.58 shows that k is an expected return that comprises a dividend yield and a capital appreciation component. P_0 is set in the marketplace so that the dividend yield, D_1/P_0, is sufficient to give shareholders their required return, given the growth rate, g. That is, if returns are too low, P_0 falls and the dividend yield increases; if returns are too high, P_0 increases and the dividend yield falls.

Determination of the Risk-Appropriate Return

E(r) is an expected return for the stock; k is an expected return that an investor requires as compensation for holding the stock. In equilibrium, E(r) must equal k. If E(r) < k, P_0 will fall and E(r) will increase; if E(r) > k, P_0 will rise and E(r) will decrease. The equilibrium expected return can be determined using the Capital Asset Pricing Model. If CAPM holds, we can, using Equation 12.53 and the condition E(r) = k, write

$$k = r_f + \beta[E(r_M) - r_f] \qquad (12.59)$$

---

* Equation 12.25 is meaningful only for g < k. When it is clear in context, we have, for simplicity, suppressed the subscript i on k and E(r) that would identify a specific security.

From Equation 12.42, $[E(r_M) - r_f]$ can be interpreted as the marginal risk premium for the market portfolio expressed as a percentage of price. Multiplying this term by the stock's beta coefficient gives us the marginal percentage risk premium for the stock.

The Relationship Between k and Market Capitalization

The relationship between k and market capitalization (the value of shares outstanding) is most simply shown for the market portfolio, for which β is unity. Let r_f and the expectation of the future share price of the market portfolio be constant, and consider the consequence of a decrease in the market portfolio's current price from P_H to P_L: the expected return for the market portfolio is higher and the risk premium paid by the market is raised in equilibrium. Thus, to maintain $E(r_M) = k_M$, the marginal risk premium required by the investor must also be higher. This is consistent with our demonstration in the section "The Market Portfolio" that, in a CAPM environment, the investor's demand curve to hold shares of the market portfolio is downward sloping. Hence the aggregate market's demand to hold shares of the market portfolio is also downward sloping. It follows that, *ceteris paribus*, k is larger for greater market capitalization, with the specific functional relationship depending on the utility functions of investors.

The discussion suggests that k is not exogenously determined, but rather depends on the size of the market portfolio. This implies that the price of the market portfolio is not an intrinsic value that can be "found" by security analysis, but rather is determined in the marketplace by the forces of demand and supply.*

The Demand to Hold Shares of a Single Asset

The determination of asset prices is less straightforward when the assumptions of the capital asset pricing model are relaxed. Nonstandard forms of the CAPM do allow for modifications of the assumptions concerning riskless borrowing and lending rates, and the absence of taxes, transaction costs, and other trading restrictions. See Elton and Gruber[12] for further discussion. One of the most critical assumptions of the CAPM, and one of the most troublesome to relax, is that investors have homogeneous expectations concerning the risk, return, and covariance characteristics of individual securities. When this assumption is relaxed, we can no longer obtain a unique market portfolio in relation to which individual asset prices may be established, given their covariances with the market.

---

* This section draws on R. Schwartz and J. Shapiro, "The Challenge of Institutionalization for the Equity Markets," in *Institutional Investors: Challenges and Responsibilities*, Arnold W. Sametz, ed. Homewood, IL: Dow Jones-Irwin, 1991, forthcoming.

This section discusses the pricing of an individual risky asset in a multi-asset environment. A formal derivation of the demand curve for a single asset along the lines followed in the previous section will not be attempted, because of the complexity of the multiasset context. Rather, we consider more broadly whether such a demand curve would be negatively inclined, upward sloping, or infinitely elastic. Following the standard practice in microstructure theory, we conclude by assuming the existence of a negatively inclined market demand curve to hold shares of a single risky asset. This demand curve is important for much of the analysis that follows in the book.

A Technical Issue

We first clarify a technical issue concerning the demand to hold shares of a financial asset. The investment decision concerns how much of one's wealth to invest in a particular asset. However, implementation of the investment decision involves the decision to buy or to sell *shares*. In other words, investors trade shares but derive utility from the dollar value of their investments. This condition differs from that of most markets, in which the resources that are traded are themselves the source of utility. Because it is shares that are traded, market equilibrium must be analyzed with regard to the demand to hold shares.

The individual's propensity to invest in an asset can be expressed as*

$$V = V(P) \qquad (12.60)$$

where $V = NP$, P is the price per share, and N is the number of shares of the asset that are held. The analysis presented in this section applies to an individual asset, and so we can, for notational simplicity, suppress the subscript i. We also suppress the time identification on P when it is clear in context that we are referring to value as of point in time 1. Note that $V/W = w$, the asset's portfolio weight. Dividing both sides of Equation 12.60 by P gives the demand to hold shares,

$$N = \frac{V(P)}{P} \qquad (12.61)$$

To explore whether Equation 12.61 is downward sloping, first differentiate it with respect to P:

$$\frac{dN}{dP} = [V'(P)P - V(P)]P^{-2}$$

$$= \left[\left(\frac{dV}{dP}\right)P - V\right]P^{-2} \qquad (12.62)$$

---

* V(P) is a general functional form; it is not V times P.

Then multiply both sides of Equation 12.62 by P/N, use $V = NP$, and simplify:

$$\frac{dN}{dP}\frac{P}{N} = \frac{dV}{dP}\frac{P}{V} - 1 \qquad (12.63)$$

The term on the left-hand side of Equation 12.63 and the first term on the right-hand side are both *elasticities,* the economist's measure of responsiveness. The first is the elasticity of N with respect to P, and the second is the elasticity of V with respect to P. Therefore, Equation 12.63 can be rewritten as

$$\eta_{N,P} = \eta_{V,P} - 1 \qquad (12.64)$$

where η is the symbol for elasticity. For any function, $y = f(x)$, the elasticity of y with respect to x is defined as the percentage change in y that results from a percentage change in x. Thus, writing the percentage change in y as dy/y and the percentage change in x as dx/x, elasticity (η) is (dy/y)/(dx/x). The expression can be rewritten in the form used in Equation 12.63, (dy/dx)(x/y). Writing the elasticity as $\eta_{y,x}$ shows explicitly that the elasticity of y is with respect to x. The function $y = f(x)$ is considered elastic if (in absolute value) $\eta > 1$, of unitary elasticity if $\eta = 1$, and inelastic if $\eta < 1$.

Equation 12.64 shows the relationship between the number of shares held (N) as a function of P and the value of holdings (V) as a function of P. With this equation, we can reason in terms of the relationship between value and price and then draw conclusions concerning the relationship between the number of shares and price (which is the demand curve to hold shares).

Before proceeding, let us assess Equation 12.64:

Case 1: $\eta_{V,P} < 0$ implies $\eta_{N,P} < -1$; here, the demand to hold shares is a negative and elastic function.

Case 2: $\eta_{V,P} = 0$ implies $\eta_{N,P} = -1$; here, the demand to hold shares is a negative function of unitary elasticity.

Case 3: $0 < \eta_{V,P} < 1$ implies $-1 < \eta_{N,P} < 0$; here, the demand to hold shares is a negative and inelastic function.

Case 4: $\eta_{V,P} > 1$ implies $\eta_{N,P} > 0$; here, an increase in the price of an asset would result in the investor's wanting to hold more shares (the demand curve is upward sloping).

The Availability of Substitutes

It is well established in microeconomics that demand elasticities depend on the availability of substitutes, that elasticities are greater the closer the substitutes are, and that demand elasticities are infinite in the presence of perfect substitutes.

Under the assumptions of the capital asset pricing model, perfect substitutes exist for individual securities. For the CAPM, the equilibrium prices of the individual risky assets that the market portfolio comprises are determined given (1) the risk-free rate of interest, (2) the investors' (homogeneous) expectations concerning future prices, (3) the investors' tastes for risk, and (4) the number of shares of the market portfolio to be held. In this context, the market demand to hold shares of any i^{th} risky asset is infinitely elastic at a price established by the ith asset's contribution to aggregate market risk, and by the market price of risk. (Note that $\eta_{V,P} = \infty$ implies $\eta_{N,P} = \infty$).

This result is perturbed when the assumptions of homogeneous expectations and unrestricted borrowing and lending at the risk-free rate are relaxed. Even if some investors view certain assets as having perfect substitutes, the market in aggregate may not, because different investors may not agree on what the perfect substitutes are. If an individual investor believes a perfect substitute exists for an individual risky asset, that investor's demand for that risky asset will be infinitely elastic over some range; however, in the absence of unrestricted borrowing and lending, the range of infinite elasticity will be bounded. In this event, the market demand for the individual risky asset will be downward sloping.

For instance, assume two assets (A and B) and two investors. Let each investor believe that A and B are perfect substitutes. This belief is reflected in each investor's having A, B indifference curves that are negatively inclined, straight lines in the space of A, B shares. (Note that these are not risk/return indifference curves, but rather indifference curves that relate two assets given the mean and variance parameters for each.) The slope of each investor's linear indifference curve reflects both the rate at which that investor would be willing to substitute shares of B for shares of A and the price at which he or she would switch from including only A in his or her portfolio to only B.

Now let the slope of the A, B indifference curves be different for the two investors (because they do not agree about the comparative riskiness of the two securities). It is clear in this case that the price change that will cause one of the investors to switch between the assets will not cause the other investor to switch. Therefore, the two investors do not switch at the same price. Accordingly, the market in aggregate will not move entirely into or out of the two assets at a single price.

The analysis of the substitution effect shows that two conditions must be satisfied for the market to have an infinitely elastic demand to hold shares of an asset:

1. Each investor must view the asset as having perfect substitutes.

2. The set of investors must have homogeneous expectations.

There are extreme conditions, and they are unlikely to prevail. Therefore, we continue to adhere to the primary law of choice: demand will be greater (but not infinitely greater) when price is lower.

The Income/Wealth Effect

Demand theory distinguishes between a substitution effect and an income or wealth effect. The income effect is primarily relevant for flow-dimensioned demand curves, and the wealth effect is primarily relevant for stock dimensioned demand curves. It is the wealth effect that we are concerned with here. These effects are as follows:

The Substitution Effect.   When the price of a good falls *in relation to* other prices, that good is substituted for others in the consumer's budget. The substitution effect is never positive. Specifically, if in a two-good universe, X becomes cheaper in relation to Y, more of X is always consumed in relation to Y, except in the extreme case of perfect complementarity.

The Income Effect.   If the consumer's *nominal* income and other prices are constant, a decrease in the price of a resource will expand the consumer's command over *all* resources, thereby increasing *real* income. Because the demand for most goods is positively related to real income, the income effect will generally reinforce the substitution effect, assuring negative inclination of the demand curve.

The Wealth Effect.   When an investor's share holdings and all other asset prices are constant, a decrease in the price of one asset will cause both an increase of wealth (additional shares of the asset can be purchased at a lower price) and a reduction of wealth (the shares an investor already owns are worth less). The net change in wealth will affect the individual's investment decision. This is called the *wealth effect*.

In general, assuming the investor's demand to hold asset shares is positively related to wealth, for a perverse wealth effect to reverse the slope of the demand curve the following must happen:

- The negative change in wealth due to the reduced value of shares already owned must exceed the positive change of wealth associated with the investor's ability to buy additional shares at a lower price.

- The *response* to the net reduction in wealth must more than offset the substitution effect associated with the share price being lower.

- The perverse wealth effect must offset the substitution effect *by enough* to make $\eta_{V,P} > 1$ (see Equation 12.64).*

---

* This requirement is more severe than its counterpart in ordinary demand theory, where all that is required to reverse the slope of the demand curve is that the perverse income effect outweigh the substitution effect.

In the preceding section, however, the derivation of an individual's demand to hold shares of the market portfolio showed that, under risk aversion, the individual's demand is a downward sloping function, regardless of initial share holdings. Furthermore, the wealth effect must be weaker for any i^{th} asset than for the portfolio of assets because the change in wealth resulting from an x percent (x%) change in the share price of the ith asset is $w_i x\% < x\%$, where $w_i < 1$ is the portfolio weight for that asset.

Therefore, we discount the possibility of a perverse wealth effect and continue to adhere to the primary law of choice: demand will be greater when price is lower.

Expectations

An investor's expected utility is positively related to expected returns, and if the return an investor expects to realize from an asset increases *(ceteris paribus)*, the dollar importance of that asset in his or her portfolio should be increased. We now assess the effect of P_1 on expected returns. This effect depends on the relationship between P_1 and $E(P_2)$. When the assumption of homogeneous expectations is relaxed, change in P_1 can cause change in $E(P_2)$ because current prices may signal information that would alter the expectations of relatively uninformed investors (see the discussion in Chapter 15).

To analyze the expectations effect, write the expected return for the asset as $E(R) = E(P_2)/P_1$, and consider the relationship between $E(P_2)$ and P_1 for four categories of investors:

1. *The rugged individualists:* Such people conduct their own security analysis, develop their own assessment of how a stock might perform in the future, and are totally unaffected by what others might think. For these people, the elasticity of $E(P_2)$ with respect to P_1 is zero.

2. *The sheep:* These investors exercise no independent judgment; rather, they simply assume that the price set on the market is the correct price. This being the case, any price change is interpreted as signaling new information on the future value share price will attain, but does not change expected returns. For these people, the elasticity of $E(P_2)$ with respect to P_1 is unity.

3. *The exaggerators:* These people assume that current price changes understate the impact of informational change. Thus they believe that any percentage increase or decrease in current price is associated with a greater percentage increase or decrease in $E(P_2)$.

4. *The rest of us:* Decision makers in this category think for themselves and come to their own conclusions, but also respect the market's

collective judgment as this is reflected in security prices. These people revise their expectations on P_2 after a change in P_1, but do so less than proportionately. Consequently, for this category, the elasticity of $E(P_2)$ with respect to P_1 is between zero and unity.

To illustrate, consider a company called Liquidity Inc. (tape symbol LIQ). Suppose that LIQ has been trading at 50, that a 20% expected annual rate of return is reasonable for the stock given its riskiness, and that the rugged individualists, the sheep, the exaggerators, and the rest of us happen to expect that one year from now the stock will be worth 60. Now suppose the price decreases to 45.

The rugged individualists still expect a future price of 60: hence, for them, $E[R] = {}^{60}\!/_{45} = 1.33$. The sheep still expect a return of 20%; hence, for them, $E[R] = E(P_2)/45 = 1.20$, which implies $E(P_2) = 54$. What about the exaggerators and the rest of us? The answer depends on how each individual's expectation is adjusted, given that price is now 45, not 50. A representative answer for a member of the rest of us category can be given. Write the individual's expectation of price one year from now, given the price today as $E(P_2|P_1)$. The expectation of P_2 could be written more explicitly as $E(P_2|P_1, \theta)$ where θ stands for all prior price history upon which current expectations might be based. This allows, for instance, for P_1 to transmit a different signal if the last preceding price were some $P' < P_1$, or if alternatively it were some $P'' > P_1$. Because θ reflects information concerning past events, it is a constant in the analysis and need not be expressed explicitly. Note that $E(P_2|P_1)$ has a one-to-one correspondence with $E(R|P_1)$, the return that is expected given today's price. For a representative member of the rest of us set, assume

$$E(P_2|P_1 = 50) = 60 \quad \text{which implies } E(R|P_1 = 50) = 1.20$$

$$E(P_2|P_1 = 45) = 58 \quad \text{which implies } E(R|P_1 = 45) = 1.29$$

The investor's portfolio decision can now be made, on the basis of the returns that are expected. For instance, we might have the following:

$$\text{Hold 100 shares at 50 [because } E(R|P_1 = 50) = 1.20]$$

$$\text{Hold 125 shares at 45 [because } E(R|P_1 = 45) = 1.29]$$

These two demand propensities are shown by points A and B in Figure 12.14. For simplicity and with no loss of generality, we here ignore the variance term. As the example has been structured, an increase of the variance term could not reverse the slope of the demand curve. This is because any price decrease would shift all points of the returns distribution to the right, causing the new distribution to dominate the old.

FIGURE 12.14   *The Demand Curve with Price Signaling*

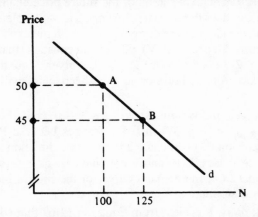

We could in principle determine other demand points in a similar way and so obtain the complete demand function. Such a function is represented by the line labeled *d* in Figure 12.14. Thus, even though expectations of the price at the end of the investment period $[E(P_2)]$ vary along the curve, desired share holdings are uniquely determined at each price. In other words, we have an unambiguous specification of the *ex ante* demand propensities and hence of the demand curve.

We may now consider whether or not the dependence of expectations on the current value of price could cause the demand curve to be positively inclined. To this end, we first show how change in an asset's expected return $E(R)$ with respect to the asset's current price (P_1) is related to the change in $E(P_2)$ with respect to P_1. The relationship is obtained as follows:

Differentiate $E(R) = E(P_2)/P_1$ with respect to P_1:

$$\frac{dE(R)}{dP_1} = \frac{[dE(P_2)/dP_1]P_1 - E(P_2)}{P_1^2} \tag{12.65}$$

Multiply both sides by $P_1/E(R)$ and rearrange:

$$\left[\frac{dE(R)}{dP_1}\right]\left[\frac{P_1}{E(R)}\right] = \left[\frac{dE(P_2)}{dP_1}\right]\left[\frac{1}{E(R)}\right] - \left[\frac{E(P_2)}{P_1}\right]\left[\frac{1}{E(R)}\right] \tag{12.66}$$

Use $E(R) = E(P_2)/P_1$ and write in elasticity form:

$$\eta_{E(R),P_1} = \eta_{E(P_2),P_1} - 1 \tag{12.67}$$

The relationship expressed by Equation 12.67 reflects the following:

- *For the sheep:* The expectation of the future price changes at precisely the same rate as does the current price ($\eta_{E(P_2),P_1} = 1$). Hence the expected return is independent of the current price. With the expected return constant, the portfolio decision (V) will remain constant (that is, $\eta_{V,P_1} = 0$, as in Case 2 in subsection 1). Thus, given Equation 12.64, the demand curve for an investor in the sheep class will be downward sloping.

- *For the rugged individualists:* $\eta_{E(P_2),P_1} = 0$, and thus by Equation 12.67, $\eta_{E(R),P_1} = -1$. When E(R) changes because P_1 changes, the portfolio decision (V) will change in the same direction as E(R). Therefore, as P_1 decreases, E(R) and V both increase as in Case 1, and hence, by Equation 12.64, the demand curve for the rugged individualist will be downward sloping.

- *For the rest of us:* It is clear from Equation 12.67 that with the response of the expected price to the current price positive and inelastic, the response of the expected return to the current price is negative (although inelastic). Again, by Equation 12.64, the demand to hold shares will be downward sloping (this is likely to fit Case 3).

- *For the exaggerators:* $\eta_{E(P_2),P_1} > 1$ for the exaggerators, and hence, from Equation 12.67, we have $\eta_{E(R),P_1} > 0$. As a consequence, the demand curve for these people may not be downward sloping (as in Case 4).

It follows that, for an individual's demand curve to be positively inclined because of the expectations effect:

1. The expectations elasticity ($\eta_{E(P_2),P_1}$) must be greater than unity (which holds only for the exaggerators).

2. The response to the change in expected returns must be *great enough* to make $\eta_{V,P} > 1$ (see Equation 12.64).

The analysis of the expectations effect shows that the response necessary for the slope of the demand curve to be perturbed is conceivable but unlikely. Therefore, we discount the possibility and continue to adhere to the primary law of choice: demand will be greater when price is lower.

Recapitulation

Having considered the possibilities for substitution, the wealth effect, and the expectations effect, we conclude that the representative investor's demand to hold shares of a single risky asset, as well as the market demand curve, will be an inverse function of price. The downward sloping demand curve represents the individual's investment decision; it is of key importance to the analysis that follows.

Appendix—Marginal Contribution of a Stock to the Variance of the Market Portfolio

The appendix shows that the derivative of the variance of the market portfolio with respect to the portfolio weight of the ith asset equals σ_{im}/σ_m. The derivative is obtained as follows. Since

$$\sigma_m = [\text{Var } (r_m)]^{1/2}$$

where $\quad \text{Var } (r_m) = \sum_{i=1}^{M} w_i^2 \sigma_i^2 + \sum_{i=1}^{M} \sum_{\substack{j=1 \\ i \neq j}}^{M} w_{ij}\sigma_{ij},$

the derivative of σ_m with respect to w_i is

$$\frac{d\sigma_m}{dw_i} = \frac{1}{2}[\text{Var } (r_m)]^{-1/2}\left[\frac{d[\text{Var } (r_m)]}{dw_i}\right] \quad (12.A1)$$

with

$$\frac{d[\text{Var } (r_m)]}{dw_i} = 2w_i\sigma_i^2 + 2\sum_{j=1}^{M} w_j\sigma_{ij} \quad (12.A2)$$

Therefore

$$\frac{d\sigma_m}{dw_i} = \frac{w_i\sigma_i^2 + \sum_{j=1}^{M} w_j\sigma_{ij}}{\sigma_m} \quad (12.A3)$$

Since $r_m = \sum_{j=1}^{M} w_j r_j$, and because* $\text{Cov}(r_i, w_j r_j) = w_j\sigma_{ij}$ and $\text{Cov}(r_i, \sum_{j=1}^{M} w_j r_j) = \sum_{j=1}^{M} w_j\sigma_{ij}$, we have

$$\sigma_{im} = \text{Cov}\left(r_i, \sum_{j=1}^{M} w_j r_j\right) = \sum_{i=1}^{M} w_i\sigma_{ij}$$

$$= w_i\sigma_i^2 + \sum_{j=1}^{M} w_j\sigma_{ij} \quad (12.A4)$$

---

* The covariance of a variable (x) with the weighted sum of two other variables $(w_y y + w_z z)$, is equal to the weighted sum of the covariance between x and y, and the covariance between x and z. The proof is

$$\text{Cov}(x, w_y y + w_z z) = E[x - \bar{x})(w_y y + w_z z - w_y \bar{y} - w_z \bar{z})]$$
$$= w_y E[(x - \bar{x})(y - \bar{y})] + w_z E[(x - \bar{x})(z - \bar{z})]$$
$$= w_y \text{Cov}(x, y) + w_z \text{Cov}(x, z)$$

Hence the numerator of (12.A3) is σ_{im}, and

$$\frac{d\sigma_m}{dw_i} = \frac{\sigma_{im}}{\sigma_m} \qquad (12.A5)$$

Q.E.D.

Suggested Reading

Allen, R. G. D. *Mathematical Analysis for Economists*. London, England: Macmillan, 1960.

Baumol, W. *Economic Theory and Operations Analysis*. 4th ed. Englewood Cliffs, NJ: Prentice Hall, 1977.

Elton, E., and Gruber, M. *Modern Portfolio Theory and Investment Analysis*. 4th ed. New York: Wiley, 1991.

Ho, T., Schwartz, R., and Whitcomb, D. "The Trading Decision and Market Clearing Under Transaction Price Uncertainty." *Journal of Finance,* March 1985.

Lintner, J. "The Valuation of Risk Assets and the Selection of Risky Investments in Stock Portfolios and Capital Budgets." *Review of Economics and Statistics,* February 1965.

Lintner, J. "Security Prices, Risk, and Maximal Gains from Diversification." *Journal of Finance,* December 1965.

Lintner, J. "The Aggregation of Investor's Diverse Judgments and Preferences in Purely Competitive Security Markets." *Journal of Financial and Quantitative Analysis,* December 1969.

Mossin, J. "Equilibrium in a Capital Asset Market." *Econometrica,* October 1966.

Pratt, J. "Risk Aversion in the Small and in the Large." *Econometrica,* January 1964.

Ross, S. "The Arbitrage Theory of Capital Asset Pricing." *Journal of Economic Theory,* December 1976.

Schwartz, R., and Shapiro, J. "The Challenge of Institutionalization for the Equity Markets." In *Institutional Investors: Challenges and Responsibilities,* Arnold W. Sametz, ed. Homewood, IL: Dow Jones-Irwin, 1991, forthcoming.

Sharpe, W. "Capital Asset Prices: A Theory of Market Equilibrium Under Conditions of Risk." *Journal of Finance,* September 1964.

Sharpe, W. *Investments,* 3d ed. Englewood Cliffs, NJ: Prentice Hall, 1985.

Notes

1. W. Baumol, *Economic Theory and Operations Analysis*. 4th ed. Englewood Cliffs, NJ: Prentice Hall, 1977.
2. E. Elton and G. Gruber, *Modern Portfolio Theory and Investment Analysis*. 4th ed. New York: Wiley, 1991.
3. Ibid.

4. W. Sharpe, "Capital Asset Prices: A Theory of Market Equilibrium Under Conditions of Risk," *Journal of Finance,* September 1964.
5. J. Lintner, "The Valuation of Risk Assets and the Selection of Risky Investments in Stock Portfolios and Capital Budgets," *Review of Economics and Statistics,* February 1965.
6. J. Mossin, "Equilibrium in a Capital Asset Market," *Econometrica,* October 1966.
7. S. Ross, "The Arbitrage Theory of Capital Asset Pricing," *Journal of Economic Theory,* December, 1976.
8. Elton and Gruber, *Modern Portfolio Theory.*
9. R. G. D. Allen, *Mathematical Analysis for Economists,* London, England: Macmillan, 1960.
10. T. Ho, R. Schwartz, and D. Whitcomb, "The Trading Decision and Market Clearing Under Transaction Price Uncertainty," *Journal of Finance,* March 1985.
11. J. Pratt, "Risk Aversion in the Small and the Large," *Econometrica,* January 1964.
12. Elton and Gruber, *Modern Portfolio Theory.*

13

Order Placement and the Determination of Market Prices

Trading is a complex activity that is separate from investing. Investment decisions involve stock selection and portfolio formation with respect to longer term risk and return relationships. Trading involves the implementation of investment decisions and buying and selling to exploit short-run price swings and arbitrage possibilities.*

Some excellent investment managers would make very poor traders, and vice versa. Successful trading requires special skills and attitudes. Good traders can sense a market, spot pricing discrepancies, and make lightning fast decisions. The long run for an investment manager may be the better part of a year or more. The long run for a trader, as of 9:30 A.M. may be early afternoon.

Trading involves strategy. Traders do not want to pay more than necessary for a purchase or accept less for a sale. At the same time, however, they do not want to miss a trade because they have bid too low or offered too high. Optimal order placement depends on the location of the agent's demand curve to hold shares of the risky asset, on his or her expectations of what the market clearing price will be, and on the design of the trading system.

The Frictionless Market

The analysis in this section assumes costless trading. The agent transmits buy/sell order functions to the market and trades the appropriate amount at whatever price is established on the market. Strategic decisions need not be made in this "frictionless" environment.

---

* The analysis presented in this chapter is based on microeconomic concepts that are set forth in Appendix A of this chapter. Microeconomic Foundations.

The Investor's Demand Curve

The demand curve of a representative investor is shown in Figure 13.1(a). The investor's current holdings are identified by the vertical line at N_0. The subscript 0 here refers to an initial share holding; alternative share holdings will be denoted by subscripts 1 and 2. Similar subscripts will be used for the price variable. P_0 is the price at which the investor would be willing to hold N_0 shares. At any price greater than P_0, the decision maker would like to hold fewer shares; at any price lower than P_0, he or she would like to hold more shares. The appendix explains how the buy and sell curves can be identified from the demand curve to hold shares. The geometry is shown in Figure 13.1(b).

If the price in the frictionless market is P_1, the investor will want to hold N_1 shares (because of the price and the signal that it conveys), and he or she will achieve this by buying Q_1 shares. If, instead, the price is P_2, the investor will want to hold N_2 shares (because of the alternative value of price and the alternative signal that is conveyed), and he or she will achieve this by selling Q_2 shares, and so forth.

Note the following about the demand curve to hold shares and the associated buy/sell order curves:

- We have suppressed the i subscript that denotes the ith asset, because the discussion in this chapter relates to the demand to hold shares of *one* particular asset. Because we now consider the full set of participants in the market for a stock, the subscript j has been introduced to identify the jth investor/trader, $j = 1, \ldots, \mathcal{S}$.

FIGURE 13.1 *Investor's Demand Curve and Buy and Sell Curves.* *(a) The Demand Curve (b) The Buy and Sell Curves*

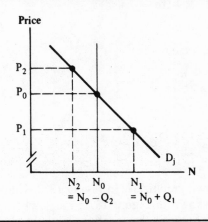
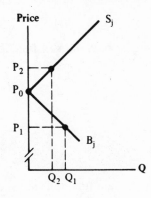

- The buy/sell functions for the individual trader branch off the price axis at a value determined by the intersection of the investor's demand curve (D_j) and the vertical line at N_0 that denotes the number of shares the jth investor holds.

- N_0 constant, the point of intersection depends on the location of the demand curve. Accordingly, shifts in D_j are associated with shifts in the buy/sell order curves shown in Figure 13.1(b).

- D_j constant, the point of intersection depends on the size of share holdings. Therefore, each trade is accompanied by a shift of the buy/sell order curves (the curves shift down with a purchase and up with a sale).

- An investor's wealth changes with each purchase or sale of shares. An investor's risk aversion measure (either absolute and/or relative) is, in general, dependent on his or her wealth, and thus the slope of the demand curve changes as the investor trades. To simplify the exposition we ignore this effect. Thus the investor's demand curve (D_j) is assumed not to shift because of a trade.

Market Equilibrium

Given each investor's order functions (the S_j and B_j trade curves) and an environment where trading is costless, each investor submits his or her complete trade curves to the market. The reason is twofold. First, the order size associated with each price along the trade curves will have been accurately written *given that* that price is in fact set on the market. Second, the environment guarantees that the investor realizes only one execution. The importance of this second consideration is shown later in relation to the opportunity costs of trading.

For the individual buy and sell functions,

$$B_j = f_j(P) \qquad (13.1)$$

$$S_j = g_j(P) \qquad (13.2)$$

the aggregate buy and sell functions are

$$B = \sum_{j=1}^{\mathscr{S}} f_j(P) \qquad (13.3)$$

$$S = \sum_{j=1}^{\mathscr{S}} g_j(P) \qquad (13.4)$$

The aggregate functions are shown graphically in Figure 13.2. Unlike the B_j and S_j curves for an investor shown in Figure 13.1, the market curves B and S can intersect each other because the locations of D_j and of the

FIGURE 13.2 *Aggregate Buy and Sell Curves*

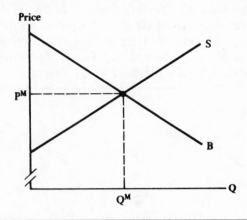

vertical line at N_0 vary across investors. When the aggregate buy and sell trade curves intersect, prices exist at or below which some investors are willing to sell, and at or above which other investors are willing to buy. Hence, trades occur. For the configuration shown in Figure 13.2, Q^M shares will trade at a price of P^M.

Trading eliminates orders from the B and S curves. After the subtraction of Q^M shares from both the B and S curves, the trade curves will have shifted to the left until the intersection point shown in Figure 13.2 is at the price axis, as shown in Figure 13.3(a).

The process of trading harmonizes the jth decision maker's investment desires with the market. As shown in Figure 13.3(b), the trade curves the jth investor submitted to the market will have resulted in the purchase of Q_1 shares at the price P^M. Figure 13.3(c) shows that, after the trade, the vertical line that denotes that investor's holdings has shifted from N_0 to $N_0 + Q_1$. Consequently, the vertical line now intersects D_j at the market price, P^M. Thus after the trade, the jth investor is holding exactly the number of shares that he or she would like to hold at the current market price.

If the investor were to submit a new set of trade curves to the market after the trade, the curves would appear as shown in Figure 13.3(d). Note that the new trade curves necessarily branch off the price axis at P^M. Because this is true for each trader, mutually profitable trading opportunities do not exist immediately after a trading session for any pairing of market participants. Therefore, one round of trading in a frictionless environment harmonizes the trading propensities of all investors and leaves no desire to recontract.

The market's aggregate demand curve to hold shares of the risky asset can now be identified: it is the curve labeled D in Figure 13.4(b). The

FIGURE 13.3   *Adjustment of an Investor's Holdings (Q) in Relation to a Market-determined Price* (P^M). *(a) Aggregate Buy and Sell Curves After Trades Have Eliminated all Crossing Orders. (b) The jth Investor's Initial Trade Curves Result in the Purchase of Q_1 Shares, at the Price P^M. (c) After the Purchase of Q_1 Shares, the Vertical Line Intersects the jth Investor's Demand Curve at $N_0 + Q_1$ Shares. (d) The jth Investor's Buy and Sell Curves Immediately After the Purchase of Q_1 Shares*

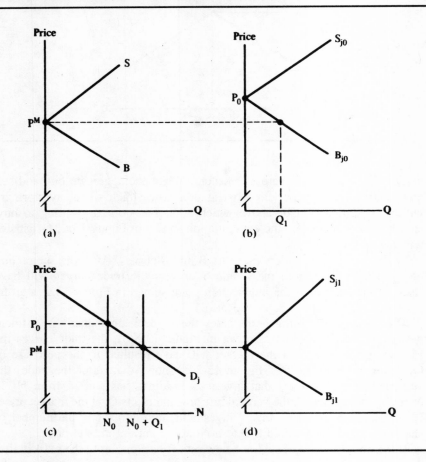

relationship between the market's trade curves, B and S [as shown in Figure 13.4(a)], and the market's demand curve, D, is the same as that which relates B_j and S_j to D_j (as shown in Figure 13.1).

Unlike the case for an individual, the market in aggregate must hold a *given* number of shares—the aggregate *number of shares outstanding* (NSO). Thus we take the vertical line at NSO as fixed and locate the aggregate

FIGURE 13.4 *Market Buy and Sell Curves and Demand Curve: (a) the Buy and Sell Curves, (b) the Demand Curve*

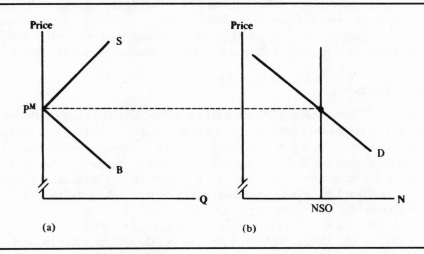

(a)　　　　　　　　　　　　　　　(b)

demand curve, D, in relation to it. In equilibrium, D crosses the vertical line at P^M, the price that has been established on the market. Alternatively stated, the equilibrium price for the market can be obtained by assessing $D = D(P)$ (the market demand equation) at $D = NSO$. Because the market in aggregate must hold the number of shares outstanding, and because this number is given, a separate supply equation is not needed to obtain a solution. (There are two equations, $D = D(P)$ and $D = NSO$, and two unknowns, D and P.)

The vertical line at NSO is not a supply curve in the following sense. If total corporate earnings, dividends, growth, and so on, are unaffected by the number of shares outstanding, then any change in NSO due, for example, to a stock split or stock dividend, would be associated with an equal but opposite percentage change in share price (for instance, a 2 for 1 stock split would result in the share price being halved). This being the case, with demand propensities constant, shifts of the vertical line at NSO would trace out a locus of equilibrium prices that is a negatively inclined, convex curve of unitary elasticity. It would be misleading to consider this curve the market demand curve for an asset. Therefore, NSO should not be interpreted as a supply curve.

Explicit Trading Costs

We begin our analysis of the nonfrictionless market by considering the explicit costs of trading: commissions, taxes, communication expenses, and so forth. These costs comprise both a *fixed* (lump sum) *component* (F) and a *variable* (per share) *component* (V). The effect of the fixed and variable costs on the trading decision is most easily considered with a *two-asset model:* cash and the risky asset. To focus on explicit costs only, we assume no transaction price uncertainty. The opportunity costs associated with transaction price uncertainty are discussed in the section "The Opportunity Costs of Trading."

Fixed Costs

Figure 13.5 shows how explicit costs affect the cash/shares budget constraint. Point B in the figure identifies the initial holdings of cash (C_0) and of the risky asset (N_0). For a given cash price of shares and with costless trading, the budget constraint is the dashed line from A to A' that passes through B. Cash is the *numeraire asset;* hence its unit price is 1. Therefore, the cash price per share for the risky asset is given in Figure 13.5 by the ratio of the line segment 0A to the line segment 0A'.

The fixed cost of trading lowers the budget constraint by the dollar amount F = AD = BE. Hence, with fixed costs alone, the budget constraint is the dashed line form D to D' that passes through E. In addition, the point B is also a part of the constraint, because the investor can remain at point B by not trading at all. An X, Y budget constraint shows the *maximum* quantity of X that can be obtained given Y. Therefore, the existence of point B causes part of the dashed line from D to D' not to be a part of the constraint. To see this, draw a horizontal and a vertical line through point B so as to identify

FIGURE 13.5 *Effect of Explicit Costs on the Cash/Shares Budget Constraint*

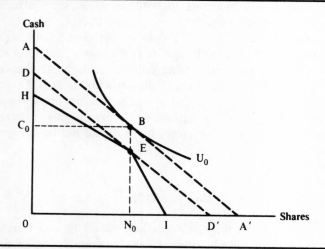

four quadrants; the section of the line DD' that passes through the quadrant to the southwest of B is not, strictly speaking, part of the budget constraint (vis-à-vis any point along this part of the line, B contains more of both cash and shares, and so must dominate). We simplify the exposition, however, by not taking further account of this technical consideration in the following diagrams or the discussion. Nothing essential is lost by the simplification, because it would never be optimal to move from B to any point that is southwest of B.

The addition of variable costs pushes the constraint farther down and to the left, to the kinked line labeled HEI. Thus the budget constraint with both fixed and variable costs is the solid line segments HE and EI and the point B. Because of the variable costs of trading, HE is flatter than DD' (fewer additional dollars are obtained when shares are traded for cash), and EI is steeper than DD' (fewer additional shares are obtained when cash is traded for shares).

The curve labeled U_0 in Figure 13.5 is the cash-shares indifference curve that passes through point B. Let U_0 be tangent to AA' at the point B. Thus the investor would want to trade only if the indifference curve were to change its slope and/or if the budget constraint were to shift because of a change in the share price of the risky asset. With the frictionless market budget constraint (AA') any change in tastes, expectations, or share price induces the investor to seek a trade.

This is not the case, however, with transaction costs, because, as Figure 13.5 shows, nonzero fixed and/or variable transaction costs cause point B to be a corner solution. Therefore, a larger (discrete) change in either tastes or in price is required to motivate a trade. Furthermore, when the investor does seek to trade, the order size will be smaller than it would be in the absence of transaction costs (budget constraint HEI defines a more restricted feasible set than does budget constraint AA').

Variable Costs

The effect of variable transaction costs on price and on the quantity of shares traded can also be seen for the aggregate market by application of a standard formulation in microeconomics, the sales tax model. The sales tax, like any other transaction cost, is a payment made by a buyer that is not received by a seller. If the difference between the payment made and the payment received is collected by the government, it is a *sales tax;* if the difference is collected by the post office, a shipping company, or a taxi driver, it is a *transportation charge;* if it is collected by a broker who brings the buyer and seller together, it is a *commission;* if it is collected by a dealer quoting a higher selling price than buying price, it is a *bid-ask spread*; and so on. Whatever it is called, the transaction cost has the same effect. To see the effect, consider Figure 13.6.

FIGURE 13.6   *Effect of Variable Transaction Costs on the Market Buy and Sell Curves*

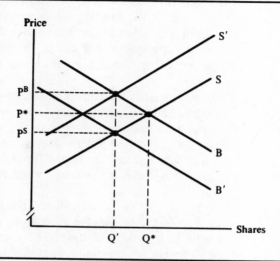

The curves labeled B and S in Figure 13.6 describe the aggregate trading desires of buyers and sellers, respectively. If trading were costless, the intersection of B and S would establish P^* and Q^* as the equilibrium price and quantity for the market. The impact of transaction costs can be seen in relation to this frictionless market result. We proceed as follows.

Write the market buy and sell equations, expressing P as a function of Q:

$$P = B(Q)$$
$$P = S(Q)$$

(13.5)

Let V be a buyer's and a seller's combined transaction cost per share traded. (The division of V between buyers and sellers is not relevant for the analysis that follows.) Thus buyers would have to pay $P^B = S(Q) + V$ per share to purchase Q shares. As far as they are concerned, the sell curve is the curve labeled S' in Figure 13.6. Alternatively viewed, sellers would receive $P^S = B(Q) - V$ per share for the sale of Q shares. As far as they are concerned, the buy curve is the curve labeled B' in Figure 13.6.

Equilibrium in this nonfrictionless market is given by the intersection of S' and B (from the viewpoint of buyers) or equivalently by the intersection of S and B' (from the viewpoint of sellers). Either way, the optimal exchange is now Q', buyers pay a price of P^B, and sellers receive a price of P^S. In summary, the effect of the variable transaction cost on the market is given by the following comparisons:

$$P^B > P^*$$
$$P^S < P^*$$
$$V = P^B - P^S$$
$$Q' < Q^*$$

Therefore, when it costs something to transact, buyers pay more, sellers receive less, and the aggregate number of shares traded is decreased.

Order Functions

A trader's buy and sell functions can be interpreted as instructions (orders) that might be submitted to the market. This is shown for buy orders (the analysis is symmetric for sell orders).

Figure 13.7 presents five alternative sets of instructions. Three different markings are used in the figure: (1) solid lines indicate that the continuous order function is operative over the range shown; (2) dashed lines indicate that the underlying propensities are not to be implemented over the range shown; (3) circles identify discrete order points along an otherwise inoperative (dashed-line) order function. In addition, it should be understood that when a sequence of orders is executed in relation to these functions, the number of shares to be bought at a price is the *difference* between the number identified on the quantity axis and the number of shares previously purchased in the sequence.

The Alternative Orders

Specifically, each of the five orders illustrated in Figure 13.7 is interpreted as follows:

- *Figure 13.7(a):* The solid line labeled B is the ordinary buy curve that was identified in relation to the individual's demand curve in Figure 13.1. Since any point along the curve is operative, the investor's instructions are to buy Q_1 shares if the price is P_1, or Q_2 shares if the price is P_2, and so on, for any arbitrarily selected price. However, if Q_1 shares are bought at P_1 and the price jumps down to P_2, then the order at P_2 is for $(Q_2 - Q_1)$ shares.

- *Figure 13.7(b):* The solid line labeled MB is related to the dashed line labeled *B* in the same way that a marginal revenue curve is related to a demand curve. As an order function, MB is to be implemented in

FIGURE 13.7 *Buyer Order Curves. (a) Order Function B. (b) Order Function MB. (c) Order Function MB'. (d) Discrete Order Points on Function B. (e) Discrete Order Point on Function RB*

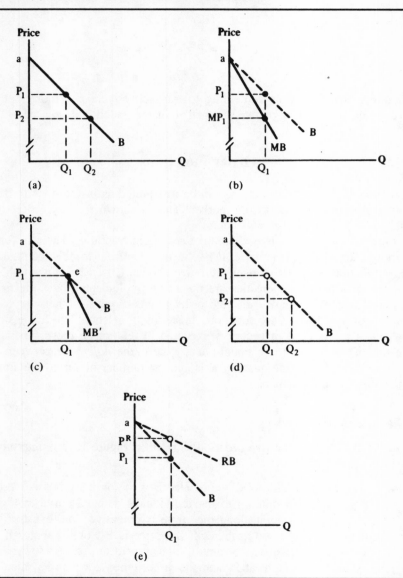

(a)

(b)

(c)

(d)

(e)

the same way as the solid line labeled B in Figure 13.7(a). The MB order function may be used when price can descend by infinitesimal steps, thereby triggering a continuous succession of executions. For this reason, MB shows, at each quantity, the price the investor is willing to pay for a marginal share, given that the number of shares shown on the quantity axis has already been bought.

- *Figure 13.7(c):* The instruction given by the order function shown in Figure 13.7(c) is that no purchases are to be made until price falls to P_1. At P_1, Q_1 shares are to be bought. If price continues to decrease, marginal shares are to be bought in accordance with the solid line labeled MB'.

- *Figure 13.7(d):* The instruction given by the order function shown in Figure 13.7(d) is either (1) buy Q_1 shares at P_1, (2) buy Q_2 shares at P_2 (if the first order has not been executed), or (3) buy Q_1 shares at P_1 and $Q_2 - Q_1$ shares at P_2. The preference ordering for the three alternatives is (2), (3), (1).

- *Figure 13.7(e):* The dashed line labeled RB is related to the dashed line labeled *B* in the same way as a reservation demand curve is related to a normal demand curve (see Chapter 6). The instruction given by the single order point shown along the dashed line RB is to buy Q_1 shares at the price P^R *or less*. An order of this type is relevant for the discussion of the periodic call market in the section "The Optimal Trading Decision."

Relationship Among the Order Functions

Writing P as a function of Q, the relationships among the curves labeled B, RB, and MB are as follows:

The equation for the curve labeled B is (see Equation 12.39)

$$P = a - 2bQ \qquad (13.6)$$

The equation for the curve labeled RB is (see Equation 12.37)

$$P = a - bQ \qquad (13.7)$$

The equation for the curve labeled MB is

$$P = a - 4bQ \qquad (13.8)$$

The curve labeled B is linear because we have assumed the investor's demand function to hold shares to be linear. We show in Appendix A that the slope (dP/dQ) of the RB curve is half that of the linear demand curve B. Equivalently, the slope of the MB curve is twice that of the B curve. To see this, first multiply equation (13.6) by Q to obtain total expenditure as a function of Q:

$$PQ = aQ - 2bQ^2 \tag{13.9}$$

Then differentiate with respect to Q to obtain the marginal expenditure as a function of Q:

$$\frac{d(PQ)}{dQ} = a - 4bQ \tag{13.10}$$

The *marginal expenditure* is the price the decision maker would be willing to pay for an incremental share, given that Q shares have already been bought. Therefore, Equation 13.10 is the equation for the curve labeled MB (Equation 13.8). For the linear case its slope (4b) is twice that of the curve labeled B (Equation 13.6).

Order Adjustment

The buy orders just identified can remain operative through a sequence of price continuations but must be adjusted after a price reversal. [In a *price continuation* a price change is followed by another price change of the same sign (a decrease is followed by a decrease, or an increase is followed by an increase). In a *price reversal* the change in price reverses direction from one transaction to the next (price goes up after a decrease or declines after an increase).] This can be demonstrated with reference to Figure 13.8. Let the solid line B_0 in Figure 13.8(b) be the trader's order function [as in Figure 13.7(a)], and assume a sequence of two negative price jumps, from P_0 to P_1 and then from P_1 to P_2. In accordance with the instruction given by the line B_0, the trader will buy Q_1 shares at P_1, and $Q_2 - Q_1$ shares at P_2. If price continues to jump down to some $P_3 < P_2$, a third purchase $(Q_3 - Q_2)$ will be appropriately identified from the order curve labeled B_0.

However, suppose a reversal occurs before the third negative price change, and that price jumps back to P_0. Then, in accordance with the sell order curve labeled S_2, the decision maker will sell Q_2 shares. If price now jumps down to P_3, the desired purchase is Q_3, not $Q_3 - Q_2$. Generalizing, we see that the buy order curve shifts after each sale (and, symmetrically, the sell order curve shifts after each purchase). Because the price reversal in the sequence of negative jumps triggers a sale, it also causes a shift of the buy order function. Notice that the direction of the shifts illustrated in Figure 13.8(b) depends on whether the transactions are buys or sells, and that the magnitude of the shifts depends upon the size of the price changes. Therefore, the revision of the order functions after any transaction depends on what the realized transaction has turned out to be.

The shifting of order functions that occurs because of a purchase or a sale means that the decision maker must transmit a considerably more detailed

FIGURE 13.8 *Adjustment of an Order Curve After a Price Reversal. (a) Trades Result in Movements Along the Investor's Demand Curve to Hold Shares. (b) Purchases Shift the Investor's Sell Order Function and Sales Shift the Investor's Buy Order Function*

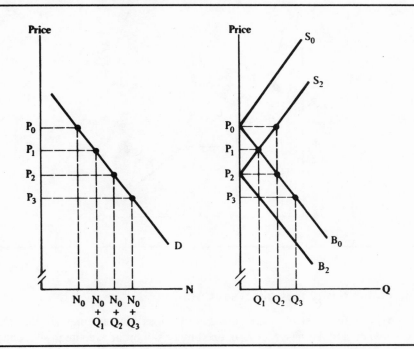

set of instructions to the market. Higher explicit costs are incurred because of the added complexity involved. However, the problem is technical and in principle it can be handled.

The Opportunity Cost of Trading

This section takes the explicit costs of trading to be zero and analyzes two opportunity costs of trading that are attributable to transaction price uncertainty. One opportunity cost relates to trades that have been made, and the other relates to trading opportunities that have been missed. Even in the absence of the explicit cost of trading, the opportunity costs affect the flow of orders to a market. Our analysis of these costs assumes a continuous market environment.

FIGURE 13.9   *Identification of the Opportunity Cost of an Intramarginal Purchase, and of the Loss of Consumer Surplus from a Trade That Was Missed*

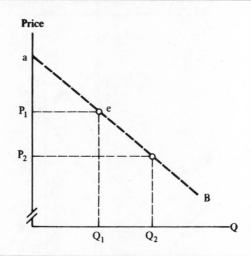

The Opportunity Cost of Trades Made

The opportunity cost of trades made is the loss of consumer surplus that occurs when a trader has more than one buy or sell order execute in sequence. The loss is the extra amount paid per share for the higher priced buy orders in a sequence or the extra price per share not received for the lower priced sell orders in a sequence. This loss can be identified precisely with reference to Figure 13.9.

Figure 13.9 shows the order set described in Figure 13.7(d): buy Q_1 shares at P_1; Q_2 at P_2; or Q_1 at P_1 and $(Q_2 - Q_1)$ at P_2. Suppose that the orders at both prices execute. Then the $\langle P_2, (Q_2 - Q_1) \rangle$ order is the *marginal* order (it just executed), and the $\langle P_1, Q_1 \rangle$ order is the *intramarginal* order (the market price could have been somewhat higher than P_2, and the order would still have executed).

The Opportunity Cost of Missing a Trade

The consumer surplus lost (the extra amount paid) as a result of the intra-marginal order's executing is $(P_1 - P_2)Q_1$. Because of this cost, one might question why the intramarginal order was written in the first place. The reason is that the decision maker does not know in advance what the transaction price will be. If the price does not fall enough to trigger the execution at P_2, the order at P_1 will be the marginal order. In such an event, its execution will yield the consumer surplus shown by the area of the triangle aP_1e, which is equal to $(a - P_1)Q_1/2$. Accordingly, if the order had not been written at P_1, this consumer surplus would have been lost. This loss of consumer surplus is the second opportunity cost of trading. It is the opportunity cost of missing a trade.

Recognition of the two opportunity costs (the extra payment made for intramarginal executions and the consumer surplus lost when a marginal order is not written) is key to understanding the trader's decision problem. These costs exist because of the very factor that distinguishes the trading decision from the investment decision: transaction prices are not known when the buy/sell orders are specified. Analyzing the trader's response to these opportunity costs show why proper specification of an order is a strategic decision.

The Submission of Discrete Order Points

The two opportunity costs of trading can be analyzed by using the alternative order sets the decision maker can submit to the market. As in the discussion of order functions, we need consider only the buy orders (the analysis on the sell side is symmetric).

Because we have assumed that the environment is prefectly competitive (any individual trader is too small to affect a market price) and that price and quantity are continuous variables, it is not necessary to take account of the possibility of partial execution of an order. That is, an individual may enter an order of discrete size at a specific price, but that order, being insignificant in relation to the market, will execute totally if the transaction price on the market reaches the order's price. The analog in the theory of the firm under competition is that, if the market price for the resource supplied by the firm reaches a level equal to the minimum point on the firm's average cost curve, the firm will enter the market, producing a (discrete) amount given by the minimum point on the firm's average cost curve. The firm, being insignificant in relation to the market, will always be able to sell the entire (discrete) amount it produces at its entry price. If the firms are continuously distributed according to the height of their cost curves, the supply curve of the industry will be a continuous, everywhere differentiable function, even though the entry quantity of each firm is not infinitesimal on the micro level. Neither need we take account of a secondary trading priority rule, such as the time priority rule that the first order placed at a price is the first to execute.

Order Function B. If the decision maker were to submit the complete buy order function labeled B in Figure 13.7(a), then with price continuations he or she would buy at a succession of points while moving down the order

FIGURE 13.10   *Analysis of the MB Order Curve*

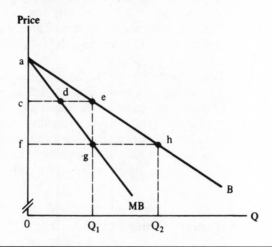

curve. This would eliminate much of the trader's consumer surplus if price were to change by discrete jumps and would eliminate *all* of the decision maker's consumer surplus if price were to change by infinitesimal jumps.

Order Function MB.   The trader can avoid the total loss of consumer surplus by submitting the curve labeled MB in Figure 13.7(b), which is reproduced in Figure 13.10. Referring to Figure 13.10, assume price drops in infinitesimal steps from $\overline{0a}$ to $\overline{0f}$.* In such a case, the investor purchases Q_1 shares at a total cost equal to the area $0agQ_1$. Since the slope (dP/dQ) of the curve MB is twice that of the curve B, it can be shown that adc and deg are equal triangles, and therefore are of equal area. Thus the area $0agQ_1$ equals the area $0ceQ_1$. Accordingly, the investor will have purchased the Q_1 shares at an average price of $\overline{0c}$.

One can now see why the investor would prefer to submit the curve MB rather than the curve B to the market. Submitting the marginal order function reduces the opportunity cost of intramarginal orders executing at higher prices. Therefore, if the price decreases to $\overline{0f}$ as discussed previously, the investor receives the consumer surplus associated with buying Q_1 shares at an average price of $\overline{0c}$, rather than no consumer surplus at all. This consumer surplus equals the area of the triangle ace, which equals the area of the triangle age.

Furthermore, by submitting the marginal order curve MB, the decision maker automatically enjoys more consumer surplus, the further the market

---

* The bar indicates that 0a is the line segment 0 to a, and that 0f is the line segment 0 to f.

price falls in the trading period. That is, as point g moves down the line MB, the associated point e (which shows the average price at which the shares are bought) moves down the line B, and the area of the triangle ace increases.

Order Function MB'. Note, however, that for the trader to benefit from buying at an average price of $\overline{0c}$, the price on the market has to fall to the lower value, $\overline{0f}$. This suggests that although the second strategy (submit the MB curve) is better than the first (submit the B curve), some other strategy may be even better. The alternative we next consider is the following order: buy Q_1 shares at P_1 and buy additional shares at lower prices according to the order function labeled MB'. This order can be analyzed with reference to Figure 13.11. Note that the order function labeled MB' in Figure 13.11 has the same slope as the order function labeled MB in Figure 13.10 and has twice the slope (dP/dQ) of the order function labeled B.

Figure 13.11(a) shows that, given the MB' order, if the market price decreases in infinitesimal steps to a value P, the decision maker's consumer surplus equals the area of the triangle aP_1e plus the area of the triangle efg. Note that the average price paid for $Q(P_1)$ shares is P_1, and that the average price paid for $Q'(P) - Q(P_1)$ shares is given by the vertical distance $gQ'(P)$ [which is why the incremental consumer surplus for $Q'(P) - Q(P_1)$ shares is given by the area of the triangle, efg]. The argument is analogous to that used previously with respect to the MB order function. If, alternatively, the

FIGURE 13.11 *Analysis of the MB' Order Curve. (a) The Opportunity Cost of Intramarginal Purchases. (b) The Opportunity Cost of Not Transacting*

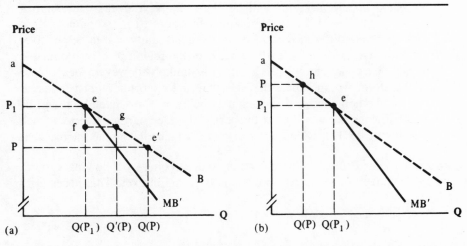

decision maker's order had been to buy Q(P) shares at the price P, his or her consumer surplus would have equaled the area of the larger triangle, aPe' Therefore, the opportunity cost of the intramarginal purchases equals the area aPe' − aP₁e − efg. Note that the line segment $\overline{ef}$ divided by the line segment $\overline{fg}$ equals b, where −b is the slope of order function B. Therefore, $(\overline{ef}) = (b)(\overline{fg}) = (b)[Q'(P) − Q(P_1)]$; hence the area of the triangle efg equals $(b)[Q'(P) − Q(P_1)]^2(\tfrac{1}{2})$.

Assume, alternatively, that the decision maker submits the same order described in the preceding paragraph, but that the price on the market does not decrease as far as P_1. Figure 13.11(b) shows that, in this case, the opportunity cost of not transacting at all equals the area of the triangle defined by the intercept parameter (a), the market price (P), and the point h.

Because the trader does not know what the transaction price will be when the order is placed, he or she cannot react to a specific opportunity cost. Rather, the trader assesses the *expected opportunity cost* (EOC) associated with an order. The change in the EOC realized by submitting order function MB' rather than order function MB is the possible loss of consumer surplus in the range P_1 to a (in Figure 13.11) if a transaction is missed, minus the possible gain of consumer surplus in the range 0 to P_1 if the intramarginal purchases between P_1 and a are avoided. Appendix B to this chapter shows that this difference in the expected opportunity cost can be expressed analytically as

$$\Delta EOC = \tfrac{1}{2}b\left\{ \int_{P_1}^{a} [Q'(P)]^2 f(P)\ dP - \int_{0}^{P_1} [Q(P_1)]^2 f(P)\ dP \right\} \qquad (13.11)$$

Note in Equation 13.11 that $Q(P_1)$ is greater than $Q'(P)$ for P in the range between P_1 and a. This suggests that, *ceteris paribus,* the change in the expected opportunity cost will be negative. Nevertheless, the sign of Equation 13.11 depends on the probability function, f(P), and on how close P_1 is to a. For the difference in the expected opportunity cost to be positive, f(P) would have to be sufficiently small over the region 0 to P_1, compared to its value over the region P_1 to a.* This is unlikely, however, for P_1 close to a. Therefore, we anticipate that the expected opportunity cost is less if P_1 is set in the neighborhood immediately below a. Consequently, it will be preferable for the decision maker to specify an order starting at a point such as e (in Figure 13.11), where e is a discrete distance below the intercept, a.

Discrete Order Points.   The trader can do even better by following a fourth strategy: convey only discrete order points to the market. This necessarily

---

* A necessary but not sufficient condition is

$$\int_{0}^{P} f(P)dP < \int_{P_1}^{a} f(P)\ dP$$

dominates the third strategy, and hence the first two strategies as well. Such a strategy is illustrated by the two order points shown in Figure 13.7(d). The dominance of this strategy for prices less than P_1 can be established by replicating the argument just presented with respect to the MB$'$ order function. To replicate the proof, simply change the origin in Figure 13.11 from 0 to $Q(P_1)$ and the intercept from a to P_1.

A Partially Collapsed Order Function.   The trader has one more alternative: reduce the order size at each price (P) in the neighborhood below the intercept a, and submit a continuous order function. To assess this alternative, consider the purchase of Q shares at an arbitrarily selected price P' that is greater than P_1 but less than a. The consumer surplus per unit purchased at this price decreases linearly from $(a - P')$ to 0, as Q increases from 0 to $Q(P')$. On the other hand, if the price on the market decreases to the value $P_1 < P'$, the additional opportunity cost per share of the intramarginal purchase equals $P' - P_1$ regardless of the number of shares purchased at the price P'. Therefore, setting Q less than Q(P) reduces the opportunity cost of missing a transaction by more than the opportunity cost of intramarginal purchases is increased, and it may be optimal for the trader to specify an order at the value P'.

Therefore, in the final analysis, the trader facing opportunity costs but not explicit costs may still submit a continuous order function to the market. That function, however, will be *partially collapsed* toward the price axis [that is, at each price we will have $0 < Q < Q(P)$]. The smaller is the probability $f(P)$ dP in the neighborhood below a, the closer the order function is to the price axis in the neighborhood below a.

Optimal Trading Decisions

We have shown that, with costly trading and transaction price uncertainty, a trader with a continuous demand curve to hold shares will submit only *discrete* order points to the market.

This section considers the optimal placement of a point order (a specific price and size) for two alternative market environments: a call market and a continuous market. In neither case is the investor forced to pick a point from his or her demand curve. Rather, an optimal order is determined, given: (1) the location of the investor's demand curve to hold shares, (2) the investor's expectation of what the transaction price will be, and (3) the design of the trading system (whether it is a call or continuous market).

Assumptions

The assumptions that define the analytic context are the following:

1. There are two distinct time spans: a trading period and an investment period. The two periods are demarcated by three points in time: point

in time T_0 is the *start of the trading period;* point in time T_1 is the *end of the trading period and the beginning of the investment period;* point in time T_2 is the *end of the investment period.* The span between T_0 and T_1 is brief (for instance, one day), and is the same for all traders. The span between T_1 and T_2 is considerably longer, and may be unique to the specific investor.

2. Participants in the market convey their orders to the market during the trading period. All trades are *settled* (shares traded are delivered and cash payments are made) at point in time T_1, the end of the trading period.

3. Each investor writes his or her order without knowing the other investors' orders. Therefore, when writing their orders, all investors face transaction price uncertainty.

4. Each trader anticipates what the transaction price will be. This anticipation is described by two parameters: an expected transaction price and the variance of the transaction price around its mean.

5. Traders make their investment decisions at point in time T_0. They do so by projecting their thoughts forward to point in time T_1 and considering the optimal share holdings for the investment period in relation to the share prices that may be established during the trading period.

6. The decision maker implements the investment decision at T_0 by making a trading decision: the specification of the specific order, set of orders, or continuous order function to convey to the market.

7. For the frictionless market all orders are batched for simultaneous execution at a single price during the trading period, as in the call market environment.

The Trader's Objective—The Maximization of Expected Consumer Surplus

The goal of the trader is the maximization of expected consumer surplus. This goal is consistent with the maximization of the expected utility of wealth (the ultimate objective of the decision maker). Consistency can be established as follows. (Note that the maximization of expected consumer surplus is identical to the minimization of the expected opportunity cost referred to in the previous section. The following analysis is based on Ho, Schwartz, and Whitcomb.)[1]

Chapter 12 shows for a two-asset universe (a risk-free asset and one risky asset) how the investor's demand function to hold shares of the risky asset can be obtained from the utility function defined on wealth. A key equation in the derivation is

$$h(P, Q \mid N_0, C_0) = c + gQ(a - bQ - P) \tag{13.12}$$

Equation 12.28 (in Chapter 12) includes a subscript 1 on the variable P to show explicitly that the price applies as of point in time T_1. This time identification is clear in context in the current chapter and thus is suppressed for simplicity. Using $P^R = a - bQ$, the equation for the reservation buy/sell function, Equation 13.12 can be rewritten as

$$h(P, Q \mid N_0, C_0) = c + gQ(P^R - P) \qquad (13.13)$$

Because c and g are parameters, the decision maker maximizes his or her expected utility, E(h), by maximizing the expected value of $Q(P^R - P)$. This term, however, is the expression for consumer surplus. Therefore, the decision maker maximizes the *expected* utility of wealth by maximizing the *expected* value of consumer surplus.

The maximization of expected consumer surplus is an intuitively appealing objective. Consumer surplus is a monetary measure of the gains of trading any given number of shares at any given price. The uncertainty for the trader is what the specific execution will be, and thus what the specific value of consumer surplus will be. That is why the trader is concerned with the *expected* value of consumer surplus; it is the probability-weighted average of the possible outcomes. The decision maker's risk aversion is reflected in the demand curve to hold shares, which is used to determine consumer surplus and need not be taken account of again. Thus we need not take account of the variance of consumer surplus.

The logic involved may be better appreciated with reference to a specific example. Consider the trader's choice between two alternative sets of instructions:

A: Buy 150 shares at $50

B: Buy 225 shares at $45

Let the outcomes associated with alternative A be the following:

Transaction	Probability	Consumer surplus[a]
1. No purchase is made	.10	–0–
2. 150 shares bought at 50	.90	$(55 - 50)150/2 = 375$

[a] We assume for the computation of consumer surplus that the order function intersects the price axis at a value of $55.

Let the outcomes associated with alternative B be the following:

Transaction	Probability	Consumer surplus
1. No purchase is made	.50	–0–
2. 225 shares bought at 45	.50	$(55 - 45)225/2 = 1125$

The expected consumer surplus for alternative A is .9(375) = 337.5. The expected consumer surplus for alternative B is .5(1125) = 562.5. The expected consumer surplus maximizing trader selects the alternative with the highest value. Therefore, alternative B is chosen over alternative A.

The Optimal Trading Decision in a Call Market Environment

All orders that transact at a trading session in a call market are executed at the same market clearing price (P^c). An investor's buy order executes if it is placed at a price equal to or greater than P^c; an investor's sell order executes if it is placed at a price equal to or less than P^c. We continue to treat buy orders only; as in preceding sections, the analysis for the specification of a sell order is symmetrical. The model in this subsection was presented by Ho, Schwartz, and Whitcomb.[2]

Let $G(x)$ be the investor's subjective probability of the clearing price being less than some value x. Assume the clearing price is normally distributed, with mean $E(P^c)$ and variance $Var(P^c)$. As established in the previous subsection, the investor maximizes his or her expected utility $[E(h)]$ by specifying a buy order price (P) and an order size (Q) that maximize the expected value of his or her consumer surplus. Because there is no purchase for $x > P$, the objective is

$$\max_{P,Q} \int_{-\infty}^{P} Q[P^R(Q) - x]G'(x)\, dx \qquad (13.14)$$

where $G'(x)\, dx$ is the probability of the clearing price equaling x, and $P^R(Q)$ is the reservation price for a buy order of size Q.

Equation 13.14 may be more easily understood with reference to Figure 13.12. Assume that an investor with the reservation buy curve RB submits an order to buy Q_1 shares at a limit price of P_1. The order will execute if P^c is equal to or less than P_1. In Figure 13.12(a), $x < P_1$, and the order would execute if P^c equaled this value. In Figure 13.12(b), $x > P_1$, and the order would not execute. If the investor's order does execute, the consumer surplus received is $Q_1(P^R - x)$. Equation 13.14 shows that the investor's *expected* consumer surplus for the P_1, Q_1 order is the probability weighted average over all x up to P_1, of the consumer surplus at each value of x.

The P_1, Q_1 order illustrated in Figure 13.12 is not an optimal order. Referring to Figure 13.12(b), we see that the investor would have received consumer surplus if his or her order had executed at the higher value of x [because $Q_1(P^R - x)$ is positive]. In general, the investor's expected consumer surplus is reduced if the limit price (P) for Q shares is less than $P^R(Q)$ (because a transaction that would yield positive consumer surplus may not be realized). Therefore, the limit price for Q_1 shares will be $P^R(Q_1)$ (the reser-

FIGURE 13.12 *Relationship Between a Market Clearing Price and a Trader's Order Price and Consumer Surplus in a Call Market Environment. (a) The Clearing Price x Is Less Than the Order Price* P_1. *(b) The Clearing Price x Is Greater Than the Order Price* P_1

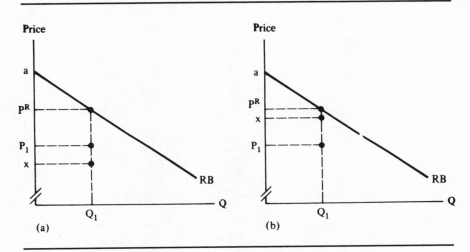

vation price for an order of size Q_1), and the objective (Equation 13.14) becomes

$$\max_{Q} \int_{-\infty}^{P^R(Q)} Q[P^R(Q) - x]G'(x) \, dx \tag{13.15}$$

Referring to Equation 13.14, this is because each integrand is positive for $P < P^R$. Each integrand is also negative for $P > P^R$. Ho, Schwartz, and Whitcomb[3] use Equation 13.15 to obtain an explicit solution for an individual's optimal order. The solution, which is illustrated in Figure 13.13, depends on the mean and variance of the clearing price, and on the parameters of the investor's order function. The specific order is obtained by setting the derivative of Equation 13.15 with respect to Q equal to zero. The solution requires solving two simultaneous equations that involve the mean and standard deviation of the clearing price, and the slope and intercept parameters of the investor's order function.[4]

Figure 13.13 shows that, in the absence of transaction price uncertainty, if the price at the call is a known value equal to $E(P^c)$, the investor will place an order for Q' shares. Ho, Schwartz, and Whitcomb show that, with transaction price uncertainty and an *expected* clearing price of $E(P^c)$, the investor's optimal order price is a value P^* greater than $E(P^c)$, and that

FIGURE 13.13   *A Trader's Optimal Buy Order in a Call Market Environment*

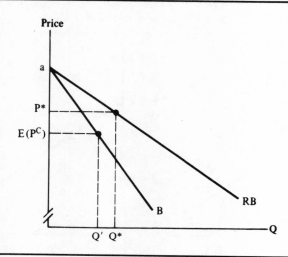

his or her optimal order size is a value Q^* greater than Q'. The reason is as follows.

The trader's order executes only if the price of the order is equal to or greater than P^c and, if it executes, it does so at the clearing price, not at its own price. Therefore, the investor obtains protection from transaction price uncertainty by specifying his or her reservation price for the order size submitted; thus we have $P^* > E(P^c)$. With this protection, the trader gambles on receiving the larger consumer surplus associated with an execution farther down and to the right, along the ordinary buy curve. The trader does so by increasing the order size somewhat ($Q^* > Q'$), and by lowering the order price somewhat (P^* is less than the reservation buy price for Q' shares).

The Optimal Trading Decision in a Continuous Market Environment

An order executes in a continuous market whenever it crosses, or is crossed by, a counterpart order. For our purpose, the continuous market can be modeled in three ways:

1. *Limit order model:* All limit orders are executed or canceled by the end of each trading session, and the trader whose decision we are analyzing is the first to submit an order in a new trading session. Therefore, this trader can submit only a limit order (there are no other limit orders

for a market order to execute against), and, if the order executes, it will do so at its own price. This model specification, which is most pertinent to the decision of a monopoly dealer, enables us to focus on only one type of order (the limit order).

2. *Hybrid model:* The trader specifies the price and size of an order before the start of a trading session, and the order is received by the market some time during the trading session. If the order price is sufficient to trigger a transaction upon its arrival, it executes as a market order at the price established by the limit order it transacts against. If the order price is not sufficient to trigger a transaction upon arrival, it is placed on the order book. If the order subsequently executes, it does so at its own limit price, as in the preceding model. This model specification, which is most pertinent for an individual who is at a distance from the trading floor, combines elements of the limit order model (the trader's order may execute at its own price) and the call market (the trader's order may execute at a price set on the market).

3. *Discretionary model:* The trader writes an order during the trading day, after learning the current bid and ask quotations. In this model, which is most pertinent to the decision of a floor trader, the trader can submit a market order or a limit order, at his or her own discretion.

These models are further analyzed by Bronfman[5] and Bronfman and Schwartz.[6]

The Limit Order Model.   We consider the limit order model first. By itself, this model is artificial, but it provides a foundation for analyzing the two that follow. To obtain a *ceteris paribus* contrast with the call market, assume the trader has the same demand curve to hold shares, and let $G(x)$ describe his or her subjective probability of the transaction price decreasing to some value x in the course of a trading day. This structures the analysis so that the only difference between the two markets is that the limit order submitted to the continuous market executes at the price of the order, not at a common market clearing price as in the call market described previously.

Because in this model the order executes at its own price, its price and size are determined by the ordinary buy function, not the reservation buy function. That is, if the order is written at the price P_1 and if it does execute, the trader wishes to purchase $Q_1 = Q(P_1)$ shares, the associated number of shares on the ordinary buy function. Therefore, the trader does not seek protection from transaction price uncertainty by submitting an order from his or her reservation curve.

Given the trader's subjective probability distribution $G(x)$, let $E(P)$ be a value such that an order at a price above $E(P)$ has a greater than 50% chance of transacting, and an order at a price below $E(P)$ has a less than 50% chance of transacting during a trading session. Figure 13.14(a) shows that, in the

FIGURE 13.14 *A Trader's Optimal Buy Order in a Continuous Market Environment. (a) For* a − E(P) *Large (a Relatively Intense Desire to Trade), the Optimal Buy Order Price* P* *Is Greater Than the Expected Price* E(P). *(b) For* a = E(P) *(a Trade Would Not Be Sought at the Expected Price), the Optimal Buy Order Price* P* *Is Less Than the Expected Price* E(P)

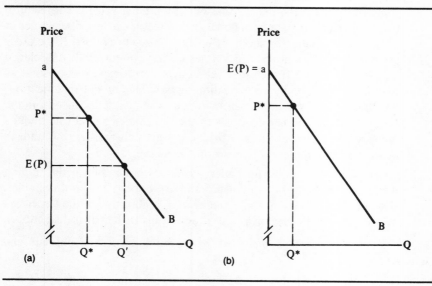

absence of transaction price uncertainty, if the price in the continuous market decreases to a known value equal to E(P), the investor places an order for Q' shares.

With transaction price uncertainty, the trader's optimal order may be placed above or below E(P), depending on the location of the order function in relation to E(P). Given the slope of the order function, the higher the intercept parameter (a) is in relation to E(P), the greater would be the decision maker's consumer surplus from trading Q' shares at the price E(P), and the larger would be his or her opportunity cost of missing such a trade. Consequently, when the value of a − E(P) is large, the trader is likely to increase the probability of realizing an execution by placing an order at a price above E(P). This is shown by the P*, Q* order along the ordinary buy function in Figure 13.14(a).

On the other hand, if a − E(P) is small, the trader would receive little consumer surplus from buying at a price equal to or greater than E(P), and therefore is likely to place an order at a price below E(P). The trader's optimal order for this second case is shown by the P*, Q* order along the ordinary buy function in Figure 13.14(b), where we have set the expected price [E(P)] equal to the intercept parameter, a. The order placed at a price below E(P) is not expected to execute, but is optimal nevertheless because of the greater consumer surplus that would be received in the event the lower price is attained.

We conclude the following from the limit order model:

1. The trader submits an order from his or her ordinary buy function.

2. The price and size of the order depend on the mean and variance of the transaction price over the trading session.

3. If at E(P) the decision maker has a strong incentive to trade [a − E(P) is large], the order price will be above E(P); if at E(P) the decision maker does not have a strong incentive to trade [a − E(P) is small], the order price will be below E(P).

4. The order transmitted to the continuous market differs from the order that would have been transmitted to a call market.

The Hybrid Model. The hybrid model is similar to the limit order model, except that it takes account of the possibility of the order executing as a market order. If it transacts as a market order, the order executes at a price below its limit price, in which event the trader would want to buy a larger number of shares. The trader takes account of the possibility of the order executing at a lower price by specifying a larger number of shares (Q) for any given limit price or, equivalently, by specifying a higher limit price for any given number of shares. Therefore, in the hybrid model, the trader picks an order above and to the right of the ordinary buy curve.

However, because the order may not execute at a market-determined price but rather at its own limit price, the trader picks a point below and to the left of his or her reservation buy curve. Therefore, in the hybrid model the trader picks an order between the ordinary buy curve (that would apply in the limit order model) and the reservation buy curve (that would apply for the call market).

The Discretionary Model. In the discretionary model, the trader knows whether the order will execute as a market order or will be placed on the book as a limit order. In this case, the limit order is a point picked from the ordinary buy function, as in the limit order model. The size (Q) of the market order is set equal to the value given by the ordinary buy function assessed at the price of the counterpart market quote. The trader selects the greater of (a) the known consumer surplus that would be realized from the market order or (b) the expected consumer surplus that would be realized from the limit order. This model is assessed further in the next section.

Orders and the Bid-Ask Spread

Further insight into order placement in a continuous market can be gained by assuming (for simplicity) that all orders are the same size and analyzing an investor's decision to place a market order or a limit order. An investor who buys at market pays the ask price; an investor who sells at market receives the bid price. For this reason, the spread is the cost of a round-trip (buying and then selling a given number of shares). Even if the investor buys at market and holds the shares for a long period of time, the spread is a cost of transacting. (Specifically, one-half of the spread is taken to be the cost of the purchase, and one-half is viewed as the cost of the sale.) To be properly assessed, the shares held in a portfolio should be evaluated at the price at which they could be sold—the bid price. If, for example, the quotes for a stock are 50 bid, 50 ¼ ask and an investor has bought at the ask, the bid must rise ¼/50 = 0.5% in order for the investor to break even on the purchase.

A public investor need not pay the spread for securities traded on an exchange. There is an alternative: submit a limit order to the market. Limit orders can also be handled by OTC dealers, but are generally not used by traders in the dealer market (see Chapter 3). If the quotes for a stock are 50 bid, 50 ¼ ask, and the investor enters a limit order to buy at 50, he or she saves the spread if the order in fact executes at 50.

As previously noted, however, placing a limit order entails the risk that the market will move away from the limit price and that the limit order will not execute. The trader, therefore, faces the dilemma of choosing between paying the spread and running the risk of not achieving an execution. The tighter the spread, the more likely the trader will be to write a market order, and the less costly will be the transaction.

Gaps in the Limit Order Book

Consider the limit order book displayed in Figure 13.15(a). The book shows buy orders from 44 ⅛ to 44 ⅜ and sell orders from 44 ⅝ to 45. The inside market is 44 ⅜ bid, 44 ⅝ ask. There are no orders on the book at prices of 44 ¼, 44 ½, and 44 ⅞. The inside spread is larger than one-eighth because there is no buy or sell order at 44 ½. The absence of orders at 44 ¼ and 44 ⅞ are "air pockets" in the limit order book. The market spread must, of course, be at least as large as the minimum allowable price change (which is one-eighth of a point for most stocks). If, for instance, the ask quotation for a stock is 44 ⅝, a bid of 44 ⅝ or higher transacts. Therefore, with one-eighth pricing and an ask at 44 ⅝, the highest allowable bid that does not transact is 44 ½.

The air pockets in the limit order book are likely to disappear if the book fills with the arrival of more orders, as shown in Figure 13.15(b).

FIGURE 13.15 *Depiction of a Limit Order Book. (a) A Relatively Thin Book. (b) The Book After Additional Orders Have Been Entered*

Buy	44	Sell		Buy	44	Sell
100	$44\frac{1}{8}$			300	$44\frac{1}{8}$	
	$44\frac{1}{4}$			100	$44\frac{1}{4}$	
300	$44\frac{3}{8}$			500	$44\frac{3}{8}$	
	$44\frac{1}{2}$				$44\frac{1}{2}$	
	$44\frac{5}{8}$	200			$44\frac{5}{8}$	400
	$44\frac{3}{4}$	100			$44\frac{3}{4}$	100
	$44\frac{7}{8}$				$44\frac{7}{8}$	
	45	300			45	400
(a)				(b)		

Contrasting Figure 13.15(b) with Figure 13.15(a) shows additional orders at some of the prices at which orders previously existed and the elimination of the air pocket at 44 ¼ on the buy side of the market. If enough additional orders were placed on the book, one would also expect the air pocket at 44 ⅞ on the sell side of the market to be eliminated.

The absence of a limit order at 44 ½, on the other hand, is apt to persist. Just why is not obvious, however, for markets comprising a very large number of traders. It is for this reason that we first establish the existence of the spread and then analyze the determinants of its size.

Assumptions

Seven assumptions facilitate modeling the existence of the gap between the buy and sell orders:

1. The trading arena is a continuous market system.
2. Public limit orders are stored on a limit order book.
3. Public limit and market orders arrive randomly during the trading day.
4. The dissemination of floor information and order transmission are instantaneous.
5. Investors specify their trading decision for one trading period.
6. Price is a continuous (rather than discrete) variable.
7. Each investor submits an order for just one round lot (100 shares).

Assumptions 4 through 7 require explanation. Instantaneous dissemination of floor information and order transmission are assumed so that market orders can be taken to execute with certainty at the posted quotes. Investors are assumed to specify their trading decision for just one trading period so that the probability of a limit order executing can be defined precisely as the probability that the order will execute within the trading period. Price is assumed to be a continuous variable to facilitate the mathematical derivation; a proof that the spread is noninfinitesimal when price is continuous suggests that spreads may indeed be greater than the minimum price change when price is discrete. Each investor is assumed to submit just one round lot order so that we need not be concerned with the probability of an order partially executing.

The spread remains (with continuous pricing) if, when we consolidate the orders of an arbitrarily large but finite number of traders, no buyer or seller places a limit order at a price infinitesimally close to a price already established by a counterpart order (a sell or a buy). To see that no trader would in fact write such an order, return to the situation described in Figure 13.15(b) and consider the decision that might be made by a representative buyer. Assume the trader's reservation price for the purchase is $50 per share.

Order Placement Strategy

The buyer can either place a limit order at any price below the market ask of 44⅝ or can submit a market order that would execute at the market ask of 44⅝. The decision involves resolving a tradeoff between the desirability of buying at a lower price and the desirability of transacting with certainty.

Expected Consumer Surplus.   We have shown that the trader's objective is to maximize the expected value of his or her consumer surplus from trading. The optimal order placement strategy can be determined with this objective in mind. As discussed, the *consumer surplus* from the purchase is the difference between the reservation price and the actual purchase price times the number of shares bought. For the case at hand, the purchase of $Q = 100$ shares at a price P gives a consumer surplus of

$$CS = Q \times 50 - Q \times P = 5,000 - 100P \qquad (13.16)$$

The graph of equation (13.16) is shown in Figure 13.16(a).

The buyer's expected consumer surplus is obtained by multiplying equation (13.16) by the probability that the order at price P will execute. Let F(P) be the probability of the market ask being equal to or less than P during the trading session; the expected consumer surplus of an order placed at the price P is therefore

$$ECS = (5,000 - 100P)F(P) \qquad (13.17)$$

FIGURE 13.16   *Relationship Between a Trader's Consumer Surplus and an Order's Price, and Between the Probability of Order Execution and an Order's Price, for a Buy Order. (a) Consumer Surplus. (b) The Probability of Order Execution*

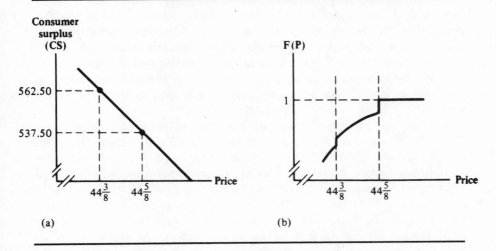

(a)   (b)

where $F(P)$ is an increasing function of P. We examine this function before considering the expected consumer surplus equation itself.

Probability of Order Execution.   The probability of the buy order executing is shown as a function of price in Figure 13.16(b). Of particular interest are the two jumps in the curve: one jump is at the market bid ($44\frac{3}{8}$), and the other is at the market ask ($44\frac{5}{8}$). The limit order of some other buyer has already set the bid and so has priority over any order placed below that price. The probability jump at the bid occurs because by placing an order at a slightly higher price than the established bid, the trader both increases the probability that a market sell order will hit the limit bid (since the new buy order decreases the spread) and gains priority in the queue.

The probability jump at the market ask occurs for the following reason. A limit buy price equal to or greater than the ask quote established on the market executes with certainty at the ask, as shown in Figure 13.16(b) by the probability being unity at $44\frac{5}{8}$ and above. [This is strictly true if the specialist has "stopped the stock" or if there is no delay in order transmission (which for simplicity, we have assumed here).] However, for any limit buy price less than the ask (but no matter how close to it), there is a finite probability that the market will move away from the buyer and that the investor's order will not execute within the trading period. Therefore, there must be a discrete probability jump to unity as the price of the buy order is increased to equal the market ask.

The thought can be stated differently. Consider the following question: Can a buyer make the probability of execution infinitesimally close to unity by writing the buy order at a price infinitesimally close to, but still below, the market ask? No, he or she cannot; a noninfinitesimal probability will remain that the ask price will increase, and that the buy limit that had been infinitesimally close to it will not be hit in the trading period. Therefore, as the buy is placed ever closer to the market ask, the probability of execution rises, but to a value that is discretely less than unity, as shown in Figure 13.16(b).

This argument can be proved mathematically for a discrete order arrival process (such as the Poisson process; see Cohen, Maier, Schwartz, and Whitcomb).[7] There is, however, an exception to the argument—for a continuous order arrival process, the probability of execution does go continuously to unity as the price of the buy order becomes infinitesimally close to the established ask. The Wiener process is one such continuous time process. The price movements associated with that process are so rapid that, if change in the market quotes were to be generated by it, and if at any instant in time the market quote were to be infinitesimally close to some value, the probability that the quote would hit that value would be infinitesimally close to unity. In a moment we will note why a continuous order arrival process is of interest; first, however, consider the significance of the probability jump to unity at the market ask.

Equation 13.17 shows that the expected consumer surplus function is obtained by multiplying the *consumer surplus* (CS) function depicted in Figure 13.16(a) by the probability function [F(P)] depicted in Figure 13.16(b). Figure 13.17 displays two alternative expected consumer surplus functions for a buy order. With CS a negative function of price (for a buy order) and F(P) a positive function of price (for a buy order), *expected consumer surplus* (ECS) is shown in both parts of the diagram as initially rising [the effect of F(P) increasing initially dominates], reaching a maximum, and then falling (the effect of CS falling eventually dominates).

The Optimal Order.   The price at which the buyer should write his or her order is given by the value at which ECS reaches a maximum. Figure 13.17(a) depicts a case in which the optimal strategy is to place a limit order above the market bid of 44⅜. Figure 13.17(b) depicts another case in which the optimal strategy is to hit the market ask of 44⅝ with a market order. The strategy that is optimal for any specific trader depends on that trader's demand function, and on his or her subjective expectation that the limit order will execute.

FIGURE 13.17 *Relationship Between a Trader's Expected Consumer Surplus and an Order's Price, for a Buy Order. (a) Case Where a Limit Order Strategy Is Optimal. (b) Case Where a Market Order Strategy Is Optimal*

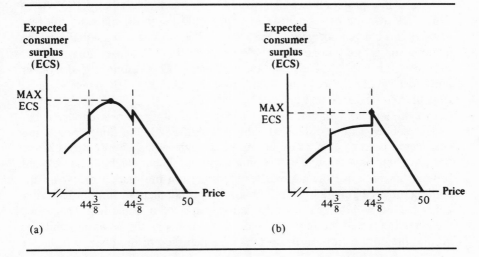

(a) (b)

Persistence of the Market Spread. Having analyzed the order placement strategy of the trader, we can now see why the market spread will persist when the market comprises a very large number of traders: (1) There are no jumps in the CS function, and the F(P) function jumps to unity at the market ask; hence the ECS function must also jump a discrete amount at the market ask. (2) Because ECS does jump a discrete amount at the market ask, the function cannot reach a maximum in the neighborhood immediately to the left of the market ask. (3) Consequently, no trader will post a buy limit at a price infinitesimally close to the price of the market ask, and therefore a noninfinitesimal market spread is preserved under aggregation.

Our formal analysis has assumed continuous pricing and has shown that the market spread is not infinitesimal. We can apply this result to understand intuitively why, with one-eighth pricing, the market spread may be greater than the minimum allowable pricing change of one-eighth of a point. The trader's selection between a limit order and a market order involves a trade-off between more consumer surplus and the certainty of execution. When the limit price of the buy order is close enough to the market ask, the incremental consumer surplus that would be lost by instead trading at the ask is relatively small, and the attractiveness of trading with certainty at the ask is relatively large. Therefore, rather than risking losing the trade in an attempt to buy at a price slightly below the ask, the buyer increases his or her price and trades with certainty at the market ask.

Alternatively viewed, it is as though the market ask exerts a gravitational pull on the new buy order, if the new buy order is sufficiently close to it. After all, if a prospective trader would very much like to buy 100 shares of a stock at a market ask of $44\frac{5}{8}$, why would he or she place a limit buy at $44\frac{1}{2}$ and chance not getting the shares? The logic applies equally to the example of a one-on-one buyer/seller negotiation. Suppose, for instance, that the asset being traded is a house in the $200,000 range. If the buyer and seller get close enough in price (say within $1,000), they typically agree to split the difference and consummate the deal.

A symmetrical situation faces a prospective seller who is choosing between placing a limit order and selling at the bid. If the limit price being considered is close enough to the market bid, the seller simply drops his or her price and hits the bid with a market order. Thus, for both buyers and sellers, the presence of quotes already posted on the market exerts on incoming orders a gravitational pull that prevents counterpart limit orders from being placed within a sufficiently narrow range of one another. Therefore, the spread between the buys and the sells remains as the book gets thicker, despite the elimination of air pockets on either side of the book.

Assessment of the Bid-Ask Model

Existence of the spread having been explained, four objectives remain: (1) to show that the spread results from the transaction costs of trading, (2) to establish the concept of an equilibrium spread for a security, (3) to analyze the size of a security's equilibrium spread, and (4) to show that the effective spread for larger orders is greater than for smaller orders.

The Market Spread and the Transaction Costs of Trading. As we have seen, the bid-ask spread is a transaction cost of trading. However, the spread exists because of other costs of trading (information and decision making costs, opportunity costs, commissions, taxes, and so on). If trading were costless, investors would transmit complete buy and sell order functions to the market; accordingly, the individual spreads would vanish, and so too would the market spread. Therefore, transaction costs account for the market spread because they cause individual investors to transmit point orders (rather than complete order functions) to the market.

In addition, with costly trading, investors do not continuously revise their orders or continuously submit new orders to the market. Therefore, with a finite population of investors, orders arrive on the market at discrete points in time, rather than continuously. We have noted that the probability jumps at the market quotes occur because order arrival is a discrete time process. It follows that the probability jumps occur because trading is not costless.

In summary, market spreads exist because of the probability jumps, the probability jumps exist because order arrival is discrete rather than continuous, and order arrival is a discrete time process because of transaction costs. Therefore, the factor that explains the existence of bid-ask spreads in markets comprising many traders is the factor that ultimately drives all of microstructure analysis: trading is not a frictionless process.

The Equilibrium Spread.   We have established that the market spread exists because no trader will place a limit order infinitesimally close to a counterpart quote already posted on the market. The actual size of the market spread for a security depends on the actual distribution of buy and sell limit orders that have been placed on the book. Furthermore, the actual market spread varies over time—new limit orders may be placed between the quotes so as to narrow the spread, and market orders may execute against the quotes so as to widen the spread. For any given stock, the wider the spread, the more likely is the next order that arrives on the market to be a limit order; conversely, the tighter the spread, the more likely is the next order that arrives on the market to be a market order. This follows from our previous discussion—the cost of trading by market order is greater the larger the spread (which makes investors more likely to select the limit order strategy). On the other hand, the tighter the spread, the more likely it is that the next investor to place an order will select the market order strategy.

The *equilibrium spread* for a stock is that spread for which the probability of the spread next increasing (because of the arrival of a market order) is equal to the probability of the spread next decreasing (because of the arrival of a limit order within the quotes).

The Size of the Equilibrium Market Spread.   The major determinant of the equilibrium spread for a security is the security's order flow. All else equal, a larger order flow is associated with a higher probability that the limit orders that set the quotes will execute. This increases the proportion of investors who will choose to place limit orders rather than market orders for any given size of the spread. This in turn implies that, when the order flow is greater, the spread must be smaller for the pressures that widen it and tighten it to be in balance.

Therefore, a major determinant of the size of spreads is the size of the market. In Chapter 14, we reach a similar conclusion with regard to price volatility, although price volatility is affected by market size in a more complex way. Furthermore, whereas the value of shares outstanding will be seen to be the appropriate measure of market size in the price volatility model, the size of the order flow is what matters in the bid-ask model.

Market Impact Effects and a Passive Trading Strategy

Market Impact

To address the issue of transaction price uncertainty in its purest form, we thus far have assumed that the investor is not large enough to have an appreciable impact on prices established in the market. That is, we have assumed a perfectly competitive environment. Accordingly, the price impact of orders has not yet been taken into account. In reality, the orders of some traders may signal information to other traders because a buy order may be viewed as a signal of positive informational change and a sell order may be viewed as a signal of negative informational change. Additionally, a limit order, because it extends a free option to other traders, gives counterpart sellers an incentive to place their orders at higher prices or counterpart buyers an incentive to place their orders at lower prices.

Even in the absence of the informational signaling and option effects, a large buy order may drive price up, and a large sell order may drive price down as the order is absorbed by the market. This market impact can be understood by relaxing the assumption used for the bid-ask model that each investor submits an order for just one round lot and considering the relationship between the size of the spread and the size of orders.

For a 100-share order, the effective spread is the inside market (because the limit orders that are posted on the market must be for at least one round lot). The trader who typically buys and sells in the neighborhood of 5,000 shares, however, does not care about the inside market if only 100 shares are posted at the bid and the ask. The effective spread for the 5,000-share trader is the difference between the price at which 5,000 shares can be bought (the effective ask for this trader) and the price at which 5,000 shares can be sold (the effective bid).

The effective spread will be larger for a larger trader for a trivial reason: a market order that is large in relation to limit orders on the book may have to transact against limit orders at more than one price if it is to execute completely. More interesting is the fact that large limit orders tend to be placed on the book at prices further from the counterpart market quotes than small limit orders. That is, the equilibrium spread between large orders is greater than the equilibrium spread between small orders. The reason for this is that the gravitational pull is stronger for larger orders.

The gravitational pull is stronger for larger orders because the probability of, for example, a 5,000-share order executing totally at any price is smaller than the probability of, for example, a 100-share order executing totally at the price. This is because the arrival of any counterpart order at the price results in the 100-share limit order executing totally; however, the counterpart order must be for at least 5,000 shares for the 5,000-share limit order to execute totally. In other words, the market is effectively thinner for larger orders.

With the probability of execution being lower, the larger order is more likely to be submitted as a market order than as a limit order at a price in the neighborhood of a large counterpart order. Therefore, a large limit order is entered at a price further from the counterpart quotes than is a smaller order. Hence the spread between the larger orders is greater than the spread between the smaller orders.

The positive relationship between the effective spread and order size explains why a trader who wishes to execute a large order quickly may have to pay an additional price concession to have the order execute totally. Larger traders, in other words, expect to incur higher execution costs because of market impact.

A Passive Trading Strategy

Traditionally, large investors in general, and institutional investors in particular, attempt to control market impact by having their orders worked by traders on an exchange floor or negotiated in the upstairs market by the trading desks of the major brokerage houses. An alternative to these active strategies exists: a Passive Trading Strategy (PTS).

PTS is a comprehensive program that calls for a trader to enter a mix of limit orders to buy or limit orders to sell a large number of securities and to update those orders more or less continuously. Passive trading has some of the characteristics of market making; but the PTS trader need not make a two-sided market and is not required to have orders continuously posted.

The strategy is most appropriate for institutional investors who place orders that are large relative to the market but small relative to their own portfolio holdings. These investors have an advantage as market makers vis-à-vis traditional dealers/specialists because they can take relatively large trading positions in a given security without materially reducing their portfolio diversification and increasing their risk. PTS can reduce market impact for these traders:

- PTS involves the placement of limit rather than market orders; therefore, the strategy does not cause market prices to change as the orders are absorbed by the market.

- PTS traders are informationless; therefore, their orders should not convey adverse informational signals to other traders when they are revealed.

- PTS may be implemented by placing limit orders on both the buy and the sell sides of the market; therefore, market impact attributable to the option characteristic of a limit order can be neutralized.

In addition to reducing trading costs, an institution may use PTS to enhance portfolio performance. That is, the PTS trader can profit from the bid-ask spread rather than incurring it as a cost. It should be noted, however, that an institution using PTS will not always earn the full spread because its limit orders may be placed inside the spread and also may not execute. At the same time, an active trader will not always pay the full spread if his or her order is negotiated.

PTS may convey benefits to the community of investors as well. Even a few passive traders of significant size would serve to narrow spreads, thereby reducing execution costs for other institutions and private investors.[8]

Appendix A—Microeconomic Foundations

The microeconomic concepts upon which this chapter and Chapter 12 are based are developed in this Appendix.

Utility

Utility is an abstract concept economists use to represent an individual's preference ordering. It is assumed that an individual seeks to maximize utility when he or she makes decisions that involve choice. The individual does this, given tastes and the set of resources over which he or she has command.

Utility cannot be measured directly. We can, however, construct utility rankings. That is, we can say that some alternative, A, contains more utility than some other alternative, B, if A is picked rather than B when both are available. Under certain conditions, we can go further and actually construct index numbers to represent the levels of utility achieved for differing quantities of a resource (good, service, or activity).

The Utility Function

A *utility function* shows the relationship between the quantity of some resource obtained and the level of utility achieved. For the moment, let X stand for the resource. Then, write the utility function for X as

$$U = U(X) \tag{13.A1}$$

where   U = the index of utility
        X = the quantity of the resource.

This function is illustrated graphically in Figure 13.A1.

FIGURE 13.A1   *Utility Function: The Relationship Between the Quantity of a Resource and the Level of Utility Achieved*

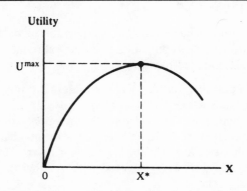

Note four points about the function:

1. $U(0) = 0$ (that is, $U = 0$ for $X = 0$). This is allowable regardless of the decision maker's unique tastes for X because, with utility being measured by index numbers, we are free to scale the function as we wish. That is, we can assign index values to any two arbitrarily selected values of X; then, the index values for all other X are uniquely given by the tastes of the decision maker. Thus we arbitrarily select $X = 0$ and assign it a value $U = 0$.

2. The curve is positively inclined for the smaller values of X. That is, the first derivative of the function, $dU/dX (= U'(X))$, is positive. This means that, initially at least, additional increments of X add to utility. Hence X is a desired resource (that is, X is a "good," not a "bad").

3. The curve is concave from below. That is, the second derivative of the function, $dU'(X)/dX (= U''(X))$, is negative. This means that successive additional increments of X result in successively smaller additions to the decision maker's utility. In other words, the decision maker has decreasing marginal utility with respect to X.

4. The curve reaches a maximum at X^*, at which point utility becomes a decreasing function of X. At X^*, marginal utility is zero ($U'(X^*) = 0$), and for $X > X^*$, marginal utility is negative ($U'(X) < 0$).

If X is free and hence the decision maker's choice of X is not constrained, we see from Figure 13.A1 that the specific quantity, $X = X^*$ will be the optimal choice. That is, setting $X = X^*$ results in the maximization of utility ($U = U^{max}$). However, if X can be obtained only at a price (that is, if something else that yields utility must be given up to get X), then some value of X less than X^* will be the optimal choice. At this point we would have

$$U'(X) = \lambda P_x \qquad\qquad 13.A2$$

where P_x =   the dollar denominated cost per unit of obtaining X
  λ =   a factor that converts this dollar value into a utility denominated measure

In the theory of consumer choice, λ is the marginal utility of income. (See the discussion in the section "Optimality.")

λ and P_x are both positive, and thus the marginal utility of X is positive at the optimal quantity of X selected. This means that we need not be concerned with the function at or to the right of its maximum at X^*. Consequently, neither need we be concerned with whether or not the function has a maximum.

This lack of concern is important: For many uses to which it is put, it is unrealistic to expect that the utility function would reach a maximum. This is because a maximum implies satiation with respect to X. Although any of us may be satiated by sufficient quantities of most specific products (refrigerators, Broadway plays, or chocolate ice cream sodas), our desire for broad product groups (consumer durables, entertainment, consumption goods, or a well diversified portfolio of financial assets) is generally thought to be unlimited.

Diminishing Marginal Utility

The concavity of the curve in Figure 13.A1 shows that the consumer has diminishing marginal utility with regard to X. The property of diminishing marginal utility was used by classical economists to explain why demand curves are negatively inclined. The modern theory of consumer choice does not require the assumption. However, a brief look at the classical argument (using current notation) is useful. At any value of P_X, the consumer selects the quantity of X that satisfies Equation 13.A2. Thus, write Equation 13.A2 for two separate price/quantity sets $< P_0, X_0 >$ and $< P_1, X_1 >$ that satisfy

$$U'(X_0) = \lambda P_0$$
$$U'(X_1) = \lambda P_1 \qquad\qquad (13.A3)$$

Let P_1 be less than P_0, and assume λ constant. [λ (the marginal utility of income) in general changes with income but can be assumed to be constant with respect to the price of X if X is taken to be a sufficiently small part of the individual's consumption basket.] We must have $U'(X_1) < U'(X_0)$. To attain this with diminishing marginal utility, we must have $X_1 > X_0$. A negatively inclined demand curve for X follows.

Utility as a Function of Wealth

X could, on the one hand, stand for the quantity of a specific good such as chocolate ice cream sodas, or it could represent a more inclusive measure of an individual's consumption. For our purposes, it is convenient to treat utility as a function of income or of wealth. Interpreted as a utility function for wealth, Equation 13.A1 would more conventionally be written as $U = f(W)$. This function is of central importance to theories of investing and trading. Several points should be noted with regard to it:

1. Consistent with Figure 13.A1, we can arbitrarily set $U(W = 0) = 0$.
2. Consistent with Figure 13.A1, we would, for small W, require that $U'(W) > 0$.
3. Contrary to Figure 13.A1, we should, over at least some values of W, allow that *increasing* marginal utility with regard to wealth ($U''(W) > 0$) is a possibility.
4. Contrary to Figure 13.A1, we do not expect the utility function defined on wealth to reach a maximum, because satiation with regard to the broadest possible definition of the economic resource does not appear likely.

Attitudes Toward Risk

A decision maker's attitude toward risk can be specified with reference to the utility (of wealth) function. Let the decision maker be offered the following fair bet: h dollars may be won with probability equal to .5, or h dollars may be lost with probability equal to .5. Using the utility function and assuming a starting wealth of W, the decision maker's utility would be $U(W + h)$ if the bet were won, or would be $U(W - h)$ if the bet were lost. Given these utility values and the probabilities of a win and a loss, the decision maker's expected utility if the bet is accepted is

$$E(U) = .5U(W + h) + .5U(W - h) \qquad (13.A4)$$

If the bet is not accepted, the decision maker's expected utility is

$$E(U) = U(W) \qquad (13.A5)$$

Assume that the act of betting provides no utility (positive or negative), and that the decision maker selects the alternative that yields maximum expected utility. Therefore, if the decision maker does not accept the bet, we must have

$$U(W) > .5U(W + h) + .5U(W - h) \qquad (13.A6)$$

Multiplying Equation 13.A6 by 2, and subtracting $[U(W) + U(W - h)]$ from both sides gives

$$U(W) - U(W - h) > U(W + h) - U(W) \qquad (13.A7)$$

Equation 13.A7 shows that the increase in the decision maker's utility, as wealth increases by h from $W - h$ to W, is greater than the increase in the decision maker's utility as wealth increases by h from W to $W + h$. Therefore, the decision maker who does not accept a fair bet must have diminishing marginal utility of wealth. Accordingly, we associate risk aversion with diminishing marginal utility. In similar fashion, risk neutrality can be associated with constant marginal utility (of wealth), and risk-seeking behavior can be associated with increasing marginal utility (of wealth).

Utility as a Function of Return

Utility as a function of wealth can be transformed into a function of the rate of return (r) or of income (I). For certain purposes, these are useful transformations to make. The transformations are made by specifying an initial wealth position (W_0), and by writing the rate of return as

$$r_T = \frac{W_T - W_0}{W_0} \qquad (13.A8)$$

and income as

$$I = r_T W_0 \qquad (13.A9)$$

where the subscript T identifies the future point in time at which the new level of wealth will be attained.

Equations 13.A8 and 13.A9 show that, given W_0, r_T and I are each linear transformations of W_T. Because transforming these variables in this way is equivalent to rescaling the original function, utility can be written as a function of either a rate of return or income, once we know utility as a function of wealth.

Indifference Curves

Indifference curves, like the utility function, are a representation of the decision maker's tastes. Indifference curves, however, give a clearer picture of the alternatives involved. The curve labeled U_0 in Figure 13.A2 is an *indifference curve*. The curve is so named because the decision maker is indifferent about the various combinations of two goods (X and Y) that lie along the curve. The consumer, for instance, is indifferent between the

FIGURE 13.A2 *Indifference Curve*

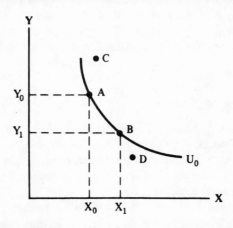

two bundles labeled A and B. Any bundle above and to the right of U_0 is preferred to any bundle on U_0, and any bundle to the left and below U_0 is inferior to any bundle on U_0. For instance, bundle C is preferred to A and B, and bundle D is inferior to A and B.

To see more precisely what is involved, write utility as a function of the quantities of the two goods, X and Y:

$$U = g(X, Y) \tag{13.A10}$$

The marginal utility of each good is the change in utility with respect to the change in the quantity of that good. That is,

$$MU_x = \frac{\partial U}{\partial X}$$

$$MU_y = \frac{\partial U}{\partial Y} \tag{13.A11}$$

Assume that MU_x and MU_y are both positive. It follows that some addition of X will make the decision maker better off, that some subtraction of Y will make the decision maker worse off, and that some combination of more X and less Y will leave the person's utility unaffected. Equivalently, some combination of less X and more Y will also leave the person's utility unaffected. This can be seen in Figure 13.A2.

In Figure 13.A2, bundle A is defined by the combination $< X_0, Y_0 >$, and bundle B is defined by the combination $< X_1, Y_1 >$. Comparing B to A, increasing X by $X_1 - X_0$ adds to the decision maker's utility exactly what decreasing Y by $Y_0 - Y_1$ subtracts. Thus the decision maker is indifferent between the two bundles. An indifference curve is the locus of all such points.

The Indifference Mapping

The utility function, Equation 13.A10, is associated with a family of indifference curves. That is, Equation 13.A10 shows the utility rating for any combination of X and Y, and each indifference curve is a contour that connects all X, Y combinations that yield the same utility. Equation 13.A10 is assumed to be a continuous function.

Every combination of X and Y has a utility rating; hence every combination of X and Y must lie on an indifference curve; and so, therefore, must bundles C and D in Figure 13.A2. Indifference curves could be drawn through the points C and D. These curves would also be downward sloping (because we have assumed MU_x and MU_y positive). Also, the curves would not cross (intersecting indifference curves imply contradictory utility statements). Finally, each curve would be convex throughout; convexity is consistent with (but does not strictly require) diminishing marginal utility. See any standard microeconomics text for a discussion of these three properties of indifference curves (negatively inclined, nonintersecting, and convex to the origin).

Note the following about a family of indifference curves:

1. The mapping is unique to the decision maker. That is, the specific addition of X that has to be made to compensate for any subtraction of Y (or vice versa) depends on the person's unique tastes for the two resources.

2. If X and Y are both desired goods (that is, if for each of them more is preferred to less), the indifference curves are negatively inclined and, throughout the mapping, preferred points lie to the northeast of less preferred points. However, if either X or Y is a bad (that is, less is preferred to more), then the indifference curves are positively inclined; the line of increasing utility slopes toward the northwest (if X is the bad) or to the southeast (if Y is the bad).

3. The objective of the decision maker is to reach the indifference curve with the highest utility rating obtainable. Finding this curve and the optimal values of X and Y is a constrained maximization problem (choice is constrained by scarcity).

The Constraint

The constraint limits the amount of utility the decision maker can attain and, by forcing the decision maker to choose among alternatives, gives rise to the economic problem. In microeconomic theory, the constraint is typically called the *budget constraint*. The budget constraint is most easily defined with respect to two goods (X and Y) that can be obtained at fixed unit prices (P_x and P_y). Assuming the decision maker allocates his or her income (I) entirely between these two goods, we have

$$I = P_x X + P_y Y \qquad (13.A12)$$

Solving for Y gives

$$Y = \frac{I}{P_y} - \frac{P_x}{P_y} X \qquad (13.A13)$$

Equation 13.A13 shows the maximum amount of Y that can be consumed for any amount of X selected. Because I, P_x, and P_y are constant, the constraint is linear. The constraint is presented graphically in Figure 13.A3.

FIGURE 13.A3 *Budget Constraint and Indifference Curves*

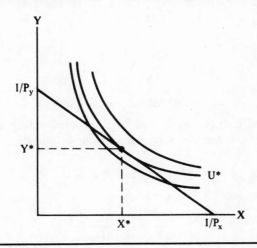

Optimality

A set of indifference curves is also shown in Figure 13.A3. One of the curves is tangent to the budget constraint. The point of tangency shows the optimal bundle of X and Y to select. The optimal quantities of X and of Y (which define the bundle) are labeled X^* and Y^*. The tangency solution also shows the maximum utility attainable; the highest indifference curve reached is labeled U^*.

The optimal solution can also be obtained analytically. The objective is to maximize $U = g(X, Y)$ subject to the constraint, $I - P_xX - P_yY = 0$. To do so, write the function

$$L = g(X, Y) + \lambda (I - P_xX - P_yY) \qquad (13.A14)$$

where λ = the Lagrangian multiplier (the Lagrangian multiplier is interpreted later).

Taking the partial derivatives of Equation 13.A14 with respect to X and Y, equating the derivatives with zero, and using Equation 13A.11 gives the following equations. We assume the second order conditions for a maximum are satisfied. See any standard microeconomics text for further discussion.

$$MU_x - \lambda P_x = 0$$
$$MU_y - \lambda P_y = 0 \qquad (13.A15)$$

This result is consistent with Equation 13.A2. Rearranging (13.A15) gives

$$\frac{MU_x}{MU_y} = \frac{P_x}{P_y} \qquad (13.A16)$$

The left-hand side of Equation 13.A16 can be interpreted. The change in utility caused by any small change in X equal to dX, and small change in Y equal to dY, is

$$dU = \frac{\partial U}{\partial X}dX + \frac{\partial U}{\partial Y}dY \qquad (13.A17)$$

$$= MU_xdX + MU_ydY$$

If the associated changes in X and Y leave total utility unchanged, the consumer remains on the same indifference curve, and thus $dU = 0$, which gives

$$MU_xdX + MU_ydY = 0 \qquad (13.A18)$$

Rearranging Equation 13.A18 gives

$$\frac{dY}{dX} = -\frac{MU_x}{MU_y} \qquad (13.A19)$$

where dY/dX is the slope of an indifference curve. (Note that with MU_x, $MU_y > 0$, the indifference curve is negatively inclined, as shown in Figure

13.A1.) Therefore, the left-hand side of Equation 13.A16 is the negative of the slope of the highest indifference curve the consumer reaches, at the point of optimality.

The right-hand side of Equation 13.A16 can also be interpreted. The change in expenditures (E) caused by any small change in X equal to dX, and small change in Y equal to dY, is

$$dE = P_x dX + P_y dY \tag{13.A20}$$

When utility is maximized, expenditures equal income, and income is constant; thus dE = 0, which gives

$$P_x dX + P_y dY = 0 \tag{13.A21}$$

Rearranging Equation 13.A21 gives

$$\frac{dY}{dX} = -\frac{P_x}{P_y} \tag{13.A22}$$

which is the slope of the constraint described algebraically by Equation 13.A13 and shown graphically in Figure 13.A3. Therefore, the right-hand side of Equation 13.A16 is the negative of the slope of the consumer's budget constraint.

We therefore see that the solution obtained analytically is consistent with the solution shown graphically in Figure 13.A3: the consumer equates the ratio of marginal utilities (MU_x/MU_y) with the ratio of prices (P_x/P_y) by selecting the specific combination $< X^*, Y^* >$ where the indifference curve labeled U^* is tangent to the budget constraint.

The Lagrangian multiplier (λ) in Equation 13.A14 can also be interpreted. The *Lagrangian multiplier* shows how the maximum realization of the objective is increased for a slight relaxation of the constraint. Here, the objective is to obtain as much utility as possible, and the constraint is relaxed by increasing income a small amount. Hence λ is the marginal utility of income. The interpretation can also be seen by rearranging 13.A15 to write $\lambda = MU_x/P_x = MU_y/P_y$. Therefore, when utility is maximized, λ equals the marginal utility per dollar spent on X, equals the marginal utility per dollar spent on Y, equals the marginal utility of a dollar of income.

The Individual's Demand Curve for X

The optimal solution, X^* and Y^*, shows how much X (and Y) the decision maker will select given the price of X (as well as the price of Y and income). Conceptually, it is a simple matter to specify some different value of P_x (keeping P_y and I constant) and to obtain a new utility-maximizing solution for the quantity of X demanded. Figure 13.A4(a) shows the utility-

FIGURE 13.A4   *Derivation of the Decision Maker's Demand Curve for X. (a) Indifference Curves and Budget Constraints. (b) Demand Curve*

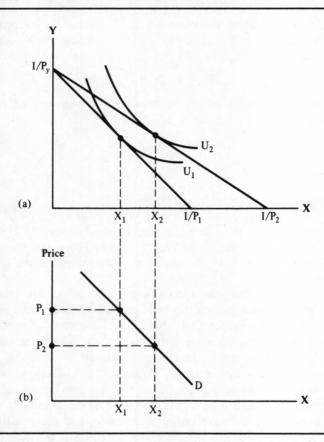

maximizing solution for X for two different prices of X (P_1 and P_2), with P_1 being greater than P_2. The information contained in Figure 13.A4(a) is then restated in Figure 13.A4(b), where the price of X is shown explicitly as the variable on the vertical axis. Figure 13.A4(b) shows that, when the price of X is P_1, X_1 units are demanded, and that when the price is P_2, X_2 units are demanded. With P_2 less than P_1, X_2 is greater than X_1.

The downward sloping line in Figure 13.A4(b) is the consumer's demand curve for X; for simplicity, we have taken the curve to be linear. The demand curve is the relationship between the price of X and the optimal selection of X, other relevant variables (other prices, income, and tastes) being constant. To keep terms clear, we refer to this demand curve as the *normal* demand curve.

Consumer Surplus

It is apparent from Figure 13.A4 that the decision maker is better off when the price of X is P_2 rather than P_1. The reason is that lowering this one price, other prices and income constant, enables the decision maker to consume more of all goods (here, X and Y). This can be seen graphically in Figure 13.A4(a) by contrasting the two budget constraints. Decreasing the price of X has shifted the X intercept to the right of I/P_1 to I/P_2; since the Y intercept, I/P_y, has not changed, the budget constraint has rotated in a counterclockwise direction around a fixed point on the Y axis. As a result, the options available to the decision maker have increased, and that person can reach a higher level of utility. This is shown in Figure 13.A4(a) by the decision maker's moving from the indifference curve labeled U_1 to the higher indifference curve labeled U_2.

The utility gained from moving along the demand curve from $< P_1, X_1 >$ to $< P_2, X_2 >$ is related to the concept of consumer surplus. In fact, what we have just shown is the *change* of consumer surplus that occurs when price decreases in the marketplace. *Consumer surplus* itself is defined as a monetary measure of the *total* gains from trade.

Consumer surplus can be defined precisely with reference to Figure 13.A5. Consider Y to be a composite commodity that might be called "money," and let the decision maker start with an initial endowment of Y and no X. This point is labeled E on the diagram. Assume indifference curves originate from the Y axis so that point E has a utility rating: E is on the indifference curve labeled U_0.

When the price of X is P_1, the consumer demands X_1 units, maximizing utility subject to the budget constraint shown graphically by the line from E to E/P_1. In total, the decision maker gives up EB units of Y to get the X_1 units of X and, in the process, increases utility from U_0 to U_1. Utility is not subject to direct measurement, and so $U_1 - U_0$ cannot be taken as a measure of the gains of trade. Nevertheless, the gain can be reflected by a dollar measure.

To obtain this dollar measure, we have drawn the two indifference curves shown in Figure 13.A5 so that the vertical distance between them is the same at all values of X. The assumption behind this construction is that the ratio of the marginal utilities of the two goods is, at a given value of X, the same for all Y. Accordingly, the line segment $\overline{AE}$ equals the line segment $\overline{CD}$. This equality is desirable because each segment has an interpretation that we wish to be consistent with the other. $\overline{AE}$ is a monetary measure of the compensatory increase in the composite commodity, money, that the decision maker would require in order to achieve the utility level U_1 without trading for X. CD is a monetary measure of the amount of the composite commodity that would have to be taken away to restore the decision maker to the initial level of utility (U_0) if that person were to trade $\overline{EB}$ units of Y for

FIGURE 13.A5   *Consumer Surplus*

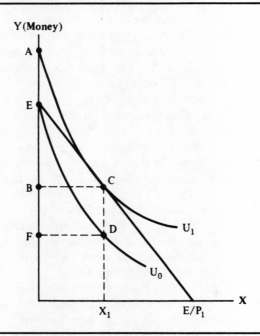

X_1 units of X. For $\overline{AE} = \overline{CD}$, each of these magnitudes is an unambiguous monetary measure of the gains of trade. The measure is called *consumer surplus*.

Reservation Prices

We have thus far focused on how much X the decision maker will demand given the price of X. We now consider the maximum amount the decision maker would be willing to pay for some specific quantity of X (for example, X_1 units). This maximum price per unit is called the *reservation price*.

To obtain the reservation price, the decision maker must be forced to choose between exactly X_1 units, and no X at all. The reason is that if a little bit less of X could be bought, the quantity of X demanded would stray from X_1. Thus, the reservation price is the highest unit price that will be paid for a quantity when the only alternative to that quantity is nothing at all. For this reason, the reservation price is sometimes referred to as an *all-or-nothing price*.

Figure 13.A5 shows that, if the price of X is P_1, the decision maker will demand X_1 units. The decision maker pays $\overline{EB}$ units of Y and gains a consumer surplus that is equivalent, in monetary terms, to $\overline{CD}$ units of Y. It is therefore clear that, at most, the decision maker would be willing to pay $\overline{EF} = \overline{EB} + \overline{CD}$ for X_1 units of X. A total expenditure of $\overline{EB} + \overline{CD}$ for X_1 units would keep the consumer on the same indifference curve (that is, would leave that person's total utility unaffected). Therefore, the reservation price per unit for X_1 units is

$$P_1^R = \frac{\overline{EB} + \overline{CD}}{X_1}$$

Clearly, P_1^R is greater than P_1.

The Normal Demand Curve and the Reservation Demand Curve

When a consumer buys an optimal amount of a good at a given price, that price reflects the marginal value of the good to the consumer (see Equation 13.A2). On the other hand, when a reservation price is paid, the consumer realizes no consumer surplus from the trade; this means that the reservation price reflects the average value of the good to the consumer. Recognizing this, we can identify the reservation demand curve and relate it to the normal demand curve defined previously.

First write the normal demand function as*

$$P = a - bX \qquad (13.A23)$$

From Equation 13.A2, $P_x = U'(X)/\lambda$. Making the substitution and integrating, we get

$$U(X)/\lambda = aX - \tfrac{1}{2}bX^2 \qquad (13.A24)$$

where $U(X)/\lambda$ is the monetary value of the total quantity of X consumed. We get the average monetary value for any quantity of X, and thereby obtain the reservation demand curve, by dividing Equation 13.A24 by X. Thus we have

$$P^R = a - \tfrac{1}{2}bX \qquad (13.A25)$$

When the normal demand curve is linear, the reservation demand curve is also linear, and the slope of the normal demand curve (dP/dX) is twice

---

* X is typically written as a function of P. The exposition is simplified here by writing the inverse function, $P = g(X)$.

FIGURE 13.A6   *Normal* (D^N) *and Reservation* (D^R) *Demand Curves*

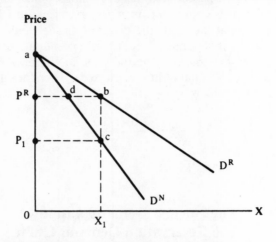

that of the reservation price demand curve, as can be seen by comparing Equations 13.A23 and 13.A25. Both of these curves are shown in Figure 13.A6, where the normal demand curve is labeled D^N and the reservation demand curve is labeled D^R.

The two demand curves can be used to derive the consumer surplus realized when the decision maker obtains X_1 units at the price P_1. In Figure 13.A5, the consumer surplus associated with this purchase is shown to be the distance $\overline{CD}$. This is because consumer surplus is the difference between the maximum total amount a consumer would be willing to pay in an all-or-nothing situation and the total amount actually paid when quantity is freely adjustable. Given the definition of the reservation price, the consumer in an all-or-nothing situation would be willing to pay $P^R X_1$ for X_1 units. But when the unit price is P_1, the total expenditure is $P_1 X_1$. Therefore, the consumer surplus shown by the distance $\overline{CD}$ in Figure 13.A5 is also given in Figure 13.A6 by the area

$$P_1 P^R bc = 0 P^R b X_1 - 0 P_1 c X_1$$

We can go one step further. Because the slope of D^N is twice that of D^R, the point d is at the midpoint of the line segment $P^R b$. Consequently, the triangle $P^R ad$ is equal to the triangle dbc, and so the area of the triangle $P_1 ac$ equals the area of the rectangle $P_1 P^R bc$. Therefore, the triangular area $P_1 ac$ under the normal demand curve is also a measure of consumer surplus.

The triangular measure of consumer surplus is useful for showing how consumer surplus changes as price changes and the decision maker moves to a new point along his or her demand curve. To see this, identify consumer surplus by the triangular area under the demand curve for two different prices. The triangular area is larger for the lower price than for the higher price; the difference in the two triangular areas is the increase in consumer surplus that results from the decrease in price.

Supply Curves

When individuals supply their labor services or their income (in the form of interest-bearing loans or equity investments) to the market, their supply decisions are made with reference to utility functions in much the same way that consumption decisions are made. The individual's supply curve is a statement of how much of a resource he or she will offer to the market as a function of price (all else constant). The major difference between the supply curve and the demand curve is that the supply curve is usually taken to be upward sloping, whereas we have shown that the demand curve is generally a downward sloping function of price.

Given a supply curve, we can also define the concepts of *producer surplus* (it is analogous to consumer surplus) and *reservation sell price* (it is

FIGURE 13.A7 *Normal Supply Curve* (S^N)*, Reservation Supply Curve* (S^R)*, and Reservation Sell Price* (P^{RS})

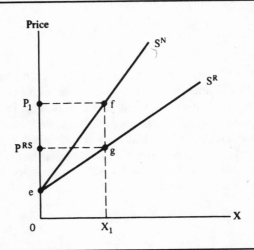

analogous to a reservation buy price). Further, we can distinguish between a normal supply curve and a reservation supply curve. These curves, along with producer surplus, are shown in Figure 13.A7, where the normal supply curve is labeled S^N, the reservation supply curve is labeled S^R, and the reservation sell price is identified as P^{RS}. In Figure 13.A7, the rectangular area $P^{RS}P_1fg$ and the triangular area eP_1f are both equal to producer surplus.

Aggregation and Market Clearing

Aggregation from Individual to Market Demand-Supply Curves

Assume that N buyers and M sellers constitute the market for X. For each ith buyer, let the demand function for X be

$$X_i = D_i(P) \tag{13.A26}$$

For each jth seller, let the supply function for X be

$$X_j = S_j(P) \tag{13.A27}$$

The *aggregate quantity* demanded and supplied at each price is the summation of all individual quantities demanded and supplied. Thus the market demand function is

$$D(P) = \sum_{i=1}^{N} X_i = \sum_{i=1}^{N} D_i(P) \tag{13.A28}$$

and the market supply function is

$$S(P) = \sum_{j=1}^{M} X_j = \sum_{j=1}^{M} S_j(P) \tag{13.A29}$$

The summation is shown graphically in Figure 13.A8 for the aggregate demand curve. For simplicity, we have taken the number of buyers to be two. At prices greater than a_2, aggregate demand is zero. Individual 2 enters the market at a price of a_2 and is the sole market participant until price drops to a_1. At the price a_1, individual 1 also enters the market (note the kink in the market demand curve at a_1). Below a_1 market demand is the aggregate of both individuals' demands. Equation 13.A28 is illustrated in Figure 13.A8 at the arbitrarily selected price P_0. At P_0:

$$D_1(P_0) = X_1$$

$$D_2(P_0) = X_2$$

$$D(P_0) = X_1 + X_2$$

FIGURE 13.A8 *Derivation of the Aggregate Demand Curve. (a) Demand Curve of Buyer 1. (b) Demand Curve of Buyer 2. (c) Combined Demand Curve for Buyer 1 and Buyer 2*

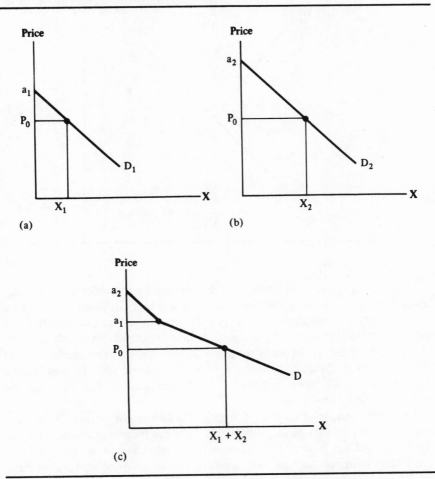

Market Clearing

A market *clears* when the price is such that the total number of units demanded in the market by buyers equals the total number of units supplied by sellers. The price that clears the market is a stable equilibrium price if a higher price would induce an excess of supply (which exerts downward pressure on price), and if a lower price would induce an excess of demand (which exerts upward pressure on price). With the demand curve downward sloping and the supply curve upward sloping, this condition is satisfied and the clearing price is a stable equilibrium price.

FIGURE 13.A9   *Determination of Equilibrium Price* (P*) *and Equilibrium Value of* X (X*)

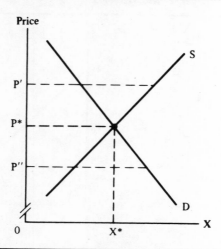

However, a second condition must also be fulfilled in order that the market clearing price be an equilibrium price: all buy and sell desires at the price must be fully and simultaneously expressed in the market. This condition is implicit in standard economic analysis, because demand and supply propensities are assumed to be fully revealed to the market. The reason is that economic theory typically assumes a frictionless world (that is, that trading in the market is a costless process). For the remainder of this appendix, we assume this condition is satisfied.

To obtain the market clearing price, let the number of buyers (N) and the number of sellers (M) be large enough so that no individual participant has significant market power; that is, assume all participants are price takers. Price takers simply "accept" the market-determined price and adjust their own demand or supply to it (price takers are too small to have a perceptible impact on the clearing price). The market clearing price is then solved for by setting Equation 13.A28 equal to Equation 13.A29. Thus the market clearing equation is

$$D(P^*) = S(P^*) \qquad\qquad (13.A30)$$

where the symbol * indicates that P is the equilibrium solution for price. Having used Equation 13.A30 to solve for P*, we can substitute P* into either Equation 13.A28 or 13.A29 and solve for X*, the equilibrium value of X.

The determination of P^* and X^* is illustrated graphically in Figure 13.A9. The solution for these variables is given by the intersection of the market demand curve (D) and the market supply curve (S). When D is downward sloping and S is upward sloping, P^*, X^* is a stable equilibrium solution: as shown in Figure 13.A9, at any price P' greater than $P*$, supply exceeds demand (which causes price to fall toward P^*), and at any price P'' less than P^*, demand exceeds supply (which causes price to rise toward P^*).

Pareto Optimality

We assess the market clearing solution (P^*, Q^*) by focusing initially on the demand side of the market. The purpose of the assessment is to show that the frictionless market achieves an efficient distribution of resources.

When P^* is established as the market price for X, each ith buyer demands the specific quantity of X given by Equation 13.A26 assessed at $P = P^*$. In equilibrium, the price (P^*) reflects the marginal value of X to the ith buyer. Assume that N buyers each allocate income over two goods, X and Y, and that the market for Y has also achieved an equilibrium solution, P_y^*, Y^*.

Equation 13.A16 shows that when any i^{th} buyer optimally allocates his or her income, the ratio of the marginal utility of the two goods is equal to the ratio of the prices. Since P_x^* and P_y^* are the same for all buyers, the ratio of marginal utilities must be the same for all buyers. That is, we must have

$$\left(\frac{MU_x}{MU_y}\right)_i = \frac{P_x^*}{P_y^*} \text{ for each buyer, } i = 1, \dots, N \qquad (13.A31)$$

Equation 13.A31 shows that when X and Y are distributed across the N buyers according to the consumer choice and market equilibrium models shown previously, it would not be possible to redistribute these resources so as to make at least one buyer better off without making at least one other buyer worse off. This concept stated in economic terminology is, the distribution of X and Y across the N buyers is Pareto optimal. *Pareto optimal* means that no one individual can be made better off without at least one other individual being made worse off.

An opportunity to trade exists whenever a distribution of resources is not Pareto optimal (assuming a market structure to handle the trade). For instance, consider two individuals (A and B) and two goods (X and Y) and let

$$\left(\frac{MU_x}{MU_y}\right)_A > \left(\frac{MU_x}{MU_y}\right)_B \qquad (13.A32)$$

Because on the margin the first individual values X relative to Y more than does the second individual, there is some (marginal) exchange of X and Y between A and B that will enable both to achieve a higher level of utility. Thus, with the inequality shown in 13.A32, the distribution of X and Y across individuals A and B is not Pareto optimal. Conversely, when equality holds, the distribution is Pareto optimal. To see this, reverse the process: if an exchange is made given that 13.A32 is initially in equality, equality cannot hold after the trade. Then, for one of the traders to have been made better off, the other trader must have been made worse off. Since no exchange exists that could make both traders better off, the equality of 13.A32 implies a Pareto optimal distribution.

The concept can be clarified with the graph shown in Figure 13.A10. The width of the box in Figure 13.A10 shows the total amount of good X available to the two traders (A and B), and the height of the box shows the total amount of good Y available to the two traders. The lower left-hand corner of the box represents the origin for trader A, and the upper right-hand corner represents the origin for trader B. Let the starting allocation of resources between A and B be given by point E.

Because A and B both gain utility from both goods, A seeks to move as far as possible to the northeast, and B seeks to move as far as possible to the southwest. Note, however, that a move in the southeasterly direction toward the point labeled F will make both individuals better off (both can reach higher indifference curves than the curves drawn through point E). At point

FIGURE 13.A10 *Determination of a Pareto Optimal Distribution of X and Y Among Traders A and B*

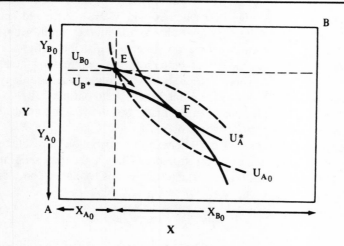

F, further trade would be undesirable. This is because for one trader to reach a higher indifference curve, the other must be forced to a lower indifference curve. The distribution represented by point F is, therefore, Pareto optimal. Notice that, at point F, the ratio of marginal utilities is the same for the two traders (because their indifference curves are tangent and thus have the same slope). The distribution represented by point E is not Pareto optimal.

The concept of Pareto optimality also applies to the quantities of X and Y that are being produced, given the cost to suppliers and the benefits to buyers. It can be shown by using the microeconomic theory of the firm that, in the competitive equilibrium we have described, each firm produces at a rate that equates the marginal cost of production with the market price of the resource produced. Thus for resources X and Y,

$$P_x^* = MC_x \text{ for each } j^{th} \text{ seller of X} \tag{13.A33}$$

and

$$P_y^* = MC_y \text{ for each } j^{th} \text{ seller of Y} \tag{13.A34}$$

Dividing Equation 13.A33 by Equation 13.A34 gives

$$\frac{P_x^*}{P_y^*} = \frac{MC_x}{MC_y} \tag{13.A35}$$

Equations 13.A31 and 13.A35 together imply

$$\left(\frac{MU_x}{MU_y}\right)_i = \frac{MC_x}{MC_y} \text{ for each buyer, } i = 1 \ldots N. \tag{13.A36}$$

Equation 13.A36 shows that, in equilibrium, X and Y are valued on the margin in the same proportion by all consumers, and that this proportion is equal to the cost on the margin of producing X, relative to the cost on the margin of producing Y. Hence both the allocation of resources for the production of X and Y, and the distribution of X and Y across buyers, are Pareto optimal.

We have described the efficiency of allocating resources according to the individual choice model and the market equilibrium model described in this chapter. When resources are so allocated, the market has accomplished its job of effecting all desired trades. When these trades have been made, there is no unsatisfied desire among market participants to trade further or to recontract. The allocation of resources is Pareto optimal; the market price is a Pareto optimal price; and we have achieved all that could be expected from a trading system. For this reason, the Pareto optimal solutions provide the ideal against which to assess solutions attained in a less than perfect trading environment.

Walrasian Tâtonnement

The Pareto optimal values of P_x^* and X^* were obtained by solving two simultaneous equations: the demand equation 13.A28 and the supply equation 13.A29. Prices and quantities, of course, are not found this way in actual markets, but rather are the result of real world processes. It is of interest, however, to consider how market clearing might be achieved if trading were a costless activity.

The French economist Leon Walras (1834–1910) envisaged buyers and sellers of a resource (X) being brought together by an auctioneer who calls out tentative prices. The process of finding a solution by a series of tentative trials is known as a *Walrasian tâtonnement*. Assume that the prices of other resources have been established and that we can focus separately on the market for X. At any price at which the demand for X exceeds supply, a higher price is called out; or, if supply exceeds demand, a lower price is called out. The *tâtonnement* process is continued until the clearing price is found. When that price is found, buyers and sellers trade optimally. As a result of the Walrasian *tâtonnement* process, X^* units are traded at a price of P^*, the solution to the two simultaneous equations.

The Time Dimension

Stocks Versus Flows

Stock refers to one way of measuring quantity, *flow* to another way. *Stocks* are quantities measured at some moment of time—the stockpile of raw materials in a warehouse, the number of loaves of bread on a supermarket shelf, the amount of money in one's pocket, the value of assets/liabilities on a balance sheet, the quantity of water in a reservoir, and so on. *Flows*, on the other hand, are quantities that are measured over some period of time—the hourly flow of water out of a reservoir, a monthly earnings figure, the number of cans of beer consumed per quarter, one's annual income, and so on.

We have been discussing two variables, quantity (X) and X's unit price (P). Is the quantity of X stock- or flow-dimensioned?

For many resources, quantity can be measured as either a stock or a flow, depending on the specific purpose of the study. That is, one could refer to car sales per year (a flow), to the total number of cars in existence at any moment in time (a stock), to the relationship between the price of cars and the frequency with which a household might buy a new car (a flow), or to the relationship between the price of cars and the number of one-car families, the number of two-car families, and so on (a stock).

Most microeconomic models treat quantity as a flow variable, and we have implicitly done so in our discussion thus far. For instance, Equation

13.A12, which is used to obtain the budget constraint, equates income (I) with total expenditure ($P_xX + P_yY$). Since income is a flow variable, then so too must be expenditures; because price in this context has no time dimension, X and Y must themselves be flow variables. For this reason, a statement such as "The quantity of X demanded is 12 units when the price per unit is $5" means that the time *rate* of consumption is 12 (for example, per day, per month, or per year, depending on the interval used to express income and consumption).

With regard to investing and trading, quantity is stock-dimensioned, not flow-dimensioned. That is, at a given price per share, the investor decides how many shares of an asset to *hold*, not how many to buy, as a rate per unit of time. Suppose, for instance, that at a price of $50 per share the investor would like to hold 150 shares, and that the investor currently has 200 shares in his or her portfolio. The decision then is simply to sell 50 shares, not to keep on selling 50 shares per day, per month, or whatever. Therefore, just as the decision to hold 150 shares is stock-dimensioned, so too is the decision to adjust the portfolio holdings by 50 shares.

The Stock-Dimensioned Demand Curve to Hold Shares

Figure 13.A11(a) shows the demand curve (labeled D) of an investor to hold shares of an asset. This curve resembles the curve labeled D^N in Figure 13.A6, and with minor exceptions it is the same. In Figure 13.A11(a), the quantity variable (the number of shares held) is denoted by the symbol N. N_0 identifies the number of shares currently held. For this demand curve, the investor would want to hold the N_0 shares at a price per share of P_0.

Given the demand to hold shares (D) and the current share holdings (N_0), we can determine the number of shares the investor would want to buy or to sell as price varies from P_0. This information is shown in Figure 13.A11(b) by the downward sloping curve labeled *Buy*, and by the upward sloping curve labeled *Sell*.

The symbol Q in Figure 13.A11 denotes the number of shares the investor would like to add to or subtract from his or her portfolio. Sell orders can be graphed as positive values of Q because the upward sloping function is labeled *Sell* (in other words, a negative buy order is equivalent to a positive sell). For instance, if the share price is P_2, Figure 13.A11(a) shows that the investor would want to hold $N_0 - Q_2$ shares. Accordingly, Figure 13.A11(b) shows that, at price P_2, he or she will seek to sell a positive number, Q_2. Alternatively, if price is P_1, the investor's optimal holdings will be $N_0 + Q_1$ shares, and the investor will want to buy Q_1 shares.

Generalizing over all values of P gives the buy and sell curves in Figure 13.A11(b). These can be found geometrically from the demand curve in Figure 13.A11(a): place a mirror on the vertical line at N_0, project the

FIGURE 13.A11 *Stock-dimensional Demand Curves. (a) Investor's Demand Curve to Hold Shares. (b) Investor's Buy and Sell Curves*

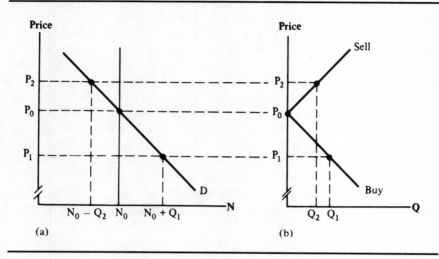

segment of the demand curve to the left of N_0 onto the quadrant to the right of N_0 (note that the mirror image is positively inclined), and change the origin from zero shares to N_0 shares.

Appendix B—The Expected Opportunity Cost of Order Placement

Equation 13.11 may be derived more formally as follows. Given the MB' order function, the opportunity cost associated with any market price (P) less than P_1 is $\frac{1}{2}[(a - P)Q(P) - (a - P_1)Q(P_1)b[Q'(P) - Q_1]^2]$, and the opportunity cost associated with any market price between P_1 and the intercept parameter (a) is $\frac{1}{2}(a - P)Q(P)$. Therefore, the *expected opportunity cost* (EOC) is

$$\text{EOC} = \int_0^{P_1} [(a - P)Q(P) - (a - P_1)Q(P_1) - b(Q'(P) - Q_1)^2] \tfrac{1}{2} f(P) \, dP$$

$$+ \int_{P_1}^a (a - P)Q(P) \tfrac{1}{2} f(P) \, dP \tag{13.B1}$$

where P is the price of the lowest priced buy order that executes, and f(P) is the probability that an order at P is the marginal order to execute. From Equation 13.B1, as P_1 is increased to the value a,

$$\lim_{P_1 \to a} EOC = \int_0^a [(a - P)Q(P) - b[Q'(P)]^2]\,\tfrac{1}{2}\, f(P)\, dP \qquad (13.B2)$$

In the limit, as P_1 goes to a, the order strategy described by the MB' order function becomes the order strategy described by the MB function. Note that $(a - P)Q(P) = b[Q(P)]^2$ and $Q(P) > Q'(P)$; thus $(a - P)Q(P)b[Q'(P)]^2 > 0$, and hence the limit is positive.

If the decision maker sets P_1 some discrete distance below the intercept, a, the expected opportunity cost associated with intramarginal purchases is less, but the EOC associated with not transacting at all is introduced. The EOC for $P_1 < a$, as compared with $P_1 = a$, can be assessed by subtracting Equation 13.B2 from Equation 13.B3 and by integrating by parts:

$$\Delta EOC = \frac{1}{2}\Bigg[\int_0^{P_1} (a - P)Q(P)f(P)\, dP - \int_0^{P_1} (a - P_1)Q(P_1)f(P)\, dP$$

$$- \int_0^{P_1} b[Q'(P) - Q_1]^2 f(P)\, dP + \int_{P_1}^a (a - P)Q(P)f(P)\, dP$$

$$- \int_0^a (a - P)Q(P)f(P)\, dP + \int_0^a b[Q'(P)]^2 f(P)\, dP \Bigg] \qquad (13.B3)$$

The first, fourth, and fifth terms on the right-hand side of Equation 13.B3 sum to zero. For P_1 close to a, Q_1 is close to zero, and thus the third term on the right-hand side of Equation 13.B3 is approximately

$$- \int_0^{P_1} b[Q'(P)]^2 f(P)\, dP$$

Canceling the first, fourth, and fifth terms; combining the third and sixth terms; and using $a - P_1 = bQ(P_1)$, gives Equation 13.11.

Suggested Reading

Biais, B. "On the Equilibrium Number of Dealers in Securities Markets." Paper presented at American Finance Association Meetings, December 1990.

Bronfman, C. "The Informational Content of Frequently Changing Prices: Implications for the Structural Organization of a Securities Market." Doctoral dissertation Graduate School of Business Administration, New York University, 1988.

Bronfman, C., and Schwartz, R. "Order Placement and Price Discovery in a Securities Market." Paper presented at American Finance Association Meetings, December 1990.

Cohen, K., Maier, S., Schwartz, R., and Whitcomb, D. *The Microstructure of Securities Markets*. Englewood Cliffs, NJ: Prentice Hall, 1986.

Cohen, K., Maier, S., Schwartz, R., and Whitcomb, D. "Transaction Costs, Order Placement Strategy, and Existence of the Bid-Ask Spread." *Journal of Political Economy*, April 1981.

Conroy, R., Harris, R., and Benet, B. "The Effects of Stock Splits on Bid/Ask Spreads." *Journal of Finance*, June 1990.

Ho, T., Schwartz, R., and Whitcomb, D. "The Trading Decision and Market Clearing Under Transaction Price Uncertainty." *Journal of Finance*, March 1985.

Roll, R. "A Simple Implicit Measure of the Effective Bid-Ask Spread in an Efficient Market." *Journal of Finance*, September 1984.

Schwartz, R., and Whitcomb, D. *Transaction Costs and Institutional Investor Trading*. Monograph Series in Finance and Economics, Salomon Brothers Center for the Study of Financial Institutions, New York University Graduate School of Business Administration, 1988, No. 1988-2/3.

Stoll, H. "Inferring the Components of the Bid-Ask Spread: Theory and Empirical Tests." *Journal of Finance*, September, 1989.

Notes

1. T. Ho, R. Schwartz, and D. Whitcomb, "The Trading Decision and Market Clearing under Transaction Price Uncertainty," *Journal of Finance*, March 1985.
2. Ibid.
3. Ibid.
4. Ibid., Appendix B.
5. C. Bronfman, The Informational Content of Frequently Changing Prices: Implications for the Structural Organization of a Securities Market. Doctoral dissertation, 1988. Graduate School of Business Administration.
6. C. Bronfman and R. Schwartz, "Order Placement and Price Discovery in a Securities Market," paper presented at the American Finance Association Meetings, Washington, DC, December 1990.
7. K. Cohen, S. Maier, R. Schwartz, and D. Whitcomb. Chapter 5, "The Bid-Ask Spread." In *The Microstructure of Securities Markets*. Englewood Cliffs, NJ: Prentice Hall, 1986.
8. See R. Schwartz and D. Whitcomb, *Transaction Costs and Institutional Investor Trading*, monograph series in Finance and Economics, Salomon Brothers Center for the Study of Financial Institutions, New York University Graduate School of Business Administration, for further discussion of PTS, No. 1988-2/3.

14

Prices and Returns

Each transaction price in a continuous market reflects the interaction of at least two orders—a buy order and a sell order. Each return that is established reflects two separate transaction prices, the price at the beginning of the period over which the return is measured and the price at the end of the period. All told, prices and returns are complex results of informational change, liquidity change, and the mechanics of the market.[*]

The Measurement of Returns

The Time Dimension

The time dimension enters the measurement of returns in a number of ways. $T + 1$ points in time establish T time intervals; t identifies the tth interval, $t = 1, \ldots, T$. The return for an interval is given an index that corresponds to the index for the interval. Thus r_t is the return over the interval $(t - 1)$ to (t). If the length of the interval is changed, then the index on the return corresponds to the point in time that demarcates the end of the longer period. That is, R_T denotes the return from 0 to T if the full span is referred to, and r_T denotes the return from $(T - 1)$ to (T) if the Tth (last) short interval

---

[*] This chapter draws heavily on K. Cohen, G. Hawawini, S. Maier, R. Schwartz, and D. Whitcomb, "Friction in the Trading Process and the Estimation of Systematic Risk," *Journal of Financial Economics,* August 1983; K. Cohen, S. Maier, R. Schwartz, and D. Whitcomb, "The Returns Generation Process, Returns Variance, and the Effect of Thinness in Securities Markets," *Journal of Finance,* March 1978; and K. Cohen, S. Maier, R. Schwartz, and D. Whitcomb, *The Microstructure of Securities Markets.* Englewood Cliffs, NJ: Prentice Hall, 1986, all used with permission.

is referred to. Using this notation, the relevant time dimensions are as follows:

- *Points in time:* The T + 1 points in time extend from the first (0) to the last (T).
- *Time intervals:* The T time interval are indexed t = 1, ..., T, with the index on each interval corresponding to the count on the price observation at the end of that interval.
- *Time span:* The overall time span is of length T, and it comprises T short intervals.
- *Interval length:* The length of each interval is point in time t, minus point in time t − 1.
- *Unit period:* Both the overall time span and the shorter time intervals are measured as multiples of a *unit period of time.* For instance, if the unit period is one day, then both the time interval t − 1 to t and the overall time span, T, are measured in days.
- *Common period:* A return measured for one interval of time (such as a week) can be expressed as a rate per some other interval (for instance, per year). Converting all time rates into a common period sometimes facilitates analysis and evaluation.
- *Compounding frequency:* Interest can be compounded once per time interval, more frequently, or, in the limit, continuously.
- *Calendar time:* For theoretical analysis, time can be treated as an abstract concept. For empirical analysis, actual price observations are located in *calendar time.* With seasonal variability, secular trends, and/or nonstationary returns distributions, the exact location of the span t = 0, ..., T in calendar time will affect the observed price behavior. Location in calendar time may be altered *in the large* by, for example, using 1990 prices instead of 1980 prices, or *in the small* by using daily opening prices instead of daily closing prices.

Prices

The term *price* can refer either to a transaction price or to a bid-ask quotation price. *Transaction prices* are prices that have been established for trades already made. *Quotation prices* are *ex ante* expressions of the willingness of buyers and sellers to trade. We generally restrict the use of the term *price* to transaction prices and refer to bid-ask prices as *quotes.* The behavior of prices and quotes is studied by analyzing their change from one point in time to another.

Price changes are *returns.* Price changes computed by using points of time that are separated by an interval of specified length (such as one day) are identified as pertaining to that period (for instance, *daily returns*). Price changes computed for a sequence of prices recorded at the points of time that trades occur are *transaction-to-transaction returns*. For the most part, we deal with returns measured for specified time intervals.

In empirical work, prices are adjusted for stock and cash dividends paid during an interval so that the return measured for the interval is the total return—capital gains plus dividends. Therefore, if the closing price of a stock at time $t - 1$ is 50, the recorded closing price at t is 49, a dividend of \$.25 a share is paid, and t is the ex-dividend date, the adjusted price at t is $49\frac{1}{4}$, and the price change from $t - 1$ to t is $49\frac{1}{4} - 50 = -\frac{3}{4}$.

Returns

Price changes (returns) can be measured as price relatives, as dollar amounts, or as percentages. Arithmetic percentages can be converted into logarithmic values or into growth rates.

Assume a time span from 0 to T divided into equal intervals indexed $t = 1, \ldots, T$.

The *price relatives* are

$$\frac{P_T}{P_0} = \left(\frac{P_1}{P_0}\right)\left(\frac{P_2}{P_1}\right) \cdots \left(\frac{P_T}{P_{T-1}}\right) \tag{14.1}$$

For the time interval 0, 1 we can write

$$P_1 = P_0 + \Delta P_1 \tag{14.2a}$$

$$P_1 = P_0(1 + r_1) \tag{14.2b}$$

$$P_1 = P_0 e^{g_1} \tag{14.2c}$$

Accordingly:

The *dollar return* is

$$\Delta P_1 = P_1 - P_0 \tag{14.3}$$

The *percentage return* is

$$r_1 = \frac{\Delta P_1}{P_0} = \frac{P_0 + \Delta P_1}{P_0} - 1 = \frac{P_1}{P_0} - 1 \tag{14.4}$$

The *logarithmic return* is

$$r_1^* = \ln(1 + r_1) \tag{14.5}$$

The *growth rate* is

$$g_1 = \ln\left(\frac{P_1}{P_0}\right) \tag{14.6}$$

where ln indicates a logarithm to the base e ($e = 2.7182\ldots$).

Generalizing for a succession of periods, $t = 1, \ldots, T$.

$$P_T = P_0 + \Delta P_1 + \cdots + \Delta P_T = P_0 + \sum_{t=1}^{T} \Delta P_t \qquad (14.7a)$$

$$P_T = P_0(1 + r_1) \ldots (1 + r_T) = P_0 \prod_{t=1}^{T} (1 + r_t) \qquad (14.7b)$$

$$P_T = P_0 e^{g_1} \ldots e^{g_T} \qquad = P_0 \prod_{t=1}^{T} e^{g_t} \qquad (14.7c)$$

For the overall time span we can also write

$$P_T = P_0 + \Delta P_T \qquad (14.8a)$$

$$P_T = P_0(1 + R_T) \qquad (14.8b)$$

$$P_T = P_0 e^{g_T} \qquad (14.8c)$$

Equations 14.7 and 14.8 give

$$\Delta P_T = \sum_{t=1}^{T} \Delta P_t \qquad (14.9a)$$

$$1 + R_T = \prod_{t=1}^{T} (1 + r_t) \qquad (14.9b)$$

$$e^{g_T} = \prod_{t=1}^{T} e^{g_t} \qquad (14.9c)$$

Taking logarithms of (14.9c) gives

$$g_T = \sum_{t=1}^{T} g_t \qquad (14.9d)$$

It follows from Equations 14.9a–14.9d that

- The average price change over the time span of length T is the arithmetic average of the price changes over the T short intervals that comprise it.
- $(1 + R_T)^{1/T}$ is the geometric mean of the $(1 + r_t)$. (The geometric mean of n observations is the nth root of the product of the n observations.)
- g_T is T times the arithmetic mean of the g_t.

Let $R_T^* = \ln(1 + R_T)$ and $r_t^* = \ln(1 + r_t)$. Then, from (14.7b) and (14.8b), we have

$$\ln\left(\frac{P_T}{P_0}\right) = R_T^* = \sum_{t=1}^{T} r_t^* \tag{14.10}$$

From (14.8b) and (14.8c) we have

$$(1 + R_T) = e^{g_T} \tag{14.11}$$

Taking logarithms of (14.11) gives

$$R_T^* = g_T \tag{14.12}$$

The growth rate g_T is, therefore, a logarithmic return.

As seen in Equation 14.7b, the $(1 + r_t)$ are multiplicative returns: it follows from Equation 14.9b that $(1 + R_T)^{1/T}$ is a geometric mean return. Multiplicative returns, geometric means, and especially the variance of multiplicative returns are cumbersome to deal with: additive returns, arithmetic means, and the variance of additive returns are not. For this reason, microstructure analysis frequently uses logarithmic returns (r^*) instead of arithmetic returns (r); the r_t^* are additive, and we can treat their arithmetic mean and variance.

Additional relationships between the arithmetic returns, logarithmic returns, and growth rates are given in the appendix to this chapter.

The Intervalling Effect

The *intervalling effect* is the way in which measures of returns behavior change as the measurement interval is varied. The relevant return measures include the following:

- Mean return (stock and index)
- The variance of returns (stock and index)
- Market model beta
- The variance of residual returns
- Market model R^2

Following the previous discussion, taking logarithms of

$$\frac{P_T}{P_0} = \left(\frac{P_1}{P_0}\right), \ldots, \left(\frac{P_T}{P_{T-1}}\right)$$

gives

$$R_T^* = \sum_{t=1}^{T} r_t^* \tag{14.13}$$

Let the short time span ($t - 1$ to t) be the unit period; the intervalling effect is the effect on each of the five measures of increasing the interval T over which the long period return, R_T^* in Equation 14.13 is measured.

Mean Return (Stock and Index).   Taking means of Equations 14.13 and assuming the returns distribution is stationary, gives

$$E(R_T^*) = \sum_{t=1}^{T} E(r_t^*)$$

$$= TE(r^*) \tag{14.14}$$

It is clear from Equation 14.14 that the mean logarithmic return increases linearly with T. For instance, the average weekly logarithmic return expressed as a rate per week is five times the average daily logarithmic return expressed as a rate per day.

The Variance of Returns (Stock and Index).   Taking the variance of Equation 14.13 gives

$$Var(R_T^*) = \sum_{t=1}^{T} \sum_{u=1}^{T} \sigma_t \sigma_u \rho_{t,u} \tag{14.15}$$

where σ_t (σ_u) is the standard deviation of returns in the tth (u^{th}) short period and $\rho_{t,u}$ is the correlation between the tth short period return and the uth short period return, $t, u = 1, \ldots, T$.

The correlation between returns affects the relationship between the variance of the long period return and the variances of the short period returns. Because of this, the intervalling effect on variance depends on the correlation pattern in security returns. This correlation is *serial correlation:* the correlation between the returns in the time series $r_1, \ldots, r_T$.

To simplify the analysis assume the following:

1. The returns distribution is stationary ($\sigma_t = \sigma_u$ for all short periods $t, u = 1, \ldots, T$).

2. $\rho_{t,u}$ is the same for all $|t - u|$. That is if $t = 8, u = 5$, and thus the returns are three short periods apart, the correlation between these two returns is identical to the correlation between any other pair of returns that are three short periods apart (the ninth return and the twelfth return, the seventh and the fourth, and so on).

From assumption (1) we have

$$\sigma_t \sigma_u = Var(r^*) \qquad \text{for all } t, u = 1, \ldots, T \tag{14.16}$$

From assumption (2) we can write

$$\rho_{t,u} = \rho_{1,1+s} \quad \text{for } s = |t - u|, s = 1, \ldots, T - 1 \quad (14.17)$$

To illustrate, consider the following. Let the correlation between the return for t = 4 and the return for u = 6 be $\rho_{4,6}$. Because $|4 - 6| = 2$, the correlation is, by assumption (2), the same as the correlation between return 1 and return 3. Using the notation in Equation 14.17 the correlation between return 1 and return 3 is $\rho_{1,1+2}$ (that is, s = 2 in this case). Equation 14.17 shows that $\rho_{4,6} = \rho_{1,3}$, an equality that follows from assumption (2).

How many $\rho_{t,u}$ are there in the series t, u = 1, ..., T that are equal to $\rho_{1,1+s}$ for any s = 1, ..., T − 1? Consider the case where T = 8 and s = 3. The pairs of returns that are three periods apart in the set of eight returns are

1, 4

2, 5

3, 6

4, 7

5, 8

There are $8 - 3 = T - s$ pairings. Generalizing for all T and s, and substituting Equations 14.16 and 14.17 into Equation 14.15 gives

$$\text{Var}(R_T^*) = T \, \text{Var}(r^*) + 2 \, \text{Var}(r^*) \sum_{s=1}^{T-1} (T - s)\rho_{1,1+s} \quad (14.18)$$

Equation 14.18 shows that the variance of logarithmic returns increases linearly with T if there is no intertemporal correlation in the returns (that is, if $\rho_{t,u} = 0$ for all $t \neq u$). It also follows that, for any value of Var(r^*), the long period variance Var(R_T^*) will be larger if the intertemporal correlations are predominantly positive and will be smaller if the intertemporal correlations are predominantly negative.

Market Model Beta. The market model beta for a stock can be written as

$$b_i = \frac{\text{Cov}(R_i^*, R_m^*)}{\text{Var}(R_m^*)} \quad (14.19)$$

From the intervalling relations defined previously for the variance term, and given that

$$\text{Cov}(R_i^*, R_m^*) = \sigma_i \sigma_m \rho_{i,m}$$

it is clear that a stock's beta will be independent of the differencing interval if there is no intertemporal correlation in security returns [that is, if $\text{Var}(R^*_{iT})$ and $\text{Var}(R^*_{mT})$ increase linearly with T, and if the cross-correlation $\rho_{i,m}$ is the same for all T]. On the other hand, intertemporal correlation in returns will introduce an intervalling effect on the beta coefficient. As discussed in Chapter 16, the use of short period returns causes beta estimates to be lower for relatively thin issues and higher for the largest issues. For a rigorous derivation of the intervalling effect bias in beta, see Cohen, Hawawini, Maier, Schwartz, and Whitcomb[1] and Cohen, Maier, Schwartz, and Whitcomb.[2]

The Variance of Residual Returns.   The *variance of residual returns* behaves in the same way as the variance of returns — it increases linearly with T in the absence of serial correlation, at a faster rate in the presence of positive serial correlation and at a slower rate if the serial correlations are predominantly negative. Residual variance is further affected if beta itself is dependent on T, with the effect depending upon the impact that the intervalling effect on beta has on the average absolute size of the residual term.

The Market Model R^2.   The squared coefficient of correlation for a regression equation shows the percentage of the variation in the dependent variable that is explained by change in the independent variable. For the market model regression,

$$R^2 = \frac{b_i^2 \text{Var}(R^*_m)}{\text{Var}(R^*_i)} \qquad (14.20)$$

There will be no intervalling effect on R^2 if there are no intertemporal correlation patterns in security returns. This is because, in the absence of such correlation, beta is independent of T, and $\text{Var}(R^*_m)$ and $\text{Var}(R^*_i)$ both change linearly with T. On the other hand, intertemporal correlations cause an intervalling effect on R^2; the effect depends upon the intervalling effect on beta and on the intervalling effect on the variance of R^*_m in relation to the intervalling effect on the variance of R^*_i.

The Intertemporal Portfolio

The section "The Measurement of Returns" shows how the return over a time span of length T is related to the returns for the T short intervals that compose it. Conceptually, the long period return is related to the short period returns, much as the return on a portfolio is related to the return on the individual securities that constitute the portfolio. The standard portfolio return is a cross-sectional average of the individual stock returns; the long period return is an intertemporal average of the returns for the individual periods. For this reason, the long period return may be considered the return on an intertemporal portfolio. Increasing T and including more short period returns in the intertemporal portfolio is similar to increasing the number of stocks in a cross-sectional portfolio.

The intertemporal portfolio, however, differs from the cross-sectional portfolio in certain respects:

- The return $(1 + R_T)$ on the intertemporal portfolio is the geometric mean of the returns [the $(1 + r_t)$] for the individual periods. In contrast, the return on the cross-sectional portfolio (R_P) is the arithmetic mean of the returns (the r_i) on the individual securities.

- All short periods have the same weight in the intertemporal portfolio. In contrast, the weights for the individual issues in a cross-sectional portfolio are specified by the decision maker.

- The size of the intertemporal portfolio (the value of T) is likely to be exogenously determined for the investor (T is no doubt larger for younger people who are just starting to accumulate wealth than for older people who are approaching retirement). In contrast, the number of shares to include in a cross-sectional portfolio is specified by the decision maker.

- The point of reference for the intercorrelation between short interval returns in an intertemporal portfolio is zero. In contrast, the point of reference for the intercorrelation between individual stock returns in a cross-sectional portfolio is unity. The reason is that if the intertemporal correlations are zero, returns variance increases linearly with T, whereas if the cross-sectional correlations are unity, the standard deviation of the portfolio return is a linear combination of the standard deviations for the individual securities.

- As T increases sufficiently for an intertemporal portfolio, the average covariance between short period returns is expected to go to zero (the correlation between distant returns is likely to be weaker than the correlation between nearby and, in particular, adjacent returns). In contrast, as additional securities are added to a randomly selected cross-sectional portfolio, there is no reason to expect a change in the average covariance between the securities.

Understanding these technical differences may help one to understand better the intervalling effect discussed earlier. There is another reason for considering the properties of the intertemporal portfolio. The value of portfolio diversification can be understood only in terms of the variance reduction attributable to stock returns not being perfectly intercorrelated; likewise, the effect of measurement interval length on returns variance can be understood only when one recognizes the implications of return not being perfectly independently distributed over time.

The diversification of an intertemporal portfolio can be contrasted with the diversification of a cross-sectional portfolio.* Assume that each security has the same weight in the cross-sectional portfolio (that is, that $k_i = 1/N$ for each ith stock, where N is the number of stocks in the portfolio). Thus the variance of the cross-sectional portfolio can be written as

$$\text{Var}(r_P) = \left(\frac{1}{N}\right)^2 \left[\sum_{i=1}^{N} \text{Var}(r_i) + \sum_{i=1}^{N}\sum_{\substack{j=1 \\ i \neq j}}^{N} \sigma_i \sigma_j \rho_{ij}\right] \qquad (14.21)$$

By writing the single sum on the right-hand side of Equation 14.21 as the average variance times the number of terms in the sum (N), and the double summation as the average covariance times the number of terms in the double summation $(N^2 - N)$, Equation 14.21 can be rewritten as

$$\text{Var}(R_P) = \left(\frac{1}{N}\right)\overline{\text{Var}}(r) + \left(\frac{N-1}{N}\right)\overline{\text{Cov}}(r_i, r_j) \qquad (14.22)$$

Equation 14.22 shows that, as N increases, $\text{Var}(R_p)$ decreases asymptotically to the average covariance, which is the systematic market risk.

The effect of T on the intertemporal portfolio can be most easily assessed for the case in which all intertemporal correlations are zero. We then have, from Equation 14.18

$$\text{Var}(R_T^*) = T\,\text{Var}(r_t^*) \qquad (14.23)$$

As previously noted, variance increases linearly with T in the absence of returns autocorrelation. Because the return R_T is expressed as a rate per T, the mean return also increases linearly with T (see Equation 14.14).

The period for which returns are expressed can be made explicit. Let $R_{T/T}^*$ identify the logarithmic return for period T expressed as a rate per T, and $R_{T/t}^*$ identify the logarithmic return for period T expressed as a rate per t. Then[†]

$$R_{T/T}^* = TR_{T/t}^* \qquad (14.24)$$

Substituting Equation 14.24 into Equation 14.23 and rearranging gives

$$\text{Var}(R_{T/t}^*) = \left(\frac{1}{T}\right)\text{Var}(r_{t/t}^*) \qquad (14.25)$$

---

* Diversification of a cross-sectional portfolio reduces portfolio variance by eliminating non-systematic (diversifiable) risk (see Chapter 12).
† Equation 14.24 is consistent with Equation 14.A12 in the appendix to this chapter.

FIGURE 14.1 *Effect of Portfolio Diversification (N) and of Holding Period Length (T) on the Variance of Portfolio Returns. (a) As N Increases,* Var(R$_P$) *Decreases Asymptotically to* $\overline{\text{Cov}}$. *(b) As T Increases,* Var(R$_{T/T}$) *Increases Linearly. (c) As T Increases,* Var(R$^*_{T/t}$) *Decreases Asymptotically to Zero*

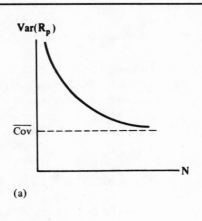

(a)

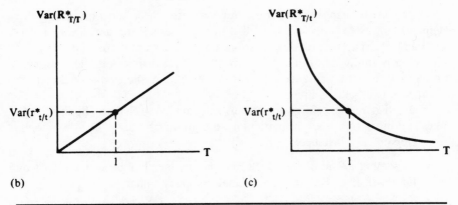

(b)   (c)

where Var($r^*_{t/t}$) is the variance of the short period (logarithmic) return expressed as a rate per t.

Equation 14.25 shows variance falling with T, much as Equation 14.22 shows variance falling with N. The only difference between the equations (Equation 14.22 has a positive asymptote whereas Equation 14.25 does not) is attributable to the different intercorrelation patterns between cross-sectional and intertemporal returns. The relationships among Equations 14.22, 14.23, and 14.25 are shown graphically by Figure 14.1(a), (b), and (c).

Equation 14.25 may seem to suggest that an investor with a longer time horizon faces lower returns variance than does an investor with a shorter time horizon (*ceteris paribus*). Equation 14.23, on the other hand, appears to suggest that an investor with a longer time horizon faces greater returns variance. Which impression is correct? The apparent contradiction can only be resolved by rephrasing the issue: *ceteris paribus*, would an investor with a longer time horizon hold a portfolio that has greater short period variance than would an investor with a shorter time horizon?

The effect of holding period length on an investor's optimal portfolio decision is itself a complex issue, with the answer's depending on the form of the investor's utility function. We will not pursue the matter here; the issue has been raised only to show the formal relationship between the intertemporal portfolio and the cross-sectional portfolio.

Factors That Account for Stock Price Changes

Broad Market Movements and Idiosyncratic Change

A stock's price changes and returns reflect shifts in the location of investor demand curves to hold shares of the stock. These shifts are due to informational change, to investor reassessments of information, and/or to the changing liquidity and liquidity needs of individual investors. The demand shifts may reflect broad-based market movements in the stock, or they may be uncorrelated across investors.

The broad market shifts are due to informational change. Such change may pertain to one stock in particular, to a group of stocks, or to all stocks in aggregate. For instance:

- News that an infallable electronic proofreader has been developed by IMB will increase the price of that company's shares.
- News that the government is going to increase the tax credit for the purchase of office equipment will increase the share price for all securities in the office equipment industry.
- News that the Federal Reserve has learned how to stabilize interest rates while lowering inflation, reducing unemployment, and accelerating economic growth will increase the price of all shares.

The demand shifts that are uncorrelated across investors are called *idiosyncratic change*. For instance:

- Upon further reflection, investor j decides that the home market for electronic proofreaders is overrated; accordingly, he calls his broker and submits an order to sell 100 shares of IMB at market.

- Upon inheriting $20,000, investor i acquires more shares of her favorite stock (Liquidity Inc.).
- Upon the receipt of a $15,000 tuition bill, Mr. Pere de Student liquidates his position in Podunk Mines.

Shifts in the Market Demand for a Stock

To consider in its pure (frictionless) form how market shifts in the demand for a stock affect share price, we make the extreme (and clearly unrealistic) assumption that all investors react identically and simultaneously to informational change. This being the case, such change will shift the market demand curve, but no trades will be made. To see this, consider Figure 14.2.

The curve labeled D_0 in Figure 14.2(a) reflects the initial market demand propensities. With NSO shares outstanding, the location of D_0 establishes P_0 as the equilibrium price of the stock. Figure 14.2(b) shows that the associated

FIGURE 14.2 *Effect of Informational Change on the Price of an Asset.* *(a) The Market Demand Curves. (b) The Market Buy and Sell Curves*

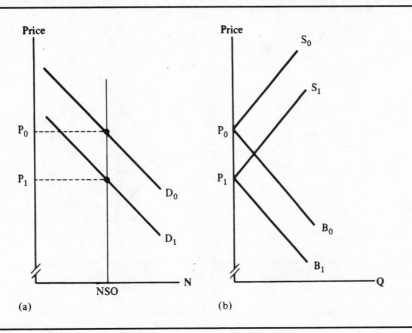

buy and sell curves are, respectively, the negatively inclined line labeled B_0 and the positively inclined line labeled S_0. Then, due to the receipt of news, let the demand curve shift to D_1, and let the associated buy and sell curves shift to B_1 and S_1. Because all investors adjust their orders simultaneously, no trades occur. However, the new equilibrium price is P_1.

Idiosyncratic Shifts

Figure 14.3 shows the impact of an idiosyncratic order on the market price of a stock. As in Figure 14.2, market demand is initially shown by the line labeled D_0, and the associated buy and sell order functions are the curves labeled B_0 and S_0.

Assume the idiosyncratic arrival of a market order to sell Q_1 shares. This order will execute against the Q_1 shares along the curve B_0, and price will decrease to P_1 (given the order function B_0, price has to decrease to this

FIGURE 14.3   *Effect of an Idiosyncratic Order on the Price of an Asset. (a) The Market Demand Curves. (b) The Market Buy and Sell Curves*

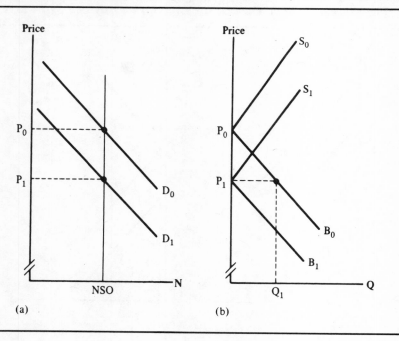

value for the Q_1 shares to be absorbed by the market). The return generated by this idiosyncratic order is, therefore, $(P_1 - P_0)/P_0$.

After the execution of the idiosyncratic order, the market demand curve has shifted down to the curve labeled D_1, and the market buy and sell order functions are the curves labeled, respectively, B_1 and S_1. As was not true with the aggregate shift, a trade has occurred as a result of the idiosyncratic order.

From Transaction-to-Transaction Returns to Periodic Returns

We have described the return that results from one aggregate demand shift or from the arrival of one idiosyncratic order. These returns occur at the points in time that something happens (that is, the aggregate demand shifts, or the idiosyncratic order arrives). Therefore, these are transaction-to-transaction returns. It may be more accurate to call these "event-to-event" returns, especially since the aggregate demand shift has not triggered any transaction. This is unusual terminology, however; thus we retain the term *transaction-to-transaction return*. Over any given interval of time (such as a trading day), a sequence of transaction-to-transaction returns is expected, and the return for the interval shows the combined impact of the individual returns that the sequence comprises. The return over a time interval of given length is, therefore,

$$r_t = \prod_{s=1}^{N_A}(1 + r_s) \prod_{k=1}^{N_1}(1 + r_k) - 1 \qquad (14.26)$$

where:

r_s = the percentage price change generated by the sth aggregate demand shift.

N_A = the number of aggregate demand shifts that occurred in the interval.

r_k = the percentage price change generated by the kth idiosyncractic order.

N_1 = the number of shares of idiosyncratic orders that arrived during the interval.

Because of the commutative property of multiplication ($xy = yx$), the return over the interval is unaffected by the sequence in which the individual percentage price changes actually occur. Therefore, the ordering of the aggregate demand shifts and the idiosyncractic order arrivals does not matter (the events are, of course, generally interspersed).

The last event (demand shift or idiosyncratic order arrival) will in all likelihood occur before the literal end of the time interval. The reason is that these events occur sporadically rather than continuously and therefore are unlikely to happen in any brief instant of time (such as at the market close). This does not affect the computation of the return for the interval. The closing price is P_t, and the return over the interval is the percentage difference between this price and the price at the start of the interval (P_{t-1}).

The Mechanics of the Market

The preceding analysis does not take account of the mechanics of the marketplace. Neither does it recognize that traders transmit order points rather than continuous order functions, or that traders do not revise their orders continuously. We here consider how the mechanics of the market affect the returns generation process. Our discussion refers to a continuous market trading regime and assumes a system in which public orders are stored on a limit order book. The discussion might seem more relevant for an exchange system than for a pure dealer market system because of our reference to a limit order book. Although this is true to some extent, the basic principles involved are applicable to both systems.

Figure 14.4 shows how the buy/sell order functions might appear at any moment in time when point orders rather than continuous order functions

FIGURE 14.4 *Buy and Sell Order Curves when Point Orders Rather Than Continuous Order Functions Are Submitted to the Market*

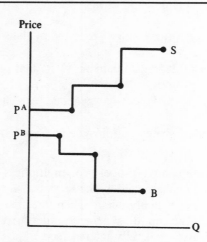

are submitted to the market. The lengths of the horizontal line segments in Figure 14.4 show the total number of shares sought for purchase or offered for sale at each price. Thus, the length of the line at P^A shows the number of shares offered at the market ask, and the length of the line at P^B shows the number of shares sought at the market bid.

The height of each vertical line segment shows the price change between orders. The minimum tick size for most stocks is one-eighth of a dollar, and therefore the minimum vertical length is one-eighth. Gaps (air pockets) in the limit order book, however, can cause price jumps of more than one-eighth. The bid-ask spread itself is the vertical distance between P^A and P^B.

The orders on the limit order book have arrived during a preceding period. Because of the cost of continuously monitoring the market and updating orders, these orders reflect decisions made in relation to an earlier information set. Therefore, if the orders had been written in light of current news and current market conditions, they would have differed somewhat. Because orders on the book are not continuously updated, the limit order book is "sticky." Quotes that are grossly out of line with current information are called *stale orders*.

The mechanics of the market include the rules by which orders are executed when multiple orders are tied at a price on the limit order book (see Chapter 2). The priority rule may be time (the first orders entered are the first to execute), size (the largest orders execute first), combinations of time and size (the New York Stock Exchange uses this procedure), or random selection. When orders are tied at a price, some traders may not realize a transaction, even if transactions are made at the prices at which their orders have been placed.

Another aspect of the market is the sequential arrival of orders following informational change. When orders are delayed, they are generally nonsynchronous with each other. The orders, of course, arrive in quick succession in highly efficient markets, and the impact of news is quickly reflected in share prices. Nonetheless, the returns generation process is affected—the orders arrive in sequence. Hence, we say order arrival is *sequential* when transaction costs and information costs cause delays in the dissemination of news, in investor reactions to news, and in order handling itself. With sequential order arrival, the demand curve does not shift as depicted in the discussion of shifts in market demand for stock; rather, the first orders to arrive on the basis of new information will interact with orders that do not reflect the news. As the informational orders arrive, trades can occur, as we showed for the idiosyncratic orders. The difference between sequential order arrival based on news and that based on idiosyncratic change is that the sequential informationally motivated orders are not independent events, whereas the idiosyncratic orders are.

The mechanics of the market also include the operations of dealers and specialists, the market makers who facilitate the process of trading. As we discuss in Chapter 7, market maker quotes reflect considerations in addition to the underlying information set. That is, a dealer or specialist buys or sells shares from a public trader simply to accommodate the public trader's demand to transact. This affects transaction prices and quotes. In the process of accommodating public traders, the dealer/specialist attains a portfolio that is not optimal from an investment point of view. The dealer's subsequent attempts to rebalance the portfolio also have an impact on the stock's price movements.

In summary, order functions in actual markets are discontinuous; price is a discontinuous variable (one-eighth of a point is generally the minimum tick size); orders arrive on the market and are revised periodically rather than continuously; the limit order book is "sticky"; quotes get "stale"; informationally motivated orders arrive sequentially rather than simultaneously; and market makers intervene in trading. These realities of the marketplace also affect the returns series that are observed. For instance, with a bid-ask spread, transaction prices may move from the bid to the ask or from the ask to the bid, simply because of the sequence in which market orders happened to arrive on the market. With a sticky limit order book and the sequential arrival of informationally motivated orders, trades that are triggered by new information may reveal outdated prices.

To understand further the extent to which returns based on either quotation prices or transaction prices may misrepresent the underlying change in market conditions, consider the following. Assume that at 3:35 P.M. on a given trading day, an order to buy 500 shares of Liquidity Inc. at $50 sets the market bid, and that this order had been placed at 10:05 A.M. on that day. Suppose further that a market order to sell 200 shares hits this bid at 3:52 P.M., and that no further orders arrive before the market's 4:00 P.M. close. In this case, both the last transaction price and the closing market bid quotation have been affected by an order that was placed a few minutes after the market opened. More than likely, information changed during the trading day, but presumably the change was not enough to induce the writer of the 500-share buy order to revise the order. Therefore, to an extent, the closing price and the return for the day have been affected by an earlier information set.

The Market Model Revisited

Having considered the returns generation process as it relates to information arrival, idiosyncratic trading, and the mechanics of the market, we return to the market model (Equation 12.24 in Chapter 12) and again consider the dichotomization of returns into a market related component ($b_i r_{mt}$) and a stock unique component (e_{it}).

1. *Informational change:* Informational change is the factor that accounts for the market-related component. If such change affects all listed securities, then it directly causes the cross-sectionally correlated market movements. If the informational change relates to one or a subset of stocks, it can in principle generate broad-based, cross-sectionally correlated returns because of portfolio rebalancing.

2. *Sequential information arrival:* Sequential information arrival means that informationally generated orders arrive nonsynchronously, not only for individual stocks, but across stocks. For this reason, even broad-based informational change generates only weakly correlated interstock price movements over very brief time intervals.

3. *Stock-specific information:* Stock-specific information generates stock unique returns if the price movements for an individual stock do not result in an appreciable amount of portfolio rebalancing.

4. *Idiosyncratic orders:* Idiosyncratic orders also generate stock unique returns.

5. *Mechanics of the market:* The mechanics of the market primarily have an impact on residual returns. However, there are exceptions. A wave of buy orders for different stocks causes many ask prices to be hit; a wave of sell orders causes many bid prices to be hit; and a cross-sectionally correlated jump of transaction prices across bid-ask spreads gives rise to a broad market movement. In such an event, the price discontinuity represented by the spread exaggerates the market related component of returns.

The Mean and Variance of Returns

This section analyzes the determinants of the mean, $E(r)$, and variance $Var(r)$, of returns. The analysis builds on the foundation developed in the preceding section. Six assumptions establish the analytical context:

1. The market comprises many traders who post quotes and who can therefore trade with each other without the services of a dealer.

2. The trading arena is a continuous market system.

3. Public limit orders are stored on a limit order book.

4. Market orders arrive sporadically during the trading day and execute against limit orders on the book.

5. The market's demand to hold shares of an asset is a linear function of price.

6. Price and quantity are continuous (rather than discrete) variables.

We begin the analysis by modeling the effect of informational change and idiosyncratic order arrival.

Informational Change

We made the extreme (and clearly unrealistic) assumption in the preceding section that investors react identically and simultaneously to informational change. We retain that assumption here to simplify the discussion, because it enables us to identify and to measure informational change as shifts in the location of the market's demand curve to hold shares [Figure 14.2(a)]. That is, instead of assuming news bits arrive in the form of statements such as "Podunk Mines is now pumping oil from its Dunkpo well," we assume news arrives in the form "the market demand curve to hold shares of Podunk Mines now crosses the vertical line at NSO at a price that is 2% higher than its previous value." The 2% figure is thus the informational change, stated as a rate of return.

This treatment is consistent with the analysis in Chapter 12, where, for a single holding period model, the intercept parameter of the linear demand curve is shown to be the present value of the expected price at the end of the period. In the context of that model, informational change would be represented by the percentage change in the intercept parameter.

Let the variable U be the returns-dimensioned value of the information bits that arrive on the market. $U > 0$ indicates a shift up of the demand curve, and $U < 0$ indicates a shift down of the demand curve. Therefore, the return generated by the arrival of one information bit is

$$\frac{\Delta P}{P} = r = U \tag{14.27}$$

Idiosyncratic Order Arrival

Assume that one sell order of size Q_1 arrives on the market. Figure 14.3 shows the price change that this one order generates. Given the buy order function labeled B_0, price has to fall from P_0 to P_1 for the Q_1 shares to be absorbed by the market. The sale eliminates Q_1 shares from the buy order function. Therefore, the market buy order function shifts to the line labeled B_1, the market sell order function shifts to the line labeled S_1, and the market demand curve to hold shares shifts to the line labeled D_1.

The size of the order (Q_1) is related to the size of the return it generates, $(P_1 - P_0)/P_0$. The return is a percentage price change. Therefore, by expressing the order size (Q_1) as a percentage of the total number of shares outstanding (NSO), we can use the standard definition of elasticity to relate the two percentage changes to each other. In Figure 14.3 the appropriate elasticity is the elasticity of D_0 at the point $\langle P_0, NSO \rangle$:

$$\eta = \frac{dN}{dP} \frac{P_0}{N}$$

where, for notational simplicity, $N = NSO$. Because D_0 is linear, the slope of the curve (dN/dP) at the point $\langle P_0, N \rangle$ equals the slope of the curve over a discrete interval. Hence

$$\frac{dN}{dP} = \frac{\Delta N}{\Delta P} \qquad (14.28)$$

Because the slope of D_0 equals the slope of B_0 (and because Q is the size of the order),

$$\frac{\Delta N}{\Delta P} = \frac{Q}{\Delta P} \qquad (14.29)$$

Thus, substituting Equation 14.29 into (14.28), and (14.28) into the expression for elasticity gives

$$\eta = \frac{Q}{\Delta P} \frac{P}{N} \qquad (14.30)$$

Rewriting Equation 14.30 shows the return generated by the sell order:

$$r = \frac{\Delta P}{P_0} = \frac{1}{\eta} \frac{Q}{N} \qquad (14.31)$$

Translating the share size of the order into the dollar value of the order shows how the return (r) is related to the investment decision that triggered the trade. Assume the investor decides to alter his or her portfolio weights by selling \$Y worth of the asset and uses the initial price, P_0, to determine the size of his or her order. Thus,

$$Q_1 = -\frac{Y}{P_0} \qquad (14.32)$$

where the minus sign shows that the order is to *sell* Q_1 shares. Treating positive Q as a purchase and negative Q as a sale avoids the need to label the buy and sell transactions separately. Substituting Equation 14.32 into (14.31) gives

$$r = -\frac{1}{\eta} \frac{Y}{NP_0} \qquad (14.33)$$

where NP_0 is the total value of shares outstanding for the stock. Therefore, letting $V = NP_0$, we have

$$r = -\frac{1}{\eta}\frac{Y}{V} \tag{14.34}$$

Equation 14.34 shows the return that is triggered by the arrival of one idiosyncratic order.

The Return over a Period of Length T

Equations 14.27 and 14.34 can be used to obtain an expression for the sequence of returns that is generated by the sequence of orders that arrive over a time interval of length T. With such an expression, we can obtain the mean and variance of returns for the time interval. Assume that informational change and idiosyncratic order arrival occur sporadically according to statistical processes with known parameters (the most reasonable process to use is the Poisson arrival process). Then, the returns for any time interval are given by Equation 14.26. Substituting Equations 14.27 and 14.34 into Equation 14.26 and rearranging gives

$$1 + r_t = \prod_{s=1}^{N_A}(1 + U_s)\prod_{k=1}^{N_I}\left(\frac{1 + Y_k}{\eta V}\right) \tag{14.35}$$

Taking logarithms of Equation 14.35 gives

$$r^* = \sum_{s=1}^{N_A}\ln(1 + U_s) + \sum_{k=1}^{N_I}\ln\left(\frac{1 + Y_k}{\eta V}\right) \tag{14.36}$$

The Expected Return

By applying the logarithmic approximation* $\ln(1+x) \cong x$ to Equation 14.36, we can more easily assess the mean and variance of returns in relation to the parameters of the right-hand side variables. From Equation 14.36, the mean return is

$$E(R_T) = T\gamma(2p - 1)E(U) \tag{14.37}$$

where T is the length of the time span over which r is measured, γ is the arrival rate parameter for the statistical process that describes the arrival of news over the interval of length T, p is the probability that any given value of U is positive, and $E(U)$ is the average absolute value of U. (See

---

* See the appendix to this chapter for a discussion of the logarithmic approximation. The approximation is reasonable for values of x where x^2 is sufficiently less than unity. The values of r_s and r_k are expected to be well below unity for transaction-to-transaction returns.

Cohen, Maier, Schwartz, and Whitcomb[3] for the derivation of Equation 14.37.) If new information is as likely to shift the aggregate demand curve up as it is to shift it down, p = .5 and the expected return is zero. If new information is more likely to shift the aggregate demand curve up, p > .5 and $E(R_T)$ is positive. $E(R_T)$ positive implies an upward drift in the security's price; such a drift may be consistent with an informationally efficient equity market in which the price sequence is described by a martingale process rather than by a random walk (see Chapter 16).

Note that $E(R_T)$ in Equation 14.37 increases linearly with T. This is consistent with the intervalling relationship for the expected return shown in the section "The Measurement of Returns."

Returns Variance

Taking variances of Equation 14.36 gives

$$\text{Var(r)} = T\gamma E(U^2) + \frac{T\mu E(Y^2)}{\eta^2 V} \qquad (14.38)$$

where μ is the arrival rate parameter for the statistical process that describes the arrival of idiosyncratic market orders over the interval of length T. Also, the elasticity, η, and the total value of shares outstanding for a stock, V, are assumed constant over the interval. See Cohen, Maier, Schwartz, and Whitcomb[4] for the derivation.

More specifically, μ is the total number of buy and sell market orders that are expected for the trading day, divided by the value of shares outstanding, V. Because the flow of idiosyncratic orders for an issue should be roughly proportionate to the issue's size, the mean arrival rate of such orders *per dollar value* of shares outstanding should, all else equal, be the same for different securities. That is, if IBM is 100 times the size of Podunk Mines, IBM should have roughly 100 times as many shareholders, and hence the total number of idiosyncratic orders that are expected to arrive in any interval of time should be roughly 100 times as large for IBM as for Podunk Mines. (As discussed later in this chapter, this simple relationship will be perturbed if larger firms attract larger shareholders.) Therefore, the parameter μ should tend to be the same for IBM as for Podunk Mines.

Assessment of the Variance Equation

The first term on the right-hand side of Equation 14.38 shows that returns variance is greater, the greater the frequency with which information changes (as reflected in the parameter γ), and the greater the price impact of the information [as measured by the variable $E(U^2)$].

The second term on the right-hand side of Equation 14.38 shows the determinants of price volatility that are related to idiosyncratic order arrival, but that are not directly related to the arrival of news. We consider each variable in that term in order:

> T: Var(r) increases linearly with the length of the measurement interval, T. The linear relationship is consistent with the previously discussed intervalling effect for the case of no serial correlation of the returns. This case is relevant here because we have assumed a random order arrival process, a zero bid-ask spread, and instantaneous and accurate price adjustments to new equilibrium values.
>
> μ: All else equal, larger μ results in larger returns variance. Rather than the direction of causality running from μ to variance, however, we expect the variance to affect μ. This is because investors who anticipate trading more frequently for liquidity needs include less volatile stocks in their portfolios (all else equal). Thus the presence of μ in the numerator of Equation 14.38 actually mitigates the effect of the other right-hand-side variables. For instance, looking at the numerator, we see that an increase of the variable $E(Y^2)$ increases Var(r). This means that μ, in response, tends to be lower (all else equal) for large $E(Y^2)$ stocks. However, the negative response of μ could not be strong enough to cause Var(r) actually to be *lower* for large $E(Y^2)$ stocks, because lower Var(r) would then itself result in *higher* μ (which would be contradictory). Similarly, if Var(r) is less for large V (or large η) securities, μ tends to be larger for large V (or large η) securities, which to some extent offsets the effect of V or η on Var(r).
>
> $E(Y^2)$: As one might expect, an increase in the size of investor orders in relation to the size of the issue (V) and the demand elasticity (η) increases the variance of returns. The derivation shows specifically that Var(r) changes linearly with $E(Y^2)$, not $E(Y)$ or $[E(Y)]^2$. The intuition behind this result is that $E(Y)$ is expected to be close to zero for all stocks (the distribution of Y spans both negative and positive values), variance cannot be a negative number, and the variable Y^2 is a reasonable reflection of what is relevant: the absolute size of the buy and sell orders. $E|Y|$ would also be intuitively reasonable; the math, however, shows that the appropriate measure is $E(Y^2)$. $E(Y^2)$ is expected to differ across stocks because of differences in the investors who select different stocks. Most importantly, institutional investors in particular tend to concentrate in large V issues, and the orders of these investors are, indeed, large.
>
> η : All else equal, returns variance is less if the demand to hold shares of the stock is more elastic. A larger elasticity means, of course, that any given percentage change in quantity is associated with a smaller percentage change in price. With regard to the case at hand, a larger

elasticity means that price does not have to change as much for an order of given size to be absorbed by the market. Note that, as is the case with order size, it is η^2, not η, that enters the equation. (Demand elasticity is negative and variance must be a positive number. η enters the derivation of Equation 14.38 as a multiplicative constant; for any multiplicative constant (c) and random variable (x), $\text{Var}(cx) = c^2\text{Var}(x)$.)

V: All else equal, price is less volatile for larger issues. The derivation shows that the value of shares *outstanding,* not the value of shares *traded,* the number of shareholders, or some other proxy for market size is the relevant measure. Because of this derivation, we generally take V to be an inverse measure of the thinness of a market.

The appearance of V in the denominator of Equation 14.38 may lead one to expect that returns variance will be lower for large V securities. We cannot be sure of this result, however—the other right-hand side variables may also be related to V. For instance, both $E(Y^2)$ and η are likely to be larger for large V securities. The reason is that security analysis is more intensive for bigger issues, more intensive security analysis is likely to make traders' expectations more homogeneous, and greater homogeneity of expectations causes the market demand curve to be more elastic. Thus we conclude the following with regard to V. A negative relationship between Var(r) and V (1) can be mitigated but not reversed by a positive relationship between μ and V, (2) can be reversed by a sufficiently strong and positive relationship between $E(Y^2)$ and V, and (3) can be reinforced by a positive relationship between η and V.

The Effects of the Market's Mechanics on Security Prices

Having assessed the *ceteris paribus* impact of the individual determinants of the mean and variance of returns, we now derive various insights concerning the effect of the market's mechanics on a security's price behavior.

Transaction costs (commissions, taxes, the opportunity costs of trading with transaction price uncertainty, and so forth) decrease expected returns and reduce the flow of orders to the market. Accordingly, these costs decrease the elasticity of the market demand curve. We see from Equation 14.38 that transaction costs therefore also increase the variance of returns.

Dealers and stock exchange specialists have the function of "making a market" by posting buy and sell quotes. Stock exchange specialists further have the "affirmative obligation" to post buy and sell quotes at those times when the sparsity of public orders would result in "unacceptably" large transaction-to-transaction price changes. The posting of quotes by dealers and specialists makes the market demand curve more elastic and thereby decreases returns variance. The affirmative obligation of the stock exchange specialist *forces* these market makers to enter their quotes more frequently for the thinner issues; this dampens any inverse relationship between Var(r) and V that might otherwise exist in an unregulated market.

The appearance of V in the denominator of Equation 14.38, and therefore the possibility of an inverse relationship between variance and V, suggests that the marketplace may give corporations a financial economy of scale; that is, a greater price stability enjoyed by larger companies simply because of their size would enable these firms to raise funds at lower cost in the new issues market.

The capital asset pricing model suggests that, in a frictionless environment, all investors would hold some fraction of the market portfolio, and that the composition of that portfolio would be the same for all investors. Therefore, when buying or selling for their own idiosyncratic reasons, investors in this frictionless environment would buy or sell shares of all stocks in proportion to each stock's weight in the market portfolio. The following would result: μV, $E(Y^2)/V^2$, and η would be the same for all stocks. To see this, recall that μ is the arrival rate per V, and therefore μV is the actual rate of order arrival for a stock. Further, when each investor holds a given fraction of the market portfolio he or she always changes his or her holdings in different assets in equal proportion ($Y_i/V_i = Y_j/V_j$ for any i^{th} and j^{th} assets). Finally, in this environment the elasticity of the demand curve to hold shares in any asset is equal to the elasticity of the demand curve to hold shares of the market portfolio. See Cohen, Maier, Schwartz and Whitcomb[5] for further discussion. Therefore, given Equation 14.38 we have that, in a frictionless environment, returns variance would not differ across stocks because of the idiosyncratic arrival of orders in the market, but rather would depend only on differential change in the information set. For this reason, evidence that returns variance is related to the size of issues would further show the impact that friction has on price behavior in the equity markets.

Appendix—Logarithmic Returns and Growth Rates

The appendix further considers the relationship between arithmetic returns, logarithmic returns, and growth returns. The difference between the *arithmetic return*, R_T, and the *logarithmic return*, $R_T^* = g_T$, is that R_T is the single period return without compounding, whereas g_T is the return for the period with *continuous* compounding. This can be seen by writing

$$P_T = P_0\left(1 + \frac{r}{m}\right)^m = P_0\left(1 + \frac{r}{m}\right)^{(m/r)r} \tag{14.A1}$$

where m is the frequency with which returns are compounded over the period T. Since

$$\lim_{x \to \infty} \left(1 + \frac{1}{x}\right)^x = e \qquad (14.A2)$$

where $e = 2.7182\ldots$ is the base of natural logarithms, the limit of Equation 14.A1 as m goes to infinity (continuous compounding) is

$$P_T = P_0 e^g \qquad (14.A3)$$

where g is used in place of r as a convention to indicate continuous compounding. In practice, g is computed by taking the log of 1 plus a rate of return.

The effect of compounding is seen by setting $T = 2$:

$$(1 + R_{T=2}) = (1 + r_1)(1 + r_2) \qquad (14.A4)$$

Expand the right-hand side and subtract 1 from both sides:

$$R_{T=2} = r_1 + r_2 + r_1 r_2 \qquad (14.A5)$$

The term $r_1 r_2$ captures the effect of compounding.

It is helpful to see specifically how the return for any period (such as 1 year) is related to the returns for the shorter intervals (for example, 12 months) that it comprises. Write R_{yr} to designate the return for the year, and $\bar{r}_{mth}$ to designate the average monthly return. Following Equations 14.8b, 14.7b, and 14.8c, respectively, the price change from P_0 to $P_{T=12}$ can be written as

$$P_{12} = P_0(1 + R_{yr}) \qquad (14.A6)$$

$$P_{12} = P_0 \prod_{t=1}^{12} (1 + r_{t(mth)}) \qquad (14.A7)$$

or as

$$P_{12} = P_0 e^{g(yr)} \qquad (14.A8)$$

We could also write

$$P_{12} = P_0(1 + \bar{r}_{mth})^{12} \qquad (14.A9)$$

From Equations 14.A7 and 14.A9 we can obtain

$$\ln(1 + \bar{r}_{mth}) = \frac{1}{12} \sum_{t=1}^{12} \ln(1 + r_{t(mth)}) \qquad (14.A10)$$

Equation 14.A10 shows that one plus the average monthly return is the *geometric mean* of the 12 individual monthly returns, plus one.

Now equate the right-hand sides of Equations 14.A6 and 14.A9:

$$1 + R_{yr} = (1 + \bar{r}_{mth})^{12} \tag{14.A11}$$

Taking logarithms of Equation 14.A11 gives

$$\ln(1 + R_{yr}) = 12\ln(1 + \bar{r}_{mth}) \tag{14.A12}$$

We thus see that the log of 1 plus the annual return expressed as a rate per year is 12 times the log of 1 plus the average monthly return expressed as a rate per month. Therefore, 1 plus the monthly return is annualized by multiplying its logarithmic value by 12 and then taking the antilog.

Now apply the logarithmic approximation, $\ln(1 + x) \cong x$, to Equation 14.A12.*

$$R_{yr} = 12\bar{r}_{mth} \tag{14.A13}$$

As might be expected, the annual return is approximately 12 times the arithmetic mean monthly return. The reason Equation 14.A13 is not a strict equality is that annualizing a monthly return by simply multiplying by 12 ignores the fact that returns generate returns (that is, that returns are compounded). Because of compounding, the arithmetic return over the time span T is not an arithmetic average of the arithmetic returns in each of the T short intervals that it comprises. Rather, the short period returns are multiplicative, and their appropriate average is the geometric mean. This is shown in Equation 14.9b.

When the arithmetic returns are multiplicative, the logarithmic returns are additive (as shown in Equation 14.10.) Therefore, the logarithmic return over the time span T is an arithmetic average of the logarithmic returns in each of the T short intervals that it comprises. This is shown in Equation 14.A10. The results are consistent: the geometric mean of arithmetic returns is the antilogarithmic value of the arithmetic mean of the logarithmic returns.

Suggested Reading

Amihud, Y., and Mendelson, H. "Trading Mechanisms and Stock Returns: An Empirical Investigation." *Journal of Finance,* July 1987.

Atchison, M., Butler, K., and Simmonds, R. "Nonsynchronous Security Trading and Market Index Autocorrelation." *Journal of Finance,* March 1987.

---

* The approximation is generally acceptable for x^2 sufficiently less than 1. For instance, if $x = 0.1, x^2 = 0.01$ (which is substantially less than 1) and the log of 1.10 is 0.1125 (which is approximately equal to x).

Black, F. "Noise." *Journal of Finance,* July 1986.

Blume, M., and Stambaugh, R. "Biases in Computed Returns: An Application to the Size Effect." *Journal of Financial Economics,* November 1983.

Cohen, K., Hawawini, G., Maier, S., Schwartz, R., and Whitcomb, D. "Friction in the Trading Process and the Estimation of Systematic Risk." *Journal of Financial Economics,* August 1983.

Cohen, K., Maier, S., Ness, W., Okuda, H., Schwartz, R., and Whitcomb, D. "The Impact of Designated Marketmakers on Security Prices: I, Empirical Evidence." *Journal of Banking and Finance,* December 1977.

Cohen, K., Maier, S., Schwartz, R., and Whitcomb, D. "The Returns Generation Process, Returns Variance, and the Effect of Thinness in Securities Markets." *Journal of Finance,* March 1978.

Cohen, K., Maier, S., Schwartz, R., and Whitcomb, D. *The Microstructure of Securities Markets,* Englewood Cliffs, NJ: Prentice Hall, 1986.

Copeland, T. "A Model of Asset Trading Under the Assumption of Sequential Information Arrival." *Journal of Finance,* September 1976.

Dimson, E. "Risk Management When Shares Are Subject to Infrequent Trading." *Journal of Financial Economics,* June 1979.

Fisher, L. "Some New Stock Market Indexes." *Journal of Business,* January 1966.

Fowler, D., and Rorke, C. H., "Risk Management When Shares Are Subject to Infrequent Trading: Comment," *Journal of Financial Economics,* August 1983.

Fowler, D., Rorke, C. H., and Jog, V. "Thin Trading and Beta Estimation Problems on the Toronto Stock Exchange." *Journal of Business Administration,* Fall 1980.

French, K., and Roll. R. "Stock Return Variances: The Arrival of Information and the Reaction of Traders." *Journal of Financial Economics,* September 1986.

Fung, W., and Rudd, A. "Pricing New Corporate Bond Issues: An Analysis of Issue Costs and Seasoning Effects." *Journal of Finance,* July 1986.

Goldman, M. B., and Beja, A. "Market Prices vs. Equilibrium Prices: Returns Variance, Serial Correlation, and the Role of the Specialist." *Journal of Finance,* June 1979.

Gottlieb, G., and Kalay, A. "Implications of the Discreteness of Observed Srock Prices." *Journal of Finance,* March 1985.

Harris, L. "Estimation of Stock Price Variances and Serial Covariances from Discrete Observations." *Journal of Financial and Quantitative Analysis,* September 1990.

Harris, L. "A Day-End Transaction Price Anomaly." *Journal of Financial and Quantitative Analysis,* March 1989.

Harris, L. "A Transaction Data Study of Weekly and Intradaily Patterns in Stock Returns." *Journal of Financial Economics,* May 1986b.

Hasbrouck, J., and Ho, T. "Order Arrival, Quote Behavior, and the Return Generating Process." *Journal of Finance,* September 1987.

Hillmer, S., and Yu, P. "The Market Speed of Adjustment to New Information." *Journal of Financial Economics,* December 1979.

Karpoff, J. "A Theory of Trading Volume." *Journal of Finance,* December 1986.

King, B. "Market and Industry Factors in Stock Price Behavior." *Journal of Business,* September 1966.

Marsh, T., and Rosenfeld, E. "Non-Trading, Market Making, and Estimates of Stock Price Volatility." *Journal of Financial Economics,* March 1986.

McInish, T., and Wood, R. "Proxies for Nonsynchronous Trading." *Financial Review,* May 1983.

McInish, T., and Wood, R. "Intraday and Overnight Returns and Day-of-the-Week Effects." *Journal of Financial Research,* Summer 1985.

McInish, T., and Wood, R. "Adjusting for Beta Bias: An Assessment of Alternate Techniques: A Note." *Journal of Finance,* March 1986.

Oldfield, G., and Rogalski, R. "A Theory of Common Stock Returns over Trading and Non-trading Periods." *Journal of Finance,* June 1980.

Oldfield, G., Rogalski, R., and Jarrow, R. "An Autoregressive Jump Process for Common Stock Returns." *Journal of Financial Economics,* December 1977.

Perry, P. "Portfolio Serial Correlation and Nonsynchronous Trading." *Journal of Financial and Quantitative Analysis,* December 1985.

Scholes, M., and Williams, J. "Estimating Betas from Nonsynchronous Data." *Journal of Financial Economics,* December 1977.

Schwartz, R., and Whitcomb, D. "The Time-Variance Relationship: Evidence on Autocorrelation in Common Stock Returns." *Journal of Finance,* March 1977.

Schwartz, R., and Whitcomb, D. "Evidence of the Presence and Causes of Serial Correlation in Market Model Residuals." *Journal of Financial and Quantitative Analysis,* June 1977.

Silber, W. "Thinness in Capital Markets: The Case of the Tel Aviv Stock Exchange." *Journal of Financial and Quantitative Analysis,* March 1975.

Smidt, S. "Continuous vs. Intermittent Trading on Auction Markets." *Journal of Financial and Quantitative Analysis,* November 1979.

Theobald, M., "The Analytic Relationship Between Intervalling and Nontrading Effects in Continuous Time." *Journal of Financial and Quantitative Analysis,* June 1983.

Theobald, M. and Price, V. "Seasonality Estimation in Thin Markets." *Journal of Finance,* June 1984.

Notes

1. K. Cohen, G. Hawawini, S. Maier, R. Schwartz, and D. Whitcomb, "Friction in the Trading Process and the Estimation of Systematic Risk." *Journal of Financial Economics,* August 1983.
2. K. Cohen, S. Maier, R. Schwartz, and D. Whitcomb, Chapters 6 and 7 in *The Microstructure of Securities Markets.* Englewood Cliffs, NJ: Prentice Hall, 1986.
3. K. Cohen, S. Maier, R. Schwartz, and D. Whitcomb, Chapter 4 in *The Microstructure of Securities Markets.* Englewood Cliffs, NJ: Prentice Hall, 1986.
4. Ibid.
5. K. Cohen, S. Maier, R. Schwartz, and D. Whitcomb, Appendix A in *The Microstructure of Securities Markets.* Englewood Cliffs, NJ: Prentice Hall, 1986.

15

Information and Prices

Information is the input that drives trading, and security prices are an output of the system. In efficient markets the information should be reflected in prices with an accuracy that leaves no investor an incentive to search for additional information or to trade. This concept may appear straightforward; it is in fact subtle:

- Informational efficiency is multifaceted. Involved are the efficient exploitation of the existing information set and the optimal allocation of resources to expand the information set. Also involved are the accuracy of the signals that prices convey and the fair and efficient dissemination of information to investors.

- Prices are both the result of information and a signal by which information is transmitted. That is, with costly information, some investors undertake research, and other investors infer information from market prices.

- The relationship between information and prices involves concepts that at first may appear paradoxical. For instance, pricing securities properly in relation to the information set eliminates the "chaos" that characterizes sloppy pricing; in frictionless markets, however, equilibrium prices change randomly over time. Another example: Securities picked by random selection would yield appropriate risk-adjusted returns if prices accurately reflect all information; but how can prices accurately reflect all information if securities are selected randomly?

- Expectation formation, decision making, market equilibrium under uncertainty, and imperfect information are only partially understood by financial economists; they remain complex subjects.

- An investor cannot achieve superior returns in the market by having good information. Rather, he or she must have *better* anticipations than the market. This feat is extremely difficult to accomplish consistently in informationally efficient markets. But it is not impossible.

367

- Even with frictionless trading and complete substantiation of the efficient market hypothesis, investor expectations need not be homogeneous in equilibrium. The existence of heterogeneous expectations in equilibrium carries an important implication: once it is allowed that investors can have different expectations, it must be allowed that some investors may have *more accurate* expectations than others.

- Security analysis can be a profitable activity even in an informationally efficient market. Over time, the truth regarding the import of any given bit of information reveals itself. As it does, some investors are shown to have been more correct than others, and, on average, we expect these people to realize higher returns. Accordingly, good security analysis can be profitable. Once an equilibrium configuration is obtained with regard to information gathering and processing, it is only *additional* analysis that would not yield sufficient returns to compensate for the marginal costs involved.

- In a world of heterogeneous expectations, market demand curves to hold shares of risky assets are negatively inclined; hence share prices can be found only by buyers and sellers meeting in the marketplace. The share prices that are established reflect not intrinsic values but rather the investment desires of the traders, as these are based on available information. In such an environment, a primary function of the securities markets is to find the prices that best represent the market's aggregate assessment of the information set.

The Information Set

Information can be classified into two broad categories: floor information and fundamental information relative to the investment decision (the basic determinants of share value).

Floor information includes knowledge of the current quotes, last transaction prices, and transaction volume. In addition, some traders take account of recent high-low prices, the daily opening price, and the previous day's close. Furthermore, it would be of value to have information on orders that have not yet executed, including knowledge of the limit order book (orders on the specialist's book are not, however, disclosed to traders), knowledge of orders held by traders in the crowd (which are partially revealed), and statements of buying or selling interest by block, institutional, and other large traders (which are partially available on systems such as AutEx).

Fundamental information relating to the investment decision pertains to the determinants of future share value. The most useful form for information to take would be a direct statement of the means, variances, and covariances of security returns (as discussed in Chapter 12). However, one can at best form expectations on means, variances, and covariances, given the information that is available:

Recent share price history: knowledge of the historic values of the means, variances, and covariances of returns, and so on.

Current financial information: information concerning current capital structure, earnings forecasts, and so on.

Current economic information: information concerning the firm's product market, the firm's competitors, national economic conditions, and so on.

Structural change: knowledge of recent acquisitions, divestitures, discoveries, regulatory change, and so on.

Organizational efficiency: knowledge of corporate structure, managerial ability, and so on.

The five categories of information pertain to the environment and to the firm whose security is being evaluated. One might view information even more broadly, however. The relevant set encompasses attributes of the decision maker—the technical knowledge and experience that allow a proper assessment of relevant facts. This information varies from formal knowledge of portfolio theory and the capital asset pricing model to the decision maker's experience and skill at assessing intangibles such as managerial ability. Information of this type may be nothing more than enlightened intuition; nevertheless, it is a key input into decision making.

Security analysis involves the assessment of share value, given fundamental information such as expected earnings, operating and financial risk, and the expected level of interest rates. Good analysts make good assessments in relation to these variables. Security analysts assess the value of a stock for their portfolios. This does not imply that they undertake a treasure hunt to find a golden number that one might call an "intrinsic value." Rather, share prices are set the way they are for most resources—in the marketplace, in relation to the forces of demand and supply. However, there are a few exceptions to this rule. Some prices are used for trading or valuation purposes outside the market in which they are established. When so used, the price can be viewed as an intrinsic value. This is commonly referred to as *derivative pricing* or as *price basing.* Derivative pricing applies when one market (such as the Cincinnati Exchange) operates within a context provided by another market (such as the NYSE). Price basing is used in relation to futures trading—the price determined in the futures market is used to set price in the related cash market.

Heterogeneous Expectations

Expectations are formed of future returns, given the current information set. Much formal analysis assumes that different investors have the same (homogeneous) expectations concerning security returns. The assumption of homogeneous expectations underlies formulations such as the standard capital asset pricing model. Even though the assumption is known to be unrealistic, models based upon it give much insight into how the market determines prices for various assets according to their risk and return characteristics.

Rational decision making may seem to imply the homogeneity of expectations. This is because such decision making considers what a rational person would conclude, given "the facts," and, presumably, what one rational person would conclude, all rational people should conclude. However, having considered the elements that the information set comprises, one may better understand why the assumption of homogeneous expectations is unrealistic.

Expectations are heterogeneous because information is costly and investors do not have perfect information. Accordingly, it is plausible for a group of investors to have homogeneous expectations only if they have perfect information. In the CAPM, the assumption of homogeneous expectations is equivalent to the assumption that decision makers have perfect information concerning the mean and variance of returns. In the real world, each investor obtains that quantity of information that is deemed to be optimal, given his or her cost of acquiring it and efficiency in processing it. For expositional simplicity we refer to the *quantity* of information as a decision variable, although the speed with which information is obtained is also of concern.

The timeliness of information affects the quality of the information, and a complete analysis should treat quantity and quality simultaneously. The costs of obtaining and the benefits of having information differ appreciably across investors. In particular, the cost of an information bit is likely to be relatively low for large institutional investors with established information gathering systems. Moreover, the larger the return on a particular information bit, the larger the dollar sum that will be invested in relation to it. That is, the cost of an information bit depends on the difficulty of getting it, but the benefit depends on the dollar magnitude of the decision to be made. Therefore, all else equal, one would expect larger investors to be better-informed investors.

Furthermore, because information is imperfect, it must be evaluated. Each investor analyzes informational inputs according to his or her past experience and knowledge. Thus assessments differ from one investor to the next, and consequently even expectations based upon commonly shared information may differ from decision maker to decision maker.

Two Decision Makers

Consider two investors, j and k. Assume these two individuals are identical in all respects (same wealth, same tastes for risk, and so on) except that j is not informed about a likely price change, and k is informed. The demand curves of the two investors are shown in Figure 15.1. Because k has received bullish information and j has not, k's demand curve (d_k) is above and to the right of j's demand curve (d_j). Assume the price P^M clears the market for the asset in one round of trading and that, as a consequence of their trades, j now holds N_j shares and k now holds N_k shares. We thus have the following results:

- The value weight of the stock is greater in k's portfolio than in j's portfolio (both started with the same wealth).
- j has obtained an optimal portfolio (given j's expectations) that, compared to k's, yields a lower expected return and a lower returns variance.
- k has obtained an optimal portfolio (given k's expectations) that has a higher expected return (in k's opinion) and a higher returns variance. The higher expected return is accounted for by the differential information. The higher variance is explained by the fact that, with a greater value weight for the stock, k does not enjoy as fully the benefit of portfolio diversification.

FIGURE 15.1 *Demand Curves of Two Traders with Heterogeneous Expectations*

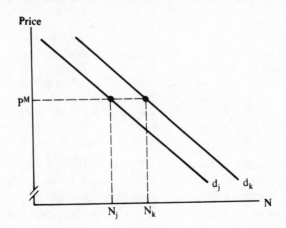

- Trade between k-type (informed) and j-type (uninformed) individuals has harmonized the trading propensities of these two investors.

- Trading has not harmonized the expectations of these investors: k still expects a higher return for the stock than does j.

The existence of heterogeneous expectations in equilibrium carries an important implication: once it is allowed that investors can have different expectations, it must also be allowed that some investors have *more accurate* expectations than others. That is, some people may be better security analysts and better decision makers than others. In equilibrium, therefore, we would expect these people to realize higher returns. It also follows that good security analysis can be a profitable activity even in informationally efficient markets. Once an equilibrium configuration is obtained with regard to information gathering and processing activities, it is only *additional* analysis that would not yield returns over and above the marginal cost involved.

Most people agree that the world is characterized by heterogeneous expectations. The homogeneous expectations assumption has pervaded the formal literature, however, and it has the potential of causing one to believe that "*the* information set" is a compilation of objective facts about which we might all agree. Unfortunately, the real world is not so transparent.

The Beauty Contest

Keynes[1] (1958, p. 156) drew a colorful parallel between stock selection and a beauty contest:

> . . . professional investment may be likened to those newspaper competitions in which the competitors have to pick out the six prettiest faces from a hundred photographs, the prize being awarded to the competitor whose choice most nearly corresponds to the average preferences of the competitors as a whole; so that each competitor has to pick, not those faces which he himself finds prettiest, but those which he thinks likeliest to catch the fancy of the other competitors, all of whom are looking at the problem from the same point of view. It is not a case of choosing those which, to the best of one's judgment, are really the prettiest, nor even those which average opinion genuinely thinks the prettiest. We have reached the third degree where we devote our intelligences to anticipating what average opinion expects the average opinion to be. And there are some, I believe, who practise the fourth, fifth and higher degrees.[1]

Keynes's analogy suggests one way of relating share prices to expectations. An investor hopes that the price of the shares he or she owns will rise in the future, so that the shares might then be sold at a profit. Whether it is because other investors in the future *think* the shares are worth more or because fundamental economic change has actually *caused* the shares to be worth more is irrelevant. What matters is only that the price does, indeed, rise. If some investors anticipate that other market participants will expect a price increase, they will buy shares and the current market price of the stock will be bid up.

The beauty contest analogy is inadequate, however, as an expectational model. For one thing, share evaluation, unlike the assessment of beauty, is not a purely subjective matter; objective information is also taken into account. Furthermore, Keynes's analogy does not allow that the judges in the stock market contest can, over time, learn how the process works, and that learned judges do not make systematic mistakes.

A Rational Expectations Model

Expectations are the link between the market value of shares and current information. This link can be considered within the context of a specific model of expectation formation: a *rational expectations* model.* The model is structured as follows:

1. The stock market contest is played repetitively in consecutive periods. The outcome of each contest is given by the share assessments established at the end of each period. Each assessment reflects what investors, at the time, anticipate shares will be worth at the end of subsequent periods.

2. Investor assessments of share values are based, in part at least, on expectations concerning the future dividend payments they will receive, and the expected stream of future dividend payments depends on the future worth of the firm.

3. At the start of each period, investors can, at a cost, obtain additional information pertaining to the economic worth of the corporation as of the end of the period. Uncertainty is not eliminated, but investors who obtain the information do form more accurate expectations than uninformed investors of the future value of share price.

There still is a beauty contest. All investors do not become informed each period (information is not costless), the uninformed still guess what the informed may have learned, and the informed anticipate that the uninformed will do so. However, with informed investors, the current value of shares is linked to future economic worth. In addition, the uninformed investors learn with experience how the contest works, and learned judges do not make systematic mistakes.

The presence of a meaningful informational signal and the absence of systematic mistakes are the essence of a rational expectations model.

---

* The exposition that follows draws on S. Grossman and J. Stiglitz, "Information and Competitive Price System," *American Economic Review*, May 1976, used with permission.

Assumptions

A rational expectations model can be used to show how market prices are determined in an environment where trading is frictionless, but where information gathering is costly. For this purpose, assume the following:

1. A succession of investment periods of length T that are identical for all decision makers; each investment period may be considered a contest period.

2. All informed investors at the start of each contest period possess an information set that applies to that single period.

3. All informed investors assess the information set the same way (homogeneous expectations). When assessed, the information is given a dollar dimension, the expected value of share price as of the end of the period.

4. Uninformed investors may have publicly available information but do not know part of the current information set possessed by informed investors.

5. The coefficient of absolute risk aversion for each investor decreases with increases in the investor's wealth.

6. Share prices at the end of each contest period are determined by the information set and by other changes that the informed traders are not themselves able to predict (such as additional informational change or changing liquidity needs).

7. Trades are made and share prices set in a frictionless Walrasian call market.

The Model

These assumptions and the investor's demand equation may be used to present the *Grossman-Stiglitz price-signaling model*. Our formulation differs from Grossman and Stiglitz[2] in that (1) we specifically assume a call market environment (Grossman and Stiglitz are silent on the point), and (2) we let liquidity trading cause the market price to be a noisy signal (Grossman and Stiglitz alternatively assume that change in the number of shares outstanding for an issue causes its price to be a noisy signal). Write the demand equation (see Chapter 12) as

$$P = \frac{E(P_T)}{R_f} - 2bN \tag{15.1}$$

where P is the share price of the risky asset at the beginning of a contest period, $E(P_T)$ is the expected value of price at the end of the contest period,

$R_f - 1$ is the risk-free rate of interest, b is the present value of the investor's risk premium, and N is the number of shares the investor wishes to hold.

Equation 15.1 shows that two parametric changes affect the location of the investor's demand curve. First, change in the expectation of the end-of-period price alters the height of the curve. Second, change in the investor's risk premium alters the slope of the curve. The investor's risk premium depends on his or her coefficient of absolute risk aversion, and this in turn depends on the investor's wealth (we have assumed diminishing absolute risk aversion). Hence, given the parameters of the utility function, the investor's demand curve depends upon his or her expectations and wealth.

To facilitate the exposition of the individual decision model, assume that all market participants but one have obtained the current information set and thus are informed traders, and consider what a single uninformed trader may be able to infer from a market-determined price. Figure 15.2 shows three alternative market demand curves. The demand curves labeled D_1 and D_2 describe identical aggregate demand conditions, except that D_1 applies when the expected value of the end-of-period price for the informed traders is $E(P_1)$, and D_2 applies when the expected value of the end-of-period price is $E(P_2)$. The third curve, D_3, reflects the same expectation of the end-of-period price $[E(P_1)]$ as does D_1, but a lower risk premium for the informed traders.

The risk premium for each informed trader changes because of cash flows (liquidity changes) that are unique to each trader. Cash inflows increase a trader's wealth and so decrease his or her coefficient of absolute risk aversion

FIGURE 15.2 *Effect of Informational Change and Liquidity Change on the Market Demand Curve*

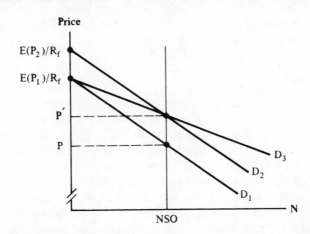

[thereby decreasing the slope (dP/dN) of his or her demand curve]. Cash outflows decrease a trader's wealth and so increase his or her coefficient of absolute risk aversion (thereby increasing the slope of his or her demand curve). Given that the price intercept of the demand curve is the same for all informed traders and that each has linear demand, the slope of the market demand curve reflects the *average* risk premium of the traders. Specifically, the slope of the market demand curve equals the negative of twice the average risk premium, divided by the number of traders.

Informational Change

Returning to Figure 15.2, assume for the moment that the market demand curve shifts only because of change in the information set. Therefore, if the informed traders' assessment of the information set leads them to expect a price of $E(P_1)$ for the end of the contest period, their aggregate demand is D_1. Thus, given the number of shares outstanding (NSO), the current equilibrium price is P. Alternatively, if the informed traders expect a price of $E(P_2)$ for the end of the contest period, their aggregate demand is D_2, and the current equilibrium price is P′. If, in the repetitive environment of the game, information alternates between the set that underlies the curve D_1 and the set that underlies the curve D_2, the uninformed trader soon learns, by relating beginning period prices to end of period results, that:

- Whenever the current market clearing price is P, the informed traders must be anticipating an end of period price of $E(P_1)$.
- Whenever the current market clearing price is P′, the informed traders must be anticipating an end of period price of $E(P_2)$.

In general, if market demand were to shift in the way described, the uninformed trader would learn to infer the current information set perfectly from the current market clearing price. If so, there would be no advantage to being an informed trader.

A Noisy Signal

If no trader were to become informed, the market price would lose its informational content. This situation is avoided, however, because the uninformed trader cannot infer the information perfectly from the current market price. The reason is that, as noted, liquidity changes that are not related to information changes also shift the market demand curve. For instance, as shown in Figure 15.2, the clearing price may change from P to P′ because (information constant) the aggregate demand curve has shifted from D_1 to D_3 for liquidity reasons. Thus the uninformed investor, knowing neither the information set nor the wealth of other traders, cannot determine upon observing the price P' whether curve D_2 or curve D_3 applies. Thus the uninformed investor does not know whether the expected end of period price is $E(P_2)$ or $E(P_1)$.

The market price, therefore, is a noisy signal. With a *noisy signal*, the uninformed trader can at best guess that the expected end of period price is $E(P_1)$ if the current price is P, or that it is $E(P_2)$ if the current price is P', and so on.

In the rational expectations model, the uninformed trader forms unbiased expectations of $E(P)$. That is, over a sufficiently large number of contest periods, the uninformed trader is correct in that the informed traders do in fact, *on average*, expect an end of period price of $E(P_1)$ when the current price is P, an end of period price of $E(P_2)$ when the current price is P', and so on. Thus the uninformed trader can infer information from the market-determined price.

The information inferred by the uninformed trader is not as precise as that obtained by the informed traders. Therefore, being informed does give traders an advantage in the marketplace. This advantage, in equilibrium, just compensates the informed traders for the additional cost of being informed.

And so we see how the market price conveys an informational signal to the uninformed trader. The relative inelasticity of the uninformed trader's demand curve is also implied by the current analysis, as we will next show.

The Demand of the Uninformed

Figure 15.3(a) shows (1) the demand of the uninformed trader if he or she were to obtain the information that implies an expected end-of-period price of $E(P_1)$ [this curve is labeled $d_u \mid E(P_1)$] and (2) the demand of the uninformed trader if he or she were to obtain the information that implies an expected end-of-period price of $E(P_2)$ [this curve is labeled $d_u \mid E(P_2)$]. Because a current price P is associated with an expected end-of-period price $E(P_1)$ and a price of P' is associated with $E(P_2)$, the demand curves in Figure 15.3 could alternatively be labeled $d_u \mid P$ and $d_u \mid P'$. We see that the uninformed trader, upon observng a market price of P and *inferring* an expected end-of-period price of $E(P_1)$, would wish to hold N shares. This same trader, upon observing a market price of P' and inferring an expected end-of-period price of $E(P_2)$, would also wish to hold N shares. Generalizing, the demand curve of the uninformed trader is the infinitely inelastic curve labeled d_u.

The uninformed trader's demand curve is infinitely inelastic because of the strict form of the model presented. We have assumed that the variance of the end-of-period price does not change as price increases from P to P', and thus that the trader's risk premium does not change. In this case, the change of the present value of the expected price equals the change of the current price {the two demand curves [$d_u \mid E(P_2)$ and $d_u \mid E(P_1)$] are parallel}.

FIGURE 15.3 *Uninformed Trader's Demand Curve with Price Signaling. (a) The Variance of End-of-Period Price Is Not Related to the Level of Prices. (b) The Variance of End-of-Period Price Increases with the Level of Prices*

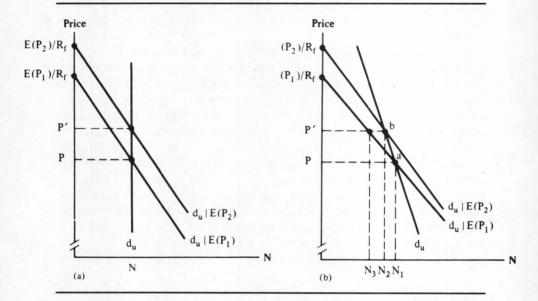

It is plausible that the uninformed investor expects the variance of the end-of-period price to be greater when $E(P)$ is greater. If so, the uninformed investor's risk premium is positively related to $E(P)$, and the demand curve labeled $d_u \mid E(P_2)$ is steeper than the demand curve labeled $d_u \mid E(P_1)$. In this case, the change of the present value of the expected price is greater than the change of the current price {the two demand curves [$d_u \mid E(P_2)$ and $d_u \mid E(P_1)$] are not parallel}. As shown in Figure 15.3(b), the uninformed investor, upon observing a market price of P, would wish to hold N_1 shares as indicated by point a or, upon observing a market price of P', would wish to hold N_2 shares as indicated by point b. The demand curve of the uninformed trader is now the relatively inelastic curve, d_u, that passes through points a and b. The demand curve labeled D_2 in Figure 15.2 may also be more steeply inclined than the curve labeled D_1 for the same reason. More generally, for d_u to be downward sloping, the curves labeled $d_u \mid E(P_2)$ and $d_u \mid E(P_1)$ in Figure 15.3 must converge more rapidly than the curves labeled D_2 and D_1 in Figure 15.2.

The intuition behind the relative inelasticity of the demand curve d_u for the uninformed trader is the following. Assume that the trader initially holds

N_1 shares, that price is initially P, and that the price then increases to P'. If the trader knew that the information set was unchanged (and that, therefore, the price increase was due to liquidity induced buying), he or she would seek to sell $N_1 - N_3$ shares to take advantage of the price increase. However, if the trader does not know whether or not information has changed, he or she will sell a smaller amount ($N_1 - N_2$ shares) because of the possibility that the price increase is attributable to bullish economic news. Generalizing, the uninformed trader's response to the price signal reduces the size of a sale for a price increase, reduces the size of a purchase for a price decrease, and thereby reduces the elasticity of the trader's demand curve.

In a frictionless market, the uninformed trader would transmit to the market the buy and sell order functions associated with the demand curve labeled d_u in Figure 15.3(b). The trader in this environment would trade the appropriate number of shares at the market-determined price, given his or her demand propensities and the information signal that the market price conveys. In addition, the model implies that:

- End-of-period price uncertainty is greater for the uninformed trader than for the informed traders (the uninformed trader is not able to conditon his or her expectations directly on the information set).
- The uninformed trader faces less uncertainty than if there were no informed traders (the market price does convey a meaningful informational signal).
- Current prices are unbiased reflections of the information set (the uninformed trader does not systematically over- or underestimate the expected end-of-period price from the signal conveyed by the current price).

Free Fall

The Grossman-Stiglitz price-signaling model can be used to show how the dynamic behavior of prices can result in the free fall experienced on 19 October 1987. We have just reasoned that an investor's demand curve to hold shares of a risky asset will be downward sloping under normal circumstances, but now note the possibility of a slope reversal under unusual conditions. One such condition is if a decrease (increase) in price conveys a sufficiently strong negative (positive) signal to investors. We now discuss this possibility with reference to Figure 15.4, which presents the demand curve of an uninformed investor with price signaling.

Assume the market generally comprises an adequate number of informed traders, and that an association has been well established between a current price of P and a relatively bullish information set, and between a current

FIGURE 15.4   *Demand of Uninformed Investor with Price Signaling.*
(a) Decrease in Price Is Not Associated with Increased Uncertainty.
(b) Decrease in Price Is Associated with Increased Uncertainty

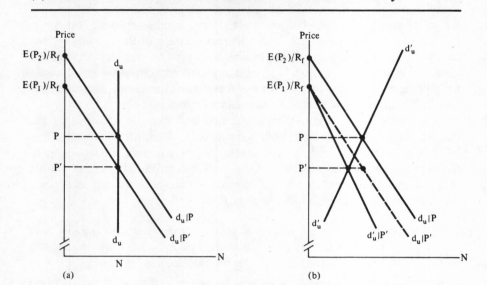

(a)

(b)

price of P' and a relatively bearish information set (where P' is less than P). Figure 15.4(a), with minor notational changes, reproduces Figure 15.3(a). The downward-sloping curve labeled $d_u \mid P$ shows what the demand of an uninformed investor would be if he or she possessed the relatively bullish information associated with P being the equilibrium price in the current period. The downward-sloping curve labeled $d_u \mid P'$ shows what the demand of an uninformed investor would be if he or she possessed the relatively bearish information associated with P' being the equilibrium price in the current period.

Note in Figure 15.4(a) that the price intercept of the "bearish" curve is below the intercept of the "bullish" curve and that the two slopes are the same. The bearish information could lower the price intercept by decreasing the price expected at the end of the investment period [$E(P_1)$ could be less than $E(P_2)$] or by increasing $R_1 - 1$, the risk-free rate of interest used in the demand model to discount the future expected price.

As shown in Figure 15.4(a), a current market price of P signals information associated with the demand curve $d_u \mid P$, and, given this demand curve and the current price of shares (P), the uninformed investor wants to hold N shares. Alternatively, a current market price of P' signals information that results in the demand curve $d_u \mid P'$, and, given this demand curve and the current price of shares (P'), the uninformed investor also wants to hold N shares. Therefore, with price signaling, the changing price does not affect the number of shares the uninformed investor wishes to hold. Hence this investor's demand curve is the vertical line labeled d_u in Figure 15.4(a).

For both informed and uninformed investors, we have again assumed that the slope of the demand curve given the information set is the same, regardless of the height of the curve. Because the slope is constant for the informed investors, the dollar change in the present value of the end-of-period price must equal the dollar change in the current price (as in Figure 15.2 and the related discussion). Note that with $E(P_2)/R_f - E(P_1)/R_f = P - P'$, we must have $d_u(P) = d_u(P') = N$, as shown in Figure 15.4(a). As previously noted, we would generally expect that, all else constant, the variance of the end-of-period price would be greater the *higher* the price and that the increase in uncertainty would be more for investors who are not directly informed of the bullish information than for those who are. Under these conditions, the demand curve of the uninformed investor would be downward sloping, as it is shown to be in Figure 15.3(b).

Alternatively, assume that a decrease in price from P to P' conveys not only a bearish signal but also increased uncertainty. In this case the demand curve of the uninformed investor conditioned on the price P' is steeper than the demand curve conditioned on the price P, as shown in Figure 15.4(b) by the curve labeled $d_u' \mid P'$. We showed in Chapter 12 that the slope of this demand curve is given by the present value of the risk premium to hold one share, where the risk premium equals one-half of the investor's coefficient of absolute risk aversion times the dollar risk attributable to holding one share of the risky asset. Thus, increasing the variance associated with the end-of-period price increases the slope of the investor's demand curve to hold shares. If the price-conditioned demand curve becomes steeper as it shifts to the left, the number of shares demanded at a price of P' is less than the number of shares demanded at a price of P. In this case, the demand curve for the uninformed investor is upward sloping, as shown in Figure 15.4(b) by the positively inclined curve labeled d_u'.

The analysis can be applied to the events of 19 October 1987. Consider the demand of investors to hold shares of the market portfolio. Initially, the changing economic environment caused the risk-free rate to rise (due to the increased level of interest rates) and the risk premium to rise (due to the increased level of uncertainty). These changes shifted down the informed investors' demand to hold shares of the market portfolio and caused the curve to be more steeply inclined. Consequently, prices fell in the New York market. Trading accelerated, and prices were pushed down further as computer sell programs were triggered in the Chicago market.

As prices dropped and the general level of uncertainty increased, the risk premium of the uninformed investors increased, and their demand curves became upward sloping. As the pace of events sped up, increasing numbers of professionals became bewildered and joined the ranks of the uninformed. At this point, a lower price was attracting insufficient buy orders from the dwindling number of investors who still believed themselves to be informed. When the positively inclined demand of the uninformed overwhelmed the market, price went into free fall. Virtually the only buyers remaining were the specialists, who were buying because of their affirmative obligation. Professionals like Laszlo Birinyi of Salomon Brothers could only observe and wonder, "What does the market know that we don't?" The answer to his question is "not much."

Recapitulation

Investors have heterogeneous expectations because information is costly. Because investors have heterogeneous expectations, risky assets do not have intrinsic values; rather, equilibrium prices are established in the marketplace.

The market price of a stock at the start of each period depends on the information set informed traders have observed. If the information is favorable, the current market price is higher because of the increased demand of the informed traders; if the news is unfavorable, the current market price is lower because of the decreased demand of the informed traders. The information set is eventually revealed publicly. The outcome of the contest depends in part on the disclosure (otherwise the information would not have value). Thus the information set establishes an association between the current and future values of price. In the repetitive environment of the contest, uninformed investors observe the association. Thus the uninformed investors learn to infer from the current market price the import that the information must have for future share value. The uninformed accordingly take account of the current price when forming their expectations, and they face less uncertainty than they would if there were no informed traders.

The inferences of the uninformed are not perfect, however. The changing liquidity needs of some traders cause current prices to have a less than perfect association with the current information set. The less than perfect association is important: if the uninformed could infer information without error from the current price, no one would become informed (information is not costless).

Informed traders invest optimally in the risky asset given their information, and uninformed traders invest optimally in the risky asset given the signal they infer from the current market price. The two groups together simultaneously set the market price in a frictionless auction. In the repetitive environment of the market, the uninformed have learned the process by which information is reflected in market prices, and they are not on average wrong in their expectations. That is, although their anticipations are less accurate than those of the informed, the uninformed do not systematically over- or underestimate the future values that share prices are expected to attain.

We have described an equilibrium. In this equilibrium, each investor realizes a rate of return that is optimal, given the riskiness of the investment and the benefits and cost of information. With a rational expectations equilibrium, all investors (both informed and uninformed) do not make systematic errors in their anticipations of future price changes, because repetitive errors of forecasting are discovered and eliminated by the players in the contest.

Rational expectations is a very useful modeling device. It gives valuable insight into necessary equilibrium conditions for a frictionless market environment, and it provides a benchmark against which to assess real world results. Furthermore, it is the best (and only truly rigorous) model of expectations formation that we have. However, the model should not be retained as an untarnished description of reality in actual markets. The truth concerning each information bit reveals itself over time, and, as this occurs, some anticipations at least are revised. The process by which heterogeneous anticipations are revised and ultimately approach unanimity may not be random, and current prices may not be unbiased reflections of current information. Most importantly, the equity markets are not a repetitive environment, and market participants do not have the opportunity to learn perfectly the parameters of the price determination process. Consequently, the rational expectations results may be perturbed.

Where do we stand now with regard to a theory of expectations? Somewhere between Keynes and rational expectations. The literature on the subject is extensive, but much still remains to be learned. The task of modeling expectations is indeed a challenge.

Informational Efficiency

This section considers five conditions for informational efficiency.

Efficiency with Regard to the Existing Information Set

Investors make decisions in relation to the information set in two ways. First, they search for situations in which they think the market has mispriced an asset given the asset's risk/return characteristics. When such a situation is found, an investor takes a position in relation to it that enables him or her to realize profits if and when prices are appropriately adjusted in the market. Second, even if all assets are appropriately priced on the market, a selection of alternative mean-variance efficient portfolios exists, and the investor uses information concerning the risk/return characteristics of securities to select an optimal portfolio (given his or her unique tastes for risk and return). The discussion that follows focuses on the first use to which information may be put and abstracts from the second.

The decision maker formulates returns expectations by assessing publicly available information, his or her own private information, and current market prices. If, on the basis of the assessment, the risk-adjusted return expected on an asset seems abnormally high, the decision maker seeks to buy additional shares. Alternatively, if the return seems abnormally low, the decision maker seeks to sell shares (if he or she is long in the asset), to short the stock, or simply to ignore the stock (if short selling is restricted). A negative return on the stock is a positive return to the investor with a short position. Therefore, by shorting a stock, a trader who is bearish in relation to the market may also anticipate positive returns.

Buying pressure increases current prices and thus decreases expected returns. Selling pressure decreases prices and thus increases expected returns. Unlimited buying or short selling unbalances the investor's portfolio, thus increasing the variance of the portfolio's returns. Therefore, appropriate buying and selling bring risk-adjusted returns into harmony with normal values for the investor. When harmony is achieved, the information set cannot be further exploited by the individual investor. Thus individual optimizing behavior leads the market to an informationally efficient outcome.

The thought can be stated somewhat differently. *Abnormal returns* on an investment are, by definition, returns that are either higher than an investor would require or lower than the investor must receive to make the investment. Therefore, abnormally high returns are "bought" (by buying the shares or shorting the stock), and abnormally low returns are "sold" (by selling shares or covering a short position). Because of the effect of purchases and sales on current prices and on portfolio diversification, transactions that exploit the abnormal returns also eliminate them. It follows that abnormal expected returns are eliminated when investors achieve portfolios that are optimal, given the information set.

Therefore, the first condition for informational efficiency—that abnormally high returns cannot be realized by exploiting the existing information set—is equivalent to the requirement that investors maximize utility by obtaining efficient portfolios, given the information that they possess.

Efficiency with Regard to Information Gathering Activities

Trade-offs.   Assume the investor anticipates a particular mean and variance of returns, given the level of price at which the stock is currently trading. Also assume that, on the basis of logic and past experience, the investor has some understanding of how a new bit of information would alter the stock's price. At a cost, the investor can attempt to obtain that information before its impact is fully reflected in market prices. If successful, he or she benefits from the price adjustment the news will trigger.

With heterogeneous expectations, an individual may also profit from information that has already been widely distributed. For instance, let there be some information bit that an individual would interpret differently than the market in the short term. If that individual were indeed more astute in his or her assessment of the information, then in the longer term that person would realize a return from it even if the news had already been assessed by others and had had its impact on market prices.

As time goes by, truth reveals itself. As it does, some investors find that their anticipations were correct, and others find that they were wrong. Therefore, the return to information includes the profits one can achieve by being more correct than the market. This is, of course, a difficult game to play, and few believe they can consistently play it with success. Nevertheless, security analysis is potentially valuable, even to decision makers who cannot beat the market by being among the first to receive news.

One need not, however, only attempt to obtain information directly— along the lines discussed previously, the investor can *infer* informational change from market prices. That is, on the basis of past experience, the investor can interpret price changes as signals (albeit noisy signals) that some new information bit has been released. Therefore, rather than directly looking for the information, the investor may decide to let the price change signal the information. This person would be a member of the "sheep" category defined in Chapter 12. In his or her opinion, a change in the stock's share price may not imply a change of the stock's risk/return characteristics.

What value might price signaling have to a member of the sheep category? From time to time new funds are invested in the market and old funds are withdrawn: knowledge (or the belief) that the risk/return characteristics of a security have not changed is relevant for portfolio decisions made in relation to these liquidity changes. In addition, the realization (or belief) that the risk/return characteristics of a security regain their previous values after the stock has adjusted to news may prevent the investor from mistakenly buying or selling after an opportunity has passed (note that nonaction itself implies a decision). In this regard, it may be advisable to act as sheep if one does not have a preferential position vis-à-vis the information flow or special insight into information's meaning. Finally, the investor may in fact benefit from signals inferred from price changes. For instance, if prices do not adjust instantly and accurately to new equilibrium values, the investor may profit from quickly entering market orders or stop loss orders (in continuous trading) or limit orders (in call market trading). Tests using filter rules have shown that trading strategies based on past price changes do in fact generate excess gross returns (although transaction costs make them, on net, unprofitable). A *filter rule* is a decision to buy if price goes up x% and to sell if price goes down x%, where the value of x sets the strength of the filter. See Alexander.[3]

Chartists in particular believe that profitable trading rules can be formulated on the basis of patterns exhibited by past price movements. Although chartism is not accepted by many, the belief that the ebb and flow of investor reactions, psychology, and so on, introduce predictable, repetitive patterns is not, per se, erroneous. The reason for questioning the premise of the chartists is that in an informationally efficient environment, the exploitation of such price patterns would eliminate the patterns. This point is clarified in Chapter 12.

In conclusion, information is valuable whether received directly or inferred from prices, and whether received before or after the market has had a chance to adjust to it. However, when it is received sooner and directly (rather than later and inferred), it is (1) more valuable and (2) more costly to obtain. This is why tradeoffs exist in information gathering.

Individual Optimality.   Consider one individual's decision of whether or not to purchase a single bit of information concerning a corporation. As discussed previously, the alternative for an investor who does not purchase the information is to make a portfolio decision regarding the corporation's stock on the basis of the stock's market price and other available information.

The value of the information bit to any specific decision maker depends upon the quality of the anticipations he or she can formulate given that information, in relation to the quality of the market's anticipations (which are reflected in the current price of the asset). The faster (in relation to other market participants) the specific individual can obtain the information bit and the better he or she is as an information processor (in relation to other market participants), the greater is the value of the information. The investor should look for information not yet gathered by others, and for information that is not highly correlated with existing information.

Suppose a specific investor is moderately efficient at obtaining and assessing information. The larger the number of other investors who are informed and the more efficient they are as information gatherers and processors, the less likely it is that that investor would realize a competitive advantage by obtaining the information bit. If the decision maker's abilities were low enough in relation to the market, then he or she might do better to let others obtain and process the information and simply to turn to price as an unbiased signal of the information.

The second condition for informational efficiency—that additional information gathering and processing activities do not generate abnormal profits— is equivalent to the requirement that an investor does indeed obtain information directly if its incremental value is greater than its incremental cost, or infer it from market prices if its incremental value is less than its incremental cost (including the opportunity cost of time).

*Market Equilibrium.** We have established that the value of additional information to each individual depends, not just on the information itself, but also on that individual's efficiency vis-à-vis others at information gathering and processing. The market is in equilibrium with respect to a piece of information if all individuals for whom that information's value exceeds its cost do obtain it and if all individuals for whom that information's value is less than its cost infer it from the market price of the asset. In such an equilibrium, the information gathering activities that are undertaken are on net profitable, but additional information gathering does not yield positive returns.

To establish the existence of an equilibrium amount of information gathering for the market, first consider a situation in which no one actively seeks additional information directly, but rather all participants base their expectations entirely on current market prices and on whatever information was publicly available in the past. The informational content of security prices declines, and prices soon convey *very* noisy signals. In such a market, an investor with even the smallest amount of additional information is able to spot some extraordinary situations—a stock paying a $15 dividend, offering much promise of dividend growth, and trading at $20 a share; some other stock trading at $75 a share although the company has slashed the dividend and is about to collapse. In such an environment, additional information gathering activities clearly are profitable.

What would the situation be if many investors were informed? The informational content of security prices would then be high, and prices would convey a far less noisy signal. In this case, all but the most efficient information processors might find that the quality of prices set in the market is too good to beat. Accordingly, rather than attempting to outguess the market, most people might simply follow the crowd. In the limit, if all share prices were to reflect all information fully and were not noisy signals, there would be no return to additional information gathering.

This may seem to imply a paradox: on the one hand, if stock prices were to reflect all information fully, no one would undertake security analysis; on the other hand, if no one were to undertake security analysis, stocks could not be appropriately priced.

There is no paradox. An equilibrium amount of information gathering exists. At one extreme, if virtually no one looks for information, the net

---

* The discussion concerning market equilibrium draws heavily on S. Grossman and J. Stiglitz, "Information and Competitive Price Systems," *American Economic Review*, May 1976, used with permission.

returns to information gathering are likely to be positive for at least the most efficient information gatherers and processors. At the other extreme, if nearly everyone looks for information, the net returns to information gathering are likely to be negative for at least the most inefficient information gatherers and processors. In equilibrium, an equilibrium number of investors is informed. Those who are informed are those who are the most efficient at the process and/or those for whom information has the greatest value. For the marginal information gatherer, the value of the information just equals the cost of obtaining it. Those for whom the value of information is less than the cost of obtaining it infer the information from prices. A market that has achieved such an equilibrium is *informationally efficient* with regard to the intensity with which information gathering activities are pursued.

The Informational Accuracy of Equilibrium Prices

Prices act as constraints that lead individuals to use resources optimally, given supply and demand conditions.* *Nonstochastic prices,* however, convey no information about the resources themselves — market participants are assumed to have complete information to begin with. On the other hand, when outcomes are uncertain and information is incomplete, prices play an important informational role. Prices are a mechanism for information transfer (from the informed to the uninformed) and for the aggregation of diverse information bits (for both informed and uninformed traders). This section considers the efficiency with which prices perform these two functions.

With a diversity of expectations in the market, a security's price reflects a weighted average opinion of all investors in the market. The more weight the market gives to the opinions of those who are better informed, the greater is the informational accuracy of the equilibrium prices. Therefore, whose expectations might the equilibrium prices reflect?

People who believe themselves to be the most efficient at information gathering and processing are those most likely to become informed traders (as noted, others will simply let price be their signal). With regard to the distribution of the informed, two factors affect the dollar strength of each person's opinion, and hence the weight of his or her conviction in the market (the *dollar strength* of an investor's opinion is the funds he or she commits to a position in light of the strength of his or her conviction). The first factor is the accuracy of the decision maker's opinion and the second is the decision maker's wealth.

---

* The discussion in this section draws on S. Figlewski, "Market 'Efficiency' in a Market with Heterogeneous Information," *The Journal of Political Economy,* August 1978, used with permission.

The dollar strength of an anticipation is correlated with the accuracy of that anticipation, to the extent that truth carries its own conviction. However, the presence of some bull- (or bear-) headed fools in the market makes the association between truth and conviction somewhat less than perfect.

The wealth an individual has realized in the financial markets is his or her reward for having invested successfully in the past, and to an extent, the quality of a decision maker's earlier anticipations is correlated with his or her current abilities as a forecaster. Therefore, current wealth should be positively related to the accuracy of current opinion. However, this association is also less than perfect. Few are able to predict consistently well over time. Furthermore, some inefficient information processors may be richly rewarded by chance, and some efficient information processors may not do well—also by chance.

With regard to the informational efficiency of equilibrium prices, we conclude that even in a market that is informationally efficient in other respects, prices are noisy signals. We may never be sure who the most efficient information processors are by spotting the consistent winners; in a large population of investors, some may win often, only by chance. Thus expectations remain heterogeneous and the market does not completely achieve informationally accurate prices.

The Informational Accuracy of Market Clearing Prices*

The preceding section considered the informational accuracy of equilibrium prices. As previously defined, *equilibrium prices* are values determined by the intersection of the aggregate buy and sell *order functions* of all traders. We now consider the informational accuracy of market clearing prices. *Market clearing prices* are values that clear all crossing buy and sell *orders* that have been written in relation to the underlying order functions (see Chapter 13). The difference between an equilibrium price and a clearing price is shown in Figure 15.5.

The downward-sloping line labeled B_j in Figure 15.5(a) is the buy order function of the jth trader. The trader's anticipations of the clearing price are shown by the bell-shaped curve drawn on the vertical axis. $E(P)$ is the expected clearing price. Let the trader submit just one order point (a single price and a single quantity) to the market. Assume a call market trading environment. Then, given the buy order function (B_j), expectations of the clearing price (as described by the bell-shaped curve), and the call market

---

* The discussion in this section draws on T. Ho, R. Schawarts, and D. Whitcomb, "The Trading Decision and Market Clearing Under Transaction Price Uncertainty," *Journal of Finance,* March 1985 and on Bronfman and Schwartz, "Price Discovery and Market Structure," paper presented at American Finance Association meetings, Washington, DC, December 1990, used with permission.

FIGURE 15.5 *A Market Clearing Price* (P') *can Differ from an Equilibrium Price* (P*). *(a) Determination of the Optimal Buy Order Point of the* j^(th) *Trader. (b) Determination of the Equilibrium Market Price* P* *by Aggregating Investor Buy and Sell Order Functions. (c) Determination of the Market Clearing Price* P' *by Aggregating Investor Buy and Sell Order Points*

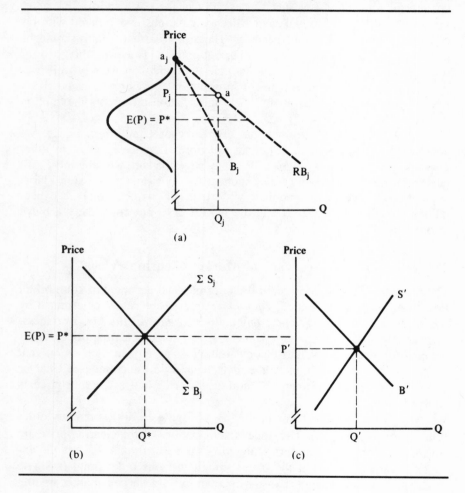

(a)

(b)   (c)

arrangement, the optimal order for the jth trader to submit is a point such as P_j, Q_j, (labeled *a*) on the curve RB_j.

The *equilibrium price* for the asset and for the trading session is shown in Figure 15.5(b) by the intersection of the aggregate buy and sell order functions. P* is the equilibrium price, and Q* is the equilibrium number of shares traded. In the case depicted in Figure 15.5(b), we have set P* equal to E(P). In other words, the representative investor has been assumed to have an unbiased, rational expectation of the clearing price. This accuracy of expectations need not be satisfied in any given trading session, however.

The asset's *clearing price* for the trading session is shown in Figure 15.5(c) by the intersection of the curves labeled B′ and S′. B′ and S′ are not aggregates of the individual order functions, but rather of the individual order points [such as the single point a, in Figure 15.5(a)]. In the case depicted in Figure 15.5(c), the market clearing price is P′, and the number of shares traded is Q′. (A similar result was obtained in Chapter 7 using a numerical analysis.)

Under transaction price uncertainty, P′, in general, differs from P*, as shown in the figure. Likewise, Q′, in general, differs from Q*. We will demonstrate this for the call market environment. Our discussion focuses on the price variable.

The simplest way to show that P′ and P* generally differ is to show the special conditions under which they will be the same. There are two conditions that must both hold: (1) buyers and sellers must all expect a clearing price of P* (the equilibrium price), and (2) the distribution of buyers and distribution of sellers must be symmetric. These two conditions hold in any given trading session only by chance. Let us consider the matter further.

Figure 15.6 shows the reservation buy and sell order curves RB_1, RB_2, RS_3, and RS_4 of four traders. All of the traders have identical and unbiased expectations of the clearing price, as reflected by the fact that each places his or her order with reference to the same expected price, E(P), with E(P) being equal to P*. The symmetry of the distribution of buyers and sellers is reflected by the symmetry between the curves labeled RB_1 and RS_3 and between the curves labeled RB_2 and RS_4. To see these symmetries, place a mirror on the horizontal line at E(P) = P* and note that the buy curves are parallel to each other, the sell curves are parallel to each other, the slopes of the sell curves are equal to the inverse of the slopes of the buy curves, $a_1 - P^* = P^* - a_3$, and $a_2 - P^* = P^* - a_4$.

Given the individual order functions, the expectations on the clearing price, and the call market environment, the specific orders that are written by the two buyers and the two sellers can be solved for analytically as discussed in Chapter 13. These orders are shown in Figure 15.6 by the circles labeled 1, 2, 3, and 4, respectively. Because the order functions are symmetrically distributed around P*, the optimal solutions for the individual orders are symmetrically distributed around P*.

If additional buy and sell order functions were to be drawn in Figure 15.6 with symmetry preserved, the additional order points would also be symmetrically distributed about P*. If a large number of these order points were then aggregated to get market buy and sell order curves [such as those labeled B′ and S′ in Figure 15.5(c)], the symmetry of the orders would be

FIGURE 15.6 *Reservation Buy and Sell Curves of Four Symmetrically Distributed Traders*

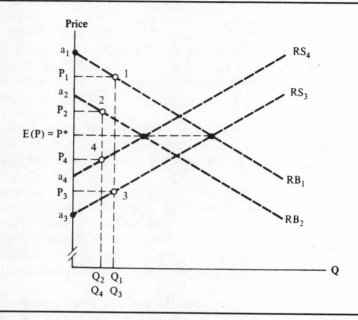

reflected in the two aggregate curves being symmetric around P*. Hence, the aggregate curves would intersect at P*. Thus the market clearing price (P') would equal the equilibrium price (P*).

There is, however, no reason to expect that investors will be symmetrically distributed at any given trading session (although on average they may be over a large number of trading sessions), and there is no reason to expect that at any given session they will all have unbiased expectations of the clearing price (although, on average, over a large number of sessions they may have unbiased expectations). When symmetry is perturbed *at any specific trading session*, P' does not equal P* for that session. Ho, Schwartz, and Whitcomb[4] and Bronfman and Schwartz[5] show this result analytically. Here we give only an intuitive explanation of what happens when we relax the assumption that the distribution of the price intercept terms for the sellers is symmetric with that of the buyers.

All traders may expect the same clearing price, but they all face transaction price uncertainty. Accordingly they all submit orders that protect them optimally in relation to that uncertainty. If the price-intercept terms are not symmetrically distributed, the intensity with which some traders wish to buy shares is not balanced by the intensity with which other traders wish to sell shares. Therefore, the intensity with which some buyers react to transaction price uncertainty is not balanced by the reaction of some sellers. This alters the relationship between the buy and sell orders that are revealed at the market call. The order functions twist, and equality between the clearing price and the equilibrium price is lost. Depending upon the specific situation, the realized clearing price could be above or below the expected clearing price, and thus above or below the equilibrium price. The deviation of the market clearing price from the equilibrium price may represent the fourth degree in Keynes's beauty contest analogy: market prices are not even accurate reflections of the average opinion about what the average opinion is.

Because the clearing price can (and in general does) differ from the equilibrium price, the informational accuracy of the market clearing price is impaired. That is why the accuracy of price discovery is an important consideration from a market's operational viewpoint (as discussed in Chapter 7).

The Dynamic Efficiency of Information Dissemination

The four efficiency criteria thus far considered concern static efficiency. We now turn to the dynamic efficiency with which information is disseminated in the investment community.

The efficiency of information dissemination has two dimensions: (1) the time needed for new information to be fully reflected in market prices and (2) the sequential order in which the information is disseminated among investors. After change has occurred in a company's fortunes, investors should learn of it quickly, and the change should be quickly reflected in market prices. This is true for both equity and efficiency: market prices provide better signals to decision makers if they reflect current, rather than outdated, information. But because information dissemination is not instantaneous, some investors are bound to receive news before others.

On 18 June 1815, Napoleon was defeated at Waterloo. A carrier pigeon took news of the British victory to Nathan Rothschild in London. In a single day, Rothschild reaped a fortune by buying shares from uninformed, and quite frightened traders (he was also credited with having saved the London Stock Exchange). Rothschild's profit was not due to the news. It was due to his having received the news first.

A tremendous amount of information is disseminated in today's markets, and only minutes may separate many investors in the receipt of news. Nonetheless, certain investors still receive information before others, and some may do so consistently. Thus we should continue to question the informational dynamic efficieny of the markets.

Investors receive information at different times for two reasons: (1) they are not equally efficient and aggressive as information gatherers, and (2) some people have a preferential position vis-à-vis the information flow. The efficiency and aggressiveness of investors should be rewarded, and they are. The returns to these people are the profits they receive from the price adjustments that occur when others lag behind them in the receipt of news. In part, it is the scramble to benefit from the price adjustments that accounts for the informational static efficiency of a market.

For some people, however, information is a by-product of a service they provide that has no relation to information gathering. The proofreader in a securities firm, the typesetter in the print shop, or the lawyer in a merger case, for instance, may receive information that has not yet been released to the public. When these people profit from their prior receipt of information, we may observe certain proofreaders, typesetters, and lawyers beng grossly overpaid for their services. No economic function is served by this overpayment. On the contrary, the feelings of inequity it can engender may have harmful repercussions.

Insiders are deemed to have a preferential and unfair advantage vis-à-vis the information flow. Accordingly, these people are restricted in their freedom to trade shares of their corporation's stock. Insiders must file with the SEC after trading, and they are not allowed to trade on news that has not yet been made public.

A tradeoff exists between the dynamic efficiency and the static efficiency of a market. The greater the flow of information in the market, the more accurate are the prices that are set and the more static efficient is the market. But the flow of information is positively related to the return to information, and the return to information is in large part the price adjustments an informed trader profits from when he or she receives the news first. Therefore, *dynamic inefficiency* motivates the informational gathering activities that make a market static-efficient.

That such a tradeoff exists is not surprising. Information gathering, like trading, is a manifestation of disequilibrium behavior. Also, as with trading, information gathering helps to repair imbalance in the market and to bring prices back to equilibrium values. It is too much to expect that the dynamic process by which equilibrium is regained will generate no undesired side effects. If we want prices that are the best possible signals of information, we must let those who have the best information (insiders included) trade with a minimum of restrictions. Alternatively, if we do not want insiders consistently to exploit the uninformed public, we must settle for prices that are noisier reflections of the information set. Making wise decisions in relation to this tradeoff is indeed difficult.

Suggested Reading

Beja, A., and Hakansson, N. "Dynamic Market Processes and the Rewards to Up-to-Date Information." *Journal of Finance*, May 1977.

Beja, A., and Hakansson, N. "On the Dynamic Behavior of Prices in Disequilibrium." *Journal of Finance*, May 1980.

Black, F. "Noise." *Journal of Finance*, July 1986.

Blanchard, O., and Watson, M. "Bubbles, Rational Expectations, and Financial Markets." In Wachtel, P. ed. *Crisis in the Economic and Financial Structure*, Lexington, MA: Lexington Books, 1982.

Copeland, T. "A Model of Asset Trading Under the Assumption of Sequential Information Arrival." *Journal of Finance*, September 1976.

DeLong, J., Shleifer, A., Summers, L., and Waldman, R. "The Economic Consequences of Noise Traders." *Journal of Political Economy*, 1990.

DeLong, J., Shleifer, A., Summers, L., and Waldman, R. "Positive Feedback Investment Strategies and Destabilizing Rational Speculation." *Journal of Finance*, June 1990.

Easley, D., and O'Hara, M. "Order Flow and Information in Securities Markets." Cornell University working paper, 1990.

Figlewski, S. "Market 'Efficiency' in a Market with Heterogeneous Information." *The Journal of Political Economy*, August 1978.

Froot, H, Scharfstein, S., and Stein, J. "Herd on the Street: Informational Inefficiencies in a Market with Short-Term Speculation." National Bureau of Economic Research, February 1990.

Garbade, K., Pomrenze, J., and Silber, W. "On the Information Content of Prices." *American Economic Review*, March 1979.

Goldman, M. B., and Sossin, H. "Information Dissemination, Market Efficiency and the Frequency of Transactions." *Journal of Financial Economics*, March 1979.

Government Accounting Office, *Securities Regulation: Efforts to Detect, Investigate, and Deter Insider Trading*. Government Accounting Office, August 1988.

Grossman, S. "An Introduction to the Theory of Rational Expectations Under Asymmetric Information." *Review of Economic Studies*, October 1981.

Grossman, S., and Stiglitz, J. "Information and Competitive Price Systems." *American Economic Review*, May 1976.

Grossman, S., and Stiglitz, J. "On the Impossibility of Informationally Efficient Markets." *American Economic Review*, June 1980.

Hellwig, R. "Rational Expectations Equilibrium with Conditioning on Past Prices: A Mean-Variance Example." *Journal of Economic Theory*, April 1982.

Hillmer, S., and Yu, P. "The Market Speed of Adjustment to New Information." *Journal of Financial Economics*, December 1979.

Ho, T., Schwartz, R., and Whitcomb, D. "The Trading Decision and Market Clearing Under Transaction Price Uncertainty." *Journal of Finance*, March 1985.

Jensen, M. "Risk, the Pricing of Capital Assets, and the Evaluation of Investment Portfolios." *Journal of Business*, April 1969.

John, K., and Mishra, B. "Information Content of Insider Trading Around Corporate Announcement: The Case of Capital Expenditures." *Journal of Finance*, July 1990.

Keynes, J. M. *The General Theory of Employment Interest and Money*. New York: Harcourt, Brace, 1958.

Scharfstein, D., and Stein, J. "Herd Behavior and Investment." *American Economic Review*, June 1990.

Schleifer, A., and Summers, L. "The Noise Trader Approach to Finance." *Journal of Economic Perspectives*, Spring 1990.

Summers, L. "Does the Stock Market Rationally Reflect Fundamental Values?" *Journal of Finance*, July 1986.

Trueman, B. "A Theory of Noise Trading in Securities Markets." *Journal of Finance*, March 1988.

Notes

1. J. M. Keynes, *The General Theory of Employment Interest and Money*, New York: Harcourt, Brace, 1958, p. 156.
2. S. Grossman and J. Stiglitz, "Informational and Competitive Price Systems," *American Economic Review*, May 1976.
3. Alexander (1961).
4. T. Ho, R. Schwartz, and D. Whitcomb, "The Trading Decision and Market Clearing Under Transaction Price Uncertainty," *Journal of Financing*, March 1985.
5. C. Bronfman and R. Schwartz, "Price Discovery and Market Structure," paper presented at American Finance Association meetings, Washington, DC, December 1990.

16

Assessing the Efficiency
of the Markets

Transaction prices must be analyzed in light of the microstructure of the markets. Market impact effects, bid-ask spread, price rounding, and imperfect price discovery all result in three related phenomena: negative intertemporal returns correlation, inflated short period returns variance, and serial cross-correlation in returns. Each is evidence of one reality: transaction prices generally differ from equilibrium values that would be achieved in a frictionless environment (an environment where trading is costless).

One must also understand that an investor cannot realize superior returns merely by having informed expectations about future returns. To enjoy excess profits, the investor must be more correct than the market. Consistently winning the guessing game is extremely difficult in informationally efficient markets, however. In fact, the informational efficiency of a market can be tested by examining whether or not traders can realize excess returns by trading on information. The null hypothesis, referred to as the *Efficient Market Hypothesis* (EMH), is that excess returns cannot be realized from information that is contained in past prices (weak form test), from information that is public (semistrong form test), or from any information (strong form test).

The EMH may be substantiated even if market prices do not reflect all information. That is, the prices at which shares are traded may reflect lagged adjustments and execution costs (bid-ask spread and market impact). The null hypothesis that price adjustment delays do not exist can be tested by analyzing the correlation between individual stock price changes and aggregate market movements over short measurement intervals. The null hypothesis that share prices are not affected by execution costs can be tested by analyzing the volatility of returns over short measurement intervals.

Intertemporal Correlation

The term *intertemporal* refers to events that occur in different time periods. For instance, if the price change for a stock in one period of time is correlated with the price change for that same stock in another period (for example, one day later), the stock's returns are said to be *intertemporally correlated*. When the return is for the same stock, this intertemporal correlation is referred to as *autocorrelation*, or as *serial correlation*.

Returns are positively autocorrelated when positive returns are more likely to be followed by other returns that are positive, and when negative returns are more likely to be followed by other returns that are negative. Therefore, if returns are positively autocorrelated, a series of price changes includes a larger number of *price continuations* (an uptick followed by other upticks, or a downtick followed by other downticks) than would be expected in a random sequence of price changes. If, on the other hand, returns are negatively autocorrelated, a series of price changes includes a larger number of *price reversals* (an uptick followed by a downtick or a downtick followed by an uptick) than would be expected in a random sequence of price changes.

The intertemporal correlation need not be between adjacent returns. With delayed price adjustments, for instance, the return in one period may be correlated with the return several periods later. The correlation between adjacent returns is called *serial correlation*, or *first order autocorrelation*. The correlation between nonadjacent returns is called *higher order autocorrelation*. The term *autocorrelation* simply means that the returns for an issue are autocorrelated, although not necessarily of first order.

The return on one stock in one period of time may also be correlated with the return on another stock in another period of time. This is *serial cross-correlation*. Serial cross-correlation exists when different stocks do not adjust simultaneously to common informational change.

Positive Intertemporal Correlation

Four factors may cause the returns for a security to be positively autocorrelated: sequential information arrival, the limit order book, market maker intervention in trading, and noninstantaneous price discovery after change in investor demand.

Sequential Information Arrival.   Copeland (1976) has shown that the sequential arrival of information (or, equivalently, the sequential adjustment of expectations) can cause a security's returns to be positively autocorrelated.

The Limit Order Book.   If orders on the book are not quickly revised after informational change, new orders based on the information transact at prices set by existing limit orders. As a series of such transactions eliminates the older orders seriatim from the book, a security's transaction price rises or falls in increments to a new equilibrium value.

Market Maker Intervention. The affirmative obligation of stock exchange specialists leads these market makers to intervene in trading when transaction-to-transaction price changes would otherwise be unacceptably large. This can cause a security's price to adjust in increments to a new equilibrium value after the advent of news.

Inaccurate Price Discovery. The term *price discovery* identifies the process by which the market finds a new equilibrium after a change in investor demand. Price discovery is inaccurate when new equilibrium values are not instantaneously achieved. Price discovery is inaccurate because investors do not instantaneously transmit their orders to the market, because orders left on the market are not continuously revised, and because, when they write their orders, investors do not know what the equilibrium prices are or will be. With inaccurate price determination, actual prices differ from equilibrium values. Some price changes are too small (they underadjust to news), and other price changes are too large (they overadjust to news). *Ceteris paribus*, if inaccurate price determination that involves partial adjustment (undershooting) predominates, returns will be positively autocorrelated.

The positive serial correlation resulting from informational change will not be very apparent in informationally efficient markets. The limit order book and specialist intervention apply to the exchanges, but not to OTC trading. Even for the exchanges, the effects of both should be apparent only in very brief period returns. This is true in part because the arrival of informationally motivated orders quickly eliminates stale orders from the book, and in part because trading is halted if informational change is substantial (so that existing orders may be revised and new, more appropriate transaction prices determined).

Negative Intertemporal Correlation

Four factors may cause negative intertemporal correlation in security returns: (1) the temporary market impact exerted by large orders, (2) the bid-ask spread, (3) price rounding, and (4) noninstantaneous price discovery after change in investor demand propensities.

Market Impact Effects. The section analyzing the mean and variance of returns in Chapter 14 shows how the arrival of one sell order changes a security's price as it interacts with the market's buy order function. The price change generated by the sell order is greater, the larger the relative size of the order (Y/V) and the lower the elasticity (η) of the market demand curve. An analogous effect would be observed for a buy order. The effective spread is expected to be greater for larger orders. In general, relatively large orders exert price pressure, and the pressure is greatest when the short run market demand is not very price responsive. Assume the arrival of a large sell order, for instance. If the book is relatively sparse and the effective spread large at the time of the order's arrival, the transaction price will be depressed so that the order may be absorbed by the relatively thin market. In this case, the lower price itself attracts new buy orders to the market (assuming the underlying demand is indeed more elastic), and price once again rises. Therefore, the initial price decrease is followed by a reversal (an increase), and the successive price changes are negatively autocorrelated.

The Bid-Ask Spread.   With a spread, orders to sell at market execute against the bid, and orders to buy at market execute against the ask. In the process, the transaction price moves between the bid and the ask. The bid and ask quotes themselves change over time with the arrival of new limit and market orders. Nonetheless, the bouncing of the transaction price between the quotes causes transaction-to-transaction price returns to be negatively autocorrelated. To see this, assume the quotes are fixed. Then if at some moment in time the last transaction in a particular stock is at the bid, the next transaction that generates a nonzero return must be at the ask, and a positive return is recorded. If the quotes remain unchanged, the next nonzero return must be negative (when a market sell once again executes at the bid). Price reversals thus occur as the transaction price moves back and forth between the bid and the ask. Even if the quotes change randomly over time, the price reversals attributed to the spread introduce negative intertemporal correlation in transaction price returns.[1]

Price Rounding.   Assume that the equilibrium price of a security is a continuous variable, but that each transaction price is rounded to the nearest one-eighth of a point. Rounding to one-eighth of a point establishes a minimum tick size (price cannot change by less than one-eighth of a point) and a minimum bid-ask spread (the spread cannot be less than one-eighth of a point). Like the spread, price rounding introduces negative serial correlation in security returns. To see this, assume that the upward drift of prices is small enough to be ignored and that the equilibrium price follows a random walk. Then, if the recorded price at point in time $t - 1$ has been rounded up, the transaction price at point in time t is likely to produce a downtick (because the transaction price at $t - 1$ was above the equilibrium price) Alternatively, if the price at $t - 1$ has been rounded down, the transaction price at t is likely to produce an uptick (because the transaction price at t − 1 was below the equilibrium price). Hence, with price rounding, positive returns are more likely to be followed by negative returns, and vice versa. The negative correlation introduced by price rounding is expected to be more pronounced for a low price stock (for which a one-eighth price change is a substantial return) than for a high price stock (for which a one-eighth price change is not a substantial return), for a low variance stock, and for returns measured over relatively short time periods. Evidence on the effect of price rounding on returns variance is presented in Table 16.1.

Inaccurate Price Discovery. With inaccurate price discovery, actual prices wander about their equilibrium values. If inaccurate price determination that involves overreaction to news (overshooting) predominates, returns are

TABLE 16.1 *Ratio of the Variance of Rounded Returns to the Variance of Unrounded Returns*

Standard deviation of unrounded returns	Price	Differencing interval ("days")					
		1	2	5	10	20	50
.002	2	12.16	8.30	5.12	3.68	2.66	1.56
	10	4.02	2.73	1.81	1.44	1.20	1.07
	50	1.26	1.21	1.03	1.00	.96	.95
	100	1.07	1.02	1.00	.99	.97	.95
.01	2	2.47	1.77	1.29	1.14	1.04	.98
	10	1.15	1.07	1.01	.99	.96	.96
	50	1.01	1.00	.99	.98	.95	.96
	100	1.00	1.00	.99	.98	.95	.96
.05	2	1.27	1.13	1.04	1.00	.97	.96
	10	1.01	1.00	.99	.98	.95	.95
	50	1.00	.99	.98	.98	.95	.96
	100	1.00	.99	.98	.98	.95	.96

Source: Schwartz and Whitcomb (June 1977), used with permission. Results reported in table are based on a simulation analysis performed by Schwartz and Whitcomb. In the study, 20 series of unrounded prices were generated for various combinations of price levels and standard deviations, using a normal returns distribution with a mean of zero. Each price was then rounded to the nearest eighth; variances were computed for each rounded series; and ratios for the matched variances were taken. Table 16.1 shows the 20-iteration averages of these ratios for each price level and standard deviation.

negatively autocorrelated. Further, Goldman and Beja have shown that returns are negatively autocorrelated if the equilibrium price changes randomly over time and if the transaction price wanders randomly about its equilibrium value.[2] The intuition behind this result is that the equilibrium price pulls the transaction price back to itself whenever the transaction price wanders away. Thus, even if the equilibrium price is following a random walk, the price discovery process causes reversals and hence negative correlation in transaction price returns.[*]

Serial Cross-Correlation

The returns for two different securities are serially cross-correlated if the price adjustments generated by a causal factor (for example, the advent of a new industrywide regulation) do not occur at the same moment in time (that is, if they are nonsynchronous).

If all price adjustments were instantaneous for all securities (as would be the case in a frictionless market), the price adjustments for different securities would be synchronous. However, the factors we have discussed in relation to returns autocorrelation also cause price adjustment delays and hence serial cross-correlation. Assume, for instance, a news bit arrives that implies a 2% upward revision in the price of two stocks, Podunk Mines and Liquidity Inc. In the very short run any or all of the following may happen, thereby causing the short run price movements to be different for the two securities:

- A large investor in Liquidity Inc. has been trying to liquidate her position for strictly personal reasons. On the other hand, a large buyer has suddenly, and for reasons known only to himself, decided that Podunk shares must be included in a well-structured portfolio.

- The last trade in Podunk occurred at the bid; the last trade in Liquidity occurred at the ask.

- The book in Podunk happens, by chance, to be unusually deep; the book in Liquidity is relatively sparse.

- Investors in Liquidity Inc. are relatively conservative; initially they believe the news will induce only a 1.5% appreciation in the share price. Investors in Podunk Mines are more optimistic; initially they anticipate a price change of 2.5%.

---

[*] Picture a man walking his dog on a leash across a field, with the dog racing randomly about the man, but never straying too far because of the leash. If the man follows a random path, the leash causes reversals in the dog's path, and thus the animal's movements are negatively autocorrelated.

- Many investors in Liquidity Inc. are otherwise occupied when the news bit arrives; many investors in Podunk Mines happen to be watching the broad tape when the news is publicly announced.

After the dust has settled, the prices of the two stocks are once again realigned. However, the paths the price adjustments follow are disparate and, in fact, largely uncorrelated.

The prices of some securities tend to adjust faster than others to changing market conditions. One would expect the large, intensely watched issues on average to lead the market and the smaller issues to lag behind. This gives rise to a pattern of serial cross-correlation where price adjustments for securities such as IBM and Exxon precede price adjustments for thinner issues such as Liquidity Inc. and Podunk Mines.

Serial cross-correlation patterns, however, are no doubt diffuse, complex, and not readily subject to exploitation by a clever trader. The reason is twofold: the time lags involved are not stable, and imperfect price discovery may entail both overshooting and undershooting.

Tests of the Efficient Market Hypothesis

Weak Form Tests

Weak form tests of the EMH focus on the informational content of the previous sequence of stock price movements. How much information should these movements contain for a market to be informationally efficient? If the market is a frictionless environment, the answer is *none*. Alternatively stated, in informationally efficient markets, above normal returns cannot be realized by using trading rules based upon past price movements.

Weak form efficiency does not require that price changes (returns) be strictly independent over time. Rather, price changes are expected to exhibit upward drift, because risk averse investors demand a positive expected return. Weak form efficiency requires only that past price changes cannot be used to improve predictions concerning the expected value of future price changes. Price changes that follow a *martingale process* satisfy this requirement.

The upward drift in stock price movements would be slight in short period (for instance, daily) intervals, and we ignore it to simplify the discussion. When the expected value of a stock's price change is zero, and when successive price changes are statistically independent and identically distributed, the security's price follows a random walk over time. (Price changes, on the other hand, can follow a martingale process even if they are statistically dependent and not identically distributed.) The *random walk* process is in essence a random number generator. The term *random walk*, and what it implies, has an interesting history.

Assume one were to leave a drunk in the middle of a large field, let him stumble around for a while and then, after some time has passed, go back and look for him. Where is the most efficient place to start looking? Because the drunk follows a random walk, knowledge of the direction of his last observed steps contains no useful information, and the best place to start looking is where the drunk was last seen.

Random walk was never the domain of the drunk alone. Bachelier (1900) reported evidence that the current price of a commodity is an unbiased estimate of the future price of the commodity. Subsequently, other students of asset price movements have reported that prices change randomly over time. See, for instance, Kendel,[3] Roberts,[4] Osborne,[5] Granger and Morgenstern,[6] and Alexander.[7] The most comprehensive review of this literature is that of Fama.[8] The curious point is that the early findings presented evidence of random walk, but an understanding of why price changes would be uncorrelated in a frictionless, informationally efficient market was not forthcoming for many years.[9]

That prices are expected to follow a random walk in informationally efficient and frictionless markets is most important. Following the empirical demonstration that, by and large, the markets are informationally efficient, we focus on deviations from random walk as evidence of operational inefficiency in nonfrictionless markets. Therefore, it is important first to understand why random walk would be evidence of informational efficiency.

To some extent a stock's price is expected to drift up over time because, as noted, shareholders expect a positive return that is commensurate with the riskiness of the stock. This drift, however, would not be very apparent in short period price movements. (A return of 36% a year is associated with a price change of less than 0.1% per day.) Accordingly, we ignore price drift in the following discussion. Instead, what is of interest are those price changes that result from changes in investor desires, information, and expectations. The question addressed is whether these price changes can be predicted or whether they are random.

Assume some investors know that in one week other investors will discover something about a stock that will drive its price up 20%. Those who are currently in the know have an opportunity to capture the 20% increase for themselves and so can make excess profits. They do this by buying the stock at the lower price.

But as the knowledgeable investors transmit their buy orders to the market, the price of the stock is bid up until these people no longer expect a further, abnormal price increase. Consequently, the price increase that was expected in a week will have been realized in the current period.

The current adjustment of price to change that is anticipated for the future means that, in equilibrium, *all* expectations are reflected in the current value of price. Accordingly, it is not possible to predict when, how, or by how much

FIGURE 16.1 *Effect of a Market Demand Shift on the Price of an Asset. (a) Determination of the Initial Equilibrium Price P_0. (b) Shifts in the Aggregate Trade Curves Change the Market Price. (c) Contrast of the Initial Equilibrium Price P_0 and the New Equilibrium Price P_1*

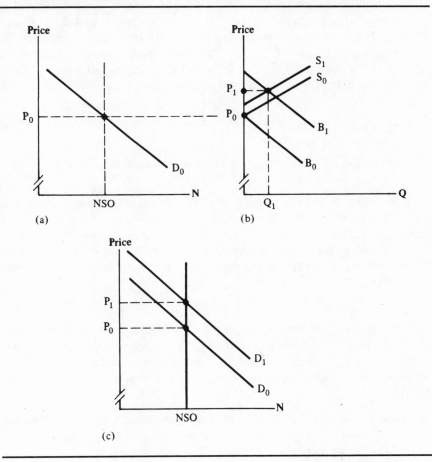

an equilibrium price will change in the future. This is because something that is *unanticipated* must occur in order for the equilibrium price to change. Therefore, in a market that is efficient in the sense that equilibrium prices are attained, market prices follow a "random walk" over time.

The random walk can be pictured for a call market environment with reference to Figure 16.1. Let the market be in the initial equilibrium position shown in Figure 16.1(a), with the aggregate demand curve being D_0, and the market price being P_0. Then, the associated trade curves will be B_0 and

S_0, as shown in Figure 16.1(b). Until the demand curve shifts for at least some trader, the market price will remain P_0.

Assume that after a short period of time has passed, some individual demand curves do shift. Perhaps there has been a change in expectations, or in the willingness of some investors to undertake risk, or in liquidity. Let the aggregate trade curves change to the lines labeled S_1 and B_1 in Figure 16.1(b). This shift causes the sell and buy curves to cross and results in Q_1 shares trading at a price of P_1. After the trade, market demand is the curve labeled D_1 in Figure 16.1(c), and the market clearing price is P_1. Once again, the market will have achieved equilibrium. In summary, this is what happened:

1. The price change is $\Delta P = P_1 - P_0$.
2. The return is $r_1 = \Delta P / P_0$.
3. After the price change, the market is in equilibrium, as it was before demand shifted.

What will the next price change be? For the reasons just discussed, this cannot be predicted. Perhaps the next shift will change price from P_1 to some new value, P_2. The next return will then be $r_2 = (P_2 - P_1)/P_1$. Because the second return (r_2) cannot be predicted before it occurs, it must be independent of everything that preceded it. Hence, r_2 must be independent of r_1. That is,

$$r_2 \neq f(r_1) \tag{16.1}$$

Nonetheless, might not the economic environment be such that information changes in a correlated fashion such that successive changes in the equilibrium prices are correlated? Abstracting from issues of operational inefficiency in a nonfrictionless market, the answer is no. The reason is as follows:

1. Aside from drift, if the sequence of price changes is not independent, knowledge of past price changes would enable investors to predict future price changes.
2. However, for these profitable predictions to be fulfilled in the future, investors could not act on them in the present. The reason is that, as is generally true with arbitrage trading, the very act of trading eliminates price patterns that can be profitably exploited.
3. It follows that a correlated sequence of price movements would suggest that investors are inept at spotting profitable price patterns.

Random walk is not caused by the pattern of information arrival, but rather by investor responses to information. Aside from long-run drift, a random walk is expected in a frictionless market that is informationally efficient.

Semistrong Form Tests

Semistrong form tests focus on the speed with which specific pieces of public information are reflected in stock prices. The announcement of a piece of information is considered an *event*, and the studies are commonly referred to as *event studies*.

One early event study established the methodology that has subsequently been used by many others: Fama, Fisher, Jensen, and Roll's analysis of the effect of stock splits on share price.[10] Stock splits are expected to increase the total value of shares because they convey a bullish signal to shareholders (since stock splits have historically been associated with strong earnings growth and increased dividends). Fama, Fisher, Jensen, and Roll (FFJR) report that, for 940 splits for NYSE stocks between 1927 and 1959, over two-thirds were followed by the announcement of a dividend increase.

FFJR examined the pattern of price changes observed in the months preceding and following splits. Specifically, they considered the difference between the actual return on a stock and the return expected, given the return on the market. (The relationship between the return on a stock and the return on the market is discussed in Chapter 12.) This difference is referred to as the *abnormal return*. They found for a sample of 622 stocks that abnormal returns tend to be considerably higher in the months preceding a stock split, that these returns continue to be somewhat higher in the months following a split for companies that do increase their dividends, and that they are somewhat lower in the months following a split for companies that do not increase their dividends.

FFJR captured these effects with the following procedure. For each stock in their sample, the month of the split was defined as month zero,* the last month before the split as month -1, the first month after the split as month $+1$, and so on, for a time span extending from month -29 to month $+30$. The abnormal return was then computed for each stock for each month. The month -29 abnormal returns were then averaged across the stocks, as were the month -28 abnormal returns, and so forth. The average abnormal returns were then cumulated, starting at month -29 and extending to month $+30$. The resulting cumulative average for all stocks is shown in Figure 16.2.

Notice that the cumulative average rises in the months preceding the split and is flat in the months following the split. As noted, FFJR also reported that the cumulative average rises somewhat after month zero for firms that do increase their dividends, and that it falls for firms that do not increase their dividends. These deviations of actual returns from expected values are evidence of the following adjustment pattern.

The considerably greater than expected returns before the split dates show that prices are adjusted upward on the basis of the optimistic signals that the

---

* Month zero is not, therefore, the same calendar month for the different stocks in the sample.

FIGURE 16.2   *Abnormal Price Changes Before and After Stock Splits*

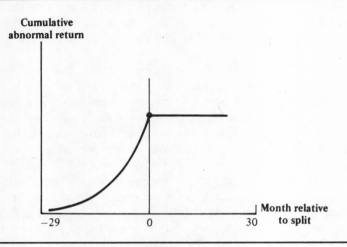

stock splits convey. It is also likely that the companies were enjoying above average and unsustainable prosperity in the two years before the split, and that the effect of this is also observed in the pattern of the residuals. The somewhat greater than expected returns after the split dates for companies that increased their dividends show the positive price responses that result when the bullish signal is confirmed. The lower than expected returns after the split dates for companies that do not increase their dividends are evidence of the negative price adjustments that occur when a bullish expectation turns out to have been unjustified.

For a large sample of stocks, the FFJR findings show that prices adjust to news before an event (for instance, before the dates of the stock splits) has occurred. Therefore, profitable trading strategies cannot be developed in relation to an event after it has occurred. A sizable number of other event studies in addition to that of Fama, Fisher, Jensen, and Roll have substantiated the informational efficiency of the market in the semistrong form of the hypothesis.

The tests of semistrong form efficiency have not, however, addressed the question of dynamic efficiency. As discussed in the previous chapter, information may be quickly reflected in prices, but some investors may nevertheless have a preferential position vis-à-vis the information flow. If so, these investors might receive and act upon information first and may receive excess profits.

Dynamic efficiency is particulary difficult to test, largely because price adjustments do occur rapidly. One would not expect to observe dynamic inefficiency in monthly price data as were used by FFJR and in many other studies. Rather, intraday prices could reveal a far more telling story. Dann, Mayers, and Raab, in their examination of the effect of block sales on transaction-to-transaction price movements, for instance, found that the price pressure caused by these sales does allow the formulation of profitable trading rules.[11] To earn a profit, however, an investor must make a purchase within *5 minutes* of the block transaction; within *15 minutes* of the transaction, prices appear to have adjusted completely to their previous levels. Given the speed with which price adjustments are made in the equity markets, one might question the inferences concerning market efficiency that have been drawn from studies based on monthly prices. If the studies had shown evidence of inefficiency, the results would have been striking. Unfortunately, the failure to demonstrate inefficiency does not carry as much conviction.

Strong Form Tests

The semistrong form of the EMH refers to news that is publicly available, the weak form refers to information that is contained in prior stock price movements, and the *strong form* refers to what remains: inside information, and that which can be "dug out" by superior security analysis. Unfortunately, academic researchers are not as a rule privy to such information. Therefore, researchers have attempted to draw inferences concerning strong form efficiency by testing whether or not investors who are most apt to enjoy this informational advantage do in fact realize excess returns.

Finding that the better informed do not make excess profits would be evidence in support of the EMH. On the other hand, observing that certain classes of investors make excess profits net of information costs may not be evidence against the EMH. The reason is twofold:

1. As discussed previously, informational efficiency requires that the marginal return to information equals the marginal cost of obtaining it. However, decreasing average and marginal returns and increasing average and marginal costs result in average returns exceeding average costs when marginal returns equal marginal costs. The reason is that a marginal value is less (greater) than an associated average value for a decreasing (increasing) average value function. Hence excess profits—such profits are sometimes referred to as *economic rent*—can be realized by some decison makers. Decision makers who undertake their own research are both producers and consumers of information. As producers they may face increasing average costs, and as consumers they may realize decreasing average returns.

2. As indicated previously: some investors do better than others simply because of luck. Therefore, larger realized returns *ex post* do not necessarily indicate that better decisions were made *ex ante*. For this

reason, excess *ex post* returns are not themselves evidence against the strong form of the EMH. Rather, to reject the hypothesis, one must demonstrate that excess returns accrue to one individual persistently (and thus are not explained by chance).

The empirical evidence shows that professional investment managers do not consistently realize superior portfolio returns. Mutual funds have been the most frequently studied of the institutions. Some of the best known studies that have shown that the funds do not outperform the market include those of Friend, Brown, Herman, and Vickers (1962), Sharpe (1966), and Jensen (1969).[12]

Insider Trading

The strong form of the EMH also refers to information possessed by insiders. Much evidence suggests that this aspect of strong form efficiency is violated, that insiders can realize abnormally high returns from trading on information they alone possess.

Insiders have an advantage vis-à-vis the information flow and can manipulate it. Further, they are able to "produce" information; for example, the management of a profitable corporation could, if unrestricted, realize personal gain by selling shares short while jeopardizing the profitability of the firm. Consequently, insider trading must be regulated.

"Insiders" are defined as the officers and directors of a corporation or any investor who owns more than 10% of a corporation's outstanding shares. Such individuals are required by the 1934 Act to report any transaction in the stock of their host corporation within 10 days after the month of the transaction. This information is contained in the *Official Summary of Securities Transactions and Holdings*, which is published monthly by the SEC. Corporate insiders are also prohibited from selling shares short and must return all short-run (six months or less) profits realized from trading their host company's stock.

SEC Rule 10b-5

It is illegal for insiders to trade on information that has not yet been made public. This restriction, imposed by SEC Rule 10b-5, known as the disclose or abstain rule, has provided the foundation for most federal enforcement concerning fraudulent conduct. The specific criteria for determining fraud under Rule 10b-5 have subsequently been established by the federal courts. To be in violation of the rule, the information used by a trader must be found to be material. That is, if revealed, the information would have to affect a contraparty's trading decision. The trader must also know that the information is unavailable to the public. An individual in possession of such nonpublic information has an obligation to disclose it before participating in a trade based upon it. A failure to disclose such information thus constitutes fraud. It is fraud, not unfairness or an inaccurate relationship between information and prices, that Section 10(b) of the 1934 Act is intended to prevent.

Merger Mania and Insider Trading

In the 1980s, insider trading was largely related to takeover activity. The complexity of Wall Street's takeover activity involved numerous people, including lawyers, accountants, typists, publishers, or others who, in the normal course of their jobs, receive information regarding merger and acquisition activity before the deals are publicly announced.

In the spring of 1986, the SEC exposed an enormous insider trading scandal. Dennis B. Levine was charged with realizing $12.6 million from trading illegally on inside information concerning corporate takeovers. Six months later, Ivan F. Boesky agreed to pay a penalty of $100 million to settle charges of trading on information illegally obtained. In March 1987, Boyd L. Jefferies agreed to plead guilty to two charges that involved securities law violations.

The Definition of Information

The definition of information is ambiguous. For example, knowledge that an important line of credit is being requested from a commercial bank is not in and of itself "information." But what if the bank indicates that the request is likely to be honored? What if the bank indicates that the request will be honored in three business days?

"Private" information is distinguished from "inside" information. Trading on the basis of private information is allowed; it is essential to the informational efficiency of the marketplace. The profits that a stock analyst earns based on his or her research are the incentive for information to be brought to light in the first place. Without this incentive, an insufficient amount of information may be supplied in the marketplace.

Arguments Against Restricting Insider Trading

Arguments both for and against insider trading restrictions are substantial. At the heart of the issue is market failure—the failure of the free market to achieve an efficient and equitable distribution of resources when the distribution of information among market participants is asymmetric. The complexity of the question is compounded by the fact that controlling insider trading is costly.

Manne was one of the first to argue against the trading restrictions.[13] According to Manne, profits realized through insider trading should be allowable as a reward for entrepreneurship. He and others have argued further that insider trading, while admittedly causing losses for those who are contraparties to the insider trades, benefits the broader community of investors by keeping prices more closely aligned with the underlying determinants of share value.

Insider trading restrictions have resulted in conflicts of interest. One department of an investment bank may, for instance, be in possession of information concerning a client firm that is relevant for customers of another department of the bank. The bank's fiduciary responsibility to the client firm dictates that the information be kept secret, but the bank's fiduciary responsibility to customers calls for disclosure. Securities firms have attempted to avoid such conflicts of interest by separating various departments with a mechanism known as a "Chinese wall." Nevertheless, investment banks at times find themselves in a no-win situation with regard to information that a client is unwilling to make public.

The following example suggests the difficulties involved. Assume the registered representatives at a brokerage house are promoting the stock of a manufacturing corporation at a time when the investment banking department of the securities firm knows that serious technological problems have emerged at one of the plants. The manufacturing corporation is unwilling to allow the securities firm to divulge the information, and a Chinese wall at the securities firm prevents the investment bankers from passing the information on to the registered reps. The brokerage firm, however, is not allowed to solicit customers without revealing all of the information that it has. They could, of course, stop trading in the client's stock; however, the very act of not trading would signal the existence of new information to the market. It appears that whichever way the securities firm turns, it will not have fully satisfied the dictates of the law.

The Difficulty of Control and Detection

Trading based on inside information is difficult to control and to detect. In a global environment trades can be made in countries where restrictions do not exist. Bank secrecy laws in Switzerland, for example, until recently prevented the disclosure of information concerning trades in U.S. stocks which were made on the basis of nonpublic information. Other places with bank secrecy laws include the Bahamas, Panama, Bermuda, and the Cayman Islands. In an environment of communications networks and complex financial operations it is exceedingly difficult to control informational leaks and to police those who might use information for their personal gain. Berg wrote in a *New York Times* article, "Wall Street is a warren of information 'networks'—cliques that exchange information regularly to win out over investors who are not part of any clique."[14] Further, an insider can, without restriction, exploit information relating to his or her own firm by trading the equity shares of a competitor, supplier, or customer firm that is also affected by the information. This further distorts the relationship between information and prices.

Beta Bias: Evidence on Lagged Price Adjustments

Although the absence of intertemporal correlation patterns in returns would confirm the efficient market hypothesis, the presence of such correlation does not imply a violation of the EMH if the patterns cannot be exploited because of their complexity and the existence of execution costs. In this section and the one that follows, it is shown that intertemporal return correlation does indeed exist. This is interpreted as a manifestation of illiquidity and inefficiencies in market operations, rather than as a refutation of the EMH.

This section presents evidence on serial cross-correlation in returns that is due to nonsynchronous (lagged) price adjustments. To this end, we use the market model

$$R_j = a + bR_M$$

where R_j is the return on an individual stock (j) and R_M is the return on the market (see Chapter 12 for further discussion of the equation). Biased estimates of the beta coefficient (b) are obtained when the market model is estimated using short period (i.e., daily) returns. The biased short period relationship is evidence of an *intervalling effect* caused by serial cross-correlation in returns.

Testing the Intervalling Effect on Beta

Beta is not subject to an intervalling effect in the absence of intertemporal correlations in security returns as discussed in Chapter 14. However, serial cross-correlation causes beta estimates obtained from short period returns to be biased downward for stocks that lag the market and to be biased upward for stocks that lead the market. Furthermore, the serial correlation causes R^2 (the square of the correlation coefficient of the market model regression equation) to be less for all stocks when shorter period returns are used for the estimation equation.[15] Therefore, we can obtain evidence on the accuracy of price determination by examining the intervalling effect on beta.

We report the findings of an analysis of the returns for 50 NYSE common stocks and for the Standard & Poor's 500 Stock Index, for the four year period 1 January 1970, to 31 December 1973.[16] The 50 stocks were selected as follows. The NYSE issues that had been listed on the Exchange throughout the four year period were ranked according to the market value of shares outstanding as of the last trading day of 1971 (the midpoint of the sample period). The array was then divided into deciles, and a random sample of five stocks was picked from each decile. Firms that did not have shares publicly held since 1965 were excluded and replaced by alternates randomly selected from the same decile.

For each of the 50 firms in the final sample, a series of 960 daily returns was used to estimate and to assess the intervalling effect on beta. A three pass regression design was employed for the study. In the first pass tests, returns for each stock were regressed on returns to the market index for 14 alternative differencing intervals ranging from 1 day to 20 days (700 first pass regressions were run). In the second pass tests, the first pass slope coefficients (beta) were regressed on differencing interval length for each stock (50 second pass regressions were run, with each based on 14 observations). In the third pass test, the second pass slope coefficients were regressed, across stocks, on the value of shares outstanding for each stock (one third pass regression was run, based on 50 observations).

First Pass Results

The first pass tests estimated beta coefficients for each of the 50 stocks (indexed by j) for each of 14 different measurement intervals (indexed by L). The market model regression equations were of the form

$$R^*_{jLt} = {}_1 a_{jL} + {}_1 b_{jL} R^*_{MLt} + e_{jLt} \qquad (16.2)$$

where $j = 1, \ldots, 50$ NYSE common stocks
$\qquad L = 1, \ldots, 6, 8, 10, 12, 14, 15, 16, 18, 20$ days
$\qquad t = 1, \ldots, 960/L$

where R^* is the logarithm of price relatives, R^*_{jLt} is the tth (log) return of length L for stock j, R^*_{MLt} is the corresponding return on the market index, e_{jLt} is the associated regression residual, and ${}_1 a_{jL}$ and ${}_1 b_{jL}$ are first pass regression coefficients.

The weaker explanatory power of the market model for shorter measurement intervals is shown by the deterioration in R^2 for the first pass regressions as the measurement interval, L, is shortened. Maximum, average, and minimum values of R^2, for the 50 stock sample, for select values of L are as follows:[17]

L	1	2	3	4	5	10	15	20
Max R^2:	.392	.486	.498	.517	.508	.525	.596	.697
Avg R^2:	.109	.164	.175	.202	.236	.305	.328	.404
Min R^2:	.020	.046	.056	.065	.077	.095	.070	.171

Second Pass Results

In the second pass tests, the 14 estimated values of beta for each stock were regressed on an inverse of the length of the differencing interval, L. The term *differencing interval* is commonly used to denote the length of the interval over which returns are measured. In this context, it has the same meaning as *measurement interval*. Because $_1b_{jL}$ is expected to approach its true value asymptotically as L increases, it cannot be a linear function of L, but may be a linear function of an inverse of L. The regression equations were of the form

$$_1b_{jL} = {_2a_j} + {_2b_j}(L)^{-.8} + e_{jL} \qquad (16.3)$$

where $_1b_{jL}$ is the first pass beta coefficient for the jth stock estimated for the Lth differencing interval, L is the length of the differencing interval, e_{jL} is the associated second pass regresson residual, and $_2a_j$ and $_2b_j$ are the second pass regression parameters.

As noted, the beta coefficient estimated by using short differencing interval returns is expected to be biased downward for stocks that lag the market and biased upward for stocks that lead the market. Therefore, since the second pass tests regressed beta on an inverse of L (specifically $L^{-.8}$), the second pass slope coefficient ($_2b_j$) is expected to be negative for stocks that lag the market and positive for stocks that lead the market. The exponent $-.8$ was selected as the value that, among several alternatives, produced the best second pass regression fit.

Table 16.2 shows the results of the second pass test. In the table, firms are ranked according to size (measured by the value of shares outstanding) from the smallest (firm 1) to the largest (firm 50). The column labeled R^2 gives the squared values of the correlation coefficients for the second pass regressions.

The slopes of the second pass regressions are negative for all but the largest issues, those of firms 44 and 48–50. This suggests that price changes

TABLE 16.2 *Summary Statistics for Second Pass Regressions*

$$_1b_{jL} = {_2}a_j + {_2}b_j(L)^{-.8} + e_{jL}$$

Firm	$_2b_j$	R^2	Firm	$_2b_j$	R^2
1	−0.936	0.607	26	−0.621	0.598
2	−0.897	0.575	27	−0.858	0.542
3	−0.738	0.710	28	−0.685	0.650
4	−0.839	0.579	29	−0.414	0.597
5	−1.150	0.496	30	−0.079*	0.047
6	−0.659	0.432	31	−0.191*	0.029
7	−0.612	0.690	32	−0.289	0.583
8	−1.296	0.671	33	−0.276*	0.188
9	−0.869	0.614	34	−0.319*	0.217
10	−0.380	0.339	35	−0.714	0.553
11	−0.313*a	0.141	36	−0.105*	0.021
12	−0.483	0.460	37	−0.312	0.522
13	−0.706	0.573	38	−0.087*	0.049
14	−0.759	0.326	39	−0.041*	0.003
15	−0.405	0.572	40	−0.117*	0.224
16	−0.476*	0.173	41	−0.350	0.352
17	−0.486	0.273	42	−0.286	0.672
18	−0.384	0.692	43	−0.010	0.271
19	−0.617	0.524	44	+0.050*	0.017
20	−0.520	0.494	45	−0.125	0.612
21	−0.367	0.413	46	−0.131	0.345
22	−0.789	0.654	47	−0.206*	0.225
23	−0.454*	0.091	48	+0.053*	0.111
24	−0.268	0.393	49	+0.122*	0.004
25	−0.429*	0.219	50	+0.432	0.712

[a] Asterisks indicate coefficients *not* significantly different from zero at the .05 significance level.

Source: Cohen, Hawawini, Maier, Schwartz, and Whitcomb, "Estimating and Adjusting for the Intervalling-Effect Bias in Beta," *Management Science*, vol. 29, no. 1, January 1983, pp. 135-138. Reprinted by permission.

lagged the market for almost all of the stocks in the sample. This is not surprising because the stratified random sampling procedure resulted in the inclusion of many small and medium size firms, whereas the market is represented by the S&P 500 index, an index of relatively large firms. The values reported in Table 16.2 suggest that the second pass regression slope parameter is more highly negative and generally more significant for the smallest companies than for the largest companies. This relationship is more rigorously assessed by the third pass test.

Third Pass Results

In the third pass test the 50 estimates of the intervalling effect as reflected by $_2b_j$, the slope parameters of the second pass regressions, were regressed on the logarithm of the value of shares outstanding for each issue. Issue size should proxy the extent to which a stock leads or lags the market: larger companies are more intensively followed by security analysts, and hence share prices for larger companies should respond more rapidly to informational change. The size of the market for a stock is also an important variable in the analysis of price volatility and the size of bid-ask spreads as discussed in Chapters 13 and 14.

The regression equation used for the third pass test was

$$_2b_j = {}_3a + {}_3b\ LVSO_j + e_j \tag{16.4}$$

where $_2b_j$ is the slope of the second pass regression for firm j, $LVSO_j$ is the logarithm of the value of shares outstanding for firm j, e_j is the associated third pass regression residual, and $_3a$ and $_3b$ are the third pass regression parameters.

Similar three pass regression tests were also run by Fung, Schwartz, and Whitcomb (1985). This latter study was based on a sample of 52 issues traded on the Paris Bourse for the period 3 January 1977 to 3 April 1980. Third pass regression results for both studies are shown in Table 16.3 (where CHMSW identifies the Cohen, Hawawini, Maier, Schwartz and Whitcomb findings, and FSW identifies the Fung, Schwartz, and Whitcomb findings).

The similarities between the two findings are striking. Despite variations in methodology used, in the time periods covered, and in the market centers

TABLE 16.3 *Results of Third Pass Regression Tests*[a]

	CHMSW	FSW
$_3a$	−2.637	−3.442
	(−11.46)	(−3.60)
$_3b$	+0.181	+0.162
	(+9.67)	(+3.23)
R^2	0.661	0.173

[a] t-statistics given in parentheses.

considered, the third pass regressions show that the intervalling effect is, as expected, significantly positively related to the value of shares outstanding. The finding does not appear to be a statistical artifact or a manifestation of noise in security returns. For the CHMSW sample, variation in the value of shares outstanding explains 66% of the variation of the second pass regression slope parameter. It would be highly unlikely that the third pass equation would have such a high explanatory power if a lead/lag pattern of the type posited did not exist in security returns. The evidence that this pattern does exist supports the hypothesis that, in the short run, stock price movements are excessively volatile because price determination in the equity markets is inaccurate.

The relationship between the value of shares outstanding and the strength of the intervalling effect is very similar but statistically weaker for Paris Bourse issues than for NYSE issues. The explanation may be that the value of shares outstanding is a poorer proxy of price adjustment delays for French stocks than for U.S. stocks. The difference may also be accounted for by the difference in the market architecture of the U.S. and French systems that existed at that time—the French market was a call system with no dealers/specialists, and the U.S. exchange markets are continuous trading systems with specialists (see Chapters 2 and 5).[18]

Execution Costs and the Correlation of Returns

Execution costs can explain the existence of intertemporal returns correlation in informationally efficient markets, as the following example suggests.

Assume the price series:

Point in time:	0	1	2	3	4
Transaction price:	50	51	52	54	57
Return:		$\frac{1}{50}$	$\frac{1}{51}$	$\frac{2}{52}$	$\frac{3}{54}$

The profitability of this series would appear to be the return one could realize from exploiting the positively autocorrelated series of returns. Alternatively assume:

Point in time:	0	1	2	3	4
Transaction price:	50	52	49	51	48
Return:		$\frac{2}{50}$	$-\frac{3}{52}$	$\frac{2}{49}$	$-\frac{3}{51}$

The profitability of this series would appear to be the return one could realize from the negatively autocorrelated series of returns. The second and fourth returns, $-\frac{3}{52}$ and $-\frac{3}{51}$, would be exploited by short sales. The random walk hypothesis is that, by appropriately buying and selling so as to exploit these return patterns, traders alter the price series (increase prices by their purchases and decrease prices by their sales) and so eliminate the patterns.

But how might the trader appropriately buy and sell so as to realize excess profits from either of the preceding returns series? Even if the trader were reasonably certain about what the price movements would be, could he or she have actually obtained any or all of the returns in the sequence? The fact is, the observed returns are the result of a process that involves market orders hitting limit orders, limit orders being stored on the limit order book, and limit orders tied at a price executing according to priority rules. Consequently, no individual trader can enter the system and, even with perfect foresight over a brief interval of time, simply realize the pattern of returns that will be measured for a stock.

The conclusion follows that deviations from random walk are not necessarily evidence against informational efficiency. The random walk test is too strict; returns autocorrelation need not imply the existence of profitable but unexploited trading opportunities because the returns that are tested for autocorrelation may be associated with price sequences at which no individual trader could have traded.

The bid-ask spread is one reason why a historic pattern of transaction price changes may not be exploited by a trader. The transactions that generate the observed price changes are triggered by orders to buy at market hitting the ask and by orders to sell at market hitting the bid. The trader who uses market orders, however, pays the spread as an execution cost, whereas the trader who uses limit orders must accept the probability that his or her limit orders will not execute.

The Effect of Execution Costs on Intertemporal Returns Correlation

This section shows that a fixed percentage cost (C) can introduce negative first order correlation in returns.

Let P_t^e be the unobservable frictionless market price at time t, and let P_t^r be the realized transaction price at point in time t.* With regard to the determination of P_t^r assume:

A1: A continuous market trading regime.

A2: All orders are for the same size (one round lot).

A3: A transaction is triggered when a market order to buy hits an ask quotation or when a market order to sell hits a bid quotation.

---

* The subsection is based on Roll, "A Simple Implicit Measure of the Effective Bid-ask Spread in an Efficient Market," *The Journal of Finance,* September 1984, used with permission.

A4: The market ask always exceeds the frictionless market price by the percentage amount C, and the market bid is always less than the frictionless market price by the percentage amount C.

A5: P_t^e follows a random walk over time.

A6: $\sigma_t = \sigma_u$ for all short periods t, u = 1, ..., T.

A7: $\rho_{t,u}$ is the same for all $|t - u|$.

C is the execution cost of trading by market orders. From assumptions A3 and A4, the realized price at time t is

$$P_t^r = \begin{cases} P_t^e(1 + C) & \text{for a market order purchase} \\ P_t^e(1 - C) & \text{for a market order sale} \end{cases} \quad (16.5)$$

where C > 0.

This simple framework can be used to show how an estimate of C might be obtained from a measure of the autocovariance of short period returns. Using the relationship $Cov(x, y) = E(xy) - E(x)E(y)$, the covariance between r_{t-1} and r_t is

$$Cov(r_{t-1}, r_t) = E(r_{t-1}r_t) - E(r_{t-1})E(r_t) \quad (16.6)$$

The expected return in any period that is attributable to the transaction price changing randomly between the bid and the ask quotations can be obtained from the following table:

P_{t-1}	P_t	r_t	Probability
Ask	Ask	0	¼
Ask	Bid	-2C	¼
Bid	Ask	+2C	¼
Bid	Bid	0	¼

Multiplying the returns by their associated probabilities and summing gives

$$E(r_t) = \tfrac{1}{4}(-2C) + \tfrac{1}{4}(2C) + \tfrac{1}{2}(0) = 0 \quad (16.7)$$

Therefore, Equation 16.6 becomes

$$Cov(r_{t-1}, r_t) = E(r_{t-1}r_t) \quad (16.8)$$

The adjacent returns r_{t-1} and r_t are given by three prices: P_{t-2}, P_{t-1}, and P_t. Each of these prices could, with equal probability, be equal to a bid or an ask quotation. Therefore, the adjacent returns could result from any of the sequences shown in the following table, with each sequence having an equal probability of occurring. Because P_t^e is assumed to follow a random walk, only those price changes that are attributable to the realized transaction price moving between the bid and the ask quotations need be considered to compute the autocovariance term. The table also shows the alternative pairings of adjacent returns, their associated probabilities of occurrence (pr), and the product $(r_{t-1})(r_t)(pr)$:

(1) P_{t-2}	(2) P_{t-1}	(3) P_t	(4) r_{t-1}	(5) r_t	(6) pr	(7) (4)(5)(6)
Ask	Bid	Bid	$-2C$	0	$\frac{1}{8}$	0
Ask	Bid	Ask	$-2C$	$+2C$	$\frac{1}{8}$	$-\frac{1}{2}C^2$
Ask	Ask	Bid	0	$-2C$	$\frac{1}{8}$	0
Ask	Ask	Ask	0	0	$\frac{1}{8}$	0
Bid	Bid	Bid	0	0	$\frac{1}{8}$	0
Bid	Bid	Ask	0	$+2C$	$\frac{1}{8}$	0
Bid	Ask	Bid	$+2C$	$-2C$	$\frac{1}{8}$	$-\frac{1}{2}C^2$
Bid	Ask	Ask	$+2C$	0	$\frac{1}{8}$	0

Summing column (7) gives the expected value of the product of adjacent returns,

$$E(r_{t-1}r_t) = -C^2 \tag{16.9}$$

Substituting into Equation 16.8 gives

$$Cov(r_{t-1}, r_t) = -C^2 \tag{16.10}$$

Equation 16.10 shows that execution costs do cause adjacent returns to be correlated. The correlation is given by term $-C^2$.

The Market Efficiency Coefficient (MEC)

The MEC measures the impact of execution costs on a stock's short period price volatility.[*] Specifically it relates the volatility of realized prices (P_t^r) to an estimate of the volatility of equilibrium prices (P_t^e). The measure is scaled so that values different from unity are evidence that realized prices, P_t^r, do not equal frictionless market values, P_t^e.

To obtain MEC, first write

$$R_T^* = \sum_{t=1}^{T} r_t^* \tag{16.11}$$

---

[*] The analysis in the remainder of this section and in the following section is based on J. Hasbrouck and R. Schwartz, "Liquidity and Execution Costs in Equity Markets," *Journal of Portfolio Management*, Spring 1988, used with permission.

where $R_T^* = \ln(1 + R_T)$
$r_t^* = \ln(1 + r_t)$
$R_T = P_T/P_0 - 1$
$r_t = P_t/P_{t-1} - 1$

Taking the variance of Equation 16.11 gives:

$$\text{Var}(R_T^*) = T \ \text{Var}(r_t^*) + 2 \ \text{Var}(r_t^*) \sum_{s=1}^{T-1} (T - s)\rho_{1,1+s} \qquad (16.12)$$

Dividing both sides of Equation 16.12 by $T[\text{Var}(r_t^*)]$ we have

$$\frac{\text{Var}(R_T^*)}{T \ \text{Var}(r_t^*)} = 1 + 2 \sum_{s=1}^{T-1} \frac{T - s}{T} \rho_{1,1+s} \qquad (16.13)$$

Equation 16.13 shows that the ratio of $\text{Var}(R_T^*)$ to $T[\text{Var}(r_t^*)]$ is greater than unity if the intertemporal correlations are predominantly positive, and less than unity if the intertemporal correlations are predominantly negative.

To assess the variance ratio, write

$$\text{MEC} = \frac{\text{Var}(R_T^*)}{T[\text{Var}(r_t^*)]}$$

$$= 1 + 2 \sum_{s=1}^{T-1} \frac{T - s}{T} \rho_{1,1+s} \qquad (16.14)$$

where MEC is the market efficiency coefficient.

For a sufficiently long interval of length T, $\text{Var}(R_T^*)$ in Equation 16.14 is an estimate of the volatility of P_T^e. Since P_T^e is assumed to follow a random walk, $\text{Var}(R_T^*)/T$ on the right-hand side of Equation 16.14 is an estimate of the volatility of P_t^e for the shorter interval of length t. $\text{Var}(r_t^*)$ itself measures the volatility of the observed price, P_t^r, over the shorter interval. Hence the MEC relates the estimated volatility of the unobservable equilibrium price to the observed volatility of the realized price over brief time intervals. An advantage of the MEC is that, unlike the standard weak form EMH tests of correlation between adjacent returns, MEC reflects the full pattern of first and higher order correlation. Negative serial returns correlation and inflated short period variance result in MECs less than unity; positive serial returns correlation and dampened short period variance result in MECs greater than unity.

The MEC is unaffected by informational change, price uncertainty, and long run market power effects. This is because these three factors affect long and short interval returns variance proportionately, and MEC assesses short period returns variance *in relation* to long period returns variance. MEC differs from unity only if returns are serially correlated. Such correlation, however, would be attributable to execution costs, not to informational change, or to price uncertainty, or to market power. The larger the execution cost, C, the greater the volatility of P_t^r in relation to the volatility of P_t^e, and hence the lower the MEC.

MEC can be measured for a stock by using different time intervals. In the empirical analysis reported in this chapter, returns variance was measured for half-hour (hh), day (d), and two day (2d) intervals. The shorter period (half-hour to two-day) MEC is*

$$MEC_S = \frac{Var(r_{2d}^*)}{24[Var(r_{hh}^*)]} \qquad (16.15)$$

The longer period (day to two day) MEC is

$$MEC_L = \frac{Var(r_{2d}^*)}{2[Var(r_d^*)]} \qquad (16.16)$$

The relationship between execution costs (C) and MEC is given by

$$C = \begin{cases} \sigma(r_{hh}^*)(\frac{1}{2} - \frac{1}{2}MEC_s)^{1/2} > 0 \\ -\sigma(r_{hh}^*)(\frac{1}{2}MEC_s - \frac{1}{2})^{1/2} < 0 \end{cases} \qquad (16.17)$$

See the appendix of this chapter for the derivation.

Determinants of MEC and of C

If a market were frictionless, one would expect to observe MECs that fluctuate randomly about unity, and estimates of C that fluctuate randomly about zero. In nonfrictionless markets, the following factors could cause MEC to be less than unity and C to be greater than zero:

- The market impact effect
- The bid-ask spread
- Price rounding
- Inaccurate price determination that involves overreaction to news (overshooting)

---

* T = 24 in equation (16.15) reflects the fact that, for the empirical study reported in the following section, the trading day comprised six hours.

The following factors could cause MEC to be greater than unity and C to be less than zero:

- Sequential information arrival
- The limit order book
- Market maker intervention
- Inaccurate price determination that involves partial adjustment to news (undershooting)

Each of the factors that cause positive returns correlation implies that a market order trader may be able to purchase shares at a price below P_t^e or may be able to sell shares at a price above P_t^e. This can be seen in relation to market maker intervention. Assume, for instance, that a transaction has occurred at some point in time $t - 1$ because a market order to sell has executed at the bid, and that the bid was below the equilibrium price. Then let the equilibrium price and the market ask rise one-half point or more by time t, let there be no intermediate transaction, and assume the arrival of a market order to buy at time t. If the specialist does not intervene, and if the ask is above the equilibrium price, the new order would cause the realized transaction price to increase by more than one-half point from the transaction at $t - 1$ to the transaction at t.

If a one-half point transaction-to-transaction price change is unacceptable to the exchange, the specialist intervenes by executing the market order to buy at a price that is closer to (for example, only one-quarter point above) the previous transaction price. This means that the market order buyer has realized an execution at a price that is less than the frictionless market price.

The case just considered implies a wealth transfer to the market order buyer. This transfer can be considered a negative execution cost. A negative execution cost is also implied by the ability of a market order buyer (seller) to obtain a price that is lower (higher) than P_t^e because of either sequential information dissemination (the market order trader receives the news before the quotes have fully adjusted), the presence of a stale limit order on the book, or inaccurate price determination that involves partial adjustment to news.

The following rule for transaction price determination is consistent with the negative cost interpretation:

$$P_t^r = \begin{cases} P_t^e(1 + C) & \text{if market order purchase and } P_t^e > P_{t-1}^e \\ P_t^e(1 - C) & \text{if market order sale and } P_t^e < P_{t-1}^e \end{cases} \quad (16.18)$$

where $C < 0$.

A market maker, of course, cannot realize a profit by giving transactions at negative C. This does not imply, however, that market making in MEC > 1, $C < 0$ stocks is unprofitable. C is a simple average that doesn't give less weight to smaller trades, and stabilizing trades need only be for 100 shares. C therefore underestimates execution costs, and market making can be profitable for MEC > 1 stocks.

As an average, C could be refined. The most meaningful adjustment to make would be to disaggregate the order flow and to compute separate MECs and Cs for large and for small trades. A contrast of MEC and of C for large and small trades would give more direct evidence of the market impact effect. However, such an analysis has not, thus far, been undertaken.

Several studies have attempted to isolate and to assess directly the price impact of block trades[19] and to measure execution costs for large orders.[20] The evidence is that price impact effects and hence execution costs are appreciable, but that the price effects vanish quickly (within approximately 15 minutes, according to Dann, Mayers, and Raab, 1977).

Empirical Analysis of MEC and of C

The Test Sample

This section summarizes the results of an analysis of the market efficiency coefficient and of execution costs that was based on a transaction record for 1209 NYSE, 200 Amex, and 651 NASDAQ/NMS issues.[21] The transaction records used comprise all trades and bid-ask quotations for all listed issues for the 42 trading days (only 41 days of prices were available for Amex issues because of collection errors) in March and April 1985. The data were collected electronically by a firm under contract to the American Stock Exchange; essentially, they constitute a transcription of the ticker tapes. All quotes are immediately posted to the tape whenever a revision occurs.

Excluded from the analysis were issues that (1) had fewer than 200 transactions during the period, (2) had stock splits or stock dividends during the period, (3) had an average price under $10, and/or (4) did not pass a 10% price reversal filter. The 10% price reversal filter screened for price increases (decreases) of 10% or more that were immediately followed by price decreases (increases) of 10% or more. Reversals of this magnitude are assumed to have resulted from recording errors. For instance, a price sequence such as 53, 35, 53, where the entry 35 is a single transcription error in the price record, causes two spurious adjacent returns of opposite sign. These errors would cause price reversals and negative serial returns correlation and hence would have depressed the value of the MEC.

The largest firms in the study are listed on the NYSE, although some very large issues are traded in the NASDAQ/NMS market. Medium size issues in the NASDAQ/NMS are similar in size to medium size NYSE issues. A disproportionate number of issues in the smallest size category (less than $100 million) are traded in the NASDAQ/NMS and Amex markets.

The NYSE and the Amex are clearly different in terms of issue size. The two exchanges, however, are very similar structurally and differ considerably from the OTC market. Therefore, an observation that the MECs and execution costs are similar for the two exchange markets but are different for the exchange and the OTC markets would suggest a significant difference in the liquidity provided by the exchange and the OTC markets.

The Measurement of MEC

The trading day during the sample period was from 10:00 A.M. to 4:00 P.M. (the trading day currently is from 9:30 A.M. to 4:00 P.M.). Half-hour returns were computed by dividing the trading day into 12 periods: 11 half-hour periods from 10:30 A.M. to 4:00 P.M. and the period from 4:00 P.M. to 10:30 A.M. on the following day. The 10:00 A.M. to 10:30 A.M. period was merged with the overnight period (which excludes the opening trade) because the overnight period is sufficiently inactive, and because markets for individual stocks do not open (that is, trading does not start) precisely at 10:00 A.M. Trading usually starts at some time during the first half-hour after the opening bell has sounded.

Returns were computed as the logarithm of price relatives. Returns variances were computed assuming the mean return to be zero: for intervals as brief as those examined in the study, the expected return is so close to zero that estimation errors would cause sample averages to be less reliable estimates than a value of zero of the true mean return. MECs were computed from the variance estimates for the half-hour, day, and two day intervals according to Equations (16.15) and (16.16).

Hypotheses Tested

Two primary hypotheses were tested empirically:

Hypothesis 1:   MECs based on short period returns variances are predominantly less than unity.

Reason: Price reversals are expected to outweigh continuations for most issues.

Hypothesis 2:   For all issues and market centers, values of MEC approach unity as the shorter period returns interval on which they are based is increased.

Reason: Serial correlation patterns are expected to decay as the measurement interval is lengthened.

Test Results

Table 16.4 presents summary statistics for MECs, execution costs (C), and other variables for the total sample and for the three market center sub-

TABLE 16.4 *Descriptive Statistics*[a]

Variable	Total sample	Amex	NYSE	NASDAQ/NMS
Number of issues	2060	200	1209	651
Number of transactions per issue	1274 (1753)	608 (963)	1593 (1970)	909 (1355)
MEC_S	0.683 (0.386)	0.862 (0.463)	0.764 (0.381)	0.488 (0.258)
MEC_L	1.015 (0.209)	1.005 (0.200)	1.027 (0.199)	0.995 (0.226)
C (percent)	0.240 (0.303)	0.123 (0.295)	0.148 (0.254)	0.438 (0.289)
Price[b]	3.158 (0.517)	2.940 (0.497)	3.289 (0.515)	2.990 (0.453)
Value of shares outstanding[b]	12.539 (1.421)	11.453 (1.065)	13.129 (1.361)	11.778 (1.006)
Average bid-ask spread ($\times$ 100)	1.375 (0.769)	1.342 (0.449)	1.065 (0.468)	1.933 (0.938)

[a] Standard deviations are given in parentheses.
[b] Logarithmic values.

samples. Transactions per issue are greatest on the NYSE followed by the NASDAQ/NMS and then the Amex. Average issue size as measured by value of shares outstanding is comparable for the Amex and NASDAQ/NMS samples and is higher for the NYSE. The average price of an issue is highest on the NYSE, followed by the NASDAQ/NMS and the Amex. The markets differ with respect to the average bid-ask spread, with the NYSE having the lowest value and the NASDAQ/NMS the highest.

Average values of MEC_S are less than unity for all market subsamples. The average MEC_S is substantially lower for the NASDAQ/NMS than for either of the exchange markets, and somewhat higher for the Amex than for the NYSE. The distribution of the MEC_S is indicated in Table 16.5. For the NASDAQ/NMS distribution, 60% of the issues are in the less than 0.5 category, whereas only 23% of the Amex and 27% of the NYSE issues are in this group. A substantial proportion of the exchange stocks have MEC_S greater than unity: 30% for the Amex and 24% for the NYSE, versus 7% for the NASDAQ/NMS.

The distribution of the MEC_S, for all three market centers, confirms hypothesis 1: the MEC measurements based on short period returns variances

TABLE 16.5   *The Percentage Distribution of MEC$_S$*

Sample	Range of MEC$_S^a$			
	<0.5	0.5–0.75	0.75–1	>1
Total	38	25	18	19
Amex	23	22	25	30
NYSE	27	27	22	24
NASDAQ/NMS	60	22	11	7

^{a} Values in table are percentages based on MEC$_S$ classification within each indicated sample: horizontal totals are 100%.
Source: Hasbrouck and Schwartz (1988), used with permission.

are predominantly less than unity. As shown in Table 16.4, the MEC$_L$ averages, on the other hand, are distributed closely about unity, and differences in the MEC$_L$ averages among the three market centers are not statistically significant. This confirms hypothesis 2: values of MEC approach unity as the shorter period returns interval on which the measure is based is increased.

Values of the execution cost (C) for the three market centers are also reported in Table 16.4. These costs were computed for each issue according to Equation 16.17, using estimates of the standard deviation of half-hour returns and of MEC$_S$. Values of C were averaged across firms to obtain the values shown in the table. Execution costs do not differ significantly between the two exchanges, but are significantly higher for the NASDAQ/NMS market than for either of the exchange markets.

The dollar magnitude of execution costs can be assessed by applying the values of C reported in Table 16.4 to a stock trading at the $20 level, roughly the average price for the entire sample. The dollar costs are as follows:

Sample	Dollar cost
Total	$.050
Amex	.025
NYSE	.030
NASDAQ/NMS	.090

Additional analysis of share price, value of shares outstanding, and market center effects on MEC and C are presented in the appendix to this chapter.

Implication

The analyses of MEC and of C suggest that the market process does cause prices to deviate from frictionless market values, that the MEC_S measure is sensitive to these deviations, and that execution costs are appreciable.

The behavior of the MEC statistic and the bias in market model beta indicate the presence of serial and serial cross-correlation in stock returns. These correlation patterns need not imply violations of the Efficient Market Hypothesis; most likely, they are manifestations of the illiquidity of the markets.

Appendix—Further Analysis of MEC

The Relationship Between MEC and C

Estimates of MEC_S can be translated into measures of C. If realized transaction prices (P_t^r) were related to underlying equilibrium prices (P_t^e) according to equation (16.5), only first order correlation ($\rho_{1.2}$) would be present in the returns series. Thus, for $\rho_{1,1+s}$ equal to zero for all $s > 1$, Equation 16.14 becomes:

$$MEC_S = 1 + \frac{2(T-1)}{T}\rho_{1.2} \qquad (16.A1)$$

Multiplying both sides of Equation 16.A1 by $Var(r_{hh}^*)$ gives

$$MEC_S Var(r_{hh}^*) = Var(r_{hh}^*) + 2\left(\frac{T-1}{T}\right)Cov(r_{hh}^*) \qquad (16.A2)$$

where $Cov(r_{hh}^*)$ is the autocovariance of the half-hour returns.

Using Equation 16.14, the left-hand side of Equation 16.A2 can be written as $Var(r_{2d}^*)/24$, which is an estimate of the volatility of P_t^e over half-hour intervals. Using this relationship and rearranging Equation 16.A2 gives

$$Var(r_{hh(r)}^*) = Var(r_{hh(e)}^*) - 2\left(\frac{T-1}{T}\right)Cov(r_{hh}^*) \qquad (16.A3)$$

where $Var(r_{hh(r)}^*)$ and $Var(r_{hh(e)}^*)$ are, respectively, the observed variance of half-hour returns and the inferred variance of half-hour returns for a frictionless environment. The second term on the right-hand side of Equation 16.A3 is the component of observed returns variance that is attributable to execution costs. Because of the price reversals and negative serial correlation introduced by $C > 0$, $Cov(r_{hh}^*)$ is expected to be negative; thus the second term on the right-hand side of Equation (16.A3) is expected to be positive, and hence the variance of half-hour returns is expected to be greater than it would be in a frictionless market.

The difference between the volatility of P_t^e and the volatility of P_t^r can be analyzed by taking T to be long enough so that the term $T/(T - 1)$ can be ignored, and by solving Equation 16.A2 for $Cov(r_{hh}^*)$:

$$Cov(r_{hh}^*) = \frac{1}{2}[Var(r_{hh}^*)(MEC_S - 1)] \tag{16.A4}$$

Given assumption (A2) (all orders are the same size), the autocovariance term can be related to the execution cost, C.

For C Positive. Substituting Equation 16.10 into 16.A4 and solving for C give

$$C = \sigma(r_{hh}^*)(\frac{1}{2} - \frac{1}{2}MEC_S)^{1/2} \tag{16.A5}$$

where $\sigma(r_{hh}^*)$ is the standard deviation of half-hour returns.

For C Negative. The relationship between MEC and C is not as readily derived for the case in which execution costs are negative (which implies MEC > 1). Equation 16.5 has to be respecified (see Equation 16.18) and Equation 16.A5 cannot be used (because MEC > 1 on the right-hand side calls for taking the square root of a negative number). The Equation used by Hasbrouck and Schwartz for estimating C for MEC > 1 is

$$C = -\sigma(r_{hh}^*)(\frac{1}{2}MEC_S - \frac{1}{2})^{1/2} < 0 \tag{16.A6}$$

Equations 16.A5 and 16.A6 give Equation 16.17 in the text.

Multivariate Analysis

Three additional hypotheses were tested by Hasbrouck and Schwartz (1988) using regression analysis:

Hypothesis 3: The values of MEC in each market center are positively related to share prices.

Reason: Price rounding effects are expected to be weaker for higher priced issues, *ceteris paribus.*

Hypothesis 4: The values of MEC in each market center are positively related to the value of shares outstanding.

Reason: Market impact effects are expected to be weaker for issues with a large value of shares outstanding.

Hypothesis 5: The values of MEC in each market center are negatively related to average percentage bid-ask spreads.

Reason: Price reversals are expected to have a lessened effect when spreads are smaller, *ceteris paribus.*

Five independent variables were included in the multiple regression tests:

1. *LVSO:* The logarithm of the value of shares outstanding for an issue in millions of dollars

2. *ABAS:* The average bid-ask spread for an issue measured as the average over all quote records of the logarithm of the ask price minus the logarithm of the bid price

3. *LP:* The logarithm of the average transaction price of an issue over the sample period

4. *DNYSE:* An intercept dummy variable that is assigned a value of 1 for all NYSE issues and a value of 0 for all other issues

5. *DAmex:* An intercept dummy variable that is assigned a value of 1 for all Amex issues and a value of 0 for all other issues

Bivariate correlations are reported in Table 16.A1. These results support hypotheses 3 through 5: the MECs are negatively related to the *average bid-ask spread* (ABAS), positively related to the *logarithmic value of share price* (LP), and positively related to the *logarithmic value of shares outstanding* (LVSO). Furt'..er, each of these relationships is appreciably stronger for the shorter interval MEC_S than for the longer interval MEC_L.

Table 16.A2 gives the results of the multivariate regression analysis used to assess the MEC_S relationships. Equations 1 through 3 show that the simple relationships reported in Table 16.A1 for LVSO, ABAS, and LP persist when market center dummy variables are included in the regression equation. The coefficients for the intercept dummy variables can be used to rank the values of MEC for the three market centers with LVSO, ABAS, and/or LP held constant. For instance, the intercept value of 0.789 in equation 2 shows that, for ABAS = 0, DNYSE = 0, and DAmex = 0, MEC_S for the NASDAQ/NMS market is 0.789. Adding DNYSE = 0.141 to 0.789 shows that, ABAS = 0, MEC_S for the NYSE market is 0.930. Adding DAmex

TABLE 16.A1   *Bivariate Correlations (Total Sample)*

	MEC_L	C	LP	LVSO	ABAS
MEC_S	.537	−.800	.422	.241	−.400
MEC_L		−.426	.247	.189	−.274
C			−.485	−.353	.614
LP				.662	−.685
LVSO					−.704

Source: Hasbrouck and Schwartz (1988), used with permission.

TABLE 16.A2   *Regressions with MEC$_S$ as Dependent Variable*[a]

Eq.	Const.	LVSO	ABAS	LP	DNYSE	DAmex	R^2
1.	−.102	.040			.214	.394	.156
	(−1.34)	(7.80)			(11.06)	(13.68)	
2.	.789		−.156		.141	.282	.202
	(30.73)		(−13.68)		(7.34)	(9.94)	
3.	−.384			.291	.189	.389	.269
	(−8.46)			(19.99)	(11.60)	(14.74)	
4.	−.307		−.016	.277	.180	.379	.270
	(−3.75)		(−1.12)	(14.01)	(9.67)	(13.51)	

[a] 2060 observations: t-statistics are given in parentheses; R^2 is corrected for degrees of freedom.
Source: Hasbrouck and Schwartz (1988), used with permission.

= 0.282 to 0.789 shows that, ABAS = 0, MEC$_S$ for the Amex market is 1.071.

The coefficients for the exchange dummy variables in all four equations in Table 16.A2 indicate that the *ceteris paribus* rankings of the three market centers by MEC$_S$ are the same as those observed in the raw averages: the Amex is the highest, followed by the NYSE, and then by the NAS-DAQ/NMS. Hypotheses 2 through 4 are also confirmed.

LP is the most significant explanatory variable. Inclusion of LP in the regression equations significantly alters the coefficients of ABAS and LVSO: inclusion of LP with ABAS (equation 4) causes the ABAS coefficient to be insignificantly different from zero (though still negative); inclusion of LP with LVSO (results not reported here) causes the coefficient of LVSO to be negative. The LP variable, however, changes neither the sign nor the significance of the market center dummy coefficients.

Table 16.A3 reports the results of the multivariate regression analysis used to assess the MEC$_L$ relationships. The overall pattern of relationships is similar to that reported in Table 16.A2 for the MEC$_S$ tests, but the values of the market center dummy coefficients are considerably more variable, the rank order relationships implied by the coefficients of the dummy variables are unstable, and the overall explanatory power of the MEC$_L$ regressions is considerably below that of the MEC$_S$ regressions. These results support hypothesis 5: they suggest that the serial correlation in daily returns is less pronounced than in half-hourly returns and, consequently, that the manifestation of market illiquidity is not detected by the variance analysis when price changes over daily and longer periods represent the shorter measurement interval.

TABLE 16.A3 *Regressions with MEC$_L$ as Dependent Variable^a*

Eq.	Const.	LVSO	ABAS	LP	DNYSE	DAmex	R^2
1.	.657	.028			−.003	.022	.035
	(14.88)	(7.71)			(−.25)	(1.30)	
2.	1.165		−8.817		−.044	−.042	.082
	(78.06)		(−13.28)		(−3.96)	(−2.55)	
3.	.694			.101	.002	.015	.062
	(24.90)			(11.24)	(.22)	(.93)	
4.	1.010		−6.842	.039	−.039	−.028	.087
	(20.31)		(−7.63)	(3.27)	(−3.44)	(−1.67)	

^{a} t-statistics are given in parentheses. R^2 is corrected for degrees of freedom.
Source: Hasbrouck and Schwartz (1988), used with permission.

Table 16.A4 reports the results of the multivariate regression analysis used to assess the behavior of C. Equations 1 through 4 parallel their counterparts in Tables 16.A2 and 16.A3. The overall pattern of results is consistent with that shown in Tables 16.A2 and 16.A3. ABAS, however, appears to be considerably more significant in the C regressions than in the MEC regressions. Nevertheless, the significance of DNYSE, DAmex, and LP in the equations that include ABAS suggests that the bid-ask spread, by itself, is not a comprehensive measure or determination of execution costs.

TABLE 16.A4 *Regressions with C ($\times$ 100) as Dependent Variable^a*

Eq.	Const.	LVSO	ABAS	LP	DNYSE	DAmex	R^2
1.	2.174	−.055			−.213	−.331	.257
	(19.55)	(−11.90)			(−15.22)	(−15.73)	
2.	.072		.208		−.110	−.192	.412
	(2.08)		(26.99)		(−8.46)	(−10.04)	
3.	2.363			−.249	−.216	−.328	.372
	(35.76)			(−23.43)	(−18.12)	(−17.03)	
4.	.971		.151	−.114	−.126	−.232	.430
	(8.53)		(14.67)	(−8.28)	(−9.73)	(−11.92)	

^{a} t-statistics are given in parentheses. R^2 is corrected for degrees of freedom.
Source: Hasbrouck and Schwartz (1988), used with permission.

Suggested Reading

Alexander, S. "Price Movements in Speculative Markets: Trends or Random Walks." *Industrial Management Review*, May 1961.

Alexander, S. "Price Movements in Speculative Markets: Trends or Random Walks No. 2." *Industrial Management Review*, Spring 1964.

Atchison, M., Butler, K., and Simonds, R. "Nonsynchronous Security Trading and Market Index Autocorrelation." *Journal of Finance*, March 1987.

Bachelier, L. *Théorie de la Spéculation*. Paris, France: Gauthier-Villars, 1900.

Beebower, G., Kamath, V., and Surz, R. "Commission and Transaction Costs of Stock Market Trading." Working paper, SEI Corporation, July 1985.

Bernstein, P. "Liquidity, Stock Markets, and Market Makers." *Financial Management*, Summer 1987.

Black, F. "Noise." *Journal of Finance*, July 1986.

Cohen, K., Hawawini, G., Maier, S., Schwartz, R., and Whitcomb, D. "Estimating and Adjusting for the Intervalling-Effect Bias in Beta." *Management Science*, January 1983.

Cohen, K., Hawawini, G., Maier, S., Schwartz, R., and Whitcomb, D. "Friction in the Trading Process and the Estimation of Systematic Risk." *Journal of Financial Economics*, August 1983.

Cohen, K., Maier, S., Schwartz, R., and Whitcomb, D. *The Microstructure of Securities Markets*, Englewood Cliffs, NJ: Prentice Hall, 1986.

Copeland, T. "A Model of Asset Trading Under the Assumption of Sequential Information Arrival." *Journal of Finance*, September 1976.

Cootner, P. *The Random Character of Stock Market Prices*. Cambridge, Mass.: The M.I.T. Press, 1964.

Dann, L., Mayers, D., and Raab, R. "Trading Rules, Large Blocks and the Speed of Price Adjustments." *Journal of Financial Economics*, January 1977.

Fama, E., "The Behavior of Stock-Market Prices." *Journal of Business*, January 1965.

Fama, E., "Efficient Capital Markets: A Review of Theory and Empirical Work." *Journal of Finance*, May 1970.

Fama, E., Fisher, L., Jensen, M., and Roll, R. "The Adjustment of Stock Prices to New Information." *International Economic Review*, February 1969.

French, K., and Roll, R. "Stock Return Variances: The Arrival of Information and the Reaction of Traders." *Journal of Financial Economics*, September 1986.

Friend, I., Brown, F., Herman, E., and Vickers, D. *A Study of Mutual Funds*. Government Printing Office, 1962.

Fung, W., Schwartz, R., and Whitcomb, D. "Adjusting the Intervalling Effect Bias in Beta: A Test Using Paris Bourse Prices." *Journal of Banking and Finance*, September 1985.

Garbade, K., and Lieber, Z. "On the Independence of Transactions on the New York Stock Exchange." *Journal of Banking and Finance*, October 1977.

Gilster, J. "Intertemporal Cross-Covariances Among Securities Which Trade Daily." Working paper, Michigan State University, 1987.

Givoli, D., and Palmon, D. "Insider Trading and the Exploitation of Inside Information: Some Empirical Evidence." *Journal of Business*, January 1985.

Goldman, M. B., and Beja, A. "Market Prices vs. Equilibrium Prices: Returns Variance, Serial Correlation, and the Role of the Specialist," *Journal of Finance*, June 1979.

Gottlieb, G., and Kalay, A. "Implications of the Discreteness of Observed Stock Prices." *Journal of Finance*, March 1985.

Granger, C., and Morgenstern, O. "Spectral Analysis of New York Stock Market Prices." *Kyklos*, January 1963.

Harris, L. *Liquidity, Trading Rules, and Electronic Trading Systems*. New York University Salomon Center Monograph Series in Finance and Economics, 1990-4.

Hasbrouck, J., and Ho, T. "Order Arrival, Quote Behavior, and the Return Generating Process." *Journal of Finance*, 1987.

Hasbrouck, J., and Schwartz, R. "Liquidity and Execution Costs in Equity Markets," *Journal of Portfolio Management*, Spring 1988.

Hawawini, G. *European Equity Markets: Price Behavior and Efficiency*. Monograph Series in Finance and Economics, Salomon Brothers Center for the Study of Financial Institutions, New York University Graduate School of Business Administration, 1984.

Jaffe, J. "The Effect of Regulation Changes on Insider Trading." *Bell Journal of Economics and Management Science*, Spring 1974.

Jensen, M. "Capital Markets, Theory and Evidence." *Bell Journal of Economics and Management Science*, Autumn 1972.

Joy, O. M., and Jones, C. "Should We Believe Tests of Market Efficiency?" *Journal of Portfolio Management*, Summer 1986.

Kendel, M. "The Analysis of Economic Time Series." *Journal of the Royal Statistical Society*, Series A, 1953.

Kraus, A., and Stoll, H. "Price Impacts of Block Trading on the New York Stock Exchange." *Journal of Finance*, June 1972.

Lo, A., and Mackinlay, C. "Stock Market Prices Do Not Follow Random Walks: Evidence from a Simple Specification Test." *Review of Financial Studies*, 1988.

Lorie, J., Dodd, P., and Kimpton, M. H. *The Stock Market: Theories and Evidence*, second edition, Homewood, Ill.: Richard D. Irwin, 1985.

Lorie, J., and Neiderhoffer, V. "Predictive and Statistical Properties of Insider Trading." *Journal of Law and Economics*, April 1968.

Malkiel, B. *A Random Walk Down Wall Street*, fourth edition, New York: W. W. Norton, 1985.

Mandelbrot, B. "Forecasts of Future Prices, Unbiased Markets, and 'Martingale' Models," *Journal of Business*, January 1966.

Marsh, T., and Rock, K. "Exchange Listing and Liquidity: A Comparison of the American Stock Exchange with the NASDAQ National Market System." American Stock Exchange Transactions Data Research Project Report Number 2, January 1986.

Neiderhoffer, V., and Osborne, M. F. "Market Making and Reversal on the Stock Exchange." *Journal of the American Statistical Association*, December 1966.

Osborne, M. F. "Brownian Motion in the Stock Market." *Operations Research*, March/April 1959.

Roberts, H. "Stock Market 'Patterns' and Financial Analysis: Methodological Suggestions." *Journal of Finance*, March 1959.

Roll, R. "A Simple Implicit Measure of the Effective Bid-Ask Spread in an Efficient Market." *The Journal of Finance*, September 1984.

Samuelson, P. "Proof That Properly Anticipated Prices Fluctuate Randomly." *Industrial Management Review*, Spring 1965.

Schwartz, R., and Whitcomb, D. "The Time-Variance Relationship: Evidence on Autocorrelation in Common Stock Returns." *The Journal of Finance*, March 1977.

Schwartz, R., and Whitcomb, D. "Evidence on the Presence and Causes of Serial Correlation in Market Model Residuals." *Journal of Financial and Quantitative Analysis*, June 1977.

Sharpe, W. "Mutual Fund Performance." *Journal of Business*, Supplement, January 1966.

Notes

1. For further discussion, see R. Roll, "A Simple Implicit Measure of the Effective Bid-Ask Spread in an Efficient Market," *The Journal of Finance*, September 1984.

2. M. B. Goldman and A. Beja, "Market Prices vs. Equilibrium Prices: Returns Variance, Serial Correlation, and the Role of the Specialist," *Journal of Finance*, June 1979.

3. M. Kendel, "The Analysis of Economic Time Series," *Journal of the Royal Statistical Society*, Series A, 1953.

4. H. Roberts, "Stock Market 'Patterns' and Financial Analysis: Methodological Suggestions," *Journal of Finance*, March 1959.

5. M. F. Osborne, "Brownian Motion in the Stock Market," *Operations Research*, March/April 1959.

6. C. Granger, "Spectral Analysis of New York Stock Market Prices," *Kyklos*, January 1963.

7. S. Alexander, "Price Movements in Speculative Markets: Trends or Random Walks," *Industrial Management Review*, May 1961.

8. E. Fama, "Efficient Capital Markets: A Review of Theory and Empirical Work," *Journal of Finance*, May 1970.

9. P. Samuelson, "Proof That Properly Anticipated Prices Fluctuate Randomly," *Industrial Management Review*, Spring 1965; B. Mandelbrot, "Forecasts of Future Prices, Unbiased Markets, and 'Martingale' Models," *Journal of Business*, January 1966; E. Fama, "The Behavior of Stock-Market Prices," *Journal of Business*, January 1965; and Fama, "Efficient Capital Markets," *The Journal of Finance,* May 1970.

10. E. Fama, L. Fisher, M. Jensen, and R. Roll, "The Adjustment of Stock Prices to New Information," *International Economic Review*, February 1969.

11. L. Dann, D. Mayers, and R. Raab, "Trading Rules, Large Blocks and the Speed of Price Adjustments," *Journal of Financial Economics*, January 1977.

12. Full citations for these works can be found in Suggested Readings, p. 434.

13. H. Manne, *Insider Trading and the Stock Market*, New York: Free Press, 1966.

14. E. Berg, *New York Times*, May 16, 1986, p. D2.
15. For further discussion, see K. Cohen, G. Hawawini, S. Maier, R. Schwartz, and D. Whitcomb, "Friction in the Trading Process and the Estimation of Systemic Risk," *Journal of Financial Economics*, August 1983; K. Cohen, S. Maier, R. Schwartz, and D. Whitcomb, *The Microstructure of Securities Markets*, Englewood Cliffs, NJ: Prentice Hall, 1986.
16. The study was undertaken by Cohen, Hawawini, Maier, Schwartz, and Whitcomb, "Estimating and Adjusting." The findings are further discussed in Cohen, Maier, Schwartz, and Whitcomb, *Microstructure*. Compatible findings are also found in W. Fung, R. Schwartz, and D. Whitcomb, "Adjusting the Intervalling Effect Bias in Beta: A Test Using Paris Bourse Prices," *Journal of Banking and Finance*, September 1985.
17. Cohen, Maier, Schwartz, and Whitcomb, *Microstructure*, p. 136.
18. For a comprehensive discussion of empirical tests of price behavior in European markets, see G. Hawawini, *European Equity Markets: Price Behavior and Efficiency*, NYU Graduate School of Business Administration, 1984.
19. A. Kraus and H. Stoll, "Price Impacts of Block Trading on the New York Stock Exchange," *Journal of Finance*, June 1972; L. Dann, D. Mayers, and R. Raab, "Trading Rules, Large Blocks and the Speed of Price Adjustments," *Journal of Financial Economics*, January 1977.
20. G. Beebower, V. Kamath, and R. Surz, "Commission and Transaction Costs of Stock Market Trading," working paper, SEI Corporation, July 1985.
21. The study was conducted by Hasbrouck and Schwartz, "Liquidity and Execution Costs."

Subject Index

National Securities Trading System (NSTS), 83–84
Negative order size, 211
Negotiation, 103–5
New York Futures Exchange (NYFE), 27, 45, 108
New York Stock Exchange (NYSE)
  after hours trading on, 93
  block trades on, 41–42, 82
  board of directors, 23
  Composite Index, 27, 108
  Consolidated Tape, 23, 32–34
  delisting, 25–26
  electronic trading in, 95
  execution costs, 125
  fixed income trading floor, 26–27
  growth of, 31
  intermarket competition, 22–23
  intermarket coordination, 44–45
  Intermarket Trading System (ITS), 35
  listing requirements, 25–26
  main trading floor, 26
  market share, 23
  market surveillance, 43–44
  members, 23–25
  vs. NASDAQ and Amex, 49–50
  odd lots, 42–43
  opening call, 205
  order handling and execution, 35–43
  order qualifications and instructions, 38–39
  order routing and information systems, 31–35
  order types, 35–38
  organizational structure of, 23–27
  vs. OTC, 47–48, 57–62
  Panel on Market Volatility and Investor Confidence, 44, 109
  as a perfectly competitive environment, 123
  price discovery, 23, 58, 60
  regulation of, 43–45
  revenues, 26
  Rule 80A, 45
  Rule 113, 59
  Rule 390, 64, 84, 169–70, 176
  Rule 394. *See* Rule 390
  as a self-regulatory organization, 43
  specialists, 24, 27–31, 59
  special rules of order execution, 40–41
  stock allocation, 25, 29
  SuperDOT, 31–32, 110

  tests of intervalling effect on share value, 414–18
  trading activity by type of investor, 198
  trading arenas, 26–27
  trading halted on, 34, 44–45
  trading priority rules, 39–40, 353
  trading volume, October 12–November 6, 1987, 4
Nikkei Index, 7
Noisy signals, 376–77, 385, 387
Nominal income, 264
Non-NASDAQ OTC (NNOTC) stocks, 52
Nonstochastic prices, 388
Normal buy curve, 188
Normal demand curve, 320, 323–25
Normal market size (NMS), 74
Not held (NH) orders, 15, 36
Null hypothesis, 397
NYSE Composite Index, 27, 108

Odd lots, 42–43, 200
Off-board trading, 177–78, 187
  restrictions on, 169–70
Offering size, 100
Office of Fair Trading, 69, 75, 76
Official Summary of Securities Transactions and Holdings (SEC), 410
One-way markets, 65, 75
Ontario Securities Commission, 84
Opening Automated Report System (OARS), 12, 30, 31
Optimality, 318–19, 386–87
Optimal order(s)
  assumptions for analyzing, 291–92
  in a call market environment, 294–96
  in a continuous market environment, 296–99
  determining, 291
  trader's goal, 292–94
Order-driven call market, 196
Order execution, probability of, 303–4
Order exposure, 172–73
Order function(s), 389
  alternative orders, 281–83
  discontinuous nature of, 354
  order adjustment, 284–85
  partially collapsed, 291
  relationship among, 283–84
  submission of discrete order points, 287–91
Ordinary demand curve, 250, 251
Overreaching, 172–73
Overshooting, 423